SACHS

100cc & 125cc ENGINES
1968 to 1975
WORKSHOP MANUAL
plus
1974 - 100cc & 125cc
Illustrated
'List of (engine) Spares'
plus
Illustrated Parts Lists for:
100cc & 125cc
1968-71 SACHS Motorcycles
1971-75 DKW Motorcycles

A Floyd Clymer Publication
This edition published in 2023 by
www.VelocePress.com

All rights reserved. This work may not be reproduced or transmitted in any form without the express written consent of the publisher.

FOREWORD

INTRODUCTION

Welcome to the world of digital publishing ~ the book you now hold in your hand was printed using the latest state of the art digital technology. The advent of print-on-demand has forever changed the publishing process, never has information been so accessible and it is our hope that this book serves your informational needs for years to come. If this is your first exposure to digital publishing, we hope that you are pleased with the results. Many more titles of interest to the classic automobile and motorcycle enthusiast, collector and restorer are available via our website at www.VelocePress.com. We hope that you find this title as interesting as we do.

NOTE FROM THE PUBLISHER

The information presented is true and complete to the best of our knowledge. All recommendations are made without any guarantees on the part of the author or the publisher, who also disclaim all liability incurred with the use of this information.

TRADEMARKS

We recognize that some words, model names and designations, for example, mentioned herein are the property of the trademark holder. We use them for identification purposes only. This is not an official publication.

INFORMATION ON THE USE OF THIS PUBLICATION

This manual is an invaluable resource for those interested in performing their own maintenance. However, in today's information age we are constantly subject to changes in common practice, new technology, availability of improved materials and increased awareness of chemical toxicity. As such, it is advised that the user consult with an experienced professional prior to undertaking any procedure described herein. While every care has been taken to ensure correctness of information, it is obviously not possible to guarantee complete freedom from errors or omissions or to accept liability arising from such errors or omissions. Therefore, any individual that uses the information contained within, or elects to perform or participate in do-it-yourself repairs or modifications acknowledges that there is a risk factor involved and that the publisher or its associates cannot be held responsible for personal injury or property damage resulting from the use of the information or the outcome of such procedures.

WARNING!

One final word of advice, this publication is intended to be used as a reference guide, and when in doubt the reader should consult with a qualified technician.

CONTENTS

CHAPTER ONE

GENERAL INFORMATION 1
    Introduction   Common tools
    Service hints   Expendable supplies
    Special tools   Safety first

CHAPTER TWO

PERIODIC SERVICE 7
    Engine operating principles   Carburetor
    Engine lubrication   Ignition
    Engine service   Clutch
    Fuel tank

CHAPTER THREE

CYLINDER HEAD, CYLINDER AND PISTON 15
    Cylinder head service   Piston removal and replacement
    Cylinder service

CHAPTER FOUR

CRANKSHAFT AND CRANKCASE 25
    Engine removal   Crankshaft seal replacement
    Lower end   Main bearing replacement
    Gear selector (one-piece lever)   Crankcase reassembly
    Gear selector (two-piece lever)   Ignition installation (Bosch)
    Crankcase separation   Ignition installation (Motoplat)
    Crankshaft removal   Drive sprocket installation
    Transmission disassembly   Gear selector installation
    Starter mechanism removal   Drive gear/clutch installation
    Inspection   Clutch side cover installation
    Measurement   Gear selector and kickstarter
    Crankshaft preassembly   Reinstallation, final assembly, and timing

CHAPTER FIVE

TRANSMISSION AND CLUTCH 45
    Clutch service   Gear selectors
    Transmission service   Shifter set-up and adjustment

CHAPTER SIX

CARBURETOR 65
    Operation   Adjustment
    Servicing   Air filter

CHAPTER SEVEN

ELECTRICAL SYSTEM 73
    Magneto ignition system   Charging system
    Electronic ignition system   Wiring diagrams (see chapters 11 & 12 also)

TROUBLESHOOTING 91

CHAPTER EIGHT

SPECIFICATIONS 92
    1001/5A   1251/6A
    1001/6A   1251/6B
    1001/6B   1251/6C
    1251/5A

CHAPTER NINE

USEFUL FORMULAS AND TABLES 102
    Conversion table   Lubricants and sealants
    Fuel and oil mixtures   Torque settings - nut and bolt

CHAPTER TEN 107
    Engine - Illustrated list of spares (1974)

CHAPTER ELEVEN 139
    1968 to 1971 SACHS Motorcycles
    Illustrated spare parts list (1968)
    Wiring diagrams

CHAPTER TWELVE 181
    1971 to 1975 SACHS/DKW Motorcycles
    Maintenance information
    Illustrated spare parts list (1972)
    Wiring diagrams

CHAPTER ONE

GENERAL INFORMATION

INTRODUCTION

Fichtel & Sachs is one of the largest and most experienced builders of proprietary motorcycle engines in the world. Over the years, their engines have been used in virtually hundreds of motorcycle makes. In today's market, Sachs engines are most commonly associated with such motorcycle manufacturers as DKW, Penton, Monark, Tyran, and Dalesman, as well as many limited-production special builders.

The information in this handbook applies to the following models:

   1001/5 A
   1251/5 A
   1001/6 A (no longer in production)
   1251/6 A (no longer in production)
   1001/6 B
   1251/6 B
   1251/6 C

NOTE: *The first 3 digits in the engine model number indicate its displacement class.*

While all late model Sachs engines of a given displacement are basically identical, variations exist in number of gears (5 or 6), cylinder construction, finning patterns, carburetion, ignition, and exhaust systems. The various engine types are shown in **Figure 1**.

SERVICE HINTS

The service procedures described are straightforward, and most of them can be performed by anyone reasonably handy with tools. However, carefully consider your own abilities and experience before attempting any operation which involves major disassembly of the engine and transmission.

Some operations require very special equipment, such as a press to disassemble and reassemble the crankshaft. This type of work should be performed by a shop equipped for it. Data provided in this handbook, such as press pressures, pre-fit temperatures, tolerances, and dimensions, will enable an experienced general machine shop to correctly perform major work if a competent motorcycle shop is not accessible to you.

Some procedures require precision measurement. Unless you have the skills and equipment to make them, it would be better to have a motorcycle shop or other specialist help in the work.

ENGINE VERSIONS

SACHS 1001/5 A
 1251/5 A
(cast iron cylinder)

SACHS 1251/5 B

(aluminium cylinder with sunburst cylinder head)
NHW-Military

SACHS 1001/5 A
 1251/5 A
 1001/6 A
 1251/6 A
 1001/6 B
 1251/6 B
 1251/6 C
(aluminium, large fin cylinder with sunburst cylinder head)

SPECIAL TOOLS

Special tools for servicing Sachs engines are shown in **Figure 2**. In some cases a similar tool that you may already have, such as a gear puller or a timing gauge, may be substituted. As far as possible, use the special tools called for. A jerry-rigged tool could damage a vital component whose replacement cost might be greater than the cost of the special tool required to do the job correctly. The tools may be purchased through dealers handling Sachs-engined products. If you are on good terms with a dealer, you may be able to borrow a tool you need from your dealer's service department.

Much of the labor charge for repairs made by dealers is for removal and disassembly of other parts to reach the defective one. It is frequently possible to do all of this yourself, then take the affected subassembly into the dealer for repair.

Once you decide to tackle a job yourself, read the entire section in this manual pertaining to it. Study the illustrations and the text until you have a good idea of what's involved. If special tools are required, make arrangements to get them before you begin work. It's frustrating to get partly into a job and then find that you are unable to complete it.

TOOLS

To properly service your motorcycle, you will need an assortment of ordinary hand tools. As a minimum, these include:

1. Combination wrenches
2. Socket wrenches
3. Plastic mallet
4. Small hammer
5. Snap ring pliers
6. Phillips screwdrivers
7. Pliers
8. Slot screwdrivers
9. Feeler gauges
10. Spark plug gauge
11. Spark plug wrench
12. Dial indicator

A tool kit, available through most motorcycle dealers, and suitable for minor servicing, is shown in **Figure 3**.

Electrical system servicing requires a voltmeter, ohmmeter or other device for determining continuity, and a hydrometer in the case of machines equipped with batteries. Hydrometers are inexpensive, and should be part of every motorcyclist's tool kit.

EXPENDABLE SUPPLIES

Certain expendable supplies are also required. These include grease, oil, gasket cement, wiping rags, silicone seal, thread locking compound such as Loctite, and cleaning solvent. Cleaning solvent is available at many service stations. Distilled water, required for battery service, is available at every supermarket. It is sold for use in steam irons, and is quite inexpensive.

If you have difficulty locating a specific product such as the Diament sealer used in assembling the lower end components, check with a dealer for his recommendation.

SAFETY FIRST

Professional motorcycle mechanics can work for years and never sustain a serious injury. If you observe a few rules of common sense and safety, you can enjoy many safe hours servicing your own machine. You can also hurt yourself or damage the bike if you ignore these rules:

1. Never use gasoline as a cleaning solvent.

2. Never smoke or use a torch in the area of flammable liquids, such as cleaning solvent in open containers.

3. Never smoke or use a torch in an area where batteries are charging. Highly explosive hydrogen gas is formed during the charging process.

4. If welding or brazing is required on the machine, remove the fuel tank to a safe distance, at least 50 feet away.

5. Be sure to use the proper size wrenches for nut turning.

6. If a nut is tight, think for a moment what would happen to your hand should the wrench slip. Be guided accordingly.

7. Keep your work area clean and uncluttered.

8. Wear safety goggles in all operations involving drilling, grinding, or the use of a chisel.

9. Do not use worn tools.

10. Keep a fire extinguisher handy. Be sure it is rated for gasoline and electrical fires.

REPAIR TOOLS AND MOUNTING JIG

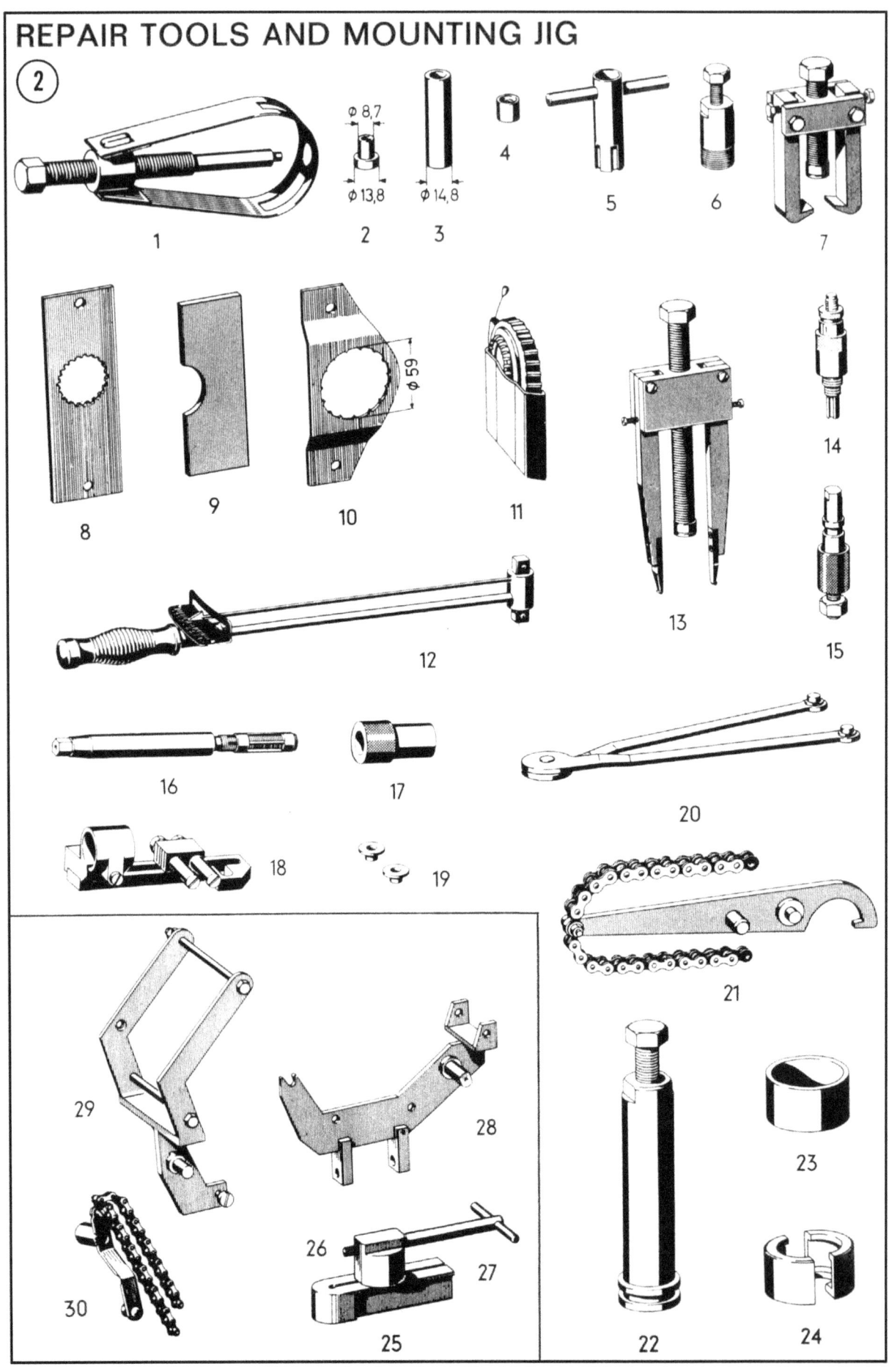

Illustr. No.	Part No.	Description	Engine							
			1001/5 A	1251/5 A	1251/5 B	1001/6 A	1251/6 A	1001/6 B	1251/6 B	1251/6 C
		Repair tools								
1	0276 065 101	Gudgeon pin extractor	x	x	x	x	x	x	x	x
2	0276 122 001	Insert bush for gudgeon pin extractor	x	x	x	x	x	x	x	x
3	0977 053 000	Guide pin for piston	x	x	x	x	x	x	x	x
4	0276 156 000	Protective cap, bore 10 mm (0.394 in.)	x	x	x	x	x	x	x	x
5	0676 021 000	Box spanner (profile)	x	x	x	x	x	x	x	x
6	0276 150 005	Puller for magneto flywheel M 26 x 1.5	x	x	x	x	x	x	x	x
7	0276 179 000	Puller for sprocket	x	x	x	x	x	x	x	x
8	0676 110 100	Locking plate for clutch hub	x	x	x	x	x	x	x	x
9	0276 019 101	Intermediate plate	x	x	x	x	x	x	x	x
10	0676 109 000	Locking plate for driving gear	x	x	x	x	x	x	x	x
11	0276 175 000	Revolution counter	x	x	x	x	x	x	x	x
12	0276 170 000	Torque spanner	x	x	x	x	x	x	x	x
13	0276 161 101	Oil seal extractor	x	x	x	x	x	x	x	x
	0276 164 100	Extractor hook 3 mm (0.118") (1 off) } spare parts for 0276 161 101								
	1476 012 000	Thrust bearing								
14	0276 135 100	Spark advance timing gauge	x	x	x	x	x	x	x	x
15	0676 027 000	Tool for extracting and inserting small end bush	x	x	x	x	x			
16	0276 159 002	Adjustable reamer P 14.0 ... 15.5 mm (0.551 ... 0.610 in.)	x	x	x	x	x			
17	0276 158 001	Guide bush No. 3, bore 17.7 mm (0.697 in.)	x	x	x	x	x			
18	0276 157 000	Guide bar	x	x	x	x	x			
19	0276 160 001	Clamping sleeve, bore 8.2 mm (0.323 in.) (1 off)	x	x	x	x	x			
20	0276 181 000	Adjustable pin spanner	1	1		1	1	1	1	1
21	0277 086 406	Hook spanner	x	x		x	x	x	x	x
	0276 180 002	Hook spanner (without illustration)			x					
22	1476 013 000	Puller sleeve assembly	x	x	x	x	x	x	x	x
	1476 011 000	Threaded sleeve } spare parts for 1476 013 000								
	1440 027 001	Screw, hexagon head								
	1476 012 000	Thrust bearing								
23	1447 009 000	Clamping ring, 58 mm (2.283 in.) I. D.	x	x	x	x	x	x	x	x
24	1476 014 010	Puller shells for inner race of magneto bearing M 20	x	x	x	x	x	x	x	x
		Mounting jig								
25	0276 081 000	Clamping base	x	x	x	x	x	x	x	x
26	0276 082 000	Swivel unit	x	x	x	x	x	x	x	x
27	0276 085 005	Clamping screw	x	x	x	x	x	x	x	x
28	0276 088 006	Mounting bracket	x	x	x	x	x	x	x	x
29	0276 131 000	Mounting bracket	x	x	x	x	x	x	x	x
30	0276 093 205	Lever	x	x	x	x	x	x	x	x

1 = for MOTOPLAT ignition set

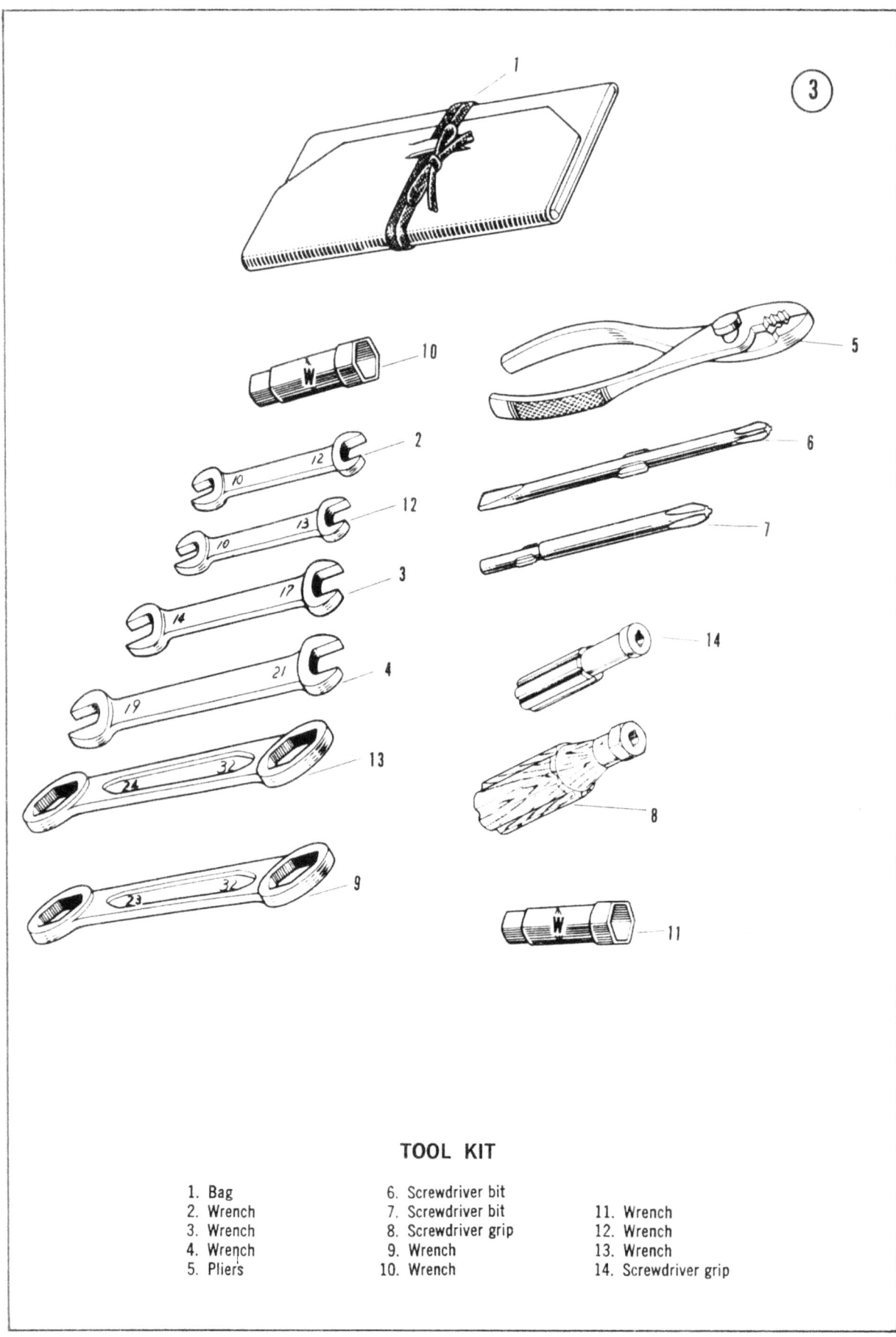

TOOL KIT

1. Bag
2. Wrench
3. Wrench
4. Wrench
5. Pliers
6. Screwdriver bit
7. Screwdriver bit
8. Screwdriver grip
9. Wrench
10. Wrench
11. Wrench
12. Wrench
13. Wrench
14. Screwdriver grip

CHAPTER TWO

PERIODIC SERVICE

This chapter describes routine periodic service of the engine, transmission, clutch, controls, and chassis components. It is suggested that the engine be serviced without removing it from the chassis except for overhaul of the crankshaft assembly, transmission, gearshift mechanism, or bearings. Operating principles of piston port two-stroke engines are also discussed in this chapter.

ENGINE OPERATING PRINCIPLES

Figures 1 through 4 illustrate operating principles of two-stroke engines. During this discussion, assume that the crankshaft is rotating counterclockwise. In **Figure 1**, as the piston travels downward, a transfer port (A) between the crankcase and the cylinder is uncovered. The exhaust gases leave the cylinder through the exhaust port (B), which is also opened by the downward movement of the piston. A fresh fuel/air charge, which has previously been compressed slightly, travels from the crankcase (C) to the cylinder through the transport port (A) as the port opens. Since the incoming charge is under pressure, it rushes into the cylinder quickly and helps to expel the exhaust gases from the previous cycle.

Figure 2 illustrates the next phase of the cycle. As the crankcase continues to rotate, the piston

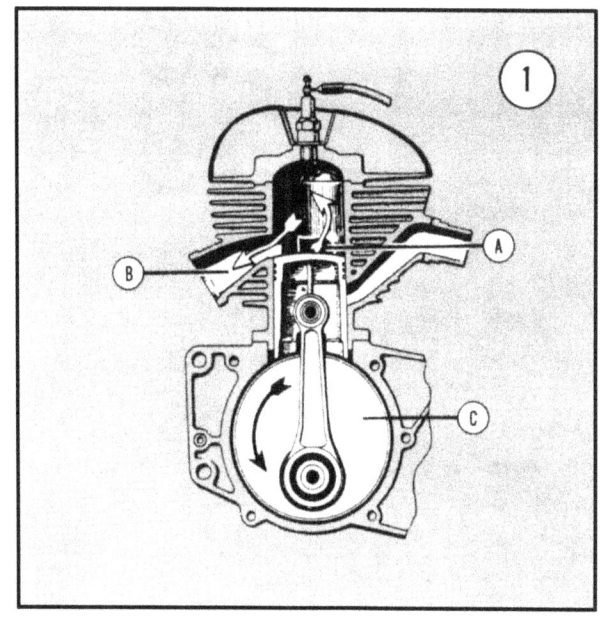

moves upward, closing the exhaust and transfer ports. As the piston continues upward, the air/fuel mixture in the cylinder is compressed. Notice also that a low pressure area is created in the crankcase at the same time. Further upward movement of the piston uncovers the intake port (D). A fresh fuel/air charge is then drawn into the crankcase through the intake port because of the low pressure created by the upward piston movement.

The third phase is shown in **Figure 3**. As the piston approaches top dead center, the spark

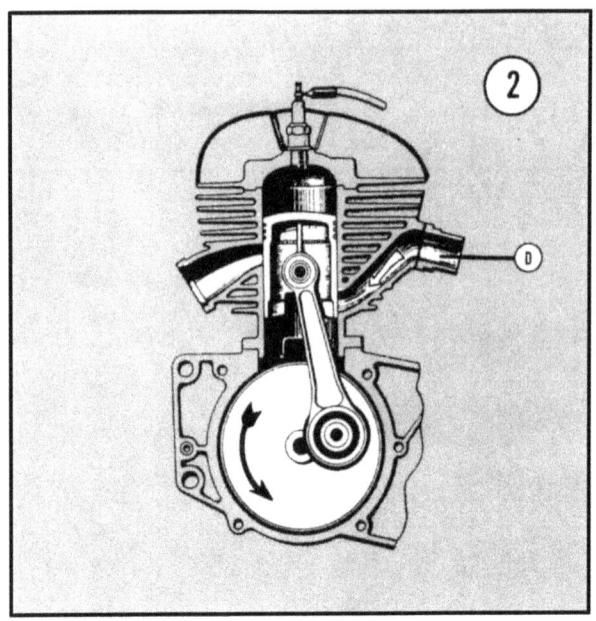

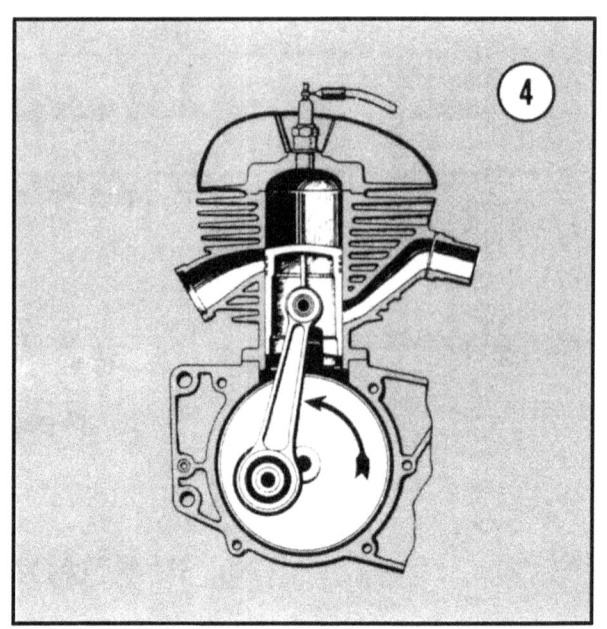

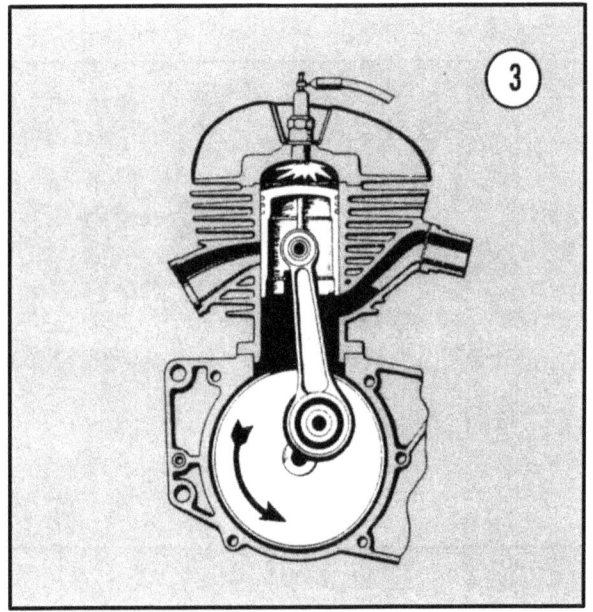

plug fires, igniting the compressed mixture. The piston is then driven downward by the expanding gases.

When the top of the piston uncovers the exhaust port, the fourth phase begins, as shown in **Figure 4**. The exhaust gases leave the cylinder through the exhaust port. As the piston continues downward, the intake port is closed and the mixture in the crankcase is compressed in preparation for the next cycle.

It can be seen from the foregoing discussion that every downward stroke of the piston is a power stroke.

ENGINE LUBRICATION

Sachs engines are lubricated by oil mixed in the fuel. Use a good grade of 2-stroke engine oil in a 4-percent (25:1) solution. Be sure to mix the oil and gasoline thoroughly together before pouring the mixture into the fuel tank. Always measure the quantities carefully; don't guess.

The Sachs factory also permits the use of SAE 40 nondetergent motor oil mixed in a 5-percent (20:1) solution. However, motor oil tends to separate from gasoline after prolonged standing. If this type of oil is used, and the motorcycle has not been ridden for several days, re-mix the fuel and oil by shaking the motorcycle from side to side and back and forth repeatedly for about a minute before starting the engine.

ENGINE SERVICE

To maintain the engine at peak efficiency, the periodic services which follow should be performed at the intervals indicated (see **Table 1**).

Air Cleaner Function

The air cleaner (**Figure 5**) removes dust and abrasive particles from the air before it enters the engine. Even very fine particles entering the engine will rapidly wear the piston, rings, cylinder, and bearings, and clog the small passages

Table I SERVICE INTERVALS

LUBRICATION AND MAINTENANCE CHART

Maintenance or lubrication point	Lubricant, quantity of lubricant, and maintenance operations	Maintenance every 1000 km - 625 mil	3000 km - 1875 mil	6000 km - 3750 mil	if necessary
	Intake silencer and micronic air filter Pull the intake silencer rearwards and take it apart. On SACHS 1251/5 B engines, lift the seat and remove upper part of intake silencer. Clean both halves of the intake silencer in gasoline. Replace the micronic air filter (1), if very dirty, by a new one; if slightly dirty, remove dust deposit by blowing cautiously. Fit the micronic air filter (open end towards the carburettor) into the intake silencer.	X			under dusty conditions
	Intake pipe and bellows Clean the intake pipe (1) and the bellows (2) also with gasoline. Replace bellows after the slightest damage by a new one.	X			
	Spark plug A provisional cleaning of the spark plug from carbon deposits can be made on the insulator foot between the electrodes. An efficient cleaning can only be achieved by means of a sandblower. **Functional check** Unscrew spark plug, fit spark plug terminal, put spark plug thread in ground contact (cylinder head) and operate starting device. If the spark plug is in good order, a strong spark must flash between the electrodes. Electrode gap 0,4+0,1 mm (0.016+0.004 in.) (see arrow).				X
	Control cables If special lubricating nipples (see arrow) are available on the wires, lubricate with light oil. If such nipples are not available, disconnect control cables and grease wire well.		X		
	Speedometer drive Remove speedometer cable, lubricate speedometer drive by pressing, with a grease gun, 2...3 cc (0.1...0.2 cu in.) of high melting point grease through the bore for the connecting screw (1).		X		
	Chain Oil roller chain with a viscous engine or gear oil. Check chain tension. Chain sag approx. 1 cm (0.39 in.)	X			
	Remove chain, clean in petrol or paraffin. Immerse in warmed chain grease, move around so that the joints and rollers are adequately lubricated everywhere.		X		

Table I SERVICE INTERVALS

LUBRICATION AND MAINTENANCE CHART

Maintenance or lubrication point	Lubricant, quantity of lubricant, and maintenance operations	Maintenance every 1000 km - 625 mil	3000 km - 1875 mil	6000 km - 3750 mil	if necessary
	Oil level check Screw out oil check plug (2). If the gear oil level is lower than the lower edge of the oil check hole, remove oil filling plug (1) and pour in SACHS gear oil or SAE 80 until oil emerges from the oil check hole. When no more oil emerges, screw in plug again.	X			
	Oil change Change the oil only when the engine is warm. Prop the vehicle up by placing a wooden block under the kick-stand. Remove oil drain plug on bottom of engine (ordinary hexagon head) and oil drain plug (3). Drain the oil, rocking the vehicle forwards and backwards in order to drain the oil completely. Restore the plugs. Remove the oil filler plug (1) and pour 600 cc. (1.3 US liq. pints) of SACHS gear oil (F & S part no. 0263 015 005) or SAE 80 oil into the hole, as described above under oil level check.			X	
	Fuel strainer Empty fuel tank. The fuel strainer is connected to the fuel cock. Hence to clean, screw off cock from fuel tank and wash strainer well in fuel. If required wash out fuel tank. Re-fit cock and re-fill fuel tank.			X	
	Carburettor Unscrew cover, remove throttle slide with jet needle. Remove Float chamber (1), unscrew main jet, needle jet and idle jet. Wash carburettor body and all components in gasoline. Jet bores and the drain bore only blow out with compressed air.			X	
Clutch	Check and adjust when necessary.	X			
Ignition set (conventional)	Check the breaker contacts and adjust when necessary, after 500, after 1000, and then every 3000 km (after 310, after 620, and then after every 1860 miles).		X		
	Lubricate the pad for the breaker cam with special BOSCH grease Ft 1 v 4.			X	
Ignition set (electronic)	Check and adjust.				X
Exhaust system	Decarbonize.				X
Cylinder wall, con-rod bearings, crankshaft bearings	Lubricate with two-stroke mixture, i. e. SACHS special engine oil in cans (F & S Part No. 0263 005 100, containing 250 cc (8.8 fl oz) pre-mixed, for 5 litres (1.3 US gal) of gasoline, or preferably two-stroke oils, or, if need be, other oils (SAE 30 or 40) of leading oil companies, to be mixed in 1:25 ratio with gasoline.				

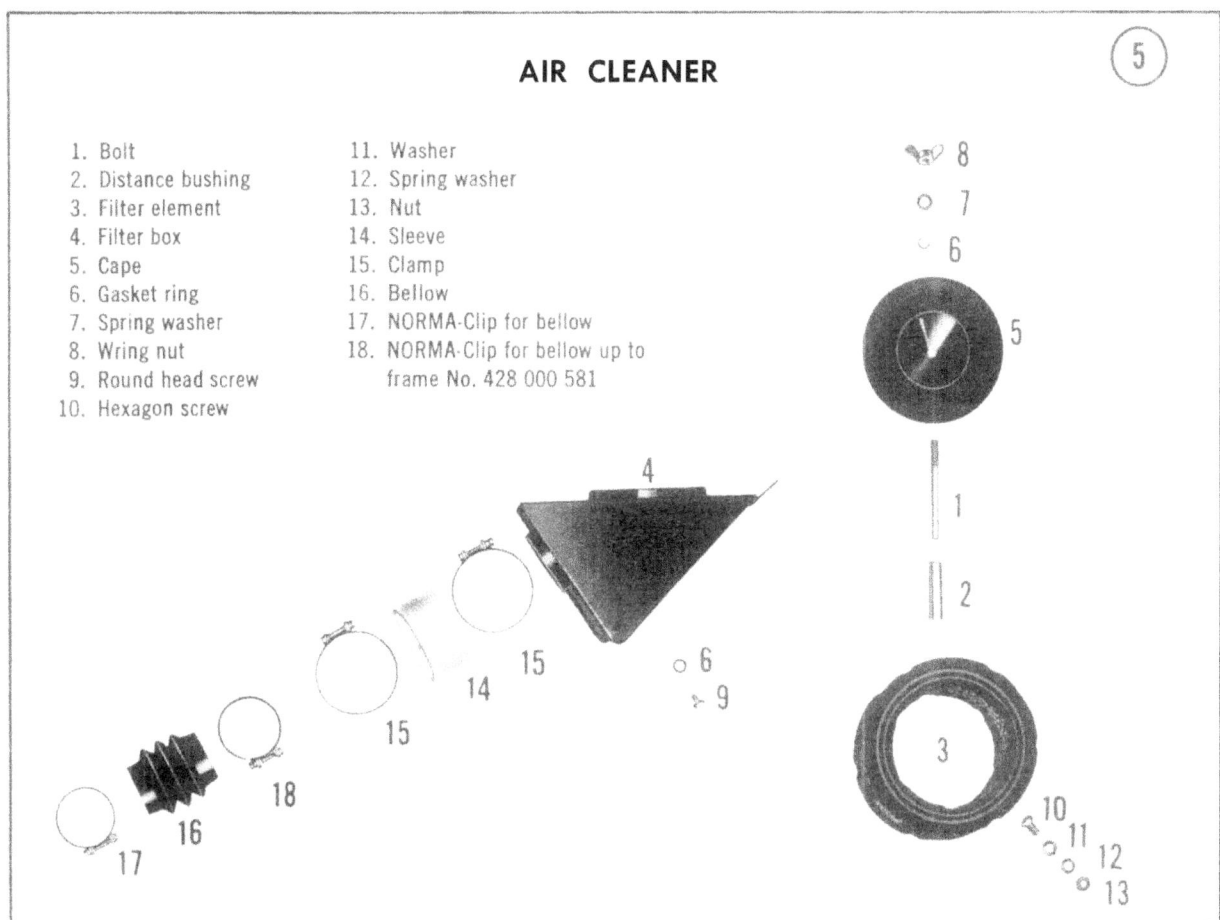

AIR CLEANER

1. Bolt
2. Distance bushing
3. Filter element
4. Filter box
5. Cape
6. Gasket ring
7. Spring washer
8. Wring nut
9. Round head screw
10. Hexagon screw
11. Washer
12. Spring washer
13. Nut
14. Sleeve
15. Clamp
16. Bellow
17. NORMA-Clip for bellow
18. NORMA-Clip for bellow up to frame No. 428 000 581

in the carburetor. The motorcycle should never be operated with the air cleaner removed, and the unit should be cleaned frequently, such as at the end of a day of trail riding or after a race. If you use your motorcycle for motocross racing, it's a good idea to have a second air cleaner element on hand to replace the first unit between motos; when the filter becomes clogged with dirt, the intake flow is restricted resulting in a decrease in engine efficiency.

Air Cleaner Servicing

1. Disassemble the air cleaner box and remove the filter element. (On motorcycles equipped with 1251/5 B engines, first lift the seat and then remove the top of the air box to gain access to the filter.)

2. Clean the inside of the air box with solvent and dry it thoroughly.

3a. On motorcycles equipped with a micronic paper filter, blow the dirt out of the filter, from the inside, with an air hose. Be careful not to rupture the filter paper. Don't wash the unit with gasoline or solvent.

NOTE: *If the filter is extremely dirty, or if it has been in service for a long time, replace it with a new one.*

3b. On motorcycles equipped with an oil-wetted foam air cleaner, thoroughly clean the filter element in kerosene and allow it to air dry. Saturate the filter with light oil and wring it out until only a light oil film remains.

4. Apply a light coat of grease to the sealing surface of the filter and reinstall it in the air box. Reinstall the cover on the air box.

5. Remove the rubber intake bellows and clean it and the intake tube in the frame with solvent. Dry them thoroughly. If the bellows is even slightly damaged or cracked, replace it. When reinstalling the bellows, make sure both ends of it are correctly seated on the mounting flanges.

Oil Change

Proper operation and long service life of the clutch and transmission requires clean oil. For motorcycles used primarily for transportation, the oil should be changed every 3,600 miles. For motorcycles used for trail riding, the oil should be changed every 1,000 miles. For motorcycles used in competition, the oil should be changed after every race.

1. Start the engine, warm it up, and shut it off.
2. Place the motorcycle on a workstand or place a block beneath the kickstand so the motorcycle is level. Place a 1-quart or larger pan beneath the engine to catch the oil. Remove the oil drain plug from the bottom of the engine (**Figure 6**) and the oil fill plug, checking plug, and level fill plug (**Figure 7**). Rock the motorcycle back and forth to drain all the oil.
3. Reinstall the bottom and side plugs.

> HINT: *Pour the old oil into a plastic bleach bottle, cap it, and discard it in the trash.*

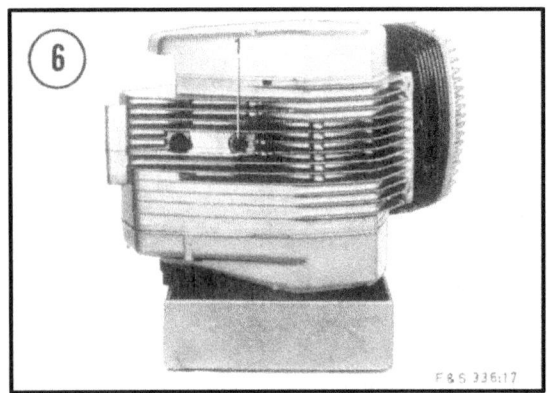

4. Fill the transmission with 20.3 ounces (600cc) of SAE 80 oil. Use a graduated beaker or a similar graduated container.

> HINT: *Plastic baby bottles make excellent graduates. They're inexpensive and are good dirt-free storage containers for the excess oil from an opened can. You'll need a plastic funnel to direct the oil into the fill hole in the top of the transmission.*

Control Cable Lubrication

If the control cables are fitted with lubrication nipples, unfasten the cover of each nipple and pour in light oil (**Figure 8**). Actuate the control to which the cable is attached several times to distribute the oil throughout the length of the cable sheath.

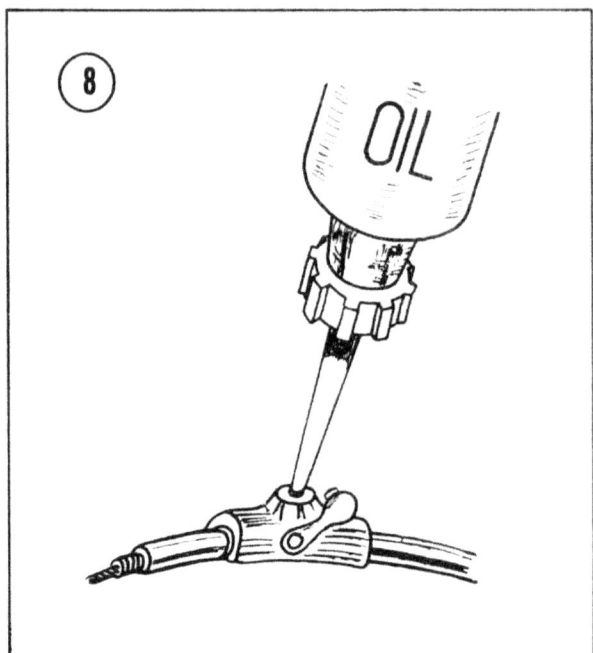

For cables without lubricating nipples, use a cable lubricator, such as the one shown in **Figure 9**, to apply lubricant to the cable.

Speedometer Drive Lubrication

Disconnect the speedometer cable at the engine and lubricate the speedometer drive with a grease gun filled with high-temperature grease.

Drive Chain Lubrication

On motorcycles used primarily for transportation, the drive chain should be lubricated and adjusted about every 600 miles, and removed, cleaned, and lubricated every 1,800 miles. The drive chain on a motorcycle used for trail riding should be lubricated and adjusted each time the motorcycle is ridden, and removed, cleaned, and lubricated after several outings. On competition

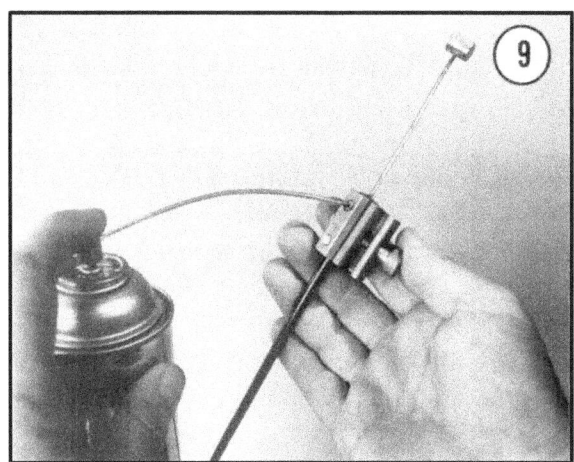

motorcycles, the chain should be removed, cleaned, lubricated and adjusted prior to each race in which is is ridden.

To clean the chain, remove it from the motorcycle, immerse it in a pan of cleaning solvent, and allow it to soak for about half an hour. Scrub the rollers and side plates with a stiff brush and rinse the chain in clean solvent to flush away loosened dirt. Hang up the chain and allow it to dry thoroughly. Lubricate the chain with a good grade of chain lubricant, carefully following the manufacturer's instructions. Reinstall the chain on the motorcycle. Use a new master link clip and install it in the direction shown in **Figure 10**.

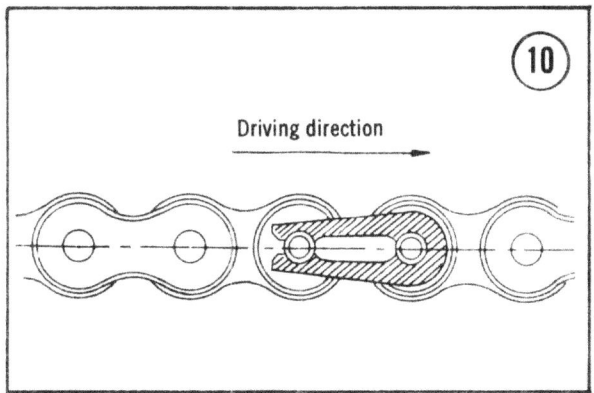

Measure the free-play of the chain with the rear wheel supported so it's free to rotate, and make sure the transmission is in neutral. Measure the maximum vertical play of the chain midway between the countershaft and the rear wheel sprockets. It should be about ⅜ in. (10mm). If adjustment is required, loosen the rear axle nut (and the brake anchor if necessary) and move the wheel backward or forward as required with the adjusters on each side of the swing arm.

Check the alignment of the rear wheel in the swing and the chain on the sprocket by sighting along the top of the chain from the rear of the motorcycle (**Figure 11**). There should be no

lateral bend in the chain. If the wheel is cocked to the right, move the left end of the axle backward with the adjuster and the right end forward. If it is cocked to the left, move the right end of the axle backward with the adjuster and the left end forward. When the wheel, chain, and sprocket are correctly aligned, recheck the vertical play of the chain and adjust it if necessary, moving both adjusters equally. Then, tighten the axle nut and the brake anchor.

FUEL TANK

The fuel tank should be removed from the motorcycle and cleaned about every 3,600 miles. Close the fuel taps and disconnect the lines. Remove the fuel tank from the motorcycle and discard the fuel that is in it. Pour about one pint of clean fuel (without oil) into the tank, install the cap, slosh the gasoline around for about a minute, and pour it out. Remove the fuel taps from the tank, disassemble them and clean them in gasoline. Check the fuel tap gaskets and replace them if they are damaged or excessively compressed. Reassemble the taps and install them in the tank. Reinstall the tank and reconnect the fuel lines. Partially fill the tank with fresh fuel/oil mixture and check for leaks around the taps and at the line connections. Tighten the taps if necessary.

CARBURETOR

The carburetor should be removed, disassembled, cleaned, and adjusted periodically. Service interval depends upon use, but a good rule of thumb is to clean the carburetor at each tune-up. For service information, refer to Chapter Six.

IGNITION

The contact breaker in conventional ignitions should be checked for condition and adjusted every 1,800 miles. Refer to Chapter Seven for service information. The electronic ignition installed on some models requires no periodic adjustment.

Spark Plug

The spark plug should be cleaned and checked and its gap adjusted every 600 miles. Plug type and gap are given in Chapter Ten. Functionally test the plug by removing it from the engine, checking and adjusting the gap, and fitting it into the cap on the high-tension terminal. Lay the plug on the head to ground it and operate the kickstart lever several times and observe the spark across the plug electrodes. If the plug is in good condition, the spark will be strong and blue in color. If it is not, replace the plug with a new one.

CLUTCH

The clutch should be checked every 600 miles and adjusted if necessary. The free-play should be 2-3mm (0.08-0.12 in.), measured between the clutch lever (3) and stop (arrow, **Figure 12**). To adjust the free-play, loosen the locknut (1) and the adjusting screw (2). Screw the cable adjuster at the hand control all the way in (**Figure 13**). The clutch lever in the case should be resting on its stop. Screw the cable adjuster out until there is 1mm (0.04 in.) of play in the hand lever before the clutch lever moves from its stop. Then lock the cable adjuster.

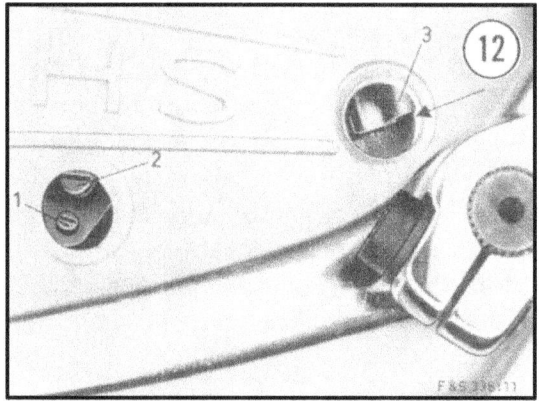

Turn the adjusting screw (Figure 12) clockwise until you can just begin to feel resistance. Turn the screw out (counterclockwise) 1/3 turn and tighten the lock screw. Check the free-play as before and repeat the above procedure if necessary until the adjustment is correct.

CARBON REMOVAL

To remove carbon from the engine, it's necessary to remove the cylinder head, cylinder, and piston as described in Chapter Three. Carbon should be removed from the engine about every 3,600 miles, or after about 40 hours of motocross competition.

CHAPTER THREE

CYLINDER HEAD, CYLINDER, AND PISTON

CYLINDER HEAD

Cylinder heads are cast from lightweight aluminum in 3 fin patterns—vertical fins (**Figure 1**), radial or sunburst fins without connecting bridges (**Figure 2**), and sunburst fins with connecting bridges (**Figure 3**).

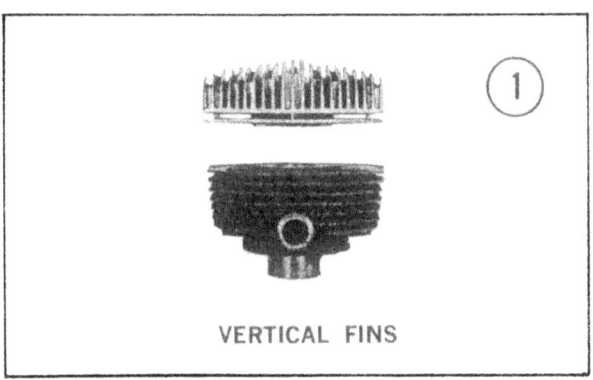

VERTICAL FINS

RADIAL FINS

RADIAL FINS WITH BRIDGES

Cylinder Head Removal

To avoid possible distortion of the cylinder head, allow the engine to cool before removal. To remove the head, proceed as follows:

1. If the engine is installed in the motorcycle, shut off the fuel taps, disconnect the lines, and remove the fuel tank from the motorcycle. Unplug the high-tension lead from the spark plug and unscrew the plug from the head. If the coil is situated in such a way that it could be damaged during work on the head, note the location of the primary leads and remove the coil from the motorcycle. On some models, it will also be necessary to remove the exhaust system.

2. Cylinder head nuts must be removed and reinstalled in the sequence specified in **Figure 4**. Loosen each nut one-half turn and repeat the

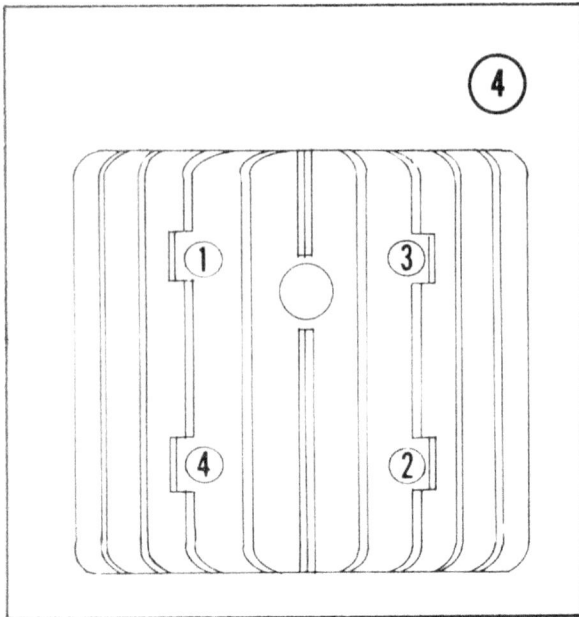

process until each nut has been loosened 2 full turns. Then, remove each nut completely and mark its location so it can be reinstalled on the stud from which it was removed.

3. Lift the cylinder head off of the cylinder, taking care not to drop washers or locating dowels into the cylinder. If necessary, tap the head with a soft-face mallet to loosen it; never pry it off because doing so may damage the fins or the sealing surface. If the engine is equipped with a head gasket, remove it.

Removing Carbon Deposits

Scrape away carbon deposits with the rounded end of a hacksaw blade. Wrap tape around the blade (see **Figure 5**) to provide a comfortable handle and prevent damage to your hand. Be careful not to scar the surface of the combustion chamber or around the seal. Small burrs resulting from gouges in the chamber will create hot spots which will cause pre-ignition and heat erosion. Gouges on the sealing surface will result in an improper seal of the combustion chamber.

After scraping, clean the head in solvent. Carefully clean the spark plug bore with a fine wire brush and blow out carbon particles with an air hose.

Cylinder Head Installation

1. On engines so equipped, install the guide dowels and a new head gasket. The inscription

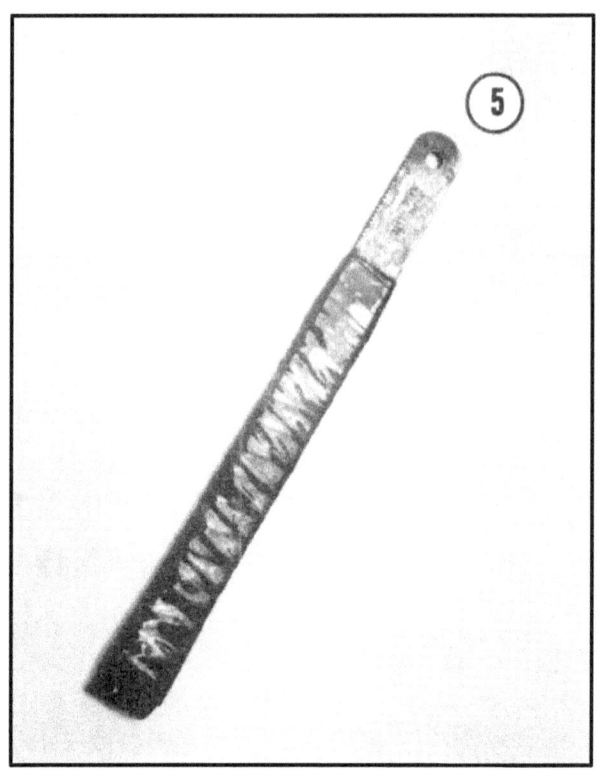

"oben" on the gasket should face up and point toward the exhaust port.

2. Reinstall the head and screw on the nuts (or bolts) making sure each one has a washer.

NOTE: *For the large sunburst head, make sure the bevelled fin is toward the front and the plug bore to the rear* **(Figure 6).**

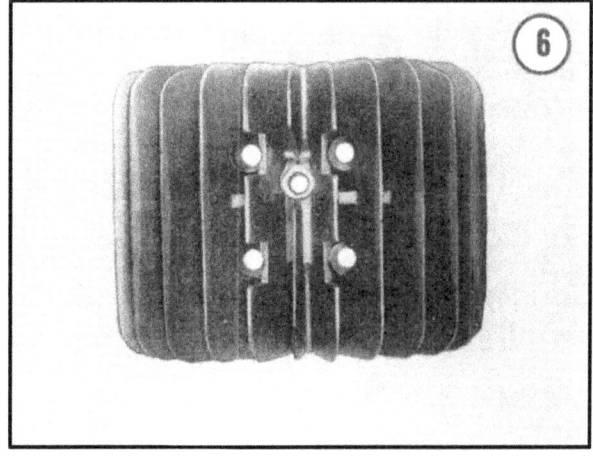

3. Tighten the nuts (bolts) with a torque wrench, in the pattern shown in Figure 4, to 12-15 ft.-lb. (1.7-2.0 kgm). Rotate the crankshaft to move the piston up and down in the cylinder after tightening each nut. Again tighten the nuts in the pattern shown, this time to the appropriate

torque value given in **Table 1**, moving the piston up and down after tightening each nut.

4. Complete the reassembly by reversing the remaining steps for removal.

Table 1 CYLINDER HEAD NUT (BOLT) TORQUE

Type	Torque
Aluminum cylinder with through-studs and nuts	18-22 ft.-lb. (2.5-3.0 kpm)
Cast iron cylinder with head bolts	22-23 ft.-lb. (3.0-3.2 kpm)

CYLINDER

There are 2 cylinder types used on Sachs engines—one-piece cast iron and two-piece cast aluminum with a pressed-in cast iron liner. The integral liner in the cast-iron cylinder is not replaceable; however, the cylinder is designed to accomodate three rebores. The cast-iron liner in aluminum cylinders will also accomodate three rebores and then may be replaced with a new liner to restore the cylinder diameter to the original dimension. Cylinder types for each model are shown in the *Specifications* section.

Cylinder Removal

1. Remove the cylinder head as described previously. In all cases, it is necessary to remove the exhaust system and carburetor.

2. On engines with a flanged cylinder base, unscrew the 4 nuts which hold the cylinder onto the crankcase.

3. Pull the cylinder up and off the studs and piston. Don't rotate the cylinder as you raise it; this could result in breakage of the rings.

Cylinder Inspection

Measure cylinder wall wear at 3 depths within the cylinder, using a cylinder gauge or inside micrometer, as shown in **Figure 7**. Measure parallel and at a right angle to the crankshaft at the locations shown in **Figure 8**. If taper exceeds 0.008 in. (0.20mm), or out-of-round

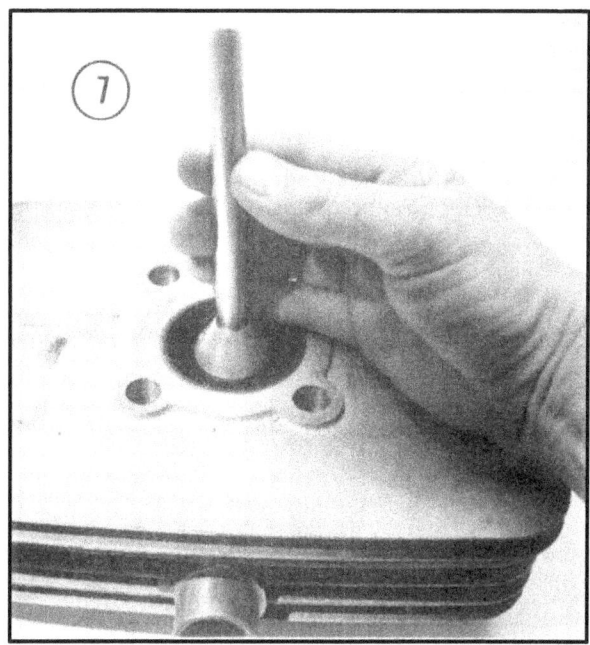

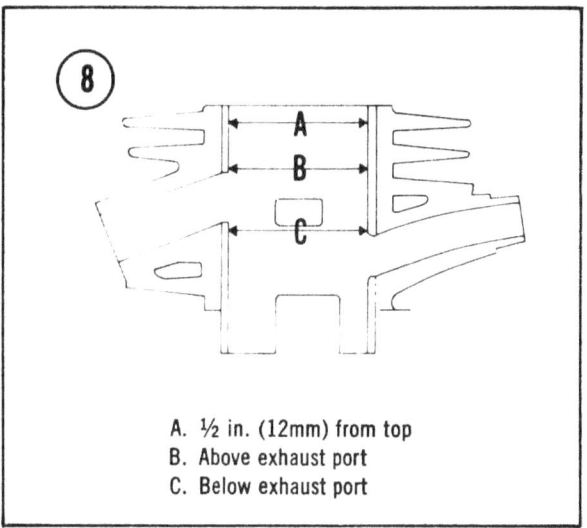

A. ½ in. (12mm) from top
B. Above exhaust port
C. Below exhaust port

exceeds 0.008 in. (0.20mm), rebore and hone the cylinder to the next oversize. After boring, radius the edges of the transfer, intake, and exhaust port (see **Table 2**).

Have the new piston on hand prior to reboring the cylinder so that it may be measured and the cylinder bored to provide the required piston-to-cylinder clearance shown in **Table 3**. Measure the piston just above the bottom of the skirt at a right angle to the pin bosses. Add the result to the desired clearance to determine the final overbore size of the cylinder.

To check the clearance of a run-in piston and bore, measure the piston and cylinder as described above and subtract the piston dimension from the cylinder dimension. If the clearance exceeds 0.008 in. (0.20mm), the cylinder should be rebored to the next oversize and a new piston fitted.

> NOTE: *Because Sachs wrist pins are mounted low in the piston, the wear pattern in the cylinder tends to become barrel shaped* **(Figure 9)**. *This condition accelerates ring wear. If this condition exists and only the rings are replaced, they will wear rapidly. If "barreling" is even only slightly evident, rebore the cylinder to the next oversize and fit a new piston.*

Cylinder Installation

1. Install a new cylinder base gasket on the studs in the crankcase (**Figure 10**). On engines with through-studs, install the alignment dowels.

2. Place a wooden block beneath the piston (**Figure 11**).

> NOTE: *The block can be made from a piece of scrap lumber or plywood cut to the dimensions shown in* **Figure 12**.

3. Make sure the rings are seated in the grooves and correctly lined up with the locating pins in the ring grooves (see **Figure 13**).

Table 2 PISTON DIAMETER

Displacement	Standard	First Oversize	Second Oversize	Third Oversize
97cc	48.0mm (1.89 in.)	48.5mm (1.91 in.)	49.0mm (1.93 in.)	49.5mm (1.95 in.)
122cc	54.0mm (2.126 in.)	54.5mm (2.147 in.)	55.0mm (2.167 in.)	55.5mm (2.186 in.)

NOTE: The inch measurement is presented only for general reference. Pistons are sized metrically.

Table 3 PISTON-TO-CYLINDER CLEARANCE

Displacement	Bore Size	Clearance
97cc	Standard 48.0mm (1.89 in.)	0.1198mm (0.00473 in.)
	First Oversize 48.5mm (1.91 in.)	0.1213mm (0.00478 in.)
	Second Oversize 49.0mm (1.93 in.)	0.1226mm (0.00484 in.)
	Third Oversize 49.5mm (1.95 in.)	0.1237mm (0.00488 in.)
122cc	Standard 54.0mm (2.13 in.)	0.1350mm (0.00532 in.)
	First Oversize 54.5mm (2.15 in.)	0.1363mm (0.00537 in.)
	Second Oversize 55.0mm (2.17 in.)	0.1375mm (0.00542 in.)
	Third Oversize 55.5mm (2.19 in.)	0.1388mm (0.00547 in.)

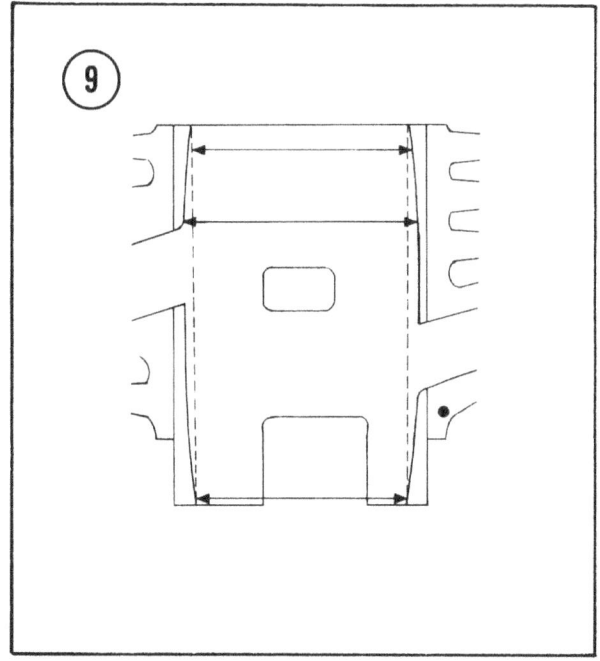

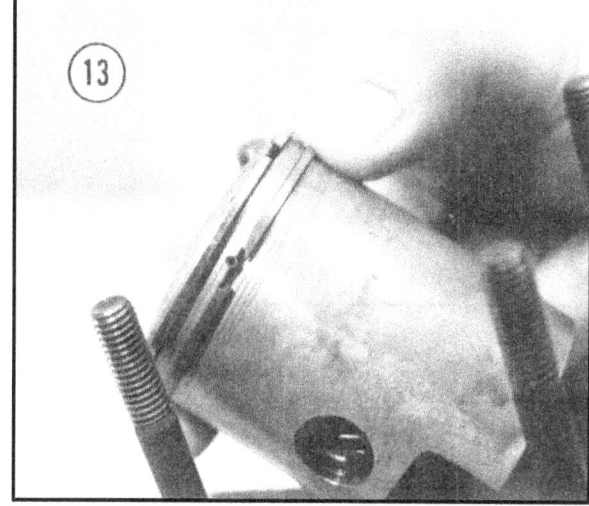

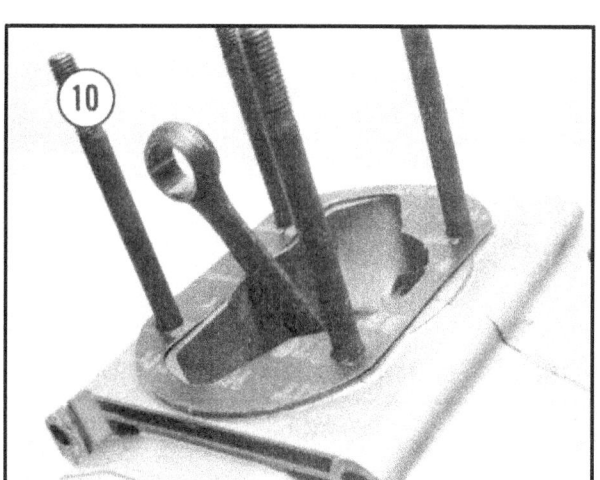

4. Oil the cylinder bore and start the cylinder onto the piston (**Figure 14**). Make sure the cylinder is correctly positioned—intake to the rear.

5. Carefully slide the cylinder down over the rings (**Figure 15**).

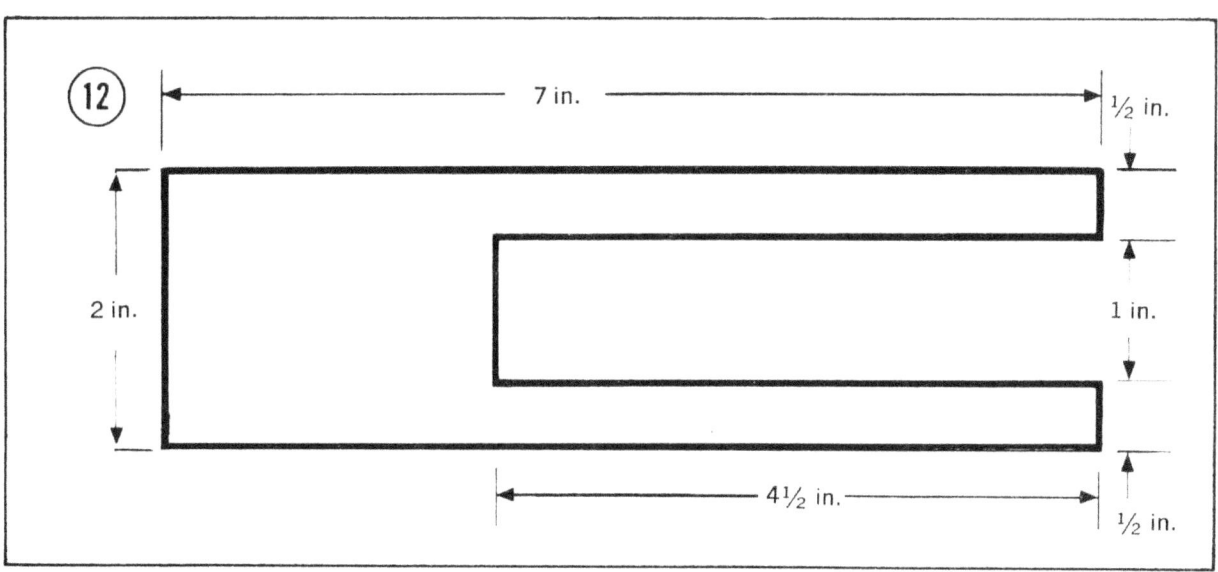

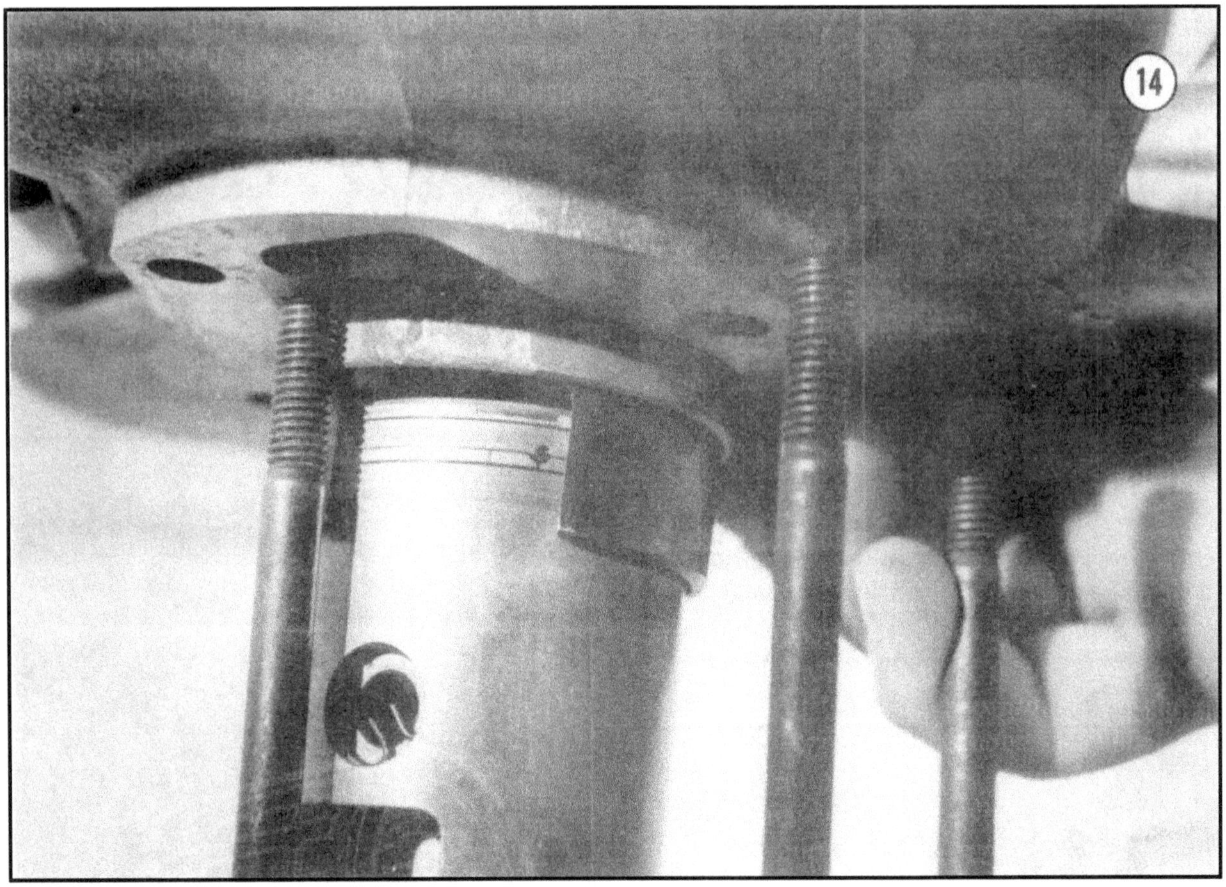
14

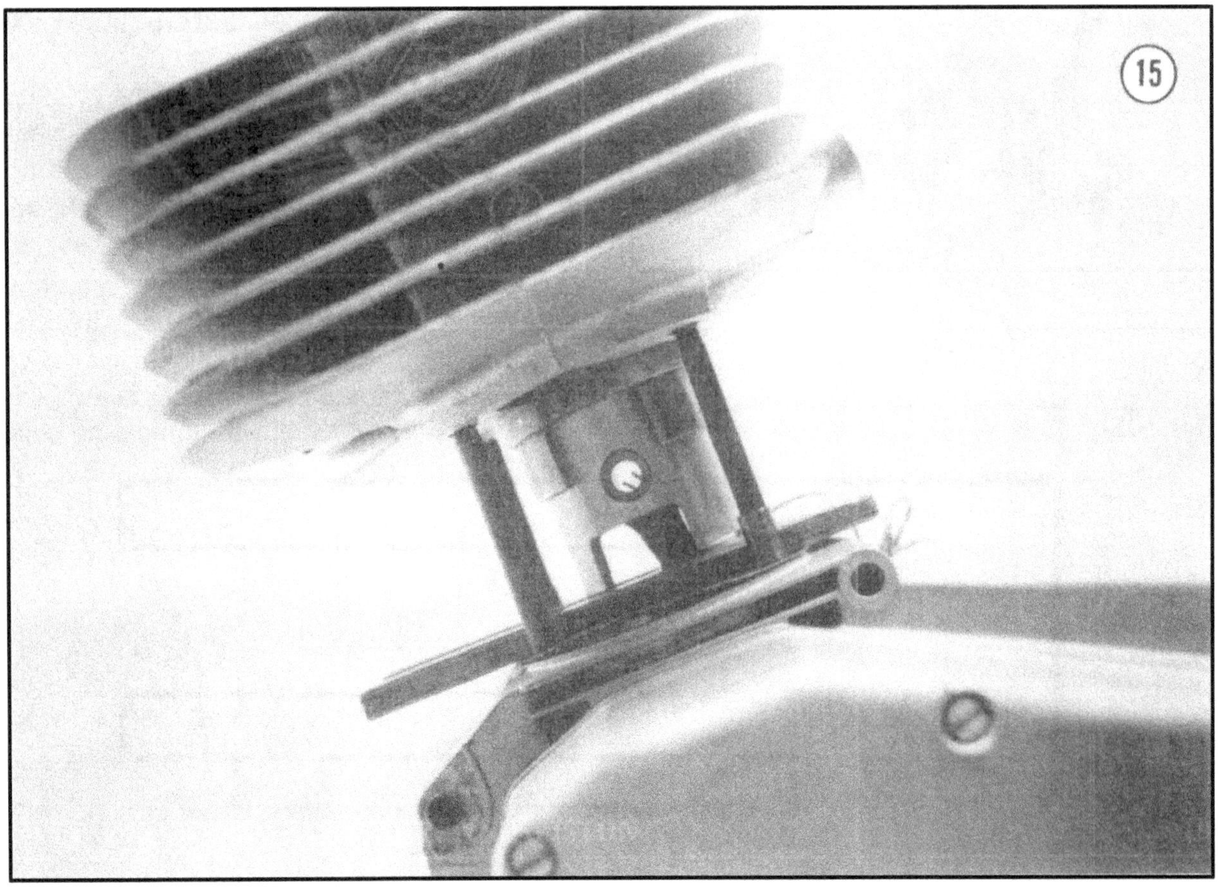
15

6. Remove the wooden block and push the cylinder all the way down onto the crankcase.

7. On engines with a flanged cylinder, install the 4 washers and nuts on the short studs and tighten the nuts to 17-19 ft.-lb. (2.4-2.6 mkg) in a diagonal pattern. Rotate the crankshaft to move the piston up and down in the cylinder after tightening each nut.

8. Install the cylinder head as discussed previously.

PISTON ASSEMBLY

Sachs pistons (**Figure 16**) are made of aluminum alloy and are fitted with 2 rings—an L or Dykes-pattern top compression ring and a rail type secondary compression ring. The wrist pin is press fitted and retained in the piston with circlips. On engines fitted with an aluminum connecting rod, the wrist pin is connected to the rod with a bronze bushing. On engines fitted with a steel connecting rod, a caged needle bearing is used on the small end of the rod.

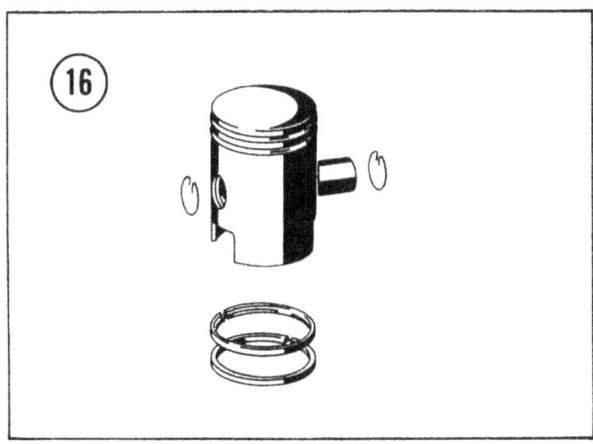

Before beginning any work on the cylinder, cylinder head, or piston, thoroughly clean the outside of the engine and adjacent areas with solvent or a good grade of engine cleaner. Flush away dirt and grime with water and thoroughly dry the engine.

Piston Removal

Allow the engine to cool thoroughly to prevent distortion of the cylinder head upon removal, then remove the head and cylinder as discussed previously.

NOTE: *On engines with aluminum connecting rods, check the wear of the pin bushing prior to removing the piston by attempting to rock the piston from side to side along the pin axis. There should be no perceptible rocking movement, although the piston should rotate freely on the axis and slide from side to side slightly.*

1. Stuff a clean, lint-free cloth into the top of the crankcase and place a wooden block beneath the piston. Remove the circlips from both sides of the piston (Figure 11).

2. Push the pin out of the piston with a pin extractor (see **Figure 17**). Be careful not to damage the rings.

3. On engines with steel connecting rods, remove the needle bearing assembly from the rod.

4. If the engine has an aluminum connecting rod and the earlier check of the bushing indicated that it is worn, press out the bushing as shown in **Figure 18** by holding the withdrawal bolt with an open-end wrench and turning the large nut clockwise.

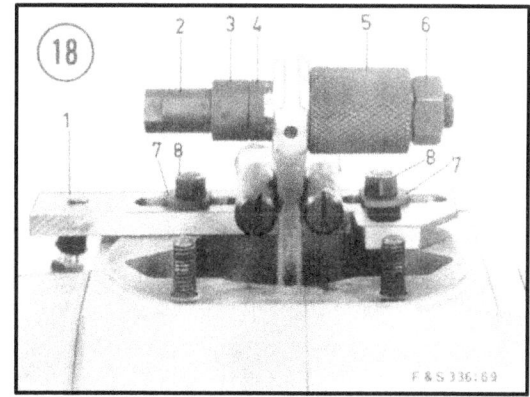

Piston Inspection

Examine the piston carefully for hairline cracks at the top edges of the transfer cutaways (see **Figure 19**). If any cracks are found, replace the piston. Check the ring lands for chips or breaks on the edges. Check the locating pins for wear. Replace the piston if there is any doubt about its condition.

Remove the rings from the piston by spreading the top ring with a thumb on each end, as shown in **Figure 20**. Remove the ring from the top of the piston and repeat the procedure for removing the secondary ring.

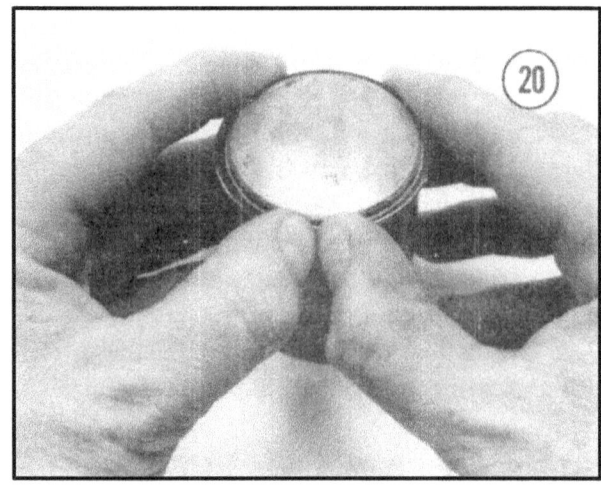

Clean the carbon from the top of the piston with the rounded end of a hacksaw blade. Clean the carbon and gum from the ring grooves with a broken ring or a groove cleaner. Any deposits left in the grooves will prevent the rings from seating correctly and may very likely result in piston seizure. Check the top of the piston for erosion of the metal and replace it if any is found. Erosion of the piston crown is very often caused by an extremely lean fuel/air mixture. This condition should be corrected immediately after a new piston has been installed and the engine reassembled.

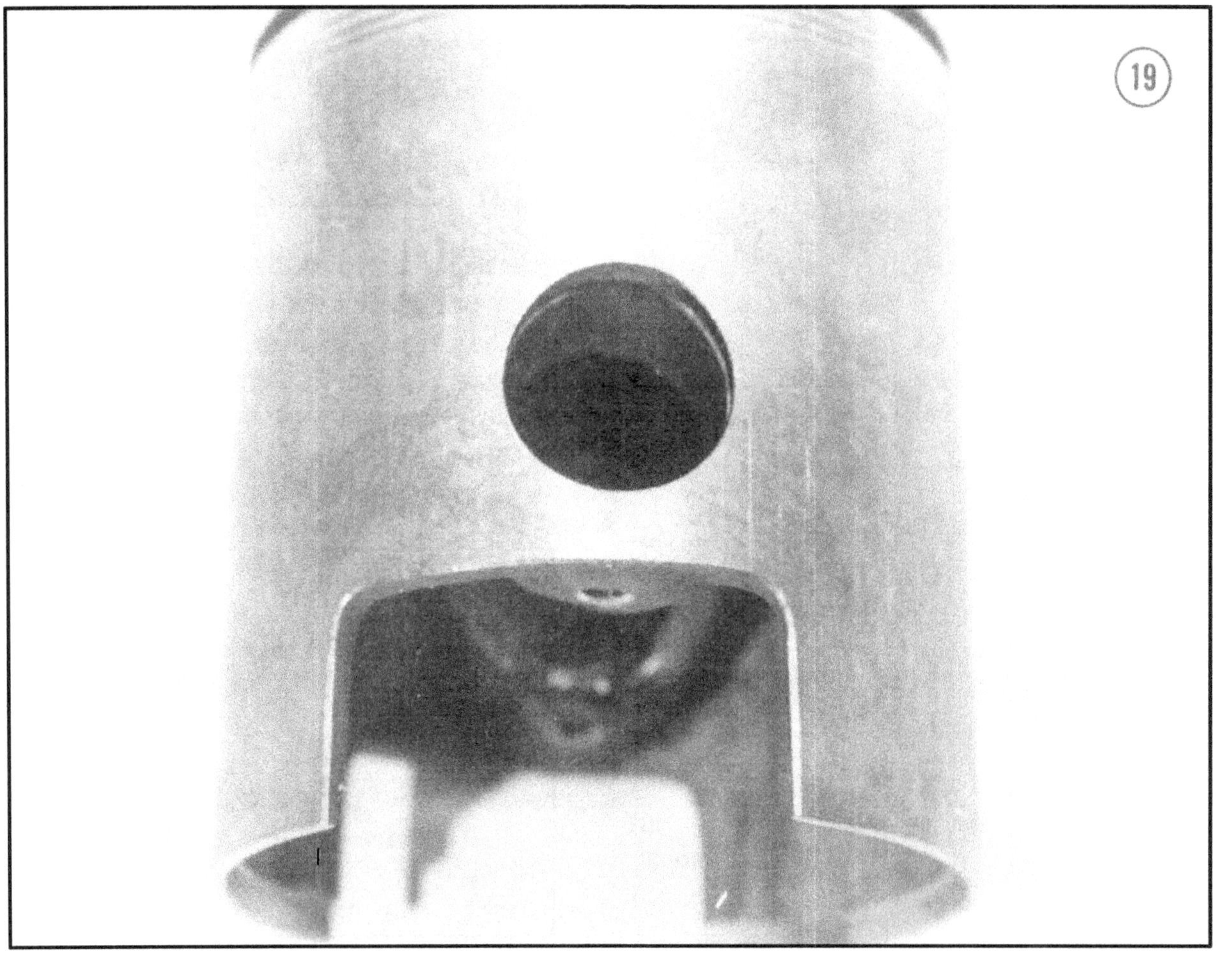

Check the skirt of the piston for brown varnish deposits. More than a slight amount is evidence of worn or sticking rings which should be replaced. Also check the skirt for galling and abrasion—a common symptom of piston seizure. If light galling is present, smooth the affected area with No. 400 emery paper or a fine oilstone. However, if galling is severe or if the piston is deeply scored, replace it.

Measure the piston for clearance in the cylinder as described earlier. Replace the piston and rebore the cylinder as described if the clearance is excessive. Measure the end gap of the rings as shown in **Figure 21**. Insert the ring about 1 in. (40mm) into the cylinder, squaring it up by pushing it into position with the head of the piston. The end gap should be 0.0025-0.0030 in. (0.063-0.076mm) for both rings. If the gap exceeds 0.0030 in. (0.076mm), replace the rings as a set. Check the end gap of new rings in the same manner as for the old.

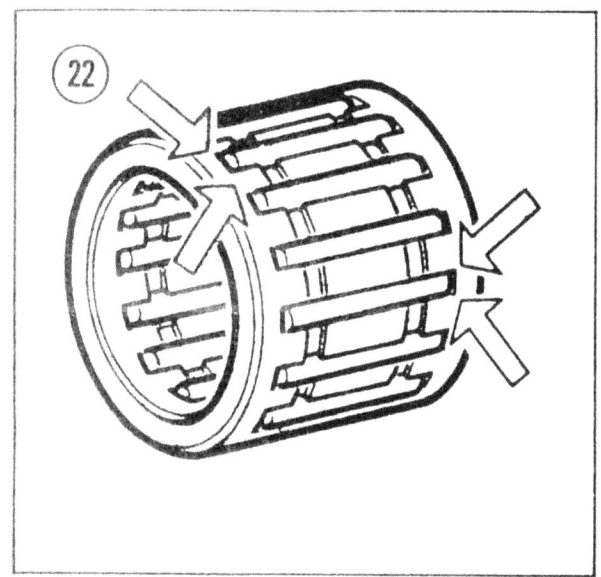

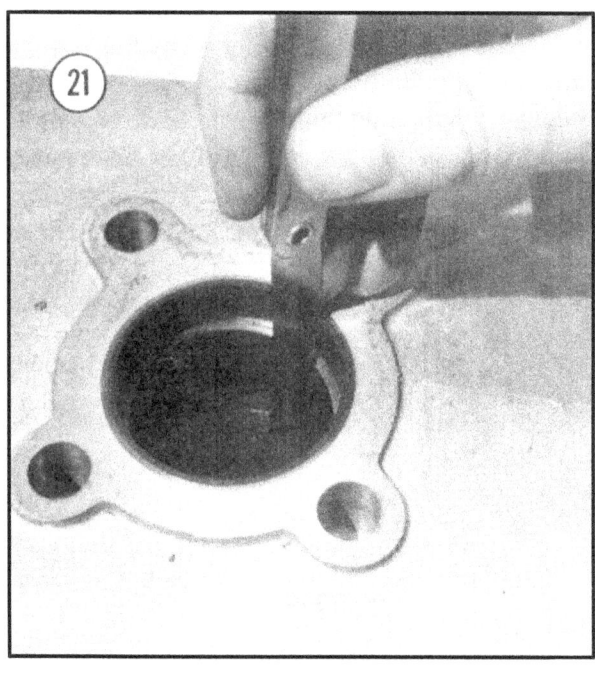

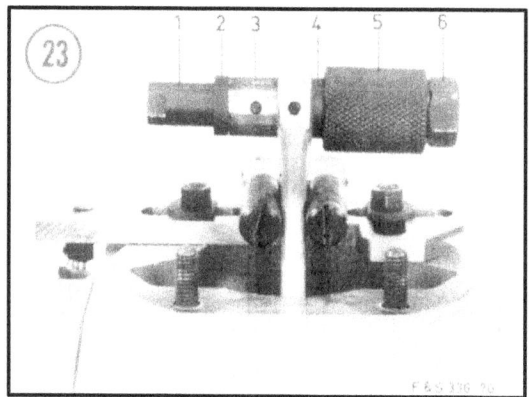

Clean the needle bearing assembly in solvent and dry it thoroughly. With a magnifying glass, examine the bearing assembly for cracks at the corners of the bearing slots, and also on the needles themselves (see **Figure 22**). If any are found, replace the bearing.

Piston Installation

1. Lightly oil the bearing and reinstall it in the upper end of the connecting rod. If the rod is bushed and a new bushing is being fitted, install the bushing and the tool as shown in **Figure 23**.

Make sure the oil hole in the bushing lines up with the oil hole in the rod. Press the bushing into the rod by holding the withdrawal bolt with an open-end wrench and turning the large nut on the tool clockwise.

> NOTE: *The bushing must be reamed to final size — 0.5916-0.5922 in. (15.015-15.030mm). This is a job which should be entrusted to an expert.*

2. Place the slotted wooden block over the top of the crankcase and set the piston on the top of the rod. The arrow on the top of the piston must point forward.

3. Lightly oil the pin and start it into the piston. Set the pin remover/installer tool in place.

4. Align the pin bosses in the piston with the connecting rod and press the pin into the piston by turning the installer bolt clockwise. Stop

when the far end of the pin has reached the inside edge of its circlip groove and remove the installer.

5. Install new circlips in both sides of the piston. Make sure they are completely seated in their grooves by rotating them slightly with the flat of a screwdriver as shown in **Figure 24**.

6. Check the installation by rocking the piston back and forth around the pin axis and from side to side along the axis. It should rotate freely back and forth but not rock from side to side.

7. Install the rings—first the bottom one, then the top—by carefully spreading the ends of the rings with the thumbs and slipping the ring over the top of the piston. Make sure the rings seat completely in the grooves, all the way around the circumference, and the ends are aligned with the locating pins.

8. Install the cylinder and cylinder head and reassemble the remaining components as described previously.

If the rings were replaced, or if the cylinder was rebored and a new piston installed, the engine must be run in at moderate speeds and loads for no less than two hours. Don't exceed 75 percent of normally allowable rpm during run in. After the first half hour, remove the spark plug and check its condition. The electrode should be dry and clean and the color of the insulation should be light to medium tan. If the insulation is white (indicating a too-lean fuel/air mixture) or if it is dark and oily (indicating a too-rich fuel/air mixture ratio), correct the condition with a jet change; both incorrect conditions produce excessive engine heat and can lead to damage of the rings, piston, and cylinder before the engine has had a chance to seat in.

CHAPTER FOUR

CRANKSHAFT AND CRANKCASE

The crankshaft assembly is made up of 2 full-circle flywheels pressed together on a hollow crankpin. The connecting rod big-end bearing on the crankpin is a needle bearing assembly. The crankshaft assembly is supported in 2 roller bearing assemblies on the drive (left) side and a single roller bearing assembly on the ignition (right) side.

The two-piece crankcase splits vertically along the centerline of the connecting rod. Disassembly, or splitting, of the crankcase yields access to both the crankshaft and the transmission. Refer to the exploded master drawing (**Figure 1**) for relationship of the crankcase and crankshaft components.

The procedure which follows is presented as a complete, step-by-step major lower-end rebuild that would be followed if an engine is to be completely reconditioned. However, if you're replacing a known failed part, the disassembly need be carried out only until the failed part is accessible; there's no need to disassemble the engine beyond that point as long as you know the remaining components are in good condition and that they were not affected by the failed part.

ENGINE REMOVAL

Before the crankcase can be split, the engine must be removed from the motorcycle. Prior to beginning work, thoroughly clean, rinse, and dry the motorcycle, paying particular attention to the engine. Refer to Chapter Three for removal of the head and cylinder and then proceed as follows.

1. Disconnect the master link from the drive chain and remove the chain from the motorcycle.
2. Loosen the clutch cable adjuster at the handlebar (**Figure 2**).

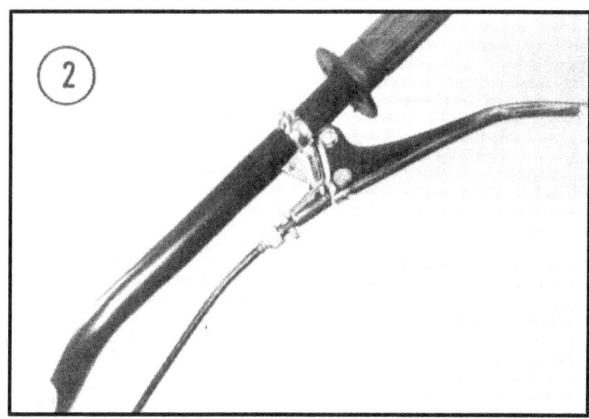

3. Disconnect the speedometer cable from the right side of the transmission (see **Figure 3**).
4. Remove the kickstarter lever (**Figure 4**).
5. Remove the gear selector pedal (**Figure 5**).

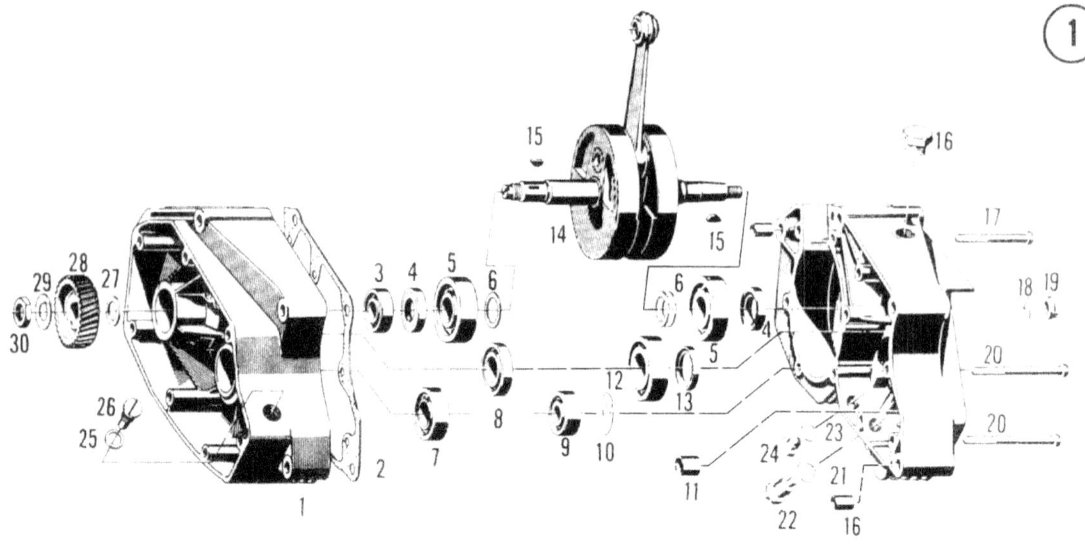

CRANKCASE AND CRANKSHAFT

1. Crankcase assembly
2. Gasket
3. Deep groove ball bearing
4. Oil seal
5. Ball bearing
6. Shim
7. Deep groove ball bearing
8. Deep groove ball bearing
9. Deep groove ball bearing
10. Profile washer
11. Washer
12. Cylindrical roller bearing
13. Oil seal
14. Crankshaft
15. Key
16. Plug screw
17. Screw
18. Spring washer
19. Collar nut
20. Screw
21. Sealing washer
22. Stop screw
23. Sealing washer
24. Oil drain plug
25. Sealing washer
26. Pivot screw
27. Washer
28. Driving pinion
29. Tab washer
30. Nut

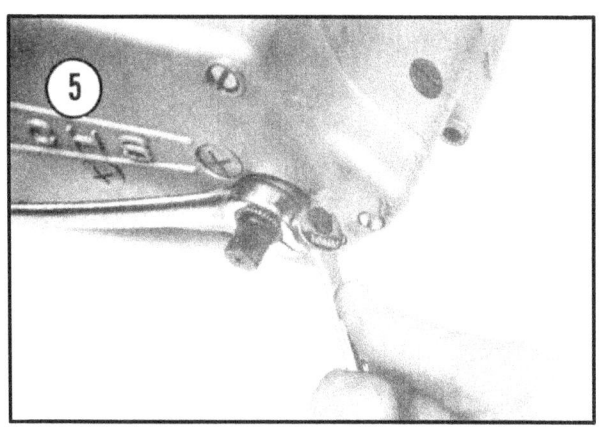

6. Place a drip pan beneath the engine and remove the drain plug (**Figure 6**), the fill plug, and the level and inspection plugs (**Figure 7**).

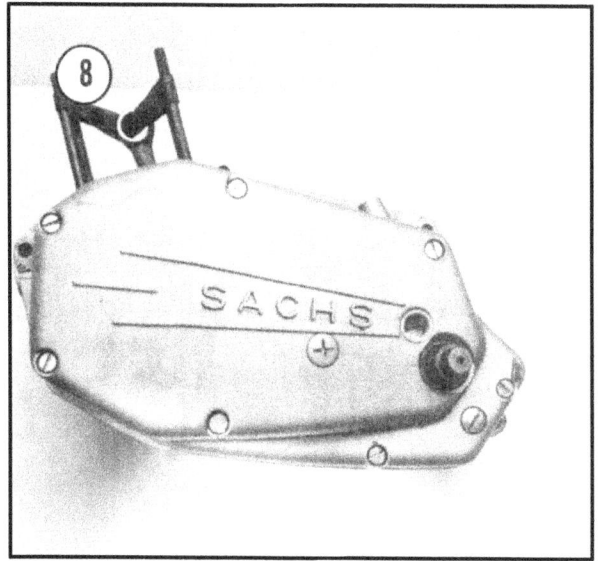

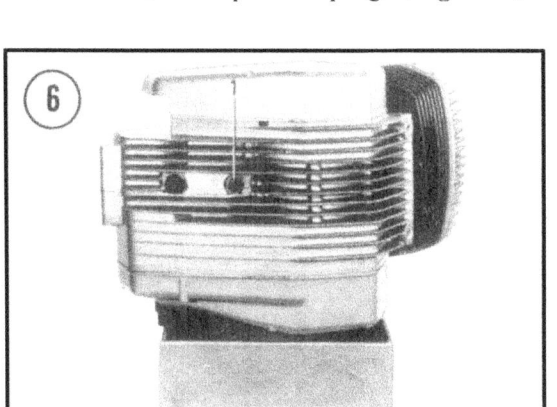

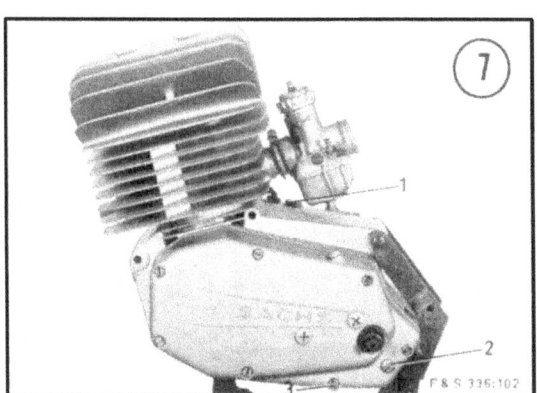

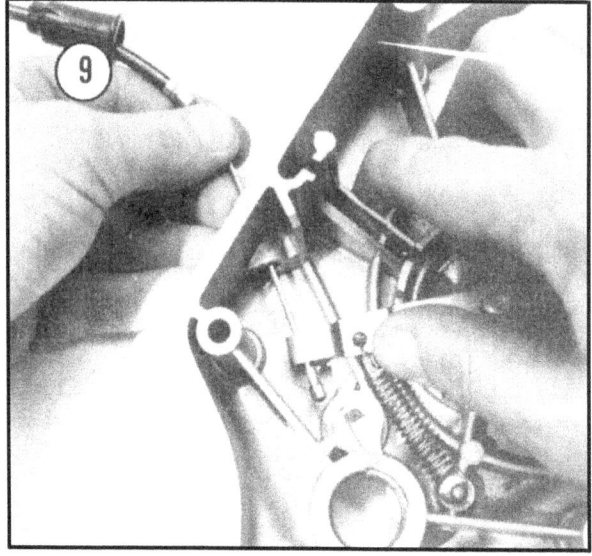

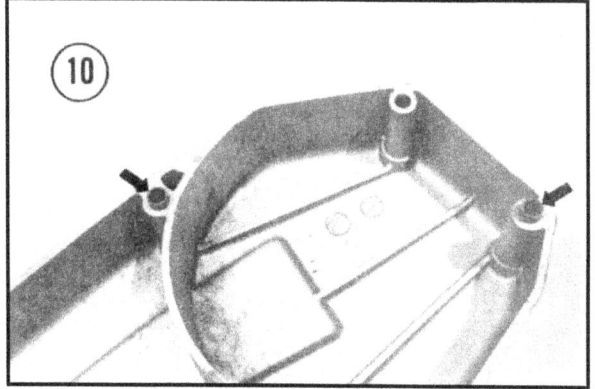

7. Remove the 7 screws from the left engine cover (**Figure 8**), pull the cover out, disconnect the clutch cable from the actuating arm (see **Figure 9**), and remove the cover.

8. Remove the 4 screws from the right engine cover and pull it off. Be careful not to lose the 2 hollow alignment dowels (**Figure 10**).

9. Unscrew the nuts from the ends of the 3 engine mounting bolts (one front, 2 rear), remove the washers, and pull out the bottom rear bolt (see **Figure 11**).

10. Get assistance and lift up the engine to take the tension off the 2 remaining bolts. Pull out

27

the top rear bolt, then the front bolt, and lift the engine out of the frame (see **Figure 12**).

LOWER END
Disassembly

1. Check the bottom of the engine for dirt and grease embedded between the fins and clean if necessary.

2. Mount the engine in a repair jig.

NOTE: *If a jig is not available, you will need assistance to hold the engine steady during some of the procedures to be carried out. In such case, set the engine on a soft wood surface, such as a piece of plywood, to prevent damage to the fins and cases.*

3. Install the chain lever on the repair jig and lay the chain of the lever over the countershaft sprocket, from left to right, as shown in **Figure 13**. Unscrew the left-hand threaded countershaft nut and remove it and the spring washer.

NOTE: *If the chain lever is not available, or if you are working without a repair jig, remove the countershaft sprocket nut with the engine in the frame before removing the drive chain. Have someone assist you by holding the rear wheel to prevent it from rotating.*

4. Install a puller on the countershaft sprocket and pull it off by turning the puller bolt clockwise (**Figure 14**).

5. Hold the flywheel with a jig lever (**Figure 15**) or a pin wrench and unscrew the left-hand threaded collar nut from the end of the flywheel.

NOTE: *When using a pin wrench to hold the flywheel on engines equipped with Motoplat electronic ignition (**Figure 16**), be careful that the pins of the wrench do not touch the timing-signal post at the front of the stator.*

6. Place the protective cap (tool No. 4) over the end of the crankshaft. Install the puller (tool No. 6) and pull off the flywheel by turning

the puller bolt clockwise (**Figure 17**). Remove the puller and protective cap (and the jig lever if it was used) and remove the flywheel from the engine.

7A. On engines equipped with Bosch contact breaker ignition, remove the 3 Phillips head screws and washers from the stator plate (**Figure 18**). Carefully pull the wiring harness and rubber grommet out of the case and remove the assembly from the engine. Insert the stator into the flywheel, wrap the entire unit in clean newspaper, and set it aside.

7B. On engines equipped with Motoplat electronic ignition, remove the 3 slotted screws and

washers from the front of stator (**Figure 19**). Carefully pull the wiring harness and rubber grommet out of the case and remove the stator from the engine and insert it into the flywheel. Remove the 3 slotted screws and washers from the base plate (**Figure 20**), remove the base plate and set it on top of the stator. Wrap the entire ignition assembly in clean newspaper and set it aside.

8. If the clutch gear is fitted with a leaf spring mounted outboard of the thrust plate (see **Figure 21**), unscrew the nut holding the spring and remove the spring and plate. The spring may be discarded; it's not essential.

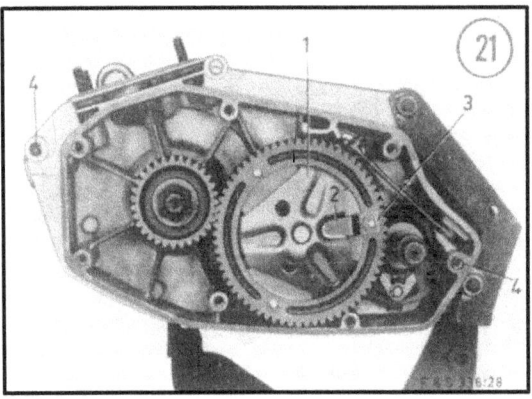

9. Remove the lock spring and shims (**Figure 22**) and pull off the clutch wheel.

10. Remove the shims from the end of the gear selector shaft (**Figure 23**).

11. Tilt the engine to its left and remove the thrust bearing from the clutch hub.

12. Fit the lock (tool No. 8) over the clutch hub splines and secure it with 2 cover retaining bolts as shown in **Figure 24**. Unscrew the clutch hub nut, remove the lock, the clutch, and the key.

13. Fit the lock (tool No. 10) over the crank gear and secure it with two cover bolts as shown in **Figure 25**. Bend back the locking tab and unscrew the sprocket nut. Remove the tab locking plate, the lock tool, the gear, and the key.

NOTE: *At this stage of disassembly, it's possible to replace the right-side crankshaft seal, provided the special seal puller (tool No. 13) is available. Also, seal removal and replacement can be accomplished with the engine in the motorcycle and without removing the head and cylinder.*

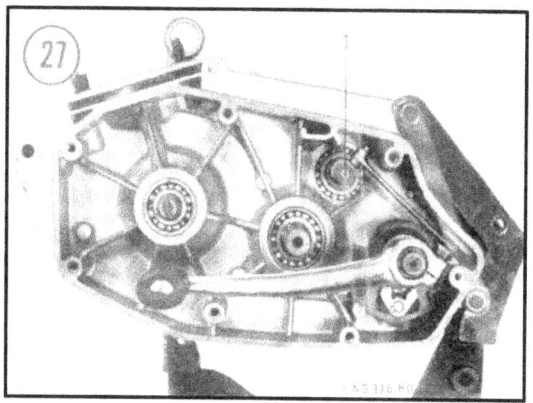

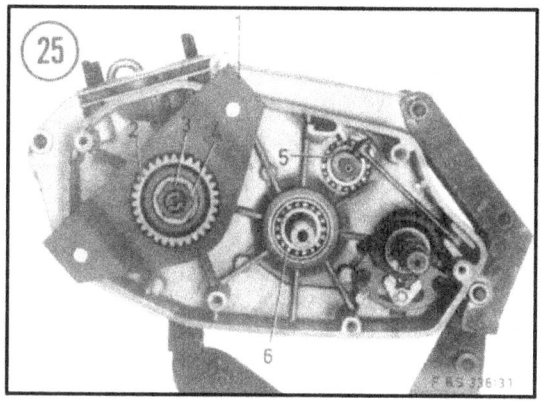

the selector boss (**Figure 28**). Lift the selector lever and pull the selector assembly off the shaft (**Figure 29**), along with the shims. If there is a gear lock on the selector mechanism (see **Figure 30**), unhook the spring and pull it out with the selector assembly.

GEAR SELECTOR REMOVAL
ONE-PIECE LEVER

1. Rotate the selector shaft clockwise to engage second gear.

2. Refer to **Figure 26** and unlock the grooved nut and unscrew it.

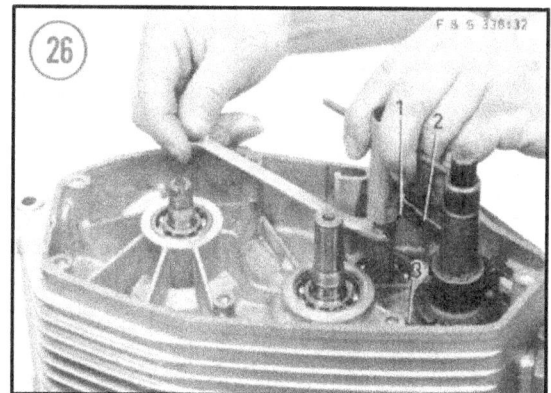

3. Remove the selector fork and slotted nut from the selector lever (**Figure 27**).

4. Remove the 2 Allen bolts and washers from

NOTE: *It's not necessary to remove the selector lever unless it has been damaged. In such case, remove the pivot bolt, sealing washer, lever, and shims (**Figure 31**). . When installing the lever, coat the threads of the pivot bolt with Loctite and screw it in with the sealing washer in place. Remember; the spacing washer fits beneath the lever, the shims fit on top.*

GEAR SELECTOR REMOVAL
TWO-PIECE LEVER

1. Rotate the selector shaft counterclockwise to engage first gear.

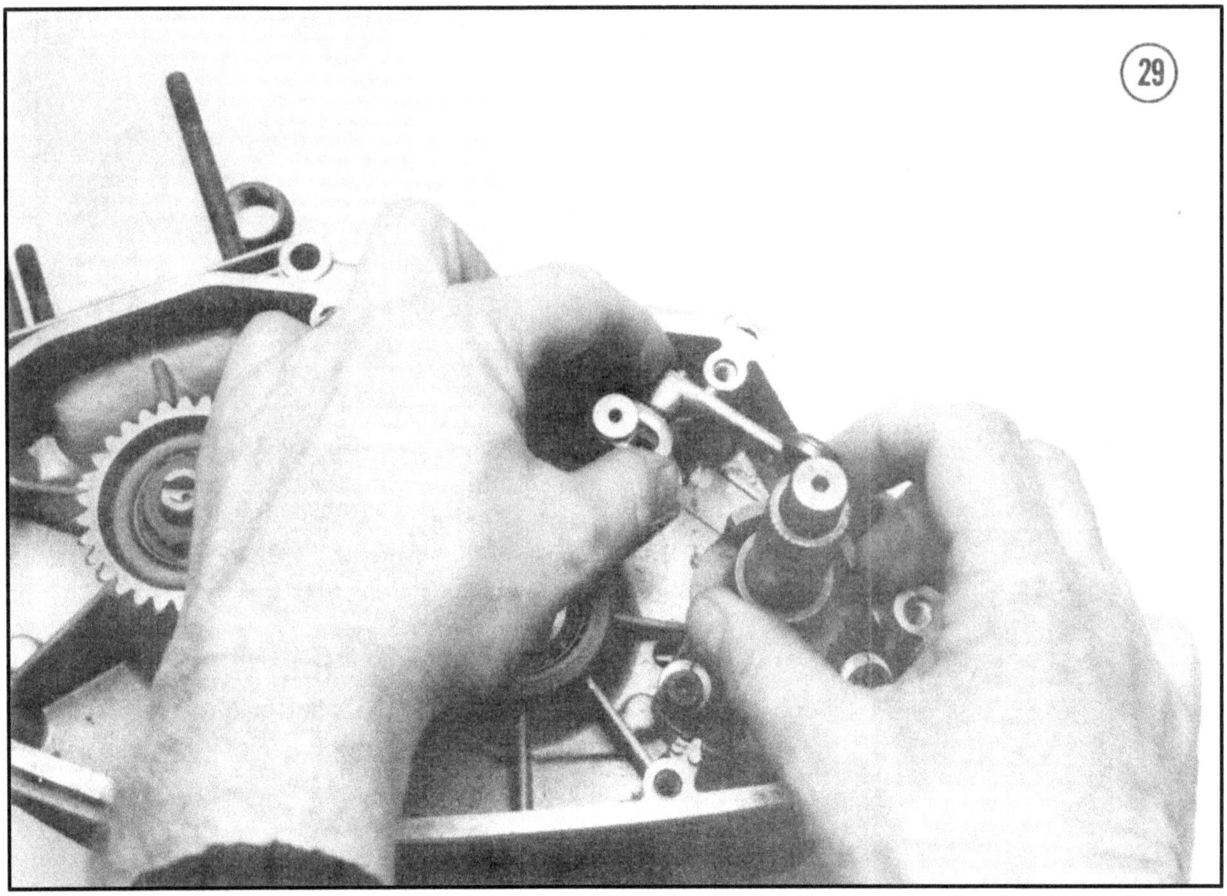

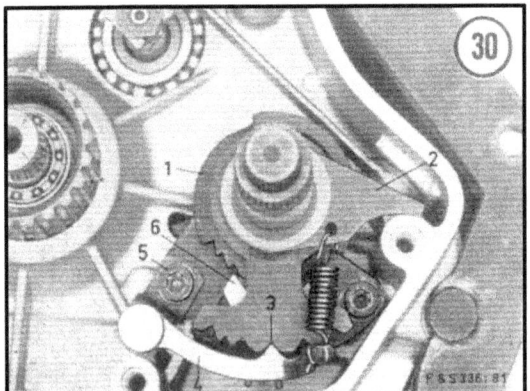

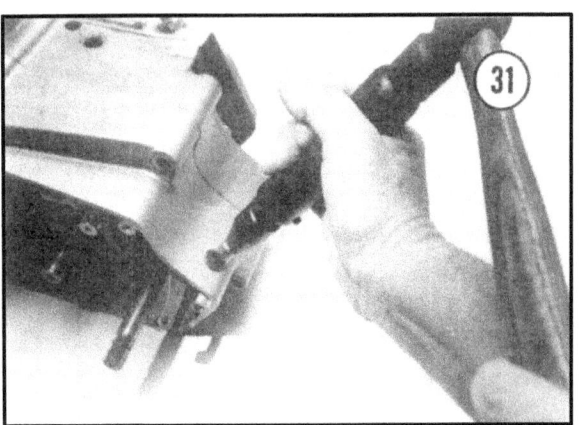

2. Refer to **Figure 32** and unscrew the nut on the top of the selector lever. Remove the lockwasher and the eccentric bolt.

3. Remove the 2 Allen bolts and washers from the selector boss.

4. Lift the selector lever and pull the selector assembly off the shaft.

5. Remove the selector fork from the lever and remove the shims. It's not necessary to remove the selector lever from the case. See the note preceding this section.

CRANKCASE SEPARATION

NOTE: *Before separating the crankcase halves, check the condition of the connecting rod big-end bearing with the crankshaft installed in the crankcase. Refer to the procedure described under* Inspection.

1. Remove the 10 slotted screws from the crankcase (**Figure 33**). The 6 screws located inside the ignition cavity are sealed with liquid sealant and may require the use of an impact screwdriver. Clean the screw threads thoroughly after removal, and remember to apply sealant to them when reassembling the crankcase halves.

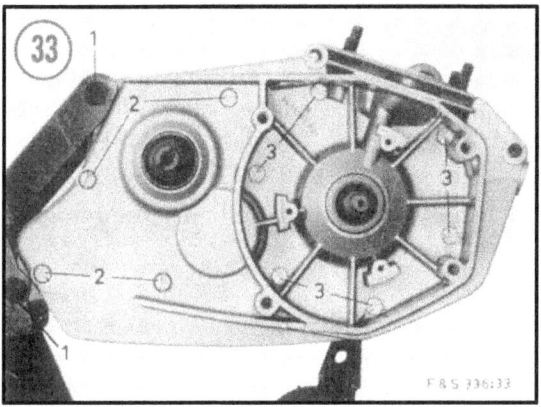

2. If a repair jig is being used, remove the crankcase from the jig and reinstall it as shown in **Figure 34**.

3. With assistance, apply pressure to the magneto-side crankcase half and tap lightly on the end of the crankshaft and transmission mainshaft to separate the cases. Lift off the magneto-side crankcase half, taking care not to lose the alignment dowels or shims (**Figure 35**).

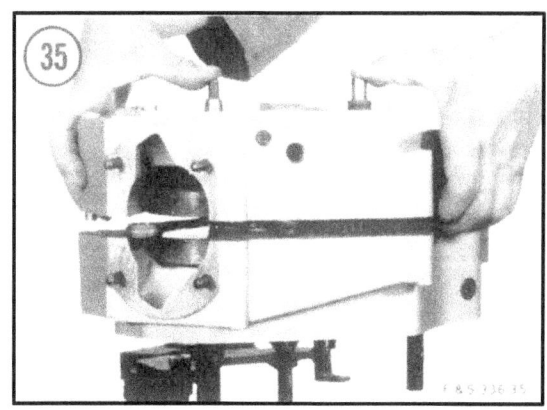

CRANKSHAFT REMOVAL

Remove the crankshaft from the clutch-side crankcase half by pulling the crank assembly straight up with a steady pressure.

TRANSMISSION DISASSEMBLY

1. Remove the layshaft and shims from the crankcase (4, **Figure 36**).

2. Remove the inner bearing race and shims from the main shaft (3, Figure 36).

3. Remove the gears and spacer rings from the main shaft, keeping them in order so they may be reassembled in the same manner (**Figure 37**).

4. Pull the main shaft out of the case, along with the washer and shims.

5. Remove the starter gear along with the thrust washer and shims.

STARTER MECHANISM REMOVAL

1. Install the kickstarter lever on the starter shaft and rotate it until the ratchet wheels lift off the stop screw (**Figure 38**).

2. Rotate the kickstarter lever forward to relax the spring, then remove the lever from the shaft and take the starter mechanism out of the case.

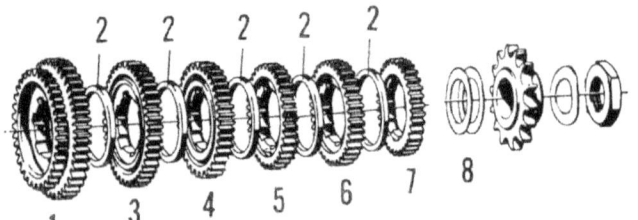

MAIN SHAFT GEARS

1. Sliding pinion 1st gear
2. Ring
3. Sliding pinion, 2nd gear
4. Sliding pinion, 3rd gear
5. Sliding pinion, 4th gear
6. Sliding pinion, 5th gear
7. Sliding pinion, 6th gear
8. Shim

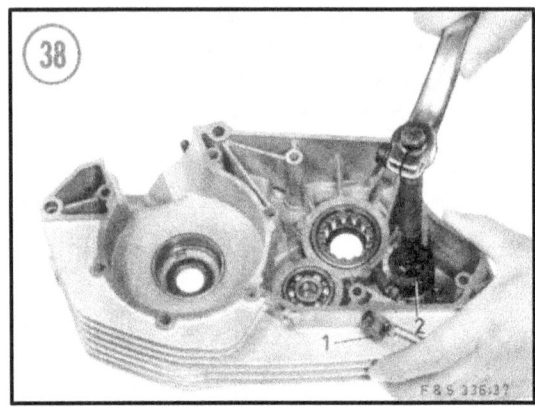

3. Remove the spacer from the case. It isn't necessary to remove the stop bolt (1, Figure 38).

INSPECTION

Check the crankcase halves for cracks or fractures in stiffening webs, around bearing bosses, and at threaded holes. While the likelihood of such damage is rare, it should be checked for, and particularly so following a catastrophic malfunction (i.e., piston breakage, bearing failure, gear breakage) or after a collision or hard spill in which the engine suffers external damage. If cracks or fractures are found, they should be repaired immediately by a reputable shop experienced in and equipped to perform repairs on precision aluminum castings.

Check the condition of the connecting rod big-end bearing by supporting the crankshaft horizontally with the crankpin in the 12 o'clock position.

NOTE: This check is most easily performed with the crankshaft installed in the crankcase.

Grasp the connecting rod firmly and pull up on it. Tap sharply on the top of the rod with a soft-face mallet. If the bearing and crankpin are in good condition there should be no movement felt in the rod. If movement is felt, or if there is a sharp, metallic click, the bearing should be replaced. This is a job which should be entrusted to a shop equipped with a press capable of separating and reassembling the crank halves and the pin.

Check the crankshaft and transmission bearings for pitting, galling, and wear. Rotate the bearings and feel for roughness and play. They should turn smoothly and evenly. There should be no radial play in the bearings. If any bearing is found faulty in any way, replace it.

Check the primary drive and transmission gears for chipped, galled, or worn teeth and replace if necessary. If both gears are worn, they should be replaced as a set, even if only one of the gears is damaged; the gears are matched as a set for correct backlash and the mixing of an old worn gear with a new gear is likely to result in premature wear or a failure which could damage other components.

Minor roughness on the surface of gear teeth may be smoothed with a fine oilstone.

MEASUREMENT

There is only one critical measurement involving the crankcase and crankshaft—axial play of the shaft in the case. Permissible axial play is 0.05-0.1mm (0.002-0.004 in.). There are several critical dimensions which must be checked in the transmission, these are covered in Chapter Five.

1. Remove the bearing cages from the main bearings (**Figure 39**).

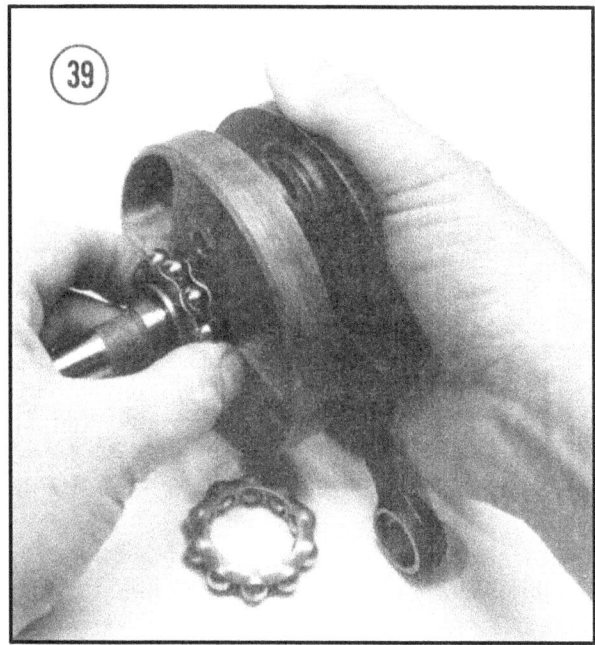

2. Pull the inner races off the crankshaft with puller shells (tool No. 24), the clamping ring (tool No. 23), and the threaded sleeve (tool No. 22) as shown in **Figure 40**. Don't mix the left-side cage or races with the right side.

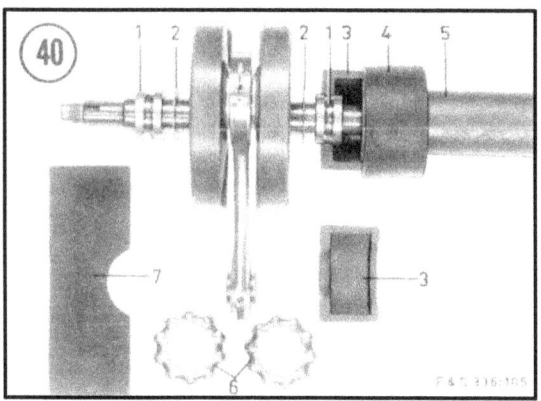

3. Assemble the entire bearings, including inner and outer races and bearing cage, in the crankcase. Make sure the bearing is correctly seated in the bore.

4. Place a gasket on the sealing surface and measure the distance from the gasket surface to the bearing inner race as shown in **Figure 41**.

5. Repeat procedure for opposing bearing.

6. Measure the width of the crankshaft across both webs as shown in **Figure 42**.

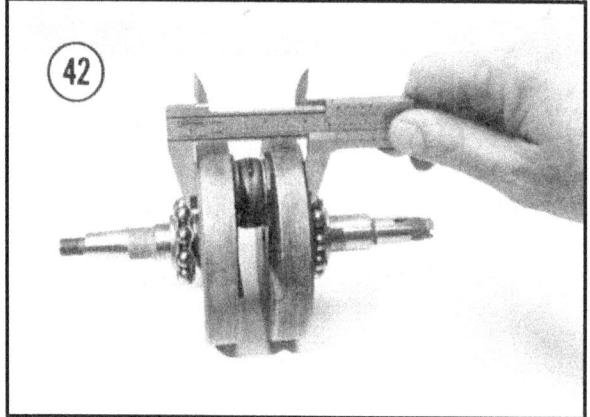

7. Add the dimensions from Steps 4 and 5 and subtract the width of the crank webs from the result to determine the actual axial play.

EXAMPLE

Distance from sealing surface to bearing inner race	
Clutch side	23.30mm (0.918 in.)
Magneto side	+33.0 mm (1.300 in.)
	56.30mm (2.218 in.)
Width of crankshaft across both webs	−54.10mm (2.131 in.)
Actual axial play	2.20mm (0.086 in.)
Permissible axial play	−0.10mm (0.0039 in.)
Difference to be taken up	2.10mm (0.0827 in.)

8. The difference in axial play is taken up with shims placed between the crank webs and the inner races of the main bearings (2, **Figure 40**). See **Table 1**.

If possible, the combined shim thickness should be the same for both sides. For instance, in the example above, a 1.0mm and 0.50 shim on each side of the crankshaft would produce

Table 1	SHIM SIZES
Thickness	
0.15mm	
0.20mm	
0.30mm	
0.40mm	
0.50mm	
0.80mm	
1.00mm	

the required play of 2.10mm. If the difference can't be taken up evenly, the thicker combination should be fitted to the clutch side of the crank.

CRANKSHAFT PREASSEMBLY

1. Fit the spacer plate (tool No. 9) (7, Figure 40) between the crank webs and support the ends of the spacer on the bed of a press or across the open jaws of a large vise.

CAUTION
Never clamp the crankshaft ends or webs in a vise, and don't install the inner races by tapping them on; such action will result in the webs being squeezed together. This will damage the big-end bearing and require its replacement.

2. Fit the shims onto the end of the crankshaft.
3. Press the bearing inner race onto the shaft firmly against the shims by screwing the threaded puller bolt into the end of the crankshaft and turning the puller sleeve clockwise (5, Figure 40).
4. Turn the crankshaft over on the bed of the press or vise and repeat the procedure for the other end.
5. Install the bearing cages on the inner races.

CRANKSHAFT SEAL REPLACEMENT

Before removing the seals from the crankcase halves, check their positions in the bores (see **Figure 43**). The new seals must be installed at the same depth as the old ones. Failure to install the seals at the correct depth can result in the seal coming in contact with the rotating bearing race or closure of the oil channel and consequent inadequate lubrication to the bearings and crankshaft.

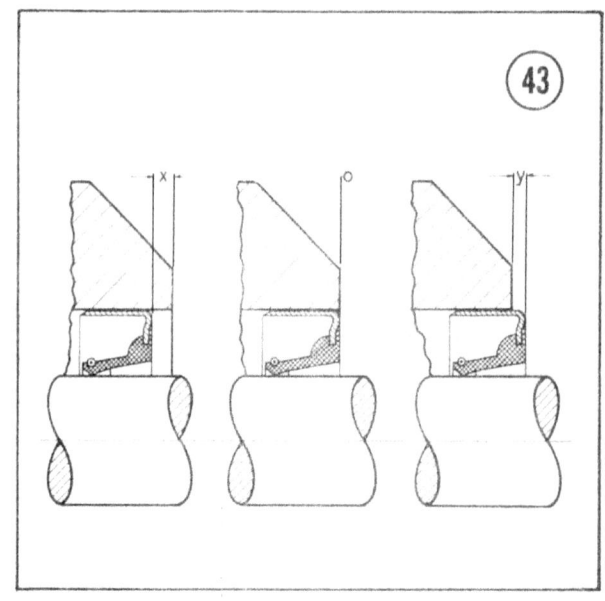

Removal

1. Place a piece of pipe with a diameter comparable to that of the seal on the seal face and tap it lightly to break any oxide bond that may have formed.

2. Install the seal puller (tool No. 13) so that both hooks are seated behind the steel rim of the seal (**Figure 44**). It may be necessary to partially disassemble the puller (see **Figure 45**) to insert the hooks and then reassemble it.

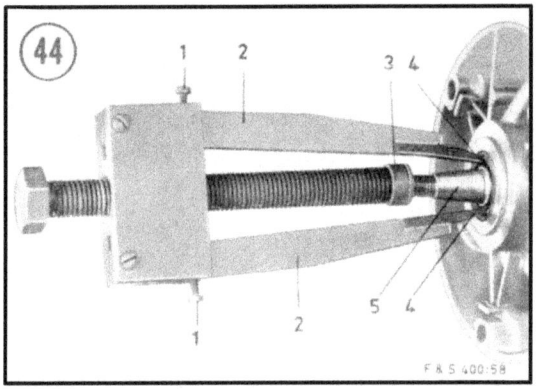

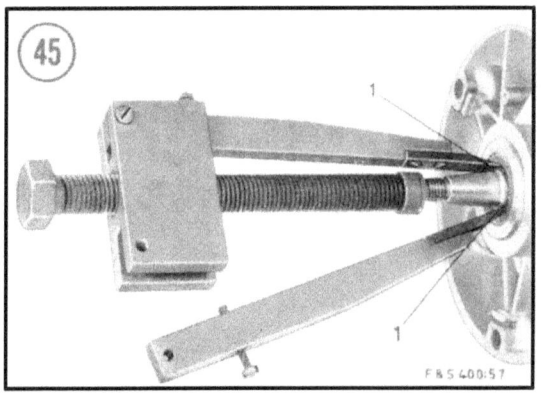

3. Press the puller arms outward equally by turning in the 2 spreader screws (1, **Figure 44**). Make sure the puller bolt and the crankshaft are in a straight line.

4. Hold the puller body to prevent it from turning and remove the seal by screwing the puller bolt clockwise.

Installation

1. Wipe seal bore with clean, lint-free cloth.

2. Fill the inner recess of the seal with high-temperature grease and lightly coat the seal lip.

3. Put a short piece of clear plastic mending tape around the sharp shoulder of the crankshaft to prevent damage to seal lip during installation.

4. Place the seal on the shaft and press it into place with a piece of pipe (**Figure 46**). Press it straight on and to the same depth as the old seal.

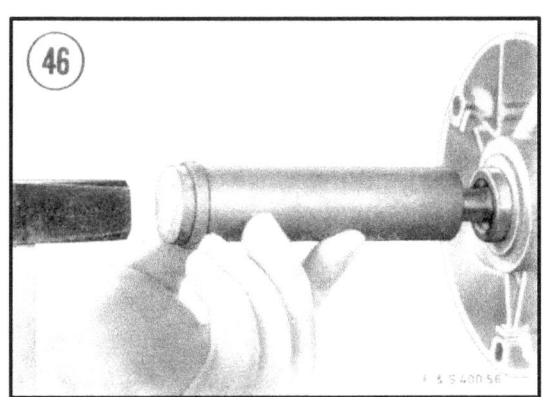

MAIN BEARING REPLACEMENT

Removal and installation of the main bearing inner races is discussed in the section of measuring and correcting crankshaft end-play. If damage has occurred to any of the bearing components—inner race, outer race, or bearing cage—the entire assembly should be replaced.

Outer Race Removal

1. Heat the crankcase halves on a hot plate to 115-140°C (250-300°F).

2. Tap the crankcase half lightly with a rubber mallet to remove the inner race and oil seal.

The transmission main- and layshaft bearings are likely to fall out at the same time. Reinstall these immediately, while the crankcase is still warm, referring to Chapter Five for their locations and positioning if necessary.

Outer Race Installation

1. Fill the recess in the face of the seal with high-temperature grease and lightly coat the seal lip. Press the seal into the bore in the ignition-side case with the sealing lip facing inward until the inner edge of the seal is flush with the inner edge of the seal bore (**Figure 47**).

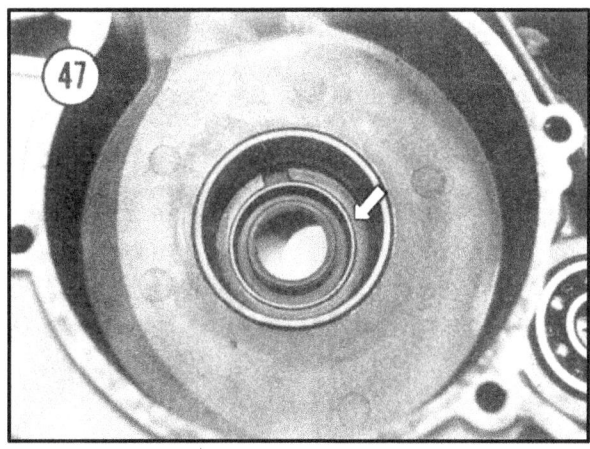

2. Press in the outer race as far as it will go. Its inner edge should contact the shoulder in the bore and its outer edge should be flush with the crankcase wall (see **Figure 48**).

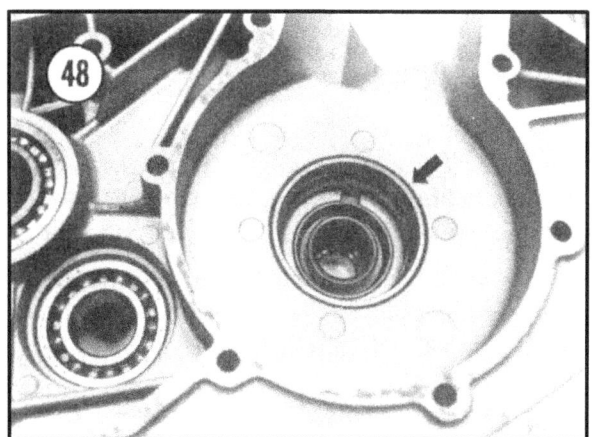

3. Install the seal and main bearing outer race in the clutch-side case in the same manner. Then, with the case still warm, press the outer ball bearing assembly into the case from the outside until its outer edge is flush with the face of the bearing boss (**Figure 49**). Again refer to Chapter Five for installation of the transmission bearings and seals.

NOTE: *Following replacement of the main bearings, measure the axial play of the crankshaft as described earlier and correct it if necessary.*

CRANKCASE REASSEMBLY

Refer to Chapter Five and reassemble the transmission and kickstarter mechanism. Then proceed as follows:

1. Fit the complete crankshaft assembly into the clutch-side case (**Figure 50**).

2. Install the 2 hollow alignment dowels in the clutch-side case.

3. Coat the mating surfaces of both crankcase halves with F&S sealant No. 40 or an equivalent gasket cement and install a new gasket over the alignment dowels. Check to see that all spacers and shims are correctly installed, referring to the disassembly procedure if necessary.

4. Assemble the 2 crankcase halves together, pushing firmly and evenly until they meet along the sealing surface.

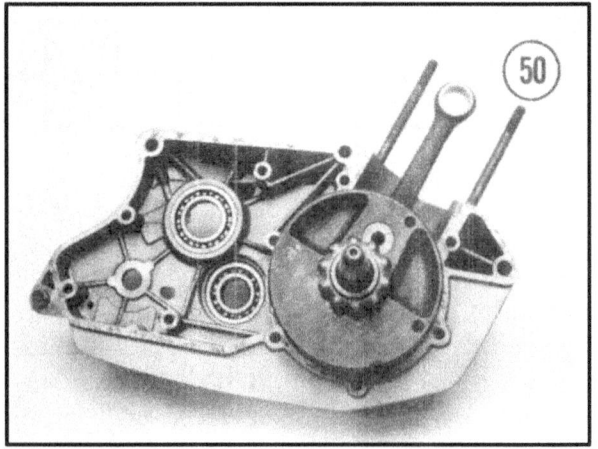

5. Coat the threads of the six 60-millimeter-long (2.36 in.) slotted screws with Diament sealant and screw them into the crankcase (see **Figure 51**).

6. Tighten the screws in the pattern shown in **Figure 52** to 5.8-7.25 ft.-lb. (0.18-1.0 mkg).

7. Screw the four 75-millimeter-long (3.0 in.) screws into the transmission portion of the crankcase (**Figure 53**).

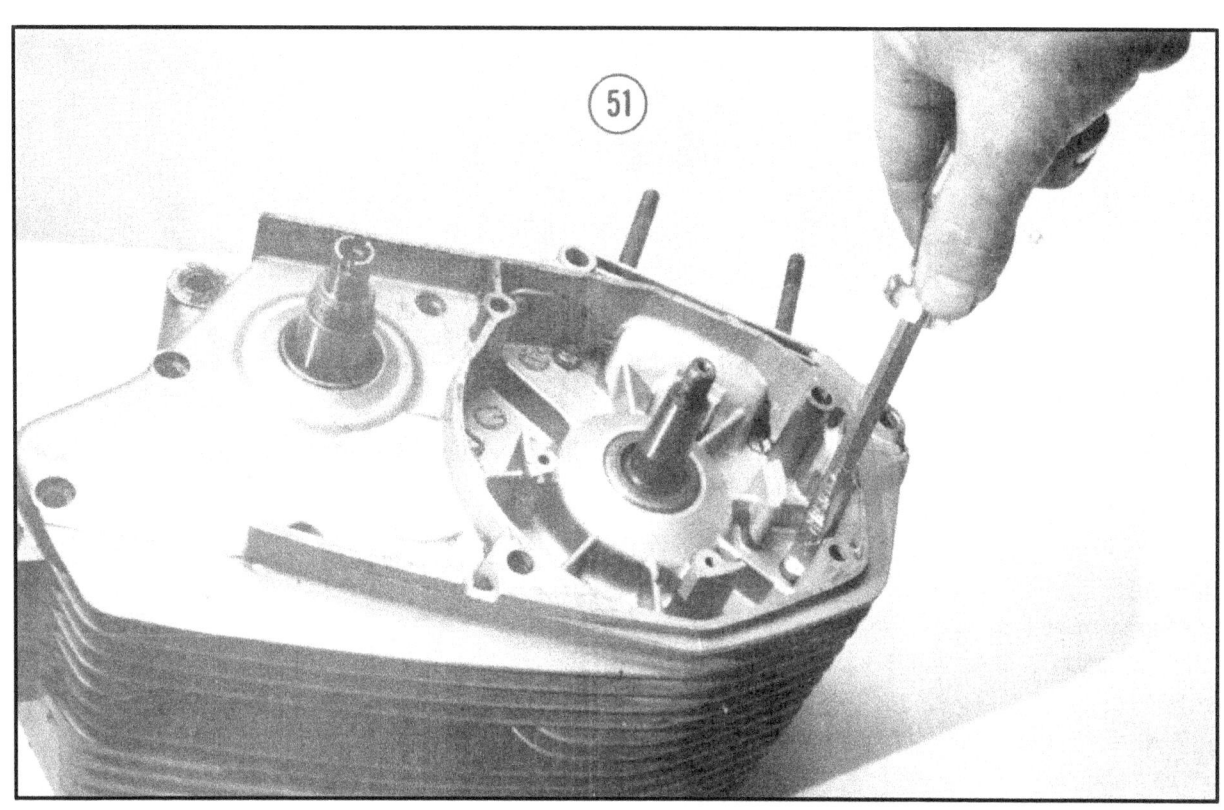

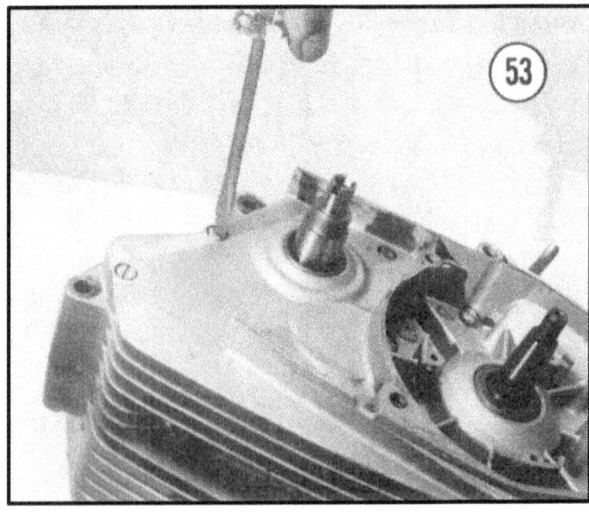

8. Screw the oil drain plug (with a sealing washer installed) into the bottom of the crankcase and tighten it to 9.4-10.85 ft.-lb. (1.3-1.5 mkg).

9. Check to make sure the crankshaft and connecting rod turn freely and smoothly and that the axial play in the shaft is barely perceptible.

IGNITION INSTALLATION (BOSCH)

If you are using a work jig, relocate the engine as shown in **Figure 54**.

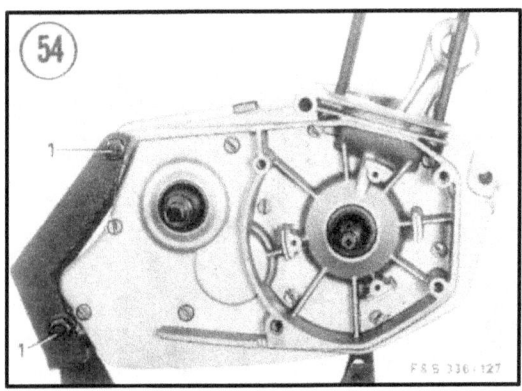

1. Degrease the tapered portion of the crankshaft and the bore in the flywheel.

2. Fit the stator plate over the shaft and onto the case. If the stator plate is not the self-aligning notched type, carefully line up the mark on the plate with the mark on the crankcase (4, **Figure 55**).

3. Coat the threads of the 3 Phillips head screws with Diament sealant and screw them into the case with their washers installed (1, Figure 55).

Tighten the screws to 2.0-4.4 ft.-lb. (0.4-0.6 mkg).

4. Set the key in the slot in the shaft (2, Figure 55) and route the electrical cable through the hole in the case. Press the rubber grommet around the cable into the hole.

5. Install the ignition flywheel on the shaft, taking care to line up the keyway with the key.

6. Hold the flywheel with a jig lever or pin wrench and install the washer and flywheel nut. Remember: it's a left-hand thread. Tighten the nut to 27.5-29 ft.-lb. (3.8-4.0 mkg).

IGNITION INSTALLATION (MOTOPLAT)

1. Degrease the tapered portion of the crankshaft and the bore in the flywheel.

2. Fit the stator plate over the shaft and onto the case. If the stator plate is not self-aligning, carefully line up the mark on the mark on the plate with the mark on the crankcase (2, **Figure 56**).

3. Coat the heads of the 3 slotted screws (1, Figure 56) with Diament sealant and install the screws with their washers. Tighten them to 2.9-4.4 ft.-lb. (0.4-0.6 mkg).

4. Route the cable of the stator body through the hole in the case. Press the rubber grommet around the cable into the hole.

5. Fit the stator body over the end of the shaft. Screw in the 3 slotted screws but don't tighten them; the stator must be able to be turned when the ignition is timed (see Chapter Seven).

6. Set the key in the slot in the shaft. Install the flywheel, taking care to line up the keyway with the key.

7. Install the washer and left-hand-threaded nut. Leave the nut slightly loose until the ignition has been timed.

8. Time the ignition in accordance with the instructions in Chapter Seven.

DRIVE SPROCKET INSTALLATION

1. Degrease the taper on the transmission main shaft and the bore of the drive sprocket.

2. Install the sprocket, washer, and left-hand-threaded nut and tighten it to 50-54 ft.-lb. (7.0-7.5 mkg).

GEAR SELECTOR INSTALLATION

Refer to Chapter Five and install and adjust the gear selector mechanism (and the gear lock if the engine is so equipped).

DRIVE GEAR/CLUTCH INSTALLATION

1. Fit the washer over the end of the crankshaft and insert the key in the keyway (**Figure 57**).

2. Install the drive gear on the shaft, taking care to line up the keyway with the key. Install a lockwasher and nut on the end of the shaft.

3. Fit the locking plate (tool No. 10) over the gear and secure it to the case with 2 screws (**Figure 58**). Tighten the nut to 50-54 ft.-lb. (7.0-7.5 mkg).

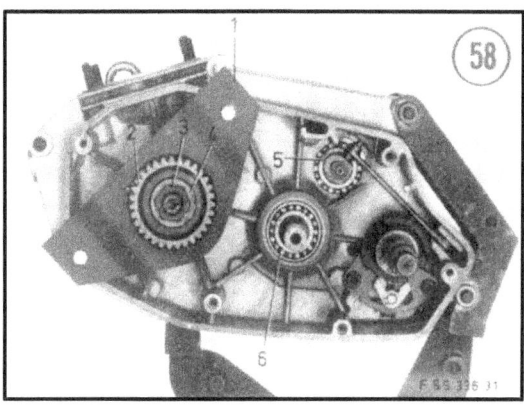

4. Insert the key into the keyway in the layshaft. Install the clutch hub on the shaft, taking care to line up the keyway with the key.

5. Place the flat washer on the shaft and screw on the nut.

6. Install the locking plate (tool No. 8) on the clutch hub and secure it with 2 screws (**Figure 59**). Tighten the nut on the main shaft to 57-65 ft.-lb. (8-9 mkg).

7. Assemble the thrust plates and ball bearing case onto the shaft (**Figure 60**). The inner plate must have its groove facing outward, and the outer plate must have its groove facing inward.

8. Preassemble the clutch as described in Chapter Five. Oil the clutch hub and fit the clutch onto it (**Figure 61**).

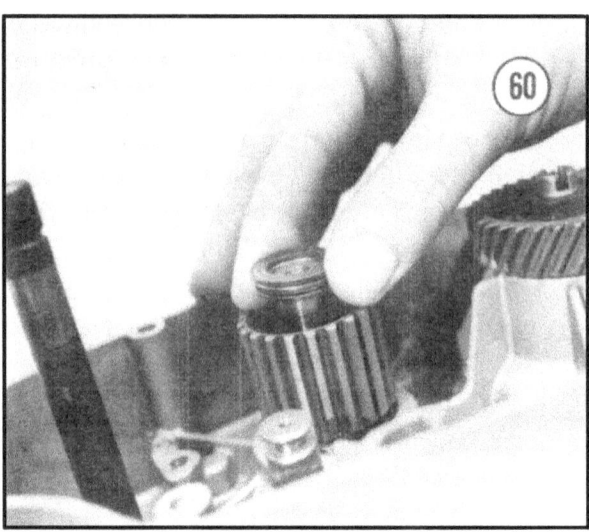

9. Add shims to the end of the shaft, up to the circlip groove, and install the circlip. Check the axial clearance of the clutch with a flat feeler gauge (**Figure 62**). It should be 0.004 (0.1 millimeter). If necessary, remove the circlip and correct the axial play by adding or removing shims as required. (See **Table 2**).

Table 2   SHIM SIZES

0.15mm (0.006 in.)
0.3 mm (0.012 in.)
0.5 mm (0.020 in.)
1.0 mm (0.40 in.)

10. Fit the pressure plate onto the clutch and install the 2 hollow alignment dowels in the case.

CLUTCH-SIDE COVER INSTALLATION

Coat the mating surface of the crankcase and the cover with F&S sealant No. 40 or an equivalent gasket cement and install the gasket over the alignment dowels in the crankcase. Set the cover in place and install the 7 slotted screws as shown in **Figure 63**. The bottommost screw must be fitted with a sealing washer because it serves as an oil drain. Tighten the screws in the pattern shown 6-7 ft.-lb. (0.8-1.0 mkg).

GEAR SELECTOR AND KICKSTARTER

Position the gear selector pedal on its shaft so it's about horizontal and install it (**Figure 64**). Slide the O-ring seal onto the shaft (**Figure 65**) and install the kickstarter lever. Tighten the pinch bolts in both levers.

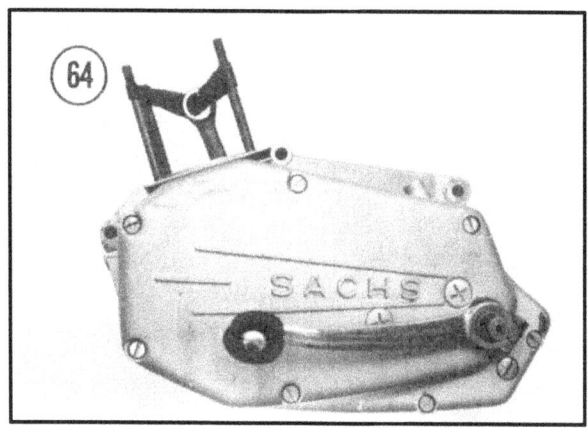

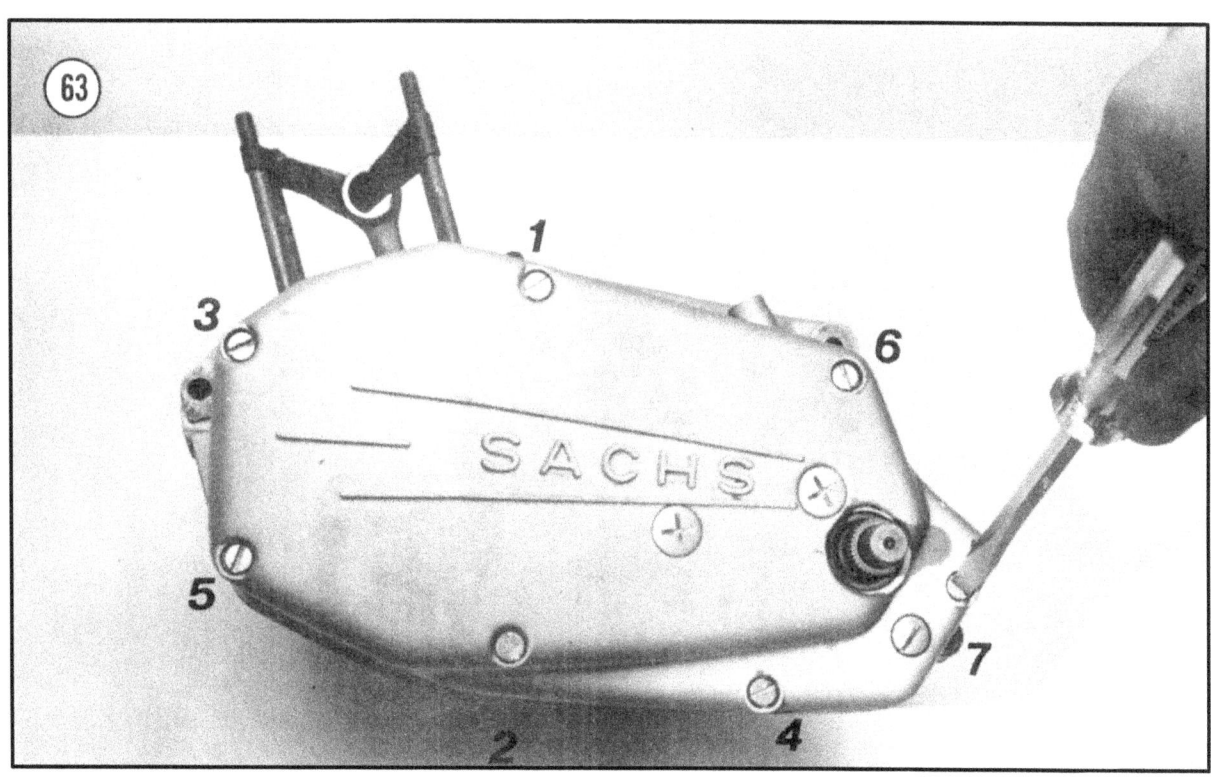

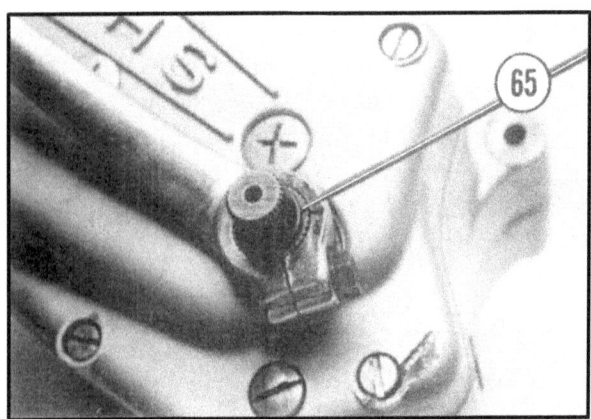

F&S sealant No. 40 or an equivalent gasket cement. Set the gasket in place over the alignment dowels. Set the cover in place, making sure the tangs inside the beveled speedometer drive gear (**Figure 66**) fit into the slot in the end of the mainshaft (**Figure 67**).

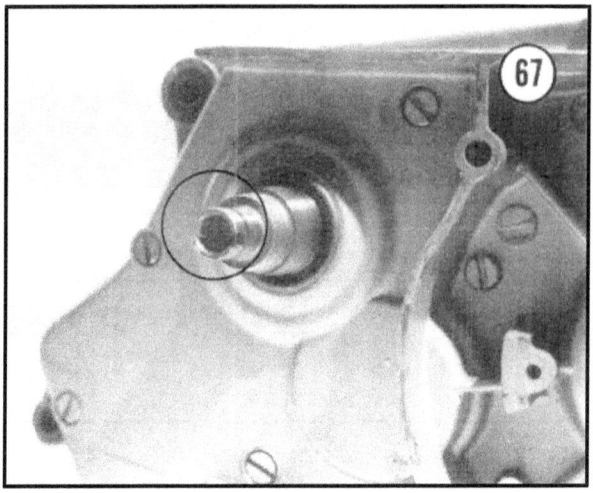

REINSTALLATION, FINAL ASSEMBLY, AND TIMING

The engine may be reinstalled in the motorcycle at this point. Reverse the removal procedure and reassemble the upper end, referring to the procedure in Chapter Three. Fill the gearbox as described in Chapter Two. Prior to installing the ignition-side cover on the engine, time the ignition in accordance with the instructions in Chapter Seven.

Install the hollow alignment dowels in the right side of the crankcase and coat the mating surfaces of the crankcase and the cover with

Screw in the four 60-millimeter-long (2.36 in.) slotted screws and tighten them to 5.6-7.3 ft.-lb. (0.8-1.0 mkg).

Reassemble the rest of the motorcycle by reversing the disassembly steps presented earlier.

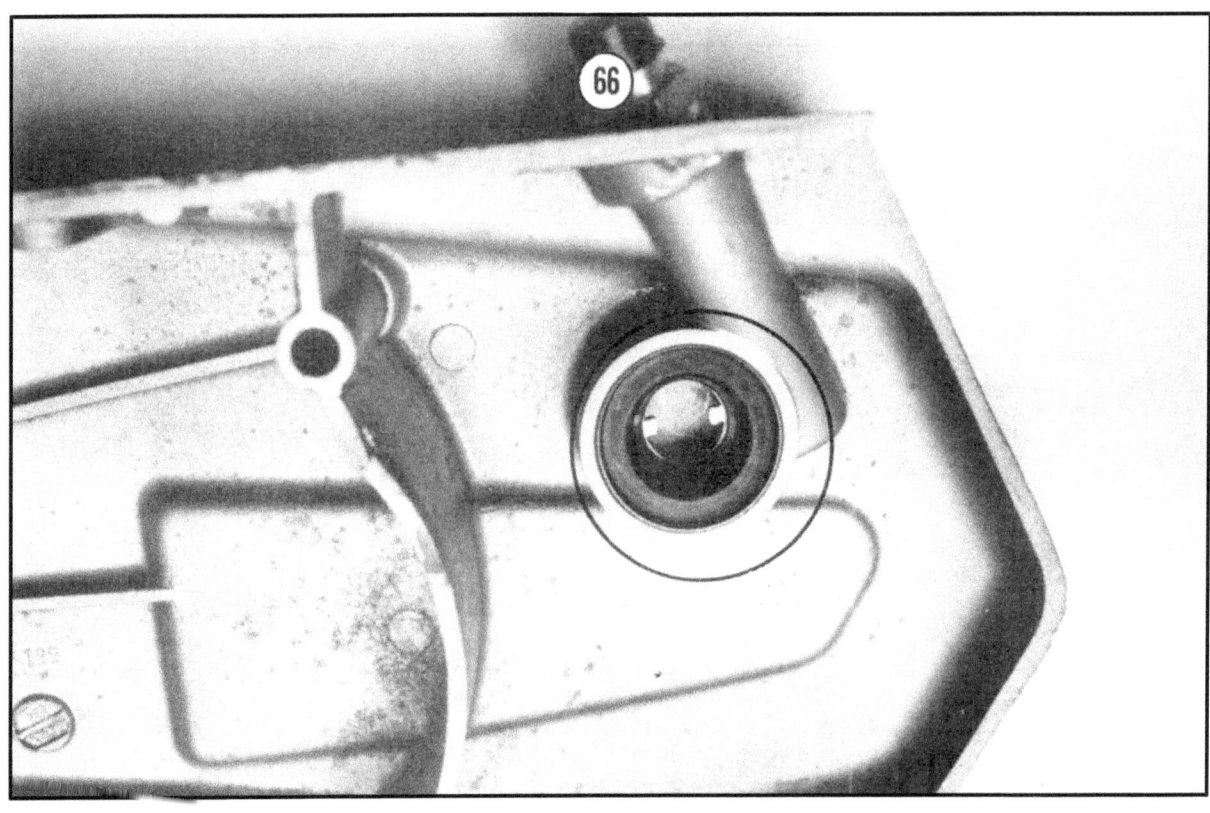

CHAPTER FIVE

TRANSMISSION AND CLUTCH

Two transmission types are used in Sachs engines—a 5-speed (**Figure 1**) and a 6-speed (**Figure 2**). Most service procedures are identical for both types. Where exceptions exist, they're noted in the text and figures. Clutches (**Figure 3**) in all models are the same.

CLUTCH

The clutch may be removed, serviced, installed, and adjusted with the engine in the motorcycle.

Removal

Removal of the clutch is discussed in Chapter Four. Be sure to drain the primary case and transmission before removing the outer cover.

Disassembly

1. Unscrew the 3 locknuts from the outer face of the layshaft gear and unscrew the 3 Allen screws which hold the clutch box on the gear (**Figure 4**). The screws should be unscrewed

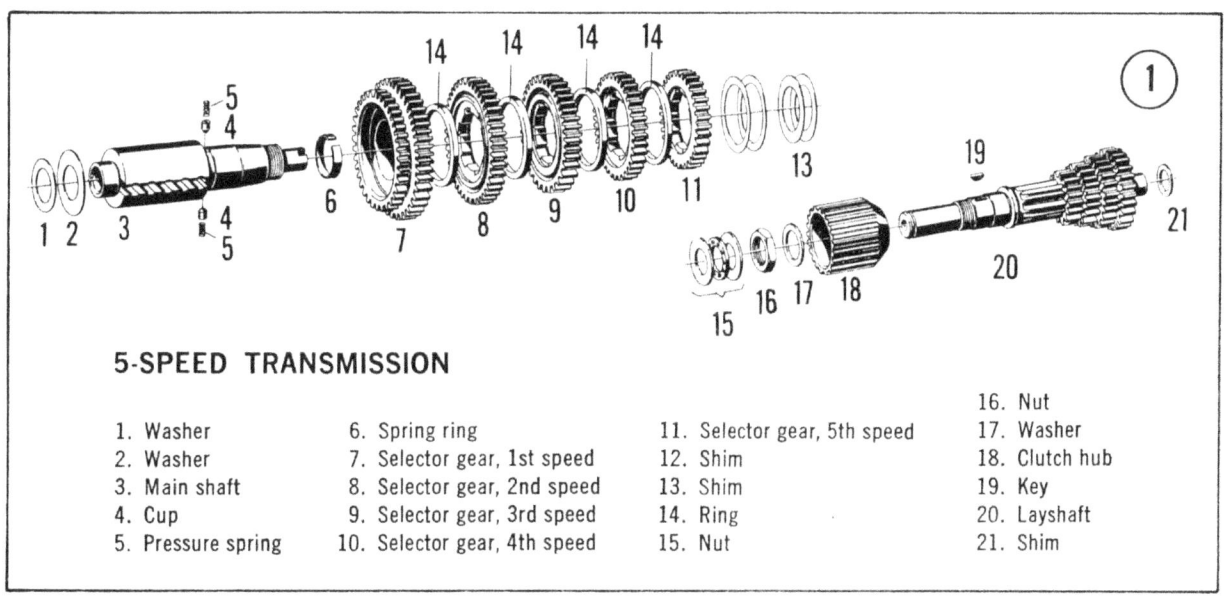

5-SPEED TRANSMISSION

1. Washer
2. Washer
3. Main shaft
4. Cup
5. Pressure spring
6. Spring ring
7. Selector gear, 1st speed
8. Selector gear, 2nd speed
9. Selector gear, 3rd speed
10. Selector gear, 4th speed
11. Selector gear, 5th speed
12. Shim
13. Shim
14. Ring
15. Nut
16. Nut
17. Washer
18. Clutch hub
19. Key
20. Layshaft
21. Shim

45

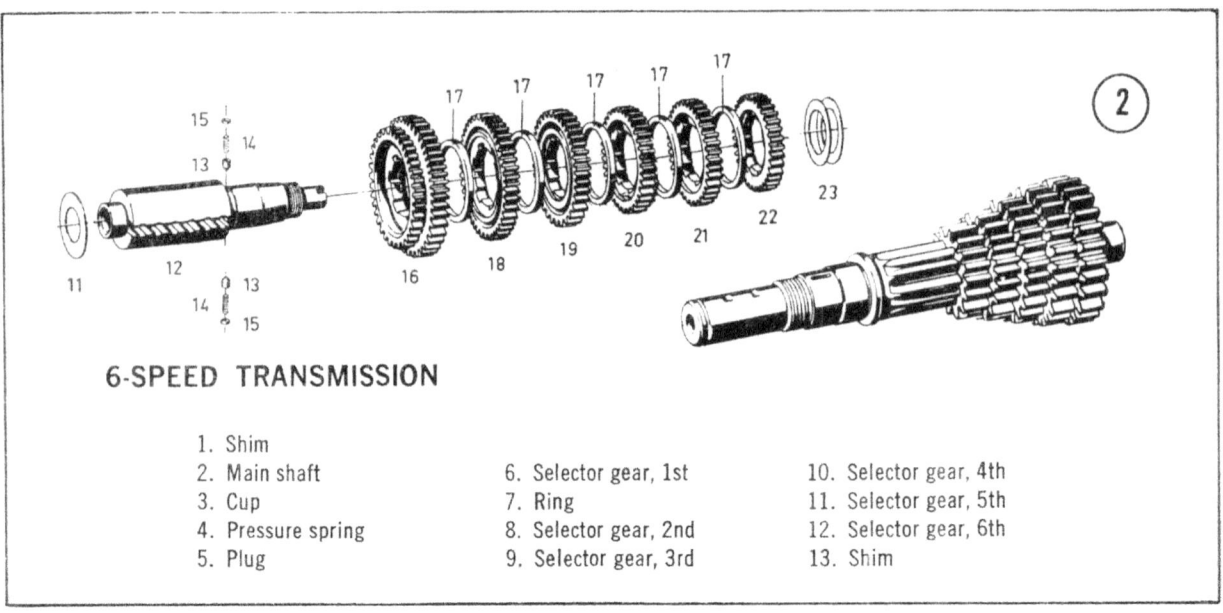

6-SPEED TRANSMISSION

1. Shim
2. Main shaft
3. Cup
4. Pressure spring
5. Plug
6. Selector gear, 1st
7. Ring
8. Selector gear, 2nd
9. Selector gear, 3rd
10. Selector gear, 4th
11. Selector gear, 5th
12. Selector gear, 6th
13. Shim

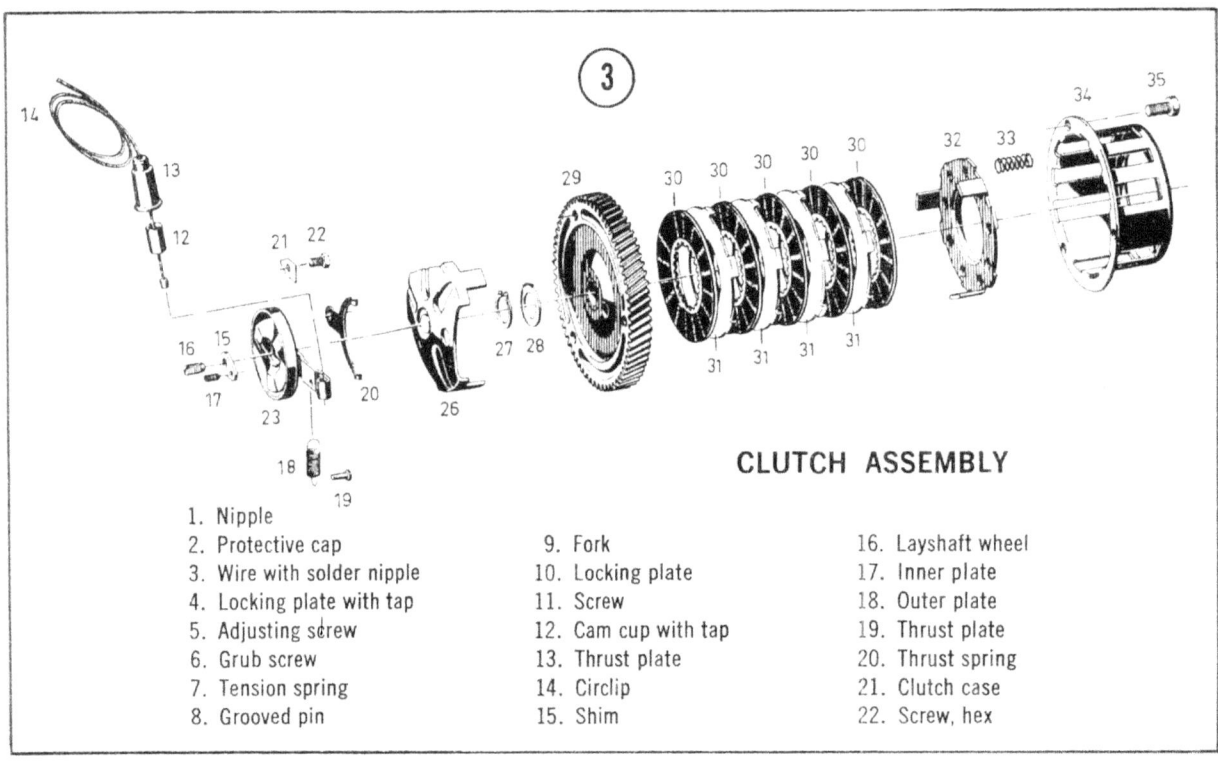

CLUTCH ASSEMBLY

1. Nipple
2. Protective cap
3. Wire with solder nipple
4. Locking plate with tap
5. Adjusting screw
6. Grub screw
7. Tension spring
8. Grooved pin
9. Fork
10. Locking plate
11. Screw
12. Cam cup with tap
13. Thrust plate
14. Circlip
15. Shim
16. Layshaft wheel
17. Inner plate
18. Outer plate
19. Thrust plate
20. Thrust spring
21. Clutch case
22. Screw, hex

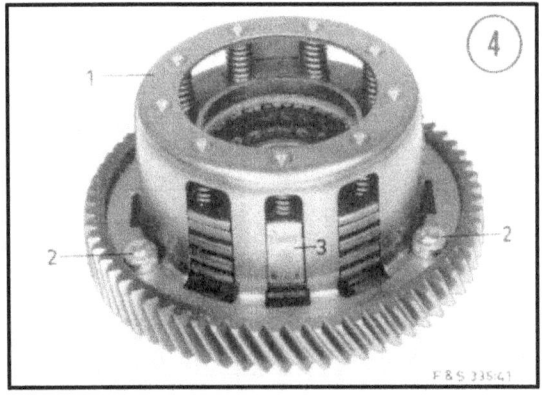

evenly, about one-half turn at a time until the spring tension has been relieved.

2. Pull off the clutch box and remove the springs and plates.

Inspection

1. Check the resiliency of the springs. They should be firm and the spacing between the coils should be even. The springs should be equal in length (**Figure 5**).

2. Examine the steel plates for galling or grooves. The friction material on the alternate plates should be uniform in thickness. If the condition of the plates is in doubt, or if the plates can be separated by pushing on the pressure plate with the clutch assembled, the plates and the springs should be replaced.

Assembly

1. Place the clutch hub over the boss on the layshaft gear (**Figure 6**) and install the plates beginning with a friction plate, alternating with a steel plate, another friction plate, and so on until all of the plates are installed. The tabs on the steel plates must point upward.

2. Install the inner pressure plate and apply a dab of grease to each of the 9 nubs. Set the springs on the pressure plate, one on each nub (**Figure 7**).

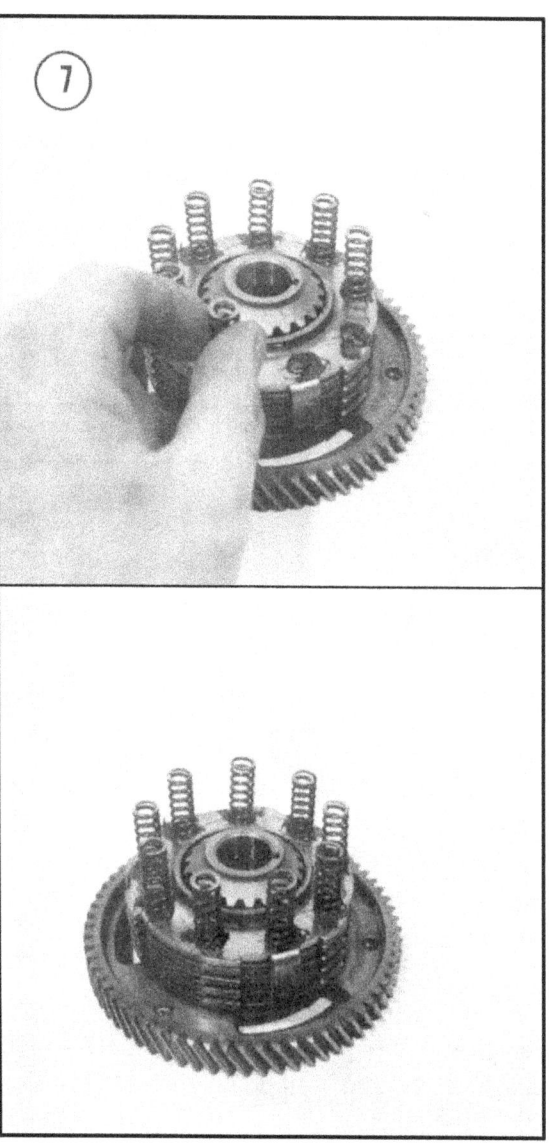

3. Install the clutch box so that its nubs engage the ends of the springs and its 3 narrow slots straddle the 3 tabs in the pressure plate (**Figure 8**). Line up the 3 holes in the flange of the clutch box with the tapped holes in the layshaft gear.

4. Coat the threads of the 3 Allen screws with liquid locking compound and screw them in evenly but not tight.

5. Reinstall the clutch hub on the layshaft and then install the assembled gear and clutch to center the plates.

6. Remove the gear and clutch assembly and tighten the 3 Allen screws to 8-7.10.8 ft.-lb. (1.2-1.5 mkg). Coat the protruding threads of the Allen screws with liquid locking compound and screw on the locknuts. Tighten them to 8-8.7 ft.-lb. (0.5-0.6 mkg).

7. Install the gear and clutch assembly, fit the shim or shims on the end of the shaft up to the circlip groove and install the circlip. The axial play of the clutch on the shaft should be 0.0039 in. (0.1mm). To check the play, push in on the clutch and insert a flat feeler gauge between the circlip and the top shim.

8. Install the outer pressure plate with its lugs engaging the inner pressure plate lugs through the slots in the layshaft gear.

9. Install the hollow alignment dowels in the crankcase and coat the sealing surface with gasket cement. Install the gasket and the outer cover. Install the 7 slotted screws (4 longest screws in the 4 forward holes) and tighten them to 5.6-7.25 ft.-lb. (0.8-1.0 kpm).

Adjustment

Adjust the clutch in accordance with the instructions in Chapter Two.

TRANSMISSION

Major transmission service requires that the engine be removed from the motorcycle, the crankcase split, and the gear train removed in accordance with the instructions provided in Chapter Four.

Service and adjustment of the gear selector mechanism (with the exeception of the selector rod and selector key), which is presented later in this chapter, can be carried out with the engine installed in the motorcycle.

Disassembly

The layshaft and its gears are a single assembly (**Figure 9**). The main shaft and its gears and spacers can be disassembled by sliding them off the drive end of the shaft with the sprocket removed (Figures 1 and 2).

The main shaft and selector rod and key are disassembled as follows:

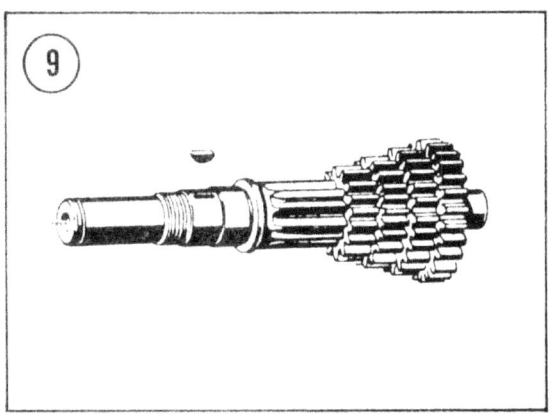

1. Gently clamp the main shaft in a vise fitted with soft jaws and unscrew (left-hand thread) the selector rod (**Figure 10**).

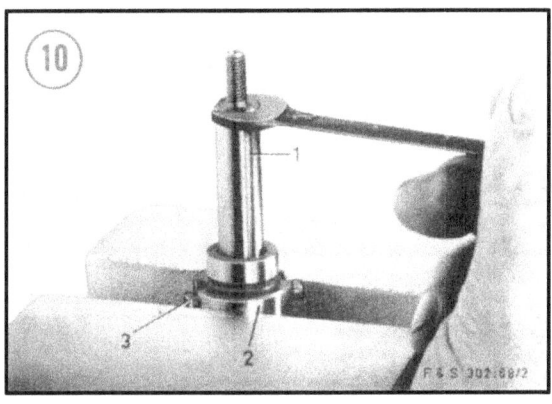

2A. If the main shaft is fitted with a spring retainer for the springs and cups (A, **Figure 11**), slide the spring back and remove the springs and cups from the shaft.

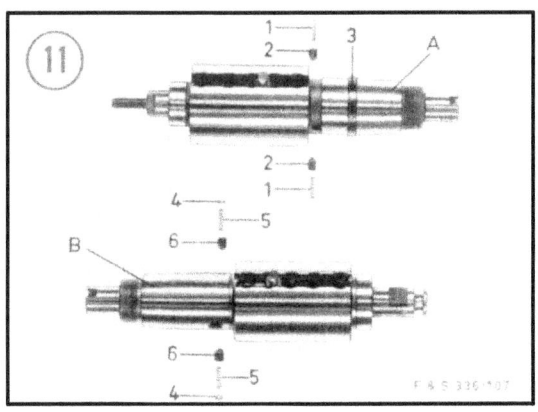

2B. If the main shaft is fitted with plugs to retain the springs and cups (B, Figure 11), remove the plugs and then the springs and cups.

3. Remove the rod and key from the main shaft.

Inspection

1. Check the gears for wear, pitting, galling, and chipped or fractured teeth and replace as necessary.

2. Check the bores in the inner bearing races for scores or galling. Rotate the bearings and feel for roughness and radial play. If either condition is present, the bearing should be replaced as described later.

3. Examine the selector rod, key, and cups for wear and replace as necessary.

> NOTE: *If bearing replacement is required, the following measurements should be performed after the new bearings have been installed.*

4. Place a new gasket on the magneto-side crankcase half and measure the distance between the inner race of the main shaft bearing and the mating surface of the crankcase as shown in **Figure 12**.

5. Measure the distance between the inner race of the main shaft bearing and the mating surface in the clutch-side crankcase half (**Figure 13**).

6. Measure the large-diameter portion of the main shaft (A or B, **Figure 14**).

7. Add the dimensions from Steps 4 and 5 and subtract the dimension determined in Step 6 from their sum.

EXAMPLE

Magneto side	42.9mm
Clutch side	12.1mm
	55.0mm
Less mainshaft width	54.1mm
Actual axial play	0.9mm
Allowable axial play	0.1mm
Difference to be compensated for	0.8mm

Appropriate shims must be fitted to the clutch side of the main shaft when the transmission is reassembled and installed in the crankcase.

8. The axial play of the layshaft should also be 0.1mm (0.0039 in.) and is determined in a

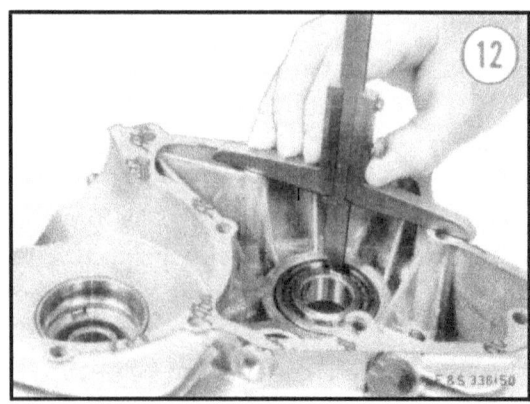

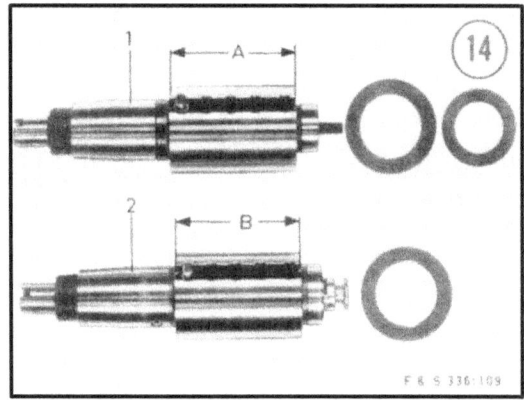

similar manner. First measure the distance of the magneto-side bearing from the mating surface with a gasket installed (**Figure 15**).

9. Measure the distance from the clutch-side bearing and the mating surface without a gasket (**Figure 16**) and add the 2 dimensions.

10. Measure the layshaft (dimension A plus dimension B in **Figure 17**) and subtract the result from the sum of the dimensions determined in Steps 8 and 9. This is the actual axial play of the layshaft. It can be corrected to the allowable axial play by adding or removing shims from the magneto-side end of the layshaft when the transmission is reassembled and installed in the crankcase. See **Table 1**.

11. The axial play of the starter shaft is also 0.1mm (0.0039 in.) and it's determined in a similar manner to that for the main shaft and layshaft. Measure the distance from the mating surface of the magneto side of the crankcase with a gasket installed (**Figure 18**).

12. Measure the distance from mating surface of the clutch-side crankcase half without a gasket to the rim of the bore for the starter ratchet (**Figure 19**).

13. Measure the starter shaft as shown in **Figure 20**. Subtract this dimension from the sum

Table 1 SHIM SIZES

Mainshaft	
Five-speed	
(large diameter)	0.3mm (0.012 in.)
	0.5mm (0.020 in.)
	0.6mm (0.024 in.)
	0.8mm (0.032 in.)
	1.0mm (0.039 in.)
(small diameter)	0.2mm (0.008 in.)
	0.3mm (0.012 in.)
	0.5mm (0.020 in.)
	0.8mm (0.032 in.)
	1.0mm (0.039 in.)
Six-speed (same as small diameter for five-speed)	
Layshaft	
All transmissions	0.2mm (0.008 in.)
	0.5mm (0.020 in.)
	1.0mm (0.039 in.)
	1.5mm (0.060 in.)

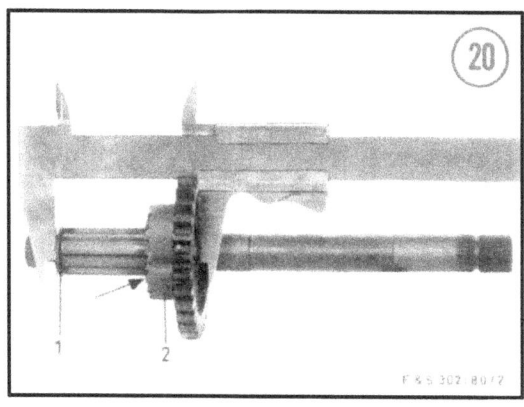

Bearing Replacement

1. Heat each crankcase half to 115-140°C (250-300°F) and tap it with a soft mallet to knock out the bearings and seals. Note the location of the washer outboard of the layshaft bearing in the magneto-side case so it may be reinstalled correctly (**Figure 22**).

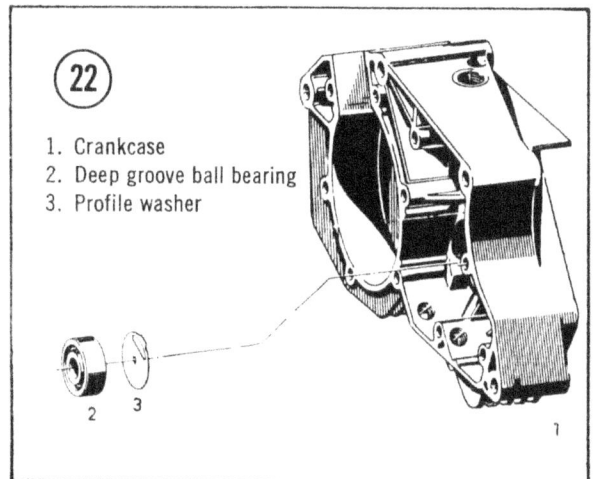

of the dimensions determined in Steps 11 and 12. This is the actual play of the starter shaft. It can be corrected by adding or removing shims between the rim of the starter bore in the clutch side of the crankcase and the ratchet gear (**Figure 21**).

2. Clean and deburr the bearing bores in the crankcases.

3. Fill the grooves in the oil seals with high-temperature grease and oil the seal lips.

4. Press the bearings and seals into the case while it is still hot. The seal lips must point inward and the outer surface of the seals must be flush with the outer edge of the bores in the cases. The flat surface of the profile washer in the layshaft bore in the magneto-side case must face inward and the washer's tab must engage the recess in the bore.

5. After the cases have cooled, repress the bearings.

> NOTE: *If the crankshaft bearings and seals were knocked out along with the transmission bearings and seals, refer to Chapter Four and reinstall them in accordance with the instructions.*

6. Refer to the section on inspection to select the appropriate shims for the transmission shafts.

Reassembly

1. Reassemble the main shaft and selector rod and key by reversing the steps for disassembly (**Figure 23**). Lightly oil all of the parts as they are assembled. Make certain the selector rod moves smoothly in the main shaft and that the detent action of the springs and cups is positive on each of the recesses in the rod. Apply liquid locking compound to the threads of the selector rod and tighten it in the selector key to 40 ft.-lb. (5.5 mkg).

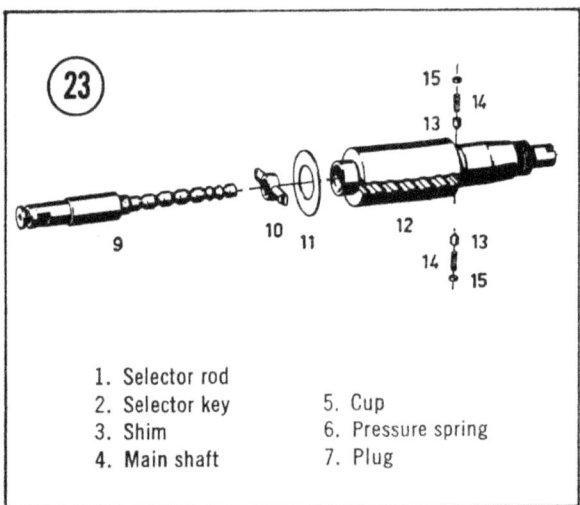

1. Selector rod
2. Selector key
3. Shim
4. Main shaft
5. Cup
6. Pressure spring
7. Plug

2. Place the shim(s) on the main shaft bearing in the clutch-side case and install the main shaft (**Figure 24**). The chamfered side of the shim must point inward.

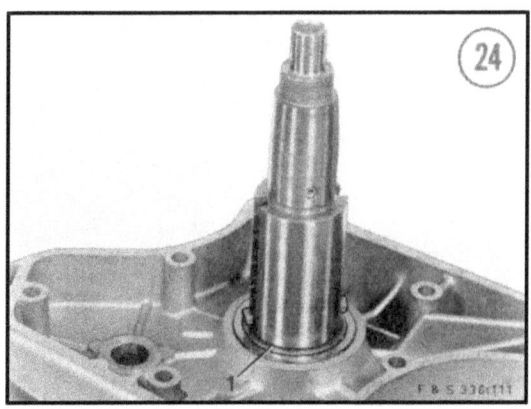

3. Oil the gears and spacers for the main shaft and install them on the shaft, beginning with the largest gear (the smaller gear of this double gear must face outward). Install a spacer and then the next smaller gear, alternating spacers with gears until they are all installed.

> NOTE: *On 5-speed transmissions, second, third, and fourth gears are reversible (not interchangeable) on the shaft. Fifth gear is recessed on the side facing fourth gear and its outer side is flat. In 6-speed transmissions, second, third, and fifth gears are reversible. Fourth gear is recessed on the side facing third gear. Sixth gear is recessed on the side facing fifth gear and its outer side is flat.*

4. Install the appropriate shim(s) beginning with the chamfered shim (chamfer facing the mainshaft collar) and install the inner race of the mainshaft bearing.

5. Install the layshaft in the transmission and fit the appropriate shims to its outer end.

6. Add the appropriate shims to the rim of the bore for the layshaft after coating them with grease and install the starter ratchet. Set the thrust washer in place on the ratchet (Figure 21).

7. Grease the rim of the starter shaft bore in the magneto-side case and install the 1mm thrust washer. Install the starter return spring in the case with the extended tang against the bottom stop in the case (**Figure 25**).

8. Slide the ratchet over the spring and engage the parallel end of the spring in the small hole in the ratchet.

9. Install the starter shaft through the ratchet and into the bore in the case. Make sure it passes through the thrust washer and is seated correctly in the case.

10. Install the kickstarter lever on the end of the shaft and turn it about ¾ turn in the starting direction. Press the ratchet down until it can be engaged with the stop screw in the case and remove the kickstarter lever.

11. Assemble the 2 crankcase halves, reassemble the rest of the engine, and install it in the motorcycle in accordance with the instructions in Chapter Four.

GEAR SELECTORS

There are 2 gear selector designs used on Sachs engines. On 100cc engines up to No. 5692 842 and 125cc engines up to No. 6318 754, the mechanism is distinguished by a one-piece lever (**Figure 26**). On subsequent engines, with both 5- and 6-speed transmissions, a 2-piece lever is used (**Figure 27**). Service and adjustment procedures for the 2 designs are distinctly different.

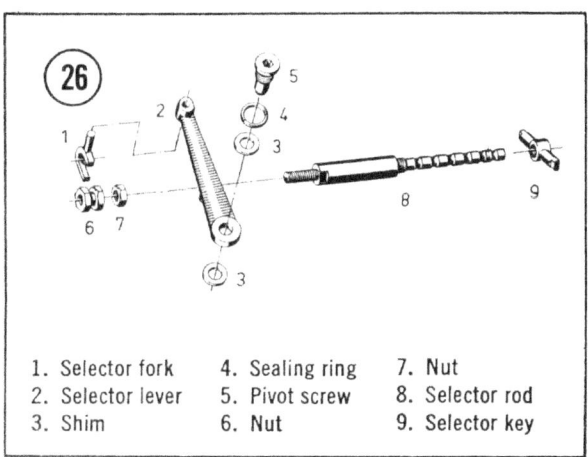

1. Selector fork
2. Selector lever
3. Shim
4. Sealing ring
5. Pivot screw
6. Nut
7. Nut
8. Selector rod
9. Selector key

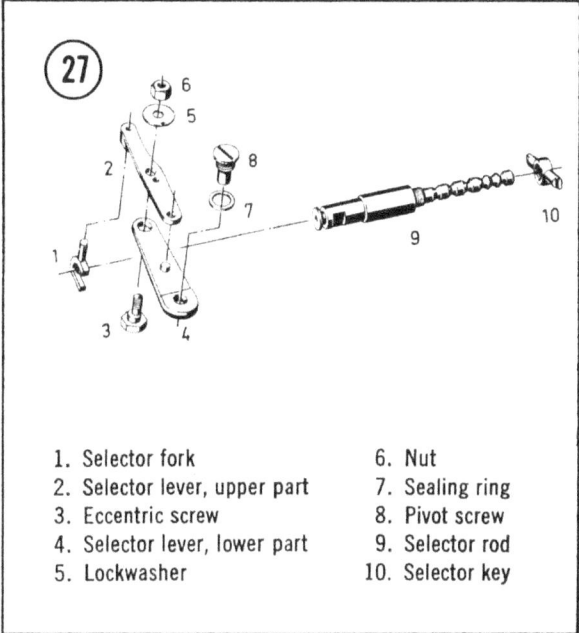

1. Selector fork
2. Selector lever, upper part
3. Eccentric screw
4. Selector lever, lower part
5. Lockwasher
6. Nut
7. Sealing ring
8. Pivot screw
9. Selector rod
10. Selector key

GEAR SELECTOR (ONE-PIECE)

Removal

Removal of the gear selector mechanism is described in Chapter Four.

Inspection

1. Check the resiliency of the springs and replace them if they are weak.

2. Examine the teeth of the pawl and selector boss for chips and wear.

3. Install the selector assembly on the kickstarter shaft and press in the adjusting plate (**Figure 28**). There should be no apparent axial play of the selector. If play exists, an appropriate shim must be installed on the shaft behind the selector mechanism; however, the selector must rotate freely on the shaft without binding.

4. Check the pathway (spiral groove) in the selector boss for wear. The edges should be sharp and even. If they are not, the selector boss should be replaced. In such cases, refer to **Figure 29** and remove the large circlip from the end of the shaft. Remove the outer shims, the selector boss, the inner shim and the pawl spring. Remove the small circlip from the end of the pawl shaft and remove the outer shims, pawl, and inner shim. Relax the spring and remove it. Remove the adjusting plate and the shim behind it and pull the selector shaft off of the kickstarter shaft.

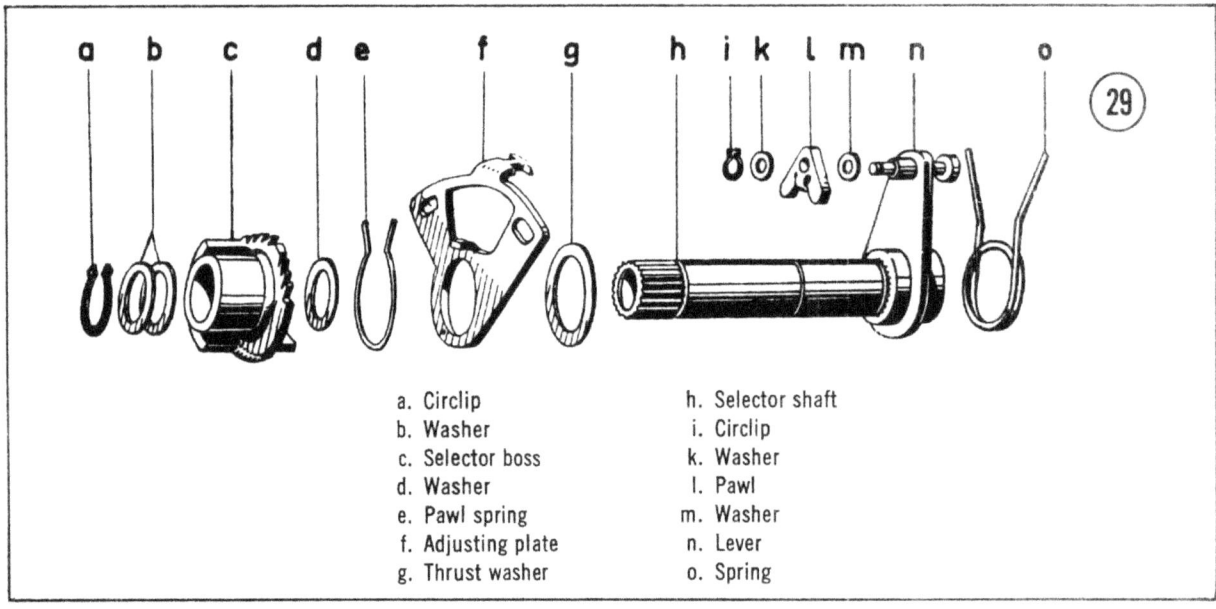

a. Circlip
b. Washer
c. Selector boss
d. Washer
e. Pawl spring
f. Adjusting plate
g. Thrust washer
h. Selector shaft
i. Circlip
k. Washer
l. Pawl
m. Washer
n. Lever
o. Spring

Assembly

1. Place a 0.5mm (0.020 in.) shim on the selector shaft and install the adjusting plate. Place a 0.5mm (0.020 in.) shim on the pawl and install the pawl with the spring tab facing inward. Add the outer shim and install the small circlip. The axial play of the pawl on the shaft should be 0.1mm (0.004 in.). Check it with a flat feeler gauge.

2. Install the pawl spring on the adjusting plate with the right end of the spring (offset) away from the plate. Cross the offset over the straight end of the spring and over the spring stop on the plate. The spring must also engage either side of the tab on the pawl (**Figure 30**).

3. Install the selector boss using appropriate shims so that the teeth of the boss line up accurately with the teeth of the pawl.

4. Fit shims to the selector shaft all the way to the circlip groove and install the circlip. There should be no perceptible axial play of the selector boss on the shaft. However, the boss must rotate freely on the shaft.

5. Install the large return spring on the inboard end of the selector shaft with the straight end toward the adjusting plate. Engage the straight end with the right side of the tab on the adjuster plate and cross the offset end over and engage it with the left side of the tab (**Figure 31**).

6. Install the shim and selector assembly on the kickstarter shaft and engage the pin on the selector lever with the pathway in the selector boss. Press the selector assembly all the way on.

7. Position the adjuster plate so the tapped holes in the case are in the center of the holes in the adjuster. Install the 2 Allen screws and tighten them (**Figure 32**).

8. Fit the gear selector pedal onto the shaft and check to see that it snaps back from both the raised and depressed positions.

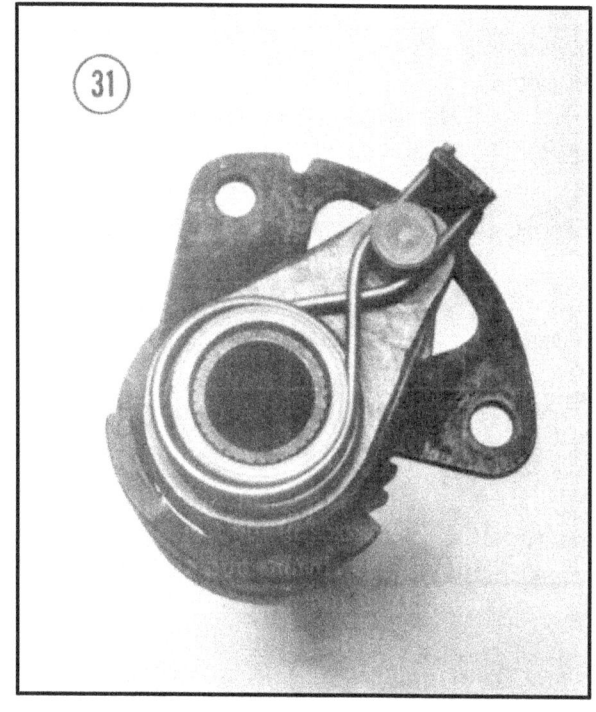

9. Screw the counter nut onto the selector rod and move the rod in or out by hand and engage third gear. You'll probably have to rotate the main shaft at the same time so that the gears will engage as the rod is moved.

10. Install the selector shoe into the end of the lever. The open end of the shoe must face the selector mechanism.

11. Fit the grooved nut into the shoe with the narrow shoulder on the nut facing outward. Screw the grooved nut all the way onto the selector rod but don't tighten it.

Adjustment

1. Install the selector pedal on the shaft and check to see that the transmission is in third gear.

2. Measure the distance between the mating surface of the crankcase (without a gasket) and the shaft of the selector shoe (**Figure 33**). This distance must be 23.2mm (0.914 in.). If necessary, screw the grooved nut in or out until the distance is correct.

3. Hold the grooved nut securely with a wrench and lock it with the counternut (**Figure 34**). Recheck the distance.

4. Shift the transmission into first gear and hold the selector pedal down, all the way against the

stop. You should be able to move the selector shoe in the nut groove (**Figure 35**). If not, loosen the Allen bolts which secure the adjusting plate to the case and rotate the stop cams as required until the selector shoe can be moved with the gear pedal pressed all the way to the bottom stop. Then tighten the Allen screws to 8.7-10.8 ft.-lb. (1.2-1.5 mkg). Shift the transmission into fifth gear and repeat the check.

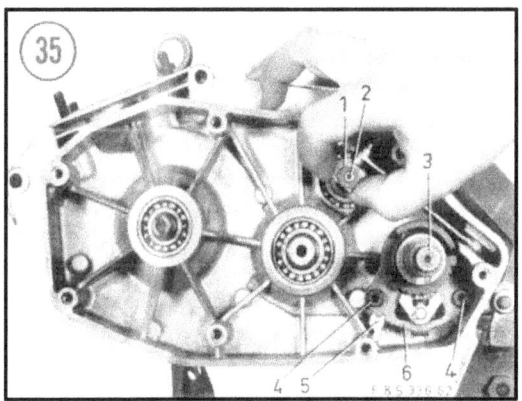

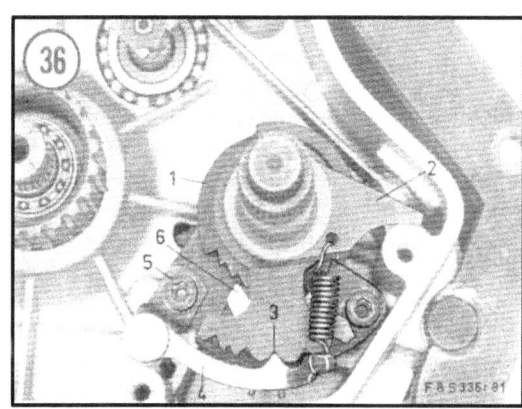

Note the position of the lock pawl in the third gear notch in the lock plate and compare it to its position in Step 2. If the gear lock is correctly adjusted, the lock pawl should rise an equal amount out of the recess in the lock plate in both directions.

4. If the lock pawl rose farther out of the notch in one direction, loosen the Allen screw (5, **Figure 36**) and center the pawl. For instance, if the pawl lifted farther out of the notch when the selector was pushed down (in the direction of second gear), move it slightly rearward and tighten the Allen screw. Recheck the action of the lock pawl as in Steps 2 and 3 and continue adjustment until the lock pawl rises out of the notch the same amount in both directions.

5. If the selector does not have a gear lock, the adjustment is complete. Reinstall the shims on the selector shaft and install the outer cover, gear selector pedal, and kickstart pedal as described in Chapter Four. If there is a gear lock on the selector, perform the following adjustment before reinstalling the cover.

5. When the adjustment of the gear lock is correct, tighten the Allen screws to 8.7-10.8 ft.-lb. (1.2-1.5 mkg) and install the outer cover, selector pedal, and kickstarter as described in Chapter Four.

Adjusting the Gear Lock

1. Install the selector pawl (4, **Figure 36**) so that its detent tip rests in the third-gear notch in the selector boss. Tighten the Allen screw (5) and install the spring between the plate (2) and the pawl.

2. Install the selector pedal on the shaft and push it downward, as though to engage second gear, and at the same time lift the rear tooth of the shifting pawl over the selector tooth with the tip of a small screwdriver so that the shifting pawl does not engage the selector but instead comes to rest against the rear stop. Note the position of lock pawl in the third gear notch in the lock plate.

3. Lift the selector pedal, as though to engage fourth gear, and lift the front tooth of the shifting pawl over the selector tooth so that the shifting pawl does not engage the selector tooth but instead comes to rest against the forward stop.

GEAR SELECTOR (TWO-PIECE)

Removal

Removal of the gear selector mechanism is described in Chapter Four.

Inspection

Inspection of the parts of the 2-piece selector assembly is the same as for the one-piece selector. Also, if the selector boss or shaft are to be replaced, they should be removed as described previously.

Assembly

1. If the selector assembly was disassembled, reassemble it in accordance with the instructions

presented previously for the selector system with the one-piece lever and proceed as follows.

2. Install the selector assembly onto the shaft and press the adjusting plate down to check the axial play. There should be no apparent play, but the selector must rotate freely. If play is present, remove the selector and add appropriate shims to the shaft. Then reinstall the selector assembly.

3. Pull the selector rod out until its end is flush with the mating surface of the case and the transmission is in first gear (**Figure 37**). It may be necessary to rotate the mainshaft to align the gears so they will mesh.

4. Loosen the nut on the selector lever (3, **Figure 38**) and install the the selector shoe in the end of the lever and onto the groove in the end of the selector rod. The open end of the shoe must face away from the selector shaft as shown in **Figure 39**.

5. Engage the pin in the rear half of the selector lever with the pathway in the selector boss. Press the selector boss down and line up the 2

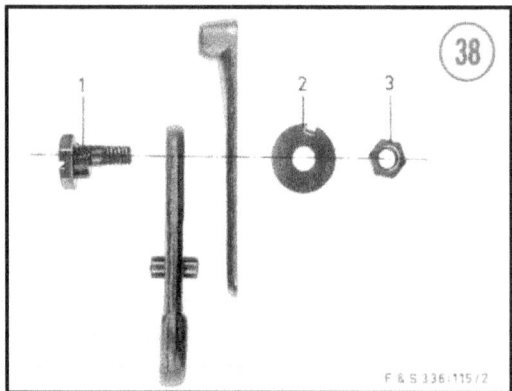

halves of the selector lever. Tighten the nut in the middle of the selector lever; make certain that the tab on the lockwasher engages the bore in the lever.

6. Install the 2. Allen screws and eccentric bushes in the adjuster plate. Turn the bushes outward and tighten the bolts (**Figure 40**).

7. Install the selector pedal and alternately depress and lift it and check to see that it snaps back to center from both directions.

Adjustment

1. Shift the transmission into first gear with the selector pedal and hold the pedal down against the bottom stop. Note the play of the selector pawl and the tooth on the selector boss (see **Figure 41**).

2. Shift the transmission into second gear and hold the pedal against the stop. Check the play of the forward selector pawl with the tooth on the selector boss. The play should be equal to the play observed in Step 1 (**Figure 42**).

3. If the play is unequal, loosen the nut in the center of the selector lever (1, **Figure 43**) and turn the eccentric bolt (4) clockwise or counterclockwise until the play between the ends of the selector pawl and the appropriate teeth in the selector boss is equal for both first and second gear, as described above. Then tighten the nut without turning the eccentric bolt and recheck the play. When the adjustment is correct, lock the nut with the tab washer.

NOTE: *The selector boss is not precisely machined. All that is necessary is to reach a reasonable compromise between the play of the front and rear pawls.*

NOTE: *If over- or under-shifting is experienced after the adjustments have been made, they can be corrected by further adjustment of the stops. If the selector undershifts in either direction, the appropriate stop should be rotated outward slightly to permit the pawl to travel farther. If the selector overshifts in either direction the appropriate stop should be rotated inward to reduce the travel of the pawl.*

4. Shift the transmission into first gear and hold the pedal against the stop. Loosen the Allen screw (4, **Figure 44**) and rotate the eccentric bushing (3) until it comes in contact with the selector pawl and tighten the screw to 8.7-10.8 ft.-lb. (1.2-1.5 mkg). Make sure the bushing does not rotate while the screw is being tightened.

5. Shift the transmission into second gear and hold the pedal against the stop. Loosen the Allen screw (2, Figure 44) and rotate the eccentric bushing (1) until it comes in contact with the selector pawl. Tighten the screw to 8.7-10.8 ft.-lb. (1.2-1.5 mkg), making sure the bushing does not rotate.

6. Remove the selector pedal and add shims to the end of the shaft until the outer face of the shim is level with the mating surface of the crankcase (**Figure 45**).

7. Install clutch and layshaft gear assembly, the outer cover, selector pedal, and kickstarter as described in Chapter Four.

SHIFTER SET-UP & ADJUSTMENT

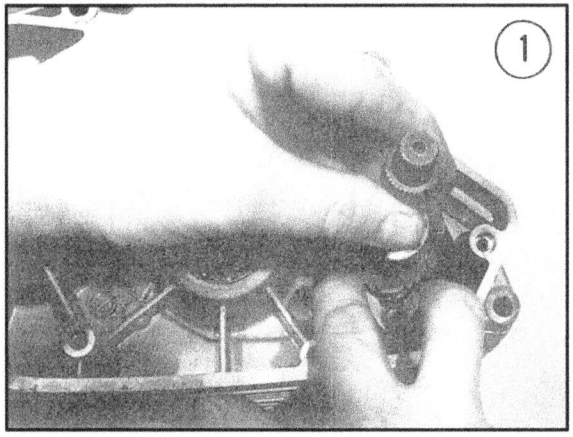

1. With the selector pedal on the shaft, move it first down and then up, allowing it to snap back each time. If the return spring is all right, the pedal will snap smartly back to center. Check the end play of the selector shaft and boss. There should be none. If you can see or feel any in-and-out movement you've already located some trouble.

2. Shift the transmission into first gear (the outer end of the selector draw rod should be level with the mating surface of the case). Unscrew the Allen screws from the adjuster plate and remove them along with their washers and eccentric bushes. Bend down the edge of the tab washer on the two-piece selector lever and unscrew the eccentric bolt and nut.

Lift the selector lever and at the same time pull the selector assembly off of the starter shaft.

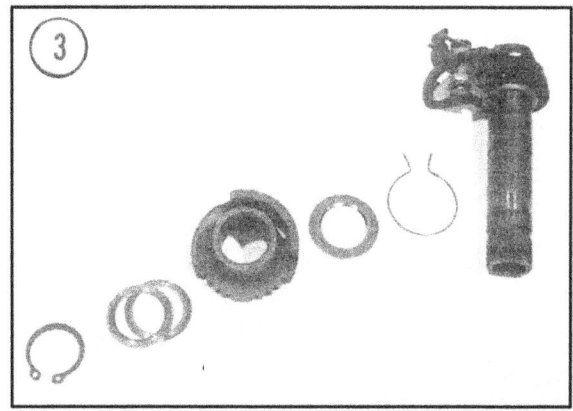

3. Check the spiral groove in the selector boss for wear. The edges must be sharp and even. Check the condition of the teeth. These too must be sharp. If there's any doubt about its condition, replace it. Remove the outer shim from the shaft, remove the circlip and the inner shims, the boss, the shim behind it, and the pawl spring. Pay close attention to the position of the pawl spring before you remove it; it has to go back in the same position with its ends crossed over one another, straddling the tang on the pawl and the tang on the adjuster plate.

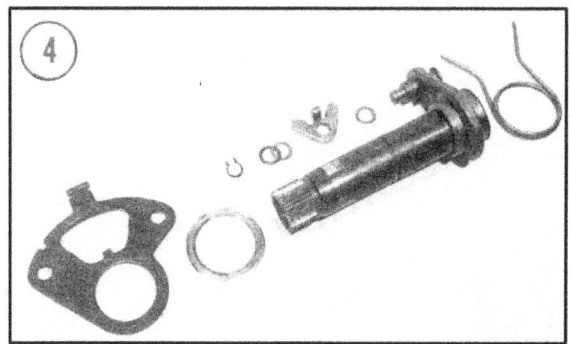

4. Remove the large return spring from the selector shaft. Check the teeth of the shifting pawl for wear. They must be sharp if the pawl is to do its job correctly. If they're not, replace it. If the pawl is in good condition you may not have to remove it but you do have to check its end play; it should be 0.1mm (0.0039 in.). The shim behind the pawl must be 0.5mm (0.020 in.). End

play can be corrected by substituting different size shims to the shaft ahead of the pawl. These shims are available through Sachs dealers in thicknesses of 0.2mm, 0.3mm, 0.5mm and 1.0mm. And while you're at it, get a new circlip.

5. If there was any end play apparent in the selector mechanism on the starter shaft it must be compensated with the shims shown here. These also are available through Sachs dealers in thicknesses of 0.2mm, 0.3mm, 0.5mm, and 1.0mm.

6. Reassemble the selector assembly and check the alignment of the teeth in the boss with the teeth of the pawl. They must line up exactly. If they do not, you must increase or decrease the thickness of the shim behind the selector boss. Place the selector shoe in the end of the selector boss and start the selector assembly onto the starter shaft. Line up the selector shoe with the groove in the selector rod and at the same time engage the pin in the selector lever with the beginning of the spiral groove in the boss. This sounds like a job for three hands, but actually all it requires is a little patience and coordination. When the selector assembly is in place, put a dab of grease on the tab washer that goes on the selector lever and set it in place, with the tang in the hole in the top of the lever. Reinstall the eccentric bolt and nut and tighten them securely but don't bend the washer over just yet.

7. Reinstall the Allen screws and eccentric bushes in the adjuster plate, rotating the bushes out as far as they will go. Tighten the screws. Install the selector pedal and check to see that it snaps back to center after it is raised and then depressed. Using the pedal, shift the transmission into first gear and carefully release it. Note the distance the pawl tooth rises out of the selector boss tooth.

8. Shift the transmission into second gear with the pedal and carefully release it. Again note the distance the pawl tooth rises out of the selector boss tooth. The return distance for both first and second gear engagement should be as nearly equal as possible.

9. The distances can be equalized by turning the eccentric bolt in the center of the selector lever clockwise or counterclockwise. Have a little patience and double check the distance in both gears until you're confident that it's as nearly equal as possible.

With your other hand, grasp the selector shoe and check its play in the groove in the selector rod. Then, shift the transmission into second gear, hold the pedal against the stop and check the play of the shoe in the groove. If the stop adjustment is correct, the play in the shoe should be about equal for both gears. Repeat this check between each gear pairing—first and second, second and third, third and fourth, fourth and fifth, fifth and sixth. Because the selector boss is not a precision machined part it's doubtful that the spacing set between first and second gear will work best for each pair up the line. You'll have to accept a compromise and it's going to take some time. Each time you make an adjustment with the eccentric bolt double check the shoe play in all of the gear pairings. Very soon, you should develop a "feel" for the best compromise in adjustment and when you're satisfied that you've reached it, stop.

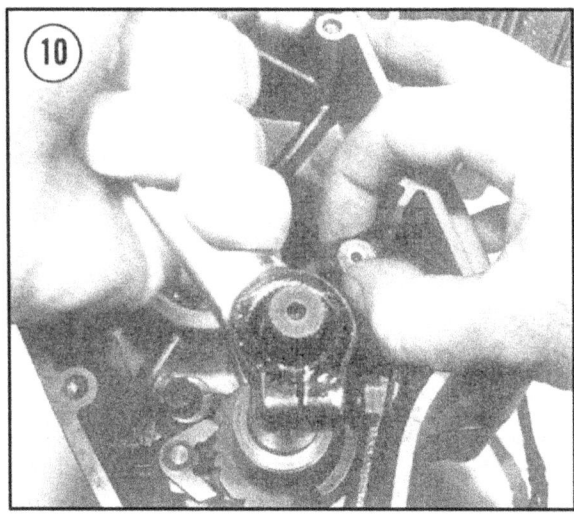

10. Once again shift the transmission into first gear but don't release the pedal; hold it firmly against the stop.

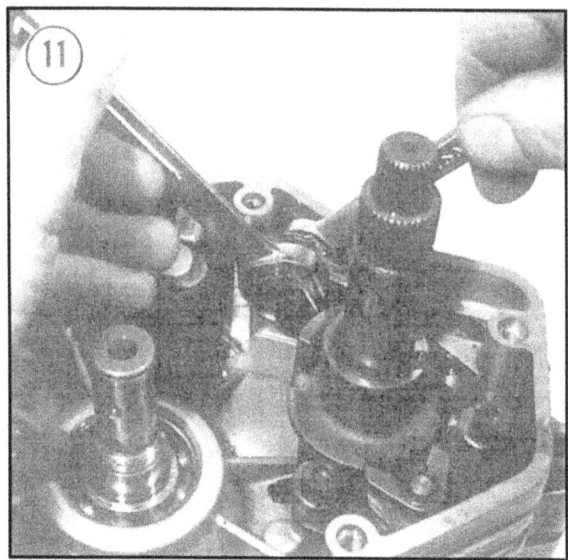

11. Retighten the nut on the eccentric bolt, without turning the bolt, and bend over the tab washer to lock everything neatly in place.

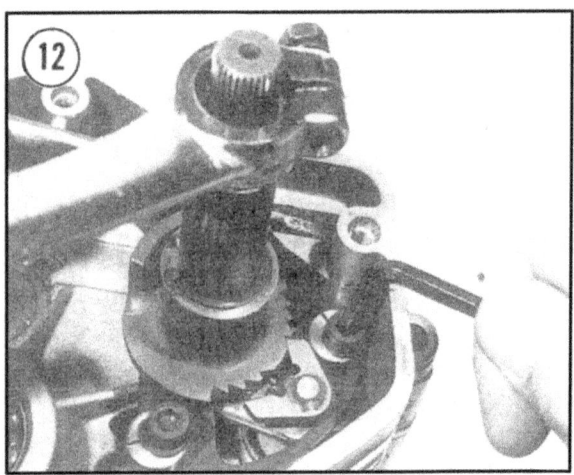

12. Now you're ready to adjust the overshift. Loosen the rear Allen screw in the adjuster plate. Shift the transmission into first gear and hold the lever against the stop. Rotate the rear eccentric bushing until it just contacts the selector pawl. Then, without moving the bushing, tighten the Allen screw to between 8.7 and 10.8 ft.-lb. (or 1.2 to 1.5 kpm, if you have a metric torque wrench).

13. Adjust the front overshift bushing in the same manner. Shift the transmission into second gear and hold it against the top. Rotate the eccentric bushing to contact the pawl and tighten the Allen screw without moving the bushing. The torque is the same.

14. Shim the outer end of the selector boss up to the level of the mating surface of the case. Reinstall the clutch (tighten the clutch hub nut to between 57.8 and 65 ft.-lb. — 8 to 9 kpm) making sure that all of the bits and pieces go back in the order they were removed. And while you're at it, you might check the axial play of the layshaft gear and clutch after you've installed the circlip. It should be 0.1mm (0.0039 in.). Coat the mating surfaces of the case and cover with gasket cement, install a new gasket over the alignment dowels, and set the cover in place. Tighten the cover screws to 6 to 7 ft.-lb., install the starter and gear selector pedals (don't forget the O-ring at the end of the selector shaft) and you're down the road!

CHAPTER SIX

CARBURETOR

For correct operation, a gasoline engine must be supplied with fuel and air mixed in proper proportions by weight. A mixture in which there is an excess of fuel is said to be rich. A lean mixture is one which contains an insufficient amount of fuel. It is the function of the carburetor to supply the correct fuel/air mixture to the engine under all operating conditions.

Sachs engines are equipped with Bing carburetors. The carburetor incorporates 4 subsystems; fuel feel, main control, idling, and starting.

OPERATION

The Bing carburetor is shown in exploded view in **Figure 1**, and in cutaway in **Figure 2**. These illustrations will be helpful in identifying individual components and their relationships.

Fuel Feed System

The fuel feed system consists of the float chamber, float, and needle valve. When fuel flowing into the float chamber reaches the correct operating level it lifts the float which raises the valve needle into the valve, cutting off the flow of fuel from the fuel tank.

As the engine consumes fuel, the level in the float chamber drops, causing the float to drop which lowers the valve needle and allows additional fuel to enter the float chamber. The needle valve serves only as a level regulator; it cannot positively shut off the fuel flow to the carburetor. Because of the likelihood of small particles becoming lodged between the needle and its seat and holding the valve open permitting a continuous flow of fuel into the float chamber, it's important that the fuel tap on the tank be closed when the engine is shut off and the motorcycle allowed to stand.

The float chamber incorporates a tickler which can be used to depress the float and allow the chamber to fill completely for cold-engine starts. This is not part of the starting system, however. The tickler tube and a hole in the top of the float chamber serve as atmospheric vents for the float chamber. If the vent hole becomes clogged, the tickler tube will act as a vent although the engine will experience fuel starvation until the vent hole is unblocked.

Main Control System

The main control system consists of the air control slide, needle, needle jet, mixing tube, and main jet. The amount of air drawn through the carburetor and into the engine is controlled by the air slide. As the slide is lifted the air flow through the carburetor increases creating a vacuum in the carburetor bore. The vacuum siphons fuel from the float chamber through the

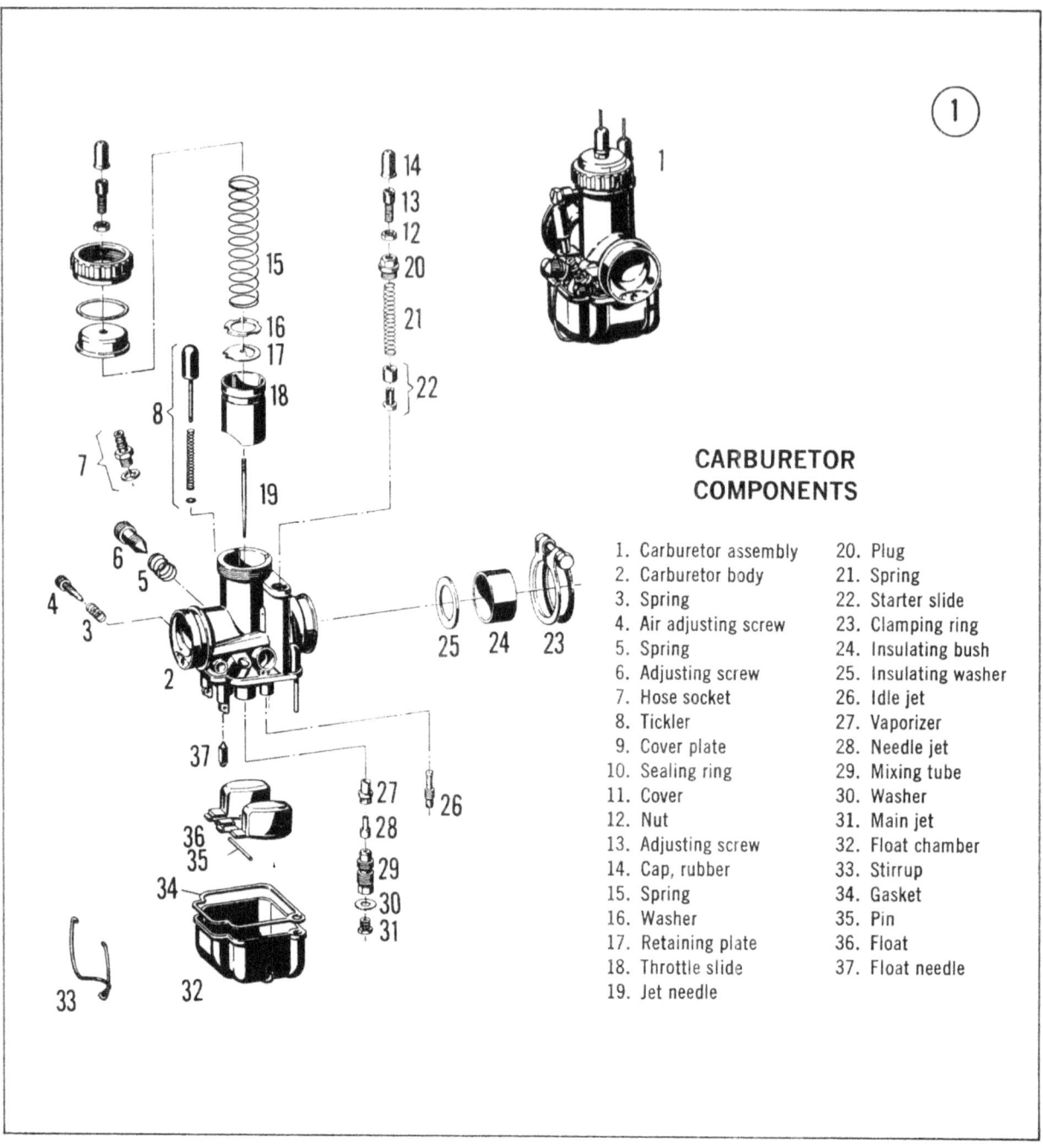

CARBURETOR COMPONENTS

1. Carburetor assembly
2. Carburetor body
3. Spring
4. Air adjusting screw
5. Spring
6. Adjusting screw
7. Hose socket
8. Tickler
9. Cover plate
10. Sealing ring
11. Cover
12. Nut
13. Adjusting screw
14. Cap, rubber
15. Spring
16. Washer
17. Retaining plate
18. Throttle slide
19. Jet needle
20. Plug
21. Spring
22. Starter slide
23. Clamping ring
24. Insulating bush
25. Insulating washer
26. Idle jet
27. Vaporizer
28. Needle jet
29. Mixing tube
30. Washer
31. Main jet
32. Float chamber
33. Stirrup
34. Gasket
35. Pin
36. Float
37. Float needle

jets where it is mixed with the incoming air. A portion of the incoming air is routed into the mixing tube where it helps to atomize the fuel passing through the jets and into the main chamber.

At partial throttle settings (from one-quarter to three-quarters full opening), fuel flow is controlled by the needle and needle jet. As the tapered needle is lifted in the needle jet, the effective flow area of the jet is increased to permit an increase of fuel flow into the incoming air stream.

At full throttle, the needle and needle jet are completely open, permitting the main jet to flow fuel at its full capacity.

Idling System

The idling system consists of an idling jet, adjustable air flow screw, and adjustable throttle stop screw.

With the air control slide closed, the vacuum in the main chamber is too low to siphon fuel through the needle jet. Air flow through the

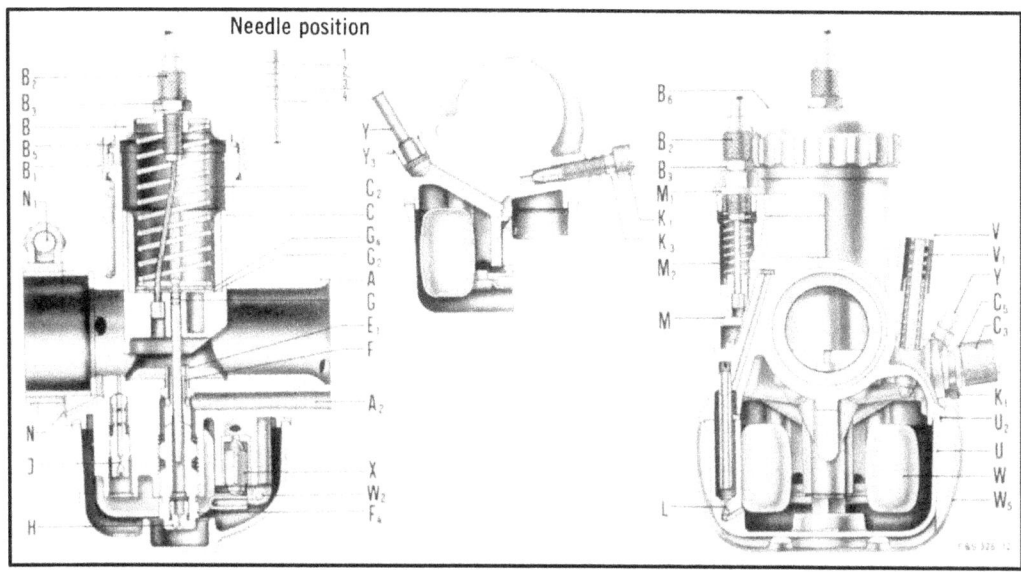

CARBURETOR COMPONENTS

- A   Carburetor body
- A_2 Compensating air passage
- B   Cover plate
- B_1 Screw cover
- B_2 Adjusting screw
- B_3 Nut
- B_5 Washer
- B_6 Safety spring
- C   Throttle valve
- C_2 Throttle valve spring
- C_3 Adjusting screw
- C_5 Spring
- E_1 Vaporiser
- F   Needle jet
- F_4 Mixing pipe
- G   Jet needle
- G_2 Retaining plate
- G_4 Washer
- H   Main jet
- J   Pilot jet
- K_1 Air regulating screw
- K_3 Spring
- L   Starting valve (fixed)
- M   Starting piston
- M_1 Screw plug
- M_2 Compression spring
- N   Clamp ring
- N_1 Clamp screw
- U   Float chamber
- U_2 Gasket
- V   Priming device
- V_1 Spring for priming device
- W   Float
- W_2 Stud
- W_5 Spring clip
- X   Float needle
- Y   Hose fitting
- Y_3 Washer

primary air hole in the bottom of the carburetor air intake passes by the air adjustment screw and through a drillway to the idling jet where it siphons fuel from the float chamber. The main air flow through the carburetor intake mixes with the fuel from the idling jet and the resulting air/fuel mixture is consumed by the engine.

Correct idling mixture is important to efficient engine operation and it must be achieved through careful adjustment of both the slide stop position and the amount of air flow to the idling jet.

Starting System

The starting system consists of a starting piston and a starting jet.

During starting, operation of the starting control lever lifts the starting piston to allow additional fuel to enter the main chamber through the starting jet. This creates a fuel-rich condition which is required for cold-engine starts.

CARBURETOR SERVICING

Major carburetor service intervals depend on use. A carburetor on a motorcycle that is used principally for transportation will usually not require attention for several thousand miles. At the extreme, for a motorcycle that is used weekly in rigorous competition, the carburetor should be serviced more frequently to ensure that it is always in top working order.

The disassembly, inspection, service, and reassembly procedures presented require that the carburetor be removed from the engine. The adjustments are carried out with the carburetor installed.

Disassembly

1. Unscrew the top ring from the carburetor and pull out the slide and needle (**Figure 3**).

2. Note the position of the retaining plate on the needle and disassemble the cable, spring, cap, needle, and slide.

3. Unscrew the starting assembly and pull it out of the carburetor (**Figure 4**).

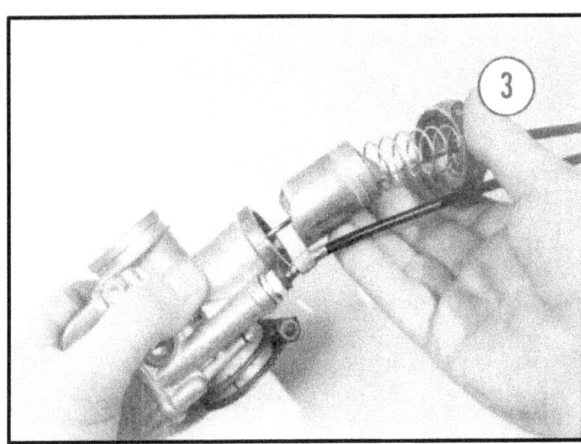

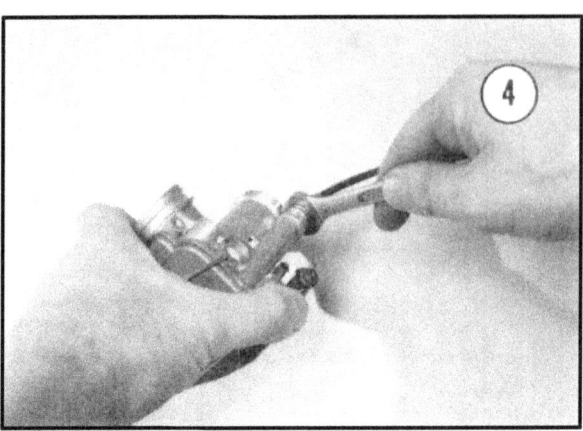

4. Unscrew the air adjusting screw and throttle stop screw (**Figure 5**).

5. Press the float chamber retaining clip forward with your thumbs and remove the float chamber (**Figure 6**).

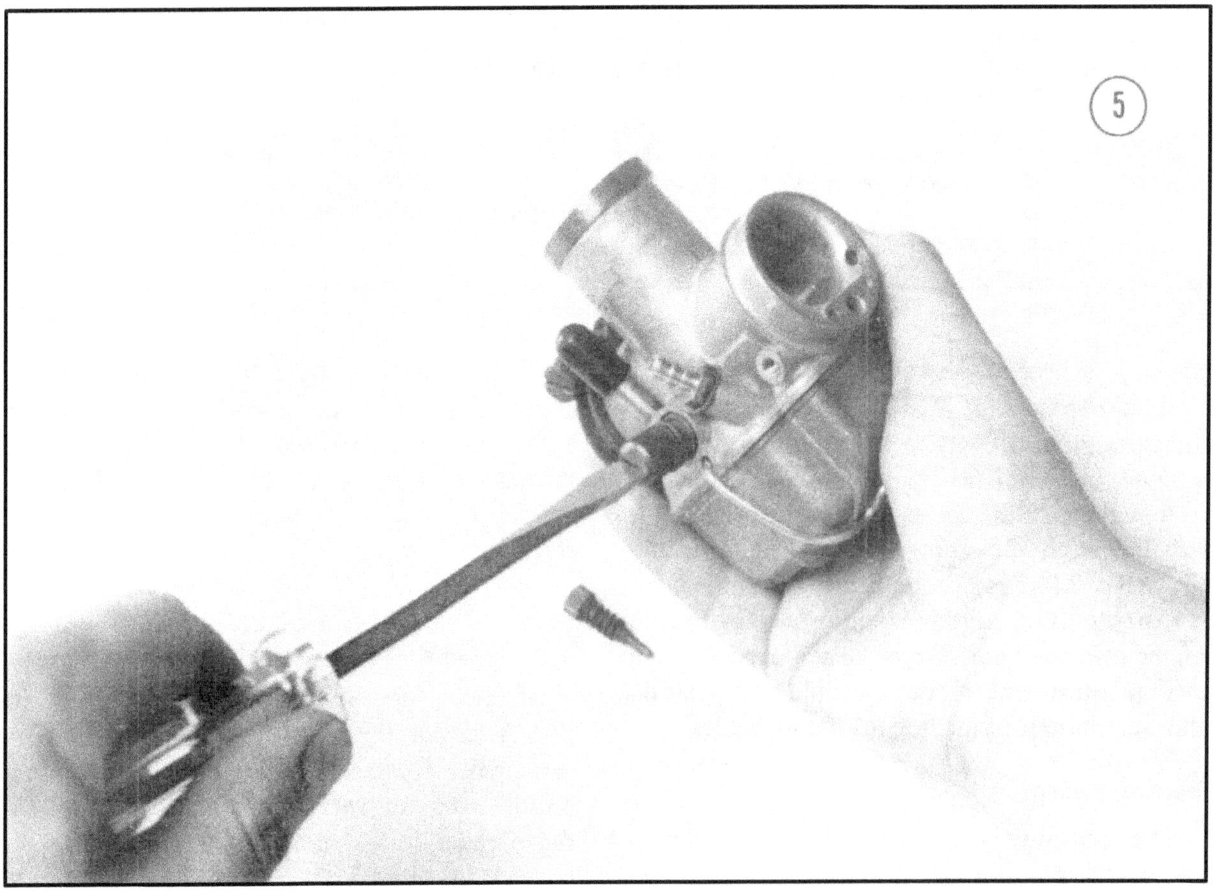

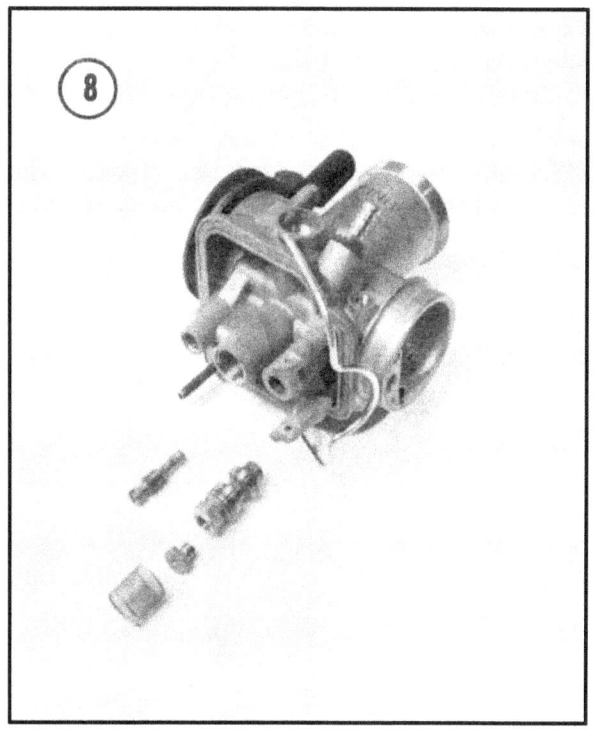

6. Slide the float hinge pin out to the side with a pair of needle-nose pliers and remove the float and needle valve (**Figure 7**).

7. Unscrew the main jet, mixing tube, and idling jet, noting their locations for reference during reassembly (**Figure 8**).

8. Push the vaporizer and needle jet out through the mixing tube port with your finger (**Figure 9**).

9. Unscrew the fuel hose nipple (**Figure 10**).

Cleaning and Inspection

1. Thoroughly clean and dry all the parts. If a special carburetor cleaning solution is used, the float, top-cap O-ring, and gaskets should be omitted from the bath and cleaned separately in common solvent.

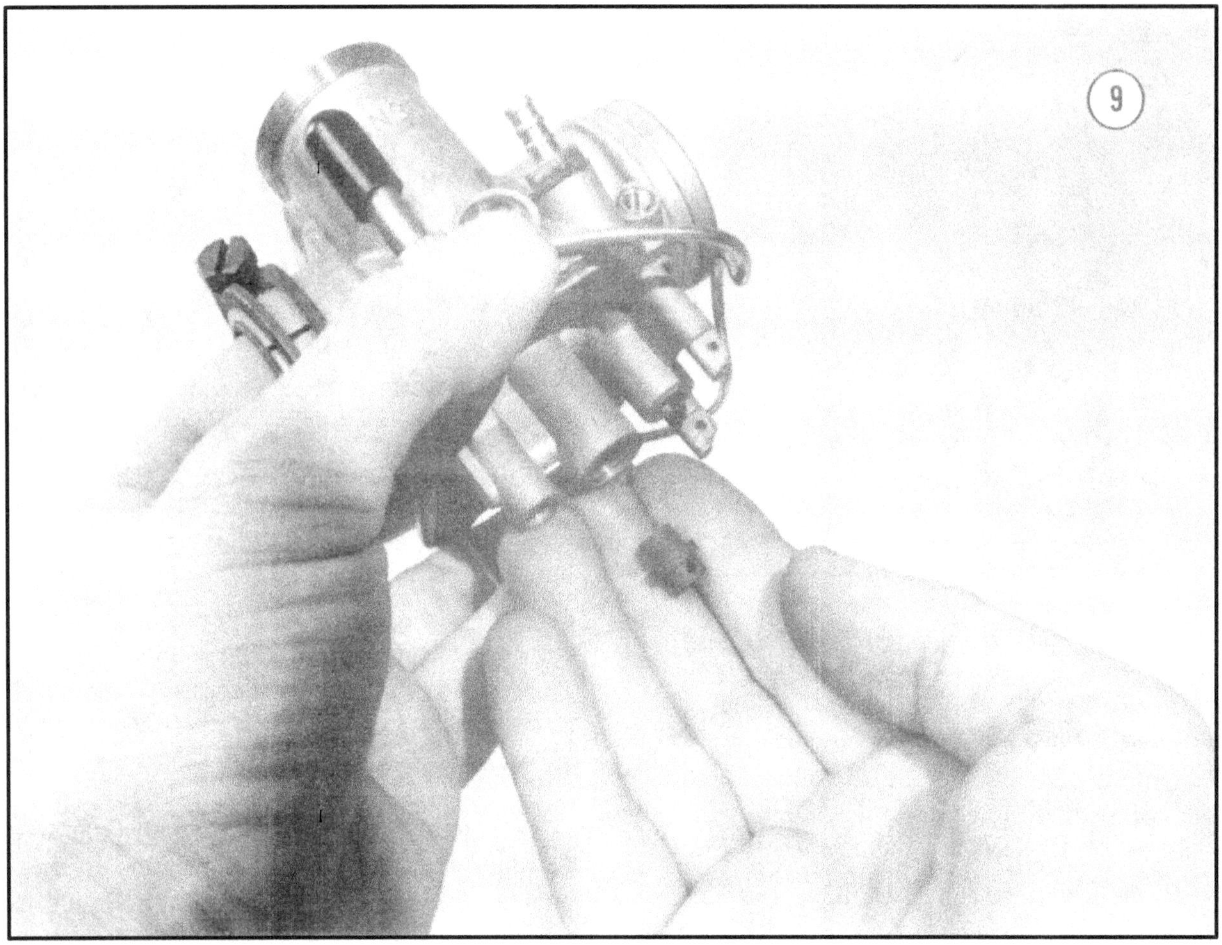

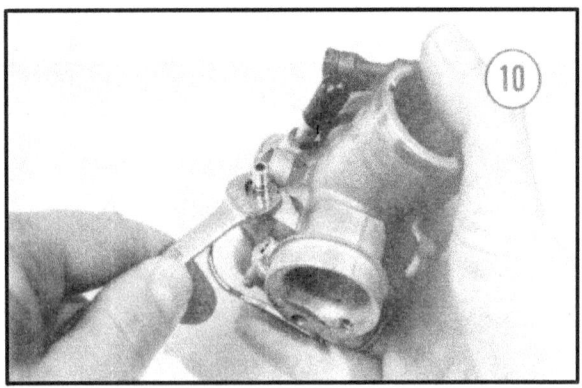

2. Blow out all the passages and jets with compressed air. Don't use wire to clean any of the orifices.

3. Check the cone of the float needle and replace it if it is scored or pitted. Also, the spring-loaded ball in the bottom of the needle should move freely in and out of its bore.

4. If the float is all brass, shake it to determine if there is any fuel in it. If there is, replace it with a new float.

5. Check the slide for scoring and galling, and if it's excessive, replace the slide.

6. Check the top-cap O-ring and replace it if it's damaged or shows signs of deterioration.

Reassembly

The carburetor is assembled by reversing the order of disassembly. The jets should be tight, but be careful not to strip their threads or the threads in the carburetor body. The float chamber gasket and the sealing ring on the fuel hose nipple should be replaced with new ones.

With the float needle valve and float reinstalled, check the float level by inverting the carburetor on a level surface. With the needle fully seated in the valve bore, the bottom of the float should be parallel to the mating surface of the float chamber as shown in **Figure 11**. The ball in the bottom of the float needle should not be compressed into the needle. If necessary, the float level can be corrected by carefully bending the brass tab on the float.

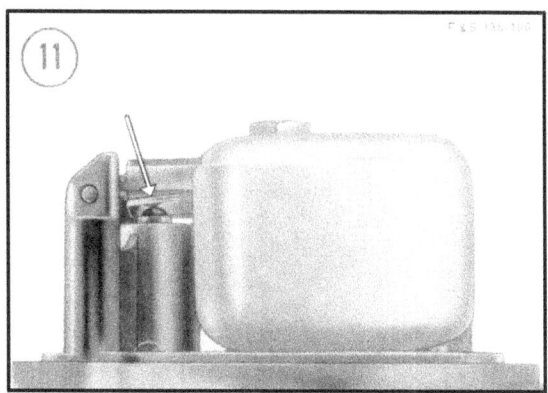

NOTE: *Late-model carburetors are fitted with an anti-surge screen at the bottom of the main jet. This device entraps gas around the main jet to prevent fuel starvation and surging when the motorcycle is operated at moderate and high speeds over undulating terrain. It's recommended that the screen be fitted in place of the flat washer on the main jet of earlier carburetors.*

When installing the slide assembly in the carburetor body, make sure the needle is seated in the needle jet and that the movement of the slide with the cap and ring installed is smooth throughout the length of the slide's travel.

Reinstall the carburetor on the engine, reconnect the control cables and fuel line, and reconnect the intake bellows between the carburetor and the air cleaner.

Carburetor Adjustment

Carburetor adjustments should be made with the engine warmed up to operating temperature.

1. Adjust the free-play in the throttle cable by turning the adjuster screw on the top of the carburetor in or out until the cable sheath can be pulled out of the carburetor top about 0.039 in. (1.0mm), **Figure 12**.

2. With the engine running, screw in the throttle stop screw (**Figure 13**) until engine speed increases slightly with the throttle completely closed.

3. Screw in the air adjustment screw (**Figure 14**) until the engine falters and then screw it out until the engine begins to run smoothly (about ½ turn).

4. Slowly unscrew the throttle stop screw to bring the engine to its lowest idle speed. For competition use, and particularly for observed trials, it's recommended that very little or no idling occur with the throttle closed.

AIR FILTER

There are two basic types of air filters used on Sachs-engine motorcycles—micronic paper element and oil-wetted foam. Service on both units is presented in Chapter Two.

CHAPTER SEVEN

ELECTRICAL SYSTEM

Operating principles, service and repair procedures for the ignition, charging, and lighting systems are presented in this chapter. Two basic systems are used on Sachs engines: Bosch magneto-generator with mechanical contact breaker ignition, and Motoplat magneto-generator with electronic ignition. Both types are flywheel-mounted systems. The 2 types are shown in **Figures 1 and 2**.

MAGNETO IGNITION SYSTEM

A magneto is a mechanically driven alternating current generator which produces the electrical energy required to fire the spark plug. On models equipped with lights, additional coils in the magneto produce the energy required to charge the battery and power the lights.

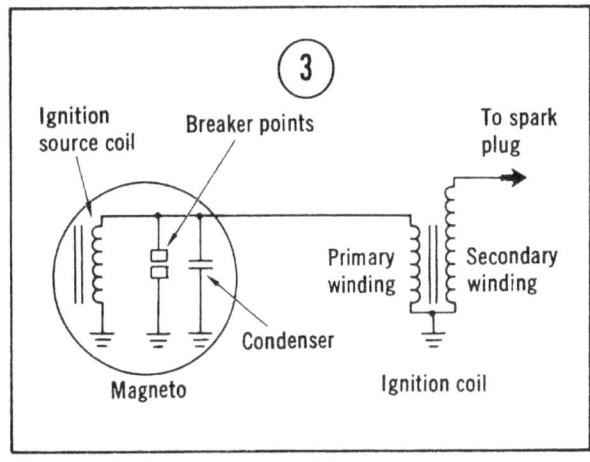

Magneto Operation

Figure 3 illustrates a typical contact-breaker magneto ignition system. As the flywheel rotates, magnets located in the flywheel move past a stationary ignition source coil inducing a current in the coil. A contact breaker, controlled by a cam attached to the crankshaft, opens at the precise instant the piston reaches its firing position. The energy produced in the source coil is then discharged to the primary side of the high-voltage ignition coil where it is increased, or stepped up to a high enough voltage to jump the gap between the spark plus electrodes.

Breaker Points

The contact breaker for Bosch ignition systems is shown in **Figure 4**. During normal operation, the contact surfaces of the points gradually burn and erode away. If the points are not badly pitted, they can be dressed with a few strokes from a point file. Never use sandpaper or emery cloth for dressing the contacts; for maximum efficiency, the contact surfaces must be flat and parallel, and sandpaper will

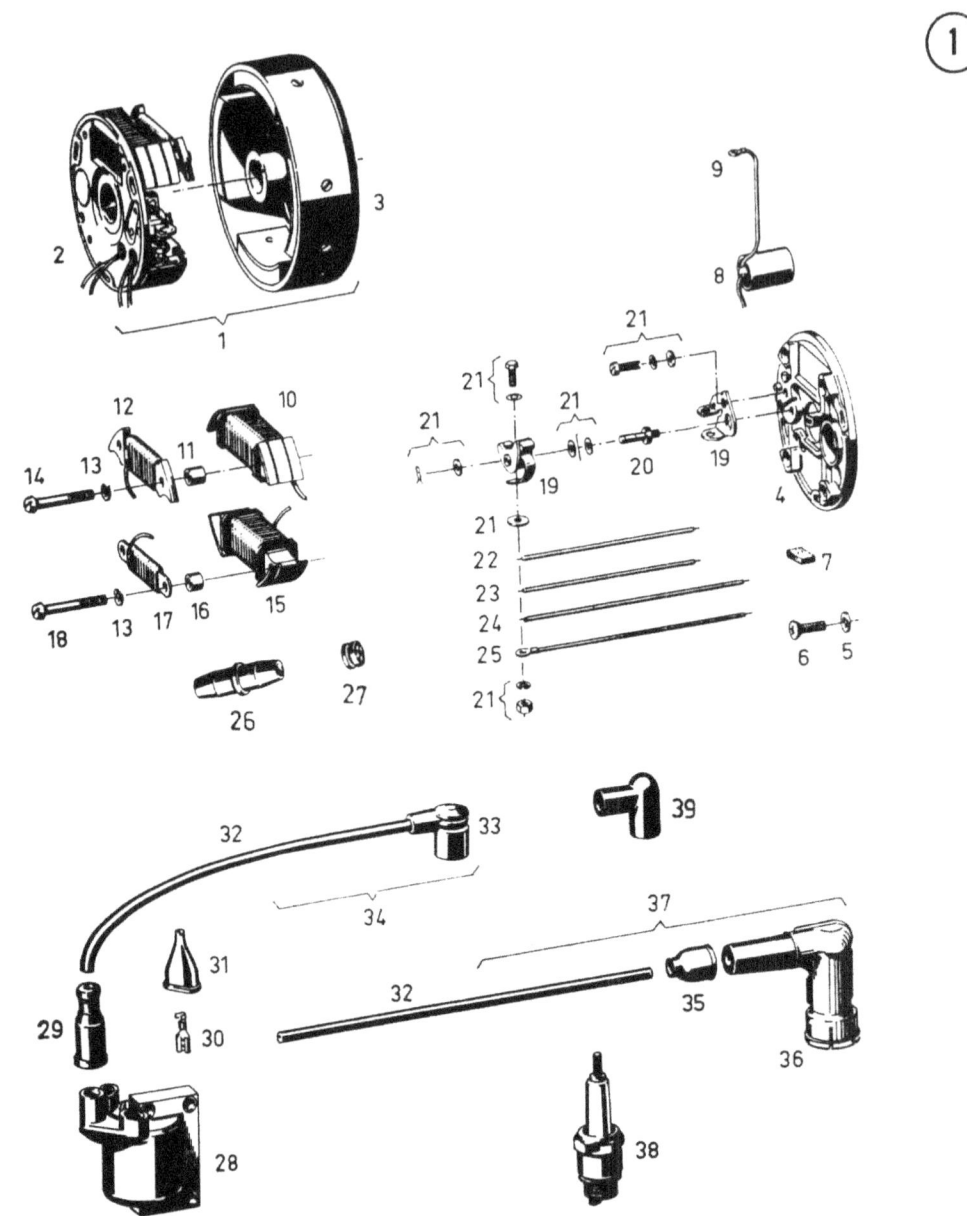

BOSCH IGNITION

1. Magneto-generator
2. Armature base plate
3. Flywheel
4. Armature base plate
5. Washer
6. Screw
7. Lubrication felt
8. Condenser
9. Cable
10. Ignition armature
11. Bush
12. Stop light armature
13. Spring washer
14. Screw, fillister head
15. Generating armature
16. Bush
17. Taillight armature
18. Screw, fillister head
19. Contact breaker set
20. Pivot pin
21. Set of spares for contact breaker
22. Lighting cable
23. Taillight cable
24. Stop light cable
25. Generating cable
26. Cable terminal
27. Rubber grommet
28. Ignition coil
29. Cap, protective
30. Cable terminal
31. Cap, protective
32. Ignition cable
33. Spark plug cap
34. Ignition cable
35. Cap, protective
36. Spark plug cap
37. Ignition cable
38. Spark plug

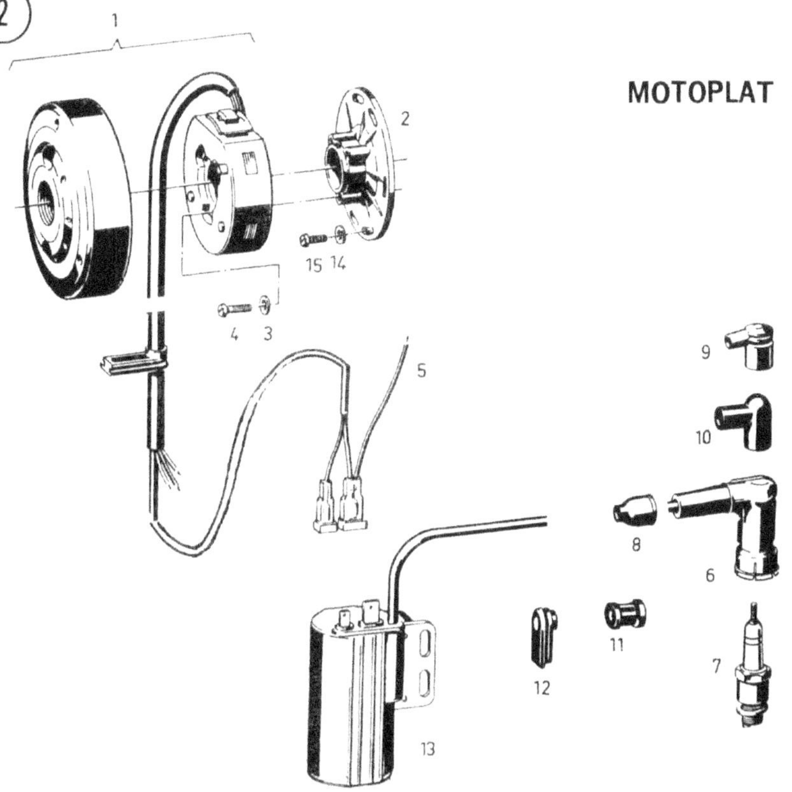

MOTOPLAT IGNITION

1. Magneto-generator
2. Base plate
3. Washer
4. Screw, fillister head
5. Short-circuit cable
6. Spark plug cap
7. Spark plug
8. Cap, protective
9. Spark plug connector
10. Spark plug connector
11. Rubber grommet
12. Rubber grommet
13. Ignition coil with cable
14. Washer
15. Screw, fillister head

round off the edges of the contacts and create the sort of condition you're attempting to correct (see **Figure 5**). If a few strokes won't correct the contact surfaces, replace the breaker assembly.

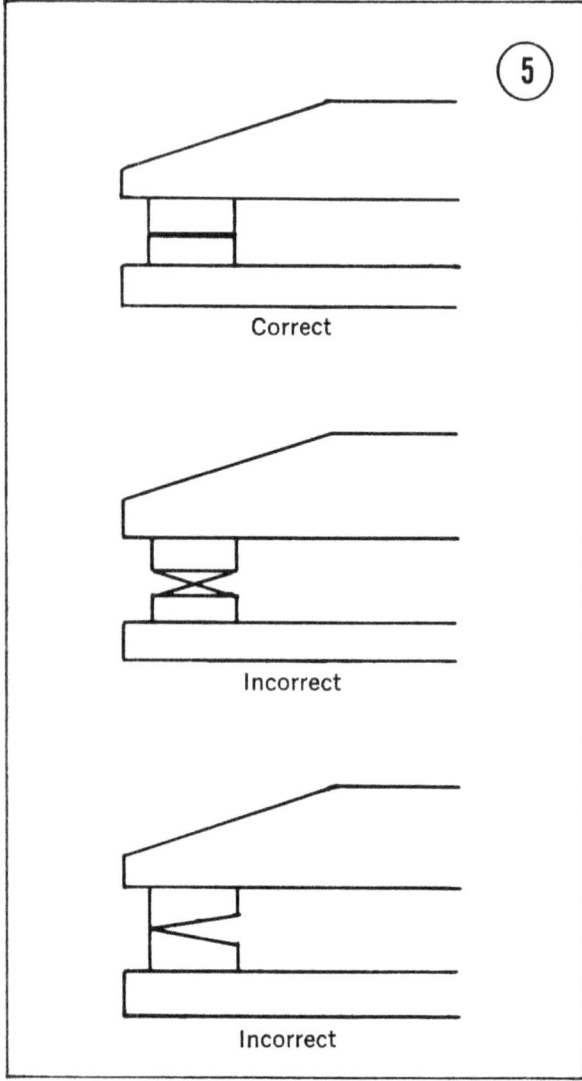
Correct
Incorrect
Incorrect

Always remove the contact breaker assembly before dressing the contacts. The time spent removing, reinstalling, and adjusting the points is preferable to risking small particles finding their way into the magneto.

Oil or dirt may get on the contacts, creating electrical resistance in them or resulting in their failure. These conditions can be caused by a defective crankshaft seal, incorrect breaker cam lubricant, or dirt getting into the magneto when the outer cover is removed. To correct these conditions, remove the contact breaker assembly and dress the contacts, clean the assembly in lacquer thinner, and lubricate the breaker cam with contact breaker lubricant. Never use oil or common grease; they break down under high temperature and frictional load and are likely to find their way to the contacts.

A weak breaker spring will allow the points to bounce at high engine speeds and cause misfiring. Usually, however, the spring will last for the life of the contacts.

Close the contacts on a piece of clean white paper, such as a business card, and pull it through the contacts. Continue to do this until no discoloration or residue remains on the card. Finally, rotate the engine and watch the contacts as they open and close. If they do not meet squarely, replace them.

Contact Breaker Replacement

1. Remove the right-side cover and the flywheel as discussed in Chapter Four.
2. Disconnect the ground (short-circuit) connection, noting the location of the insulation washers for reference during reassembly, as shown in **Figure 6**.
3. Remove the spring clip from the end of the pivot shaft. Pull off breaker arm and shims.
4. Remove the slotted screw and pull off the contact carrier (**Figure 7**).
5. Reverse the above steps to install a new breaker assembly. Grease the pivot shaft with contact breaker lubricant (Bosch Ft 1 v4 or an equivalent) before installing the breaker arm. With the breaker arm installed, check the alignment of the contacts and correct it if necessary by adding or removing shims. Knead the lubricating felt with contact breaker lubricant and apply some to the groove in the rubbing portion of the arm. Be sure the terminals are clean and tight and that there is no oil or grease between the contact carrier and the stator baseplate.

Condenser Replacement

The condenser should be routinely replaced with the points.

1. Unsolder the condenser leads (**Figure 8**).
2. Pull the condenser out of the stator baseplate (**Figure 9**).

6

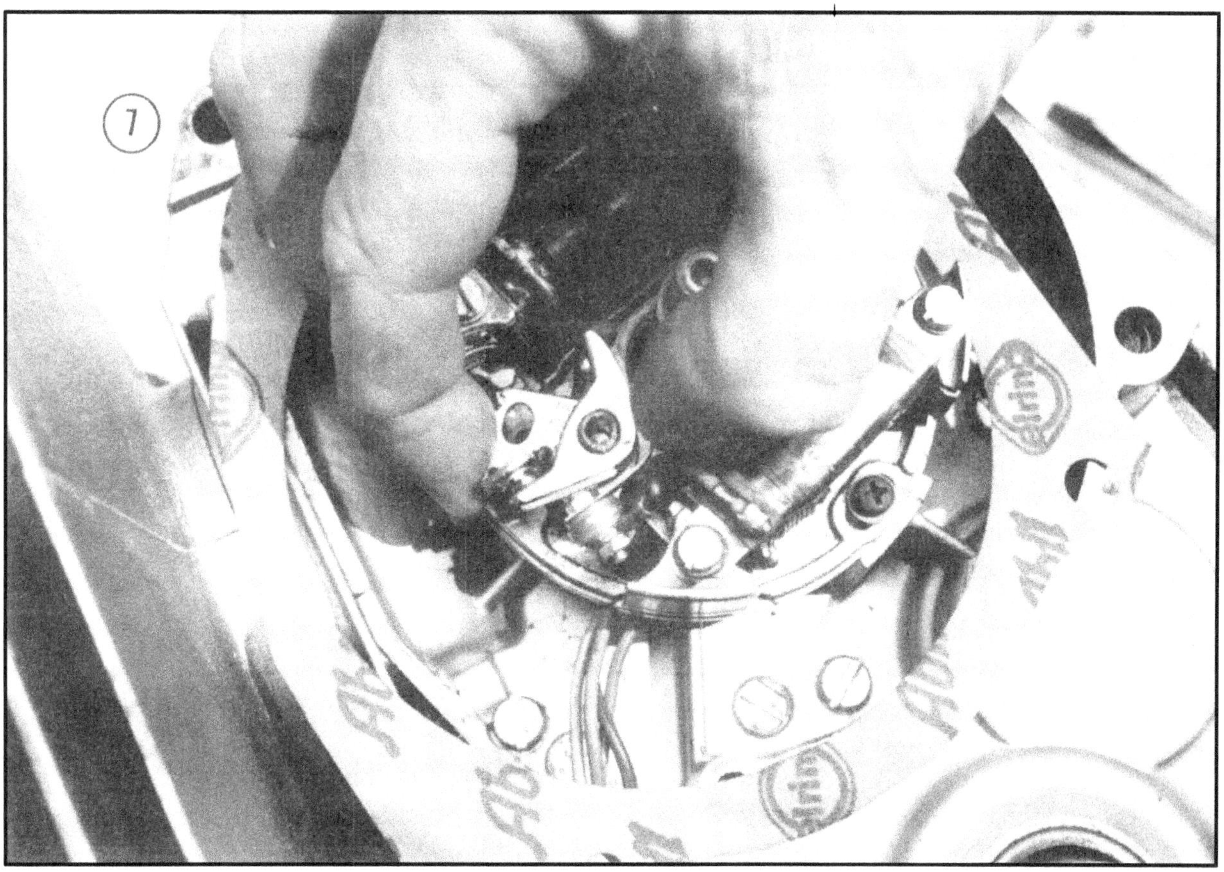

7

77

3. Remove any oxidation burrs from the condenser boss.

4. Install a new condenser in the boss and caulk it with silicone sealer (**Figure 10**).

5. Solder the condenser leads to the terminals.

Adjusting Contact Gap

The gap of the contact breaker is adjusted with the flywheel installed.

1. Rotate the flywheel counterclockwise and line up the timing mark "M" with the mark on the crankcase (**Figure 11**). The contacts should be closed.

2. Slowly rotate the flywheel clockwise. The contacts should begin to open immediately. If not, time the ignition in accordance with the instructions which follow.

3. Continue to rotate the flywheel clockwise until the contacts are at their maximum opening. Measure the gap with a flat feeler gauge. It should be 0.0014-0.0018 in. (0.35-0.45mm). If necessary, adjust the gap by loosening the locking screw (**Figure 12**) and moving the breaker plate as required.

4. Tighten the locking screw and recheck the adjustment.

5. Again check the ignition timing and adjust if necessary.

Ignition Timing

Any change in contact breaker gap, including that occuring through normal wear of the contacts and the rubbing block, will alter ignition timing. For this reason, ignition timing should be checked and corrected each time the contact breaker is serviced or replaced. Severe engine damage can result from a spark that is too far advanced, and a late or retarded spark can cause overheating and loss of power.

The ignition timing described employs a Sachs timing gauge (tool No. 14). However, a similar plunger or dial type timing gauge can be used.

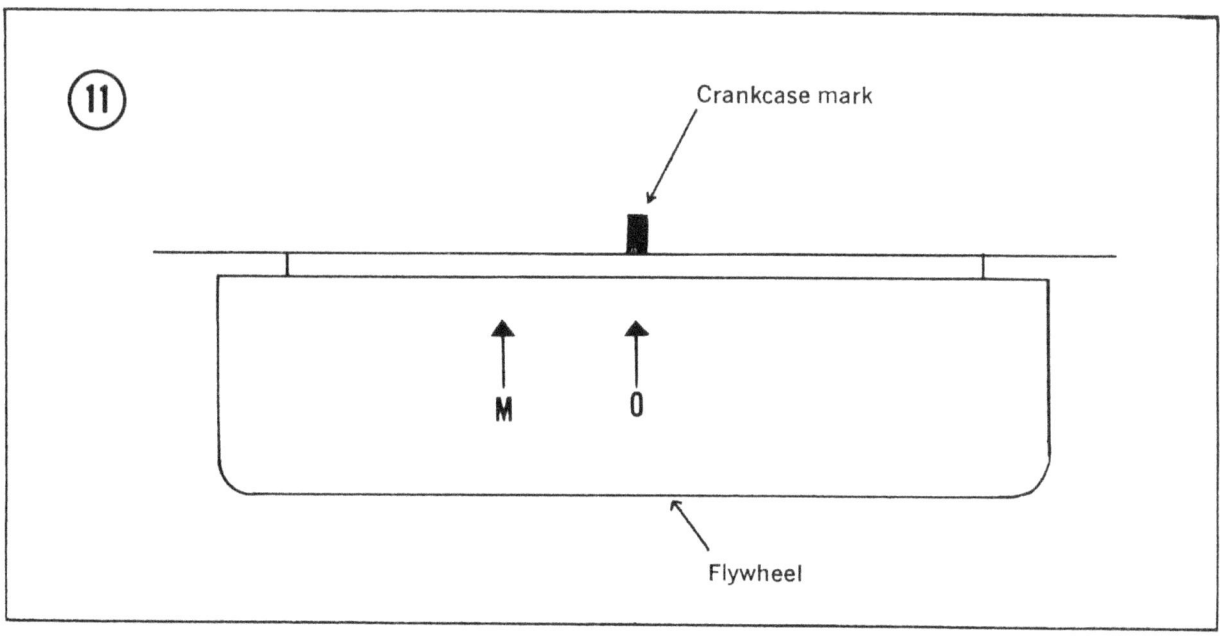

⑫

1. Remove the spark plug from the cylinder head and install the timing gauge (**Figure 13**). Remove the right-side engine cover.

⑬

2. Rotate the flywheel counterclockwise as viewed from the ignition side to bring the piston to TDC as indicated by the timing gauge. The "O" mark on the flywheel should line up with the mark on the crankcase (**Figure 14**).

3. Continue to rotate the flywheel and line up the "M" mark on the flywheel with the mark on the crankcase (Figure 11). The contact breaker should be closed.

4. Slowly rotate the flywheel clockwise—in the direction of rotation during engine operation—and observe the contact breaker. If the timing is correct, the breaker should begin to open.

5. If the timing is not correct, loosen the 3 screws in the stator plate and rotate the plate as required. The screws can be loosened and tightened through the openings in the flywheel (**Figures 15A through 15C**). To advance the timing, rotate the stator counterclockwise. To retard it, rotate the stator plate clockwise. After adjusting the stator, tighten the screws.

Establishing Timing Marks

If the flywheel and crankcase do not have ignition timing marks, these should be established to facilitate future ignition servicing.

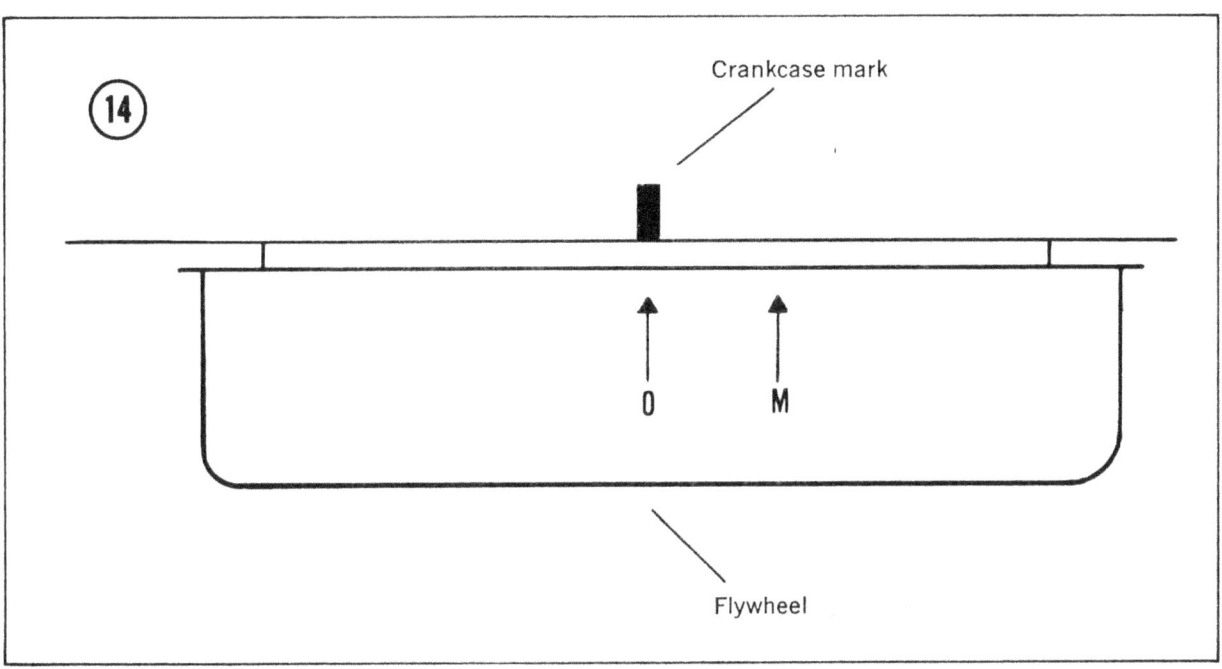

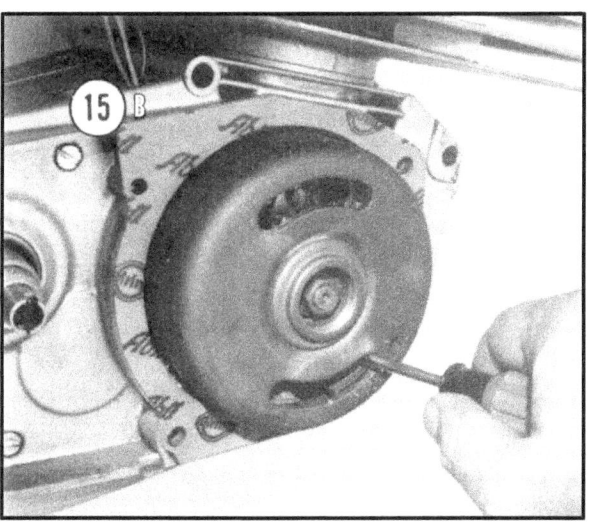

1. With a timing gauge installed in the spark plug bore in the head, rotate the crankshaft to bring the piston to TDC.

2. Make a mark on the crankcase and a corresponding mark on the flywheel with a chisel. Scribe an "O" on the flywheel at the mark. This establishes TDC.

3. Screw in the adjusting nut (see **Figure 16**) until it just touches the bushing.

4. Turn the nut back 2½ to 3 turns. This establishes the piston at the firing position before TDC. The firing position is 2.5-3.0mm (0.098-0.118 in.) before TDC. Each complete turn of the adjuster nut on the timing gauge corresponds

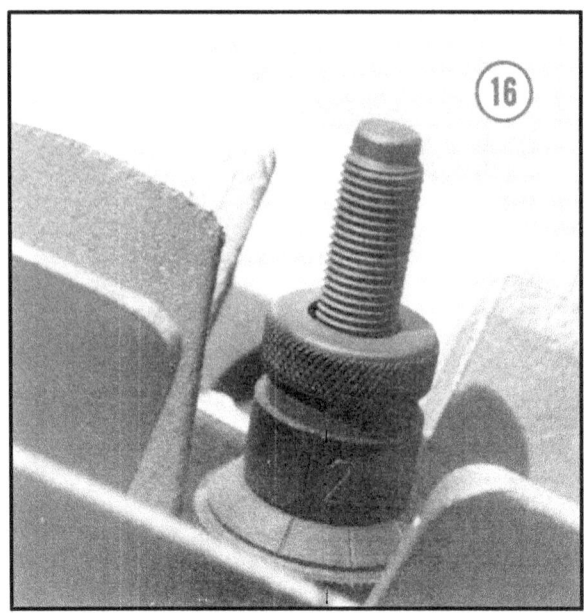

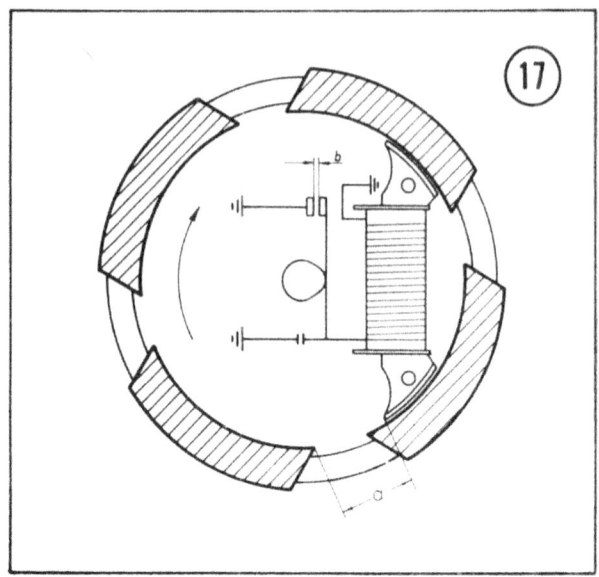

to 1.0mm (0.039 in.). The marks on the adjuster nut correspond to 0.25mm (0.00985 in.), and the marks on the bush correspond to 0.1mm (0.00394 in.).

5. Rotate the flywheel counterclockwise until the adjusting nut just touches the bush. Check to see that the piston is in contact with the rod in the timing gauge. Apply a chisel mark to the flywheel in line with the mark on the crankcase. This establishes the firing position.

Pole Shoe Gap

The pole shoe gap (a, **Figure 17**) should be 22-25mm (0.867-0.985 in.) with the flywheel set at the firing position ("M"). The pole shoe gap may be corrected by adjusting the contact breaker gap, within the limits of 0.0014-0.0018 in. (0.35-0.45mm) prescribed for the contact breaker gap.

Armature Replacement

If a functional test of the generator indicates that one or more of the 4 armatures is faulty, they may be replaced individually. However, armature replacement shouldn't be attempted unless you have access to a Bosch centering plate and ring; these special tools are required to accurately set the air gap between the armature cores and the magneto flywheel.

1. Remove the right-side cover and the flywheel as described in **Chapter Four**.

2. Remove the 3 Phillips-head screws which hold the stator baseplate in place (**Figure 18**) and carefully pull the wiring harness out of the hole in the crankcase.

3. Pass the wiring harness through the hole in the centering plate and set the stator in place (**Figure 19**). Install the bolt in the centering tool and tighten it by hand.

4. Remove faulty armature cores and install new ones.

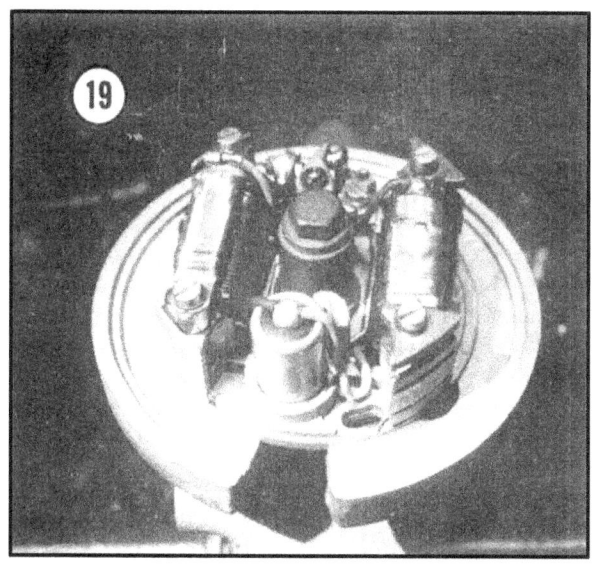

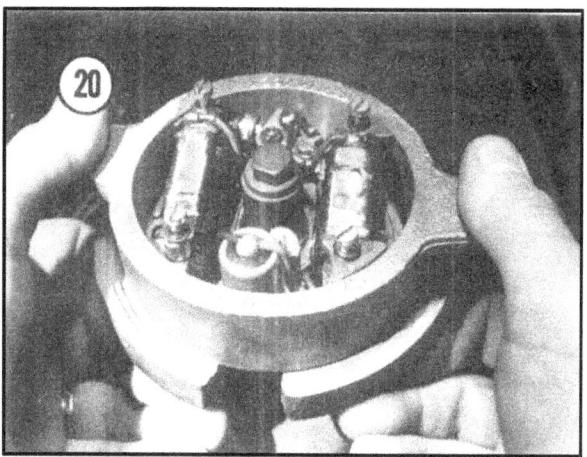

5. Set the centering ring in place (**Figure 20**). Press the armatures up tight against the ring and tighten the retaining screws.

6. Remove the ring, unscrew the centering bolt, and reinstall the stator on the engine, taking care to line up the timing mark. Reinstall the flywheel and check ignition timing as discussed earlier.

Ignition Coil

The ignition coil is a step-up transformer which increases the low voltage produced by the magneto to a high voltage required to jump the spark plug gap. The only service required is periodic inspection of the electrical leads to make sure they are clean and tight, and checking to see that the coil is mounted securely.

If the functional condition of the coil is in doubt, there are several checks which should be made.

1. Using an ohmmeter, measure the resistance between the primary wire and ground as shown in **Figure 21**. Resistance should be about 1 ohm.

2. Measure the resistance between the high-tension lead and ground as shown in **Figure 22**. It should be 3,000 ohms.

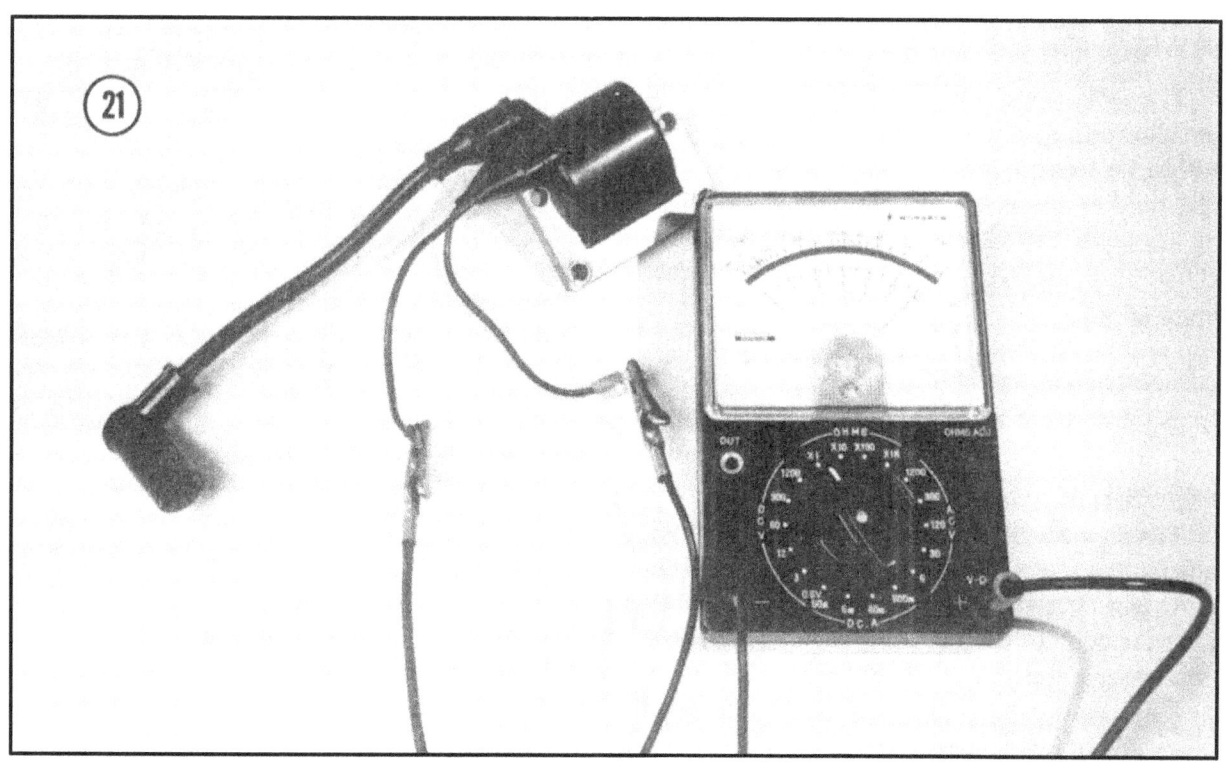

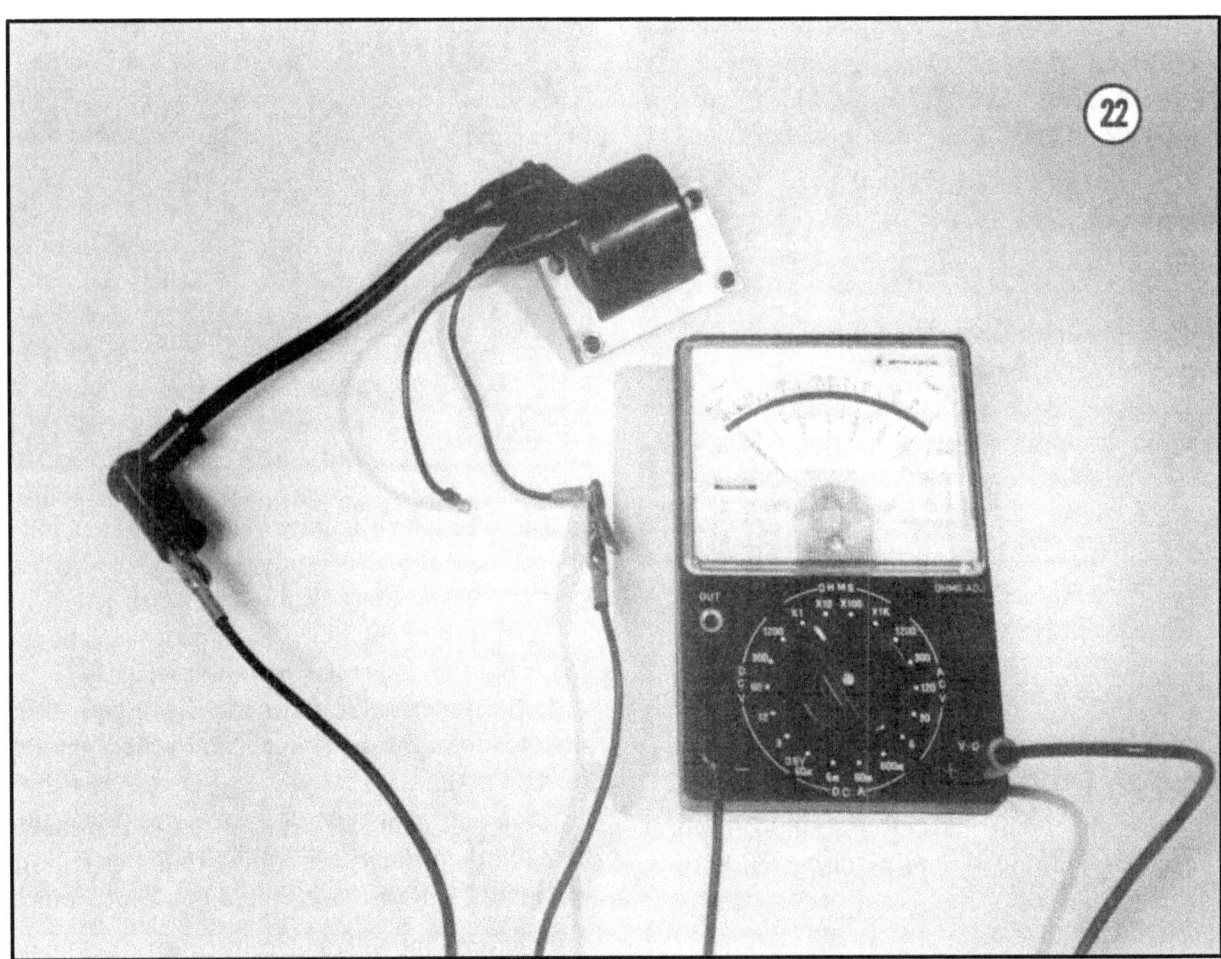

3. If the meter indicates an open circuit (no continuity) in **Step 2**, unplug the high-tension lead from the coil and test it again as shown in **Figure 2**. If the resistance is now correct, the trouble is in the high-tension lead. It may be a bad connection at the spark plug cap or an internal break in the wire. Make sure the connection is good and check the lead for continuity, and if an open circuit is still indicated, replace the high-tension lead. However, if an open circuit is indicated between the primary and high-tension leads of the coil itself, the coil is defective and must be replaced.

Condenser

The condenser requires no service other than checking to see that its connections are clean and tight. It should be routinely replaced each time the contact breaker is replaced. To test the condenser, connect it to the battery—negative to negative, positive to positive—and allow it to charge for a few seconds. Then, quickly disconnect it and touch one condenser lead to the other. If there is a spark, the condenser may be assumed to be all right.

Troubleshooting

The magneto-generator is a simple device which should give little trouble. If problems are suspected, perform the following checks with all the wiring disconnected.

1. Block the contact breaker open with a business card or similar piece of paper.

2. Disconnect both of the contact leads and with an ohmmeter set at its highest range, check that the movable breaker is not shorted to ground. If the ohmmeter registers at all, replace the points.

3. Check the condenser and replace it if there is any doubt about its condition.

4. Examine temperature coils for chafing and check them individually for shorts and continuity. Replace any coils that are faulty.

5. Check the flywheel for cracks or movement at the point where the cam is pressed into it. If the cam moves, the "E" gap (which ensures maximum energy from the primary ignition pulse) will not be correct and the flywheel must be replaced.

ELECTRONIC IGNITION SYSTEM

Some Sachs engines are equipped with Motoplat electronic ignition. This system has no mechanical contact breaker, cam, or any adjustable components. The system requires no servicing other than periodic checks of the connections to make sure they are clean and tight. It's virtually unaffected by dust and dampness but care should still be taken to keep it clean and dry when the right-side cover is removed from the engine.

The Motoplat electronic ignition system can be installed on Sachs engines currently fitted with conventional contact breaker ignition with no modifications.

System Operation

Figure 23 is a diagram of a typical electronic ignition system. Alternating current produced by a source coil located in the magneto is rectified to direct current by a diode in the electronic unit. This current charges a capacitor. A trigger pulse, produced by a signal coil in the magneto, is developed each time the piston reaches firing position. This pulse is the equivalent of the opening of a contact breaker. It is applied to the gate of a diode which connects the capacitor to the primary side of the high-voltage coil. The pulse to the gate of the diode signals the diode to conduct. It thus provides a discharge path for the capacitor to the coil primary. This voltage is then stepped up in the coil to a value which is sufficient to jump the spark plug gap.

Testing

The Motoplat electronic can be tested with an ohmmeter with a 0-10,000 ohm range. Always make sure the polarity is correct for a test hookup and never attempt to test the ignition components with a voltmeter.

The stator and coil need not be removed from the motorcycle to be tested, but the flat connectors must be disconnected from the coil,

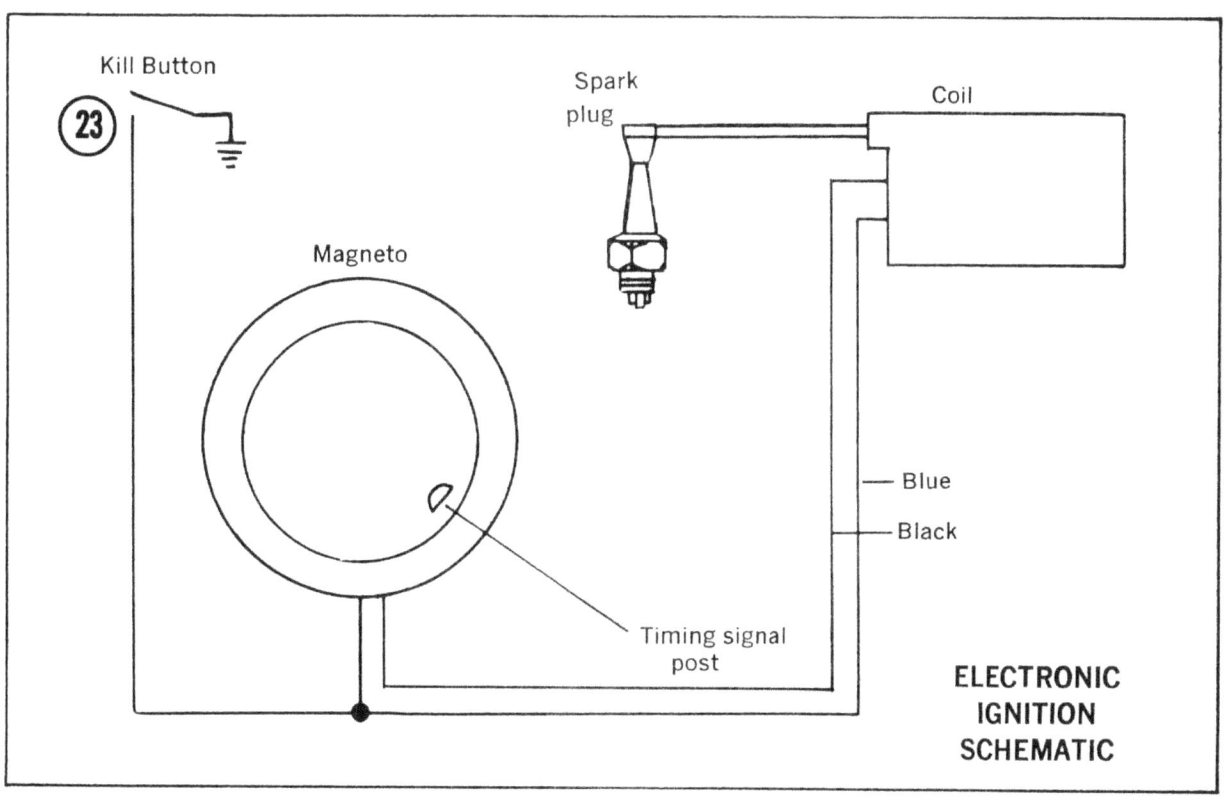

the spark plug cap removed from the high-tension lead, and the blue ignition lead disconnected from the No. 2 terminal of the ignition switch (or kill button).

1. Connect the ohmmeter test leads to the flat terminals on the ignition coil (**Figure 24**) and read the resistance of the primary winding. It should be 20-30 ohms. If it is not within this range, the coil is defective and should be replaced.

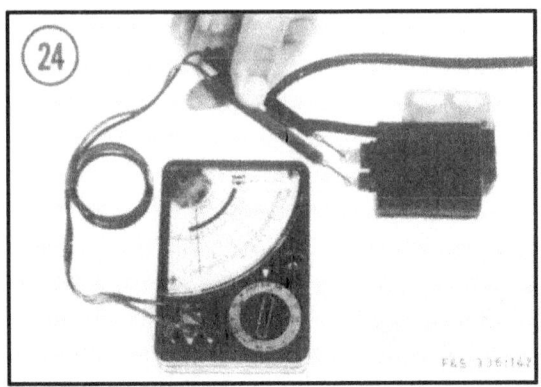

2. Test the coil secondary winding by connecting one test lead to ground and the other to the high-tension lead (**Figure 25**). The reading should be 7,000-9,000 ohms.

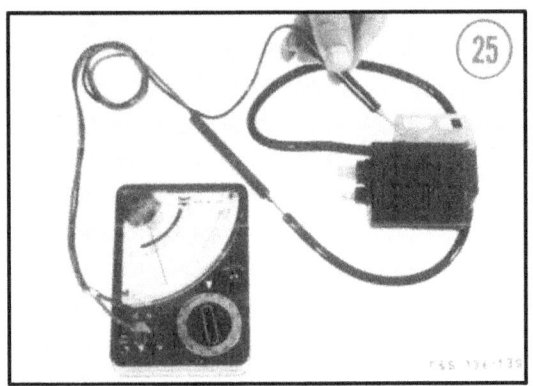

3. Connect one ohmmeter lead to the blue ignition wire and the other to ground (**Figure 26**). The meter should indicate either infinity or 8,000-9,000 ohms. Reverse the ohmmeter leads and the meter should read the opposite of the first reading; i.e., if the meter indicated infinity for the first polarity, it should indicate 8,000-9,000 ohms for the opposite polarity, and vice versa. If resistance is 0 in both directions, the diode is defective, and if it is infinity in both directions, there is a break in the stator. In

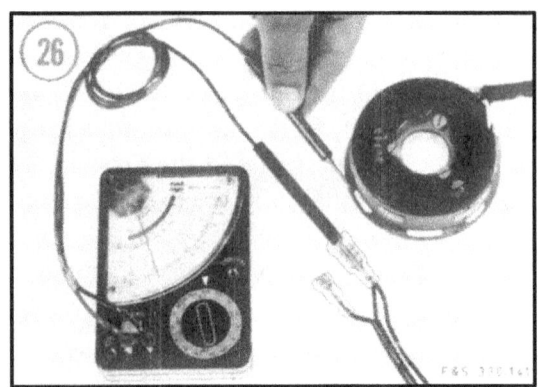

either case, both the stator and flywheel must be replaced as a set.

4. Test the ignition signal coil by connecting one ohmmeter lead to the blue ignition lead and the other ohmmeter lead to the black ignition lead (**Figure 27**). The reading should be approximately 20 ohms. If it is less, there is a short in the signal coil and the stator and flywheel must be replaced as a set.

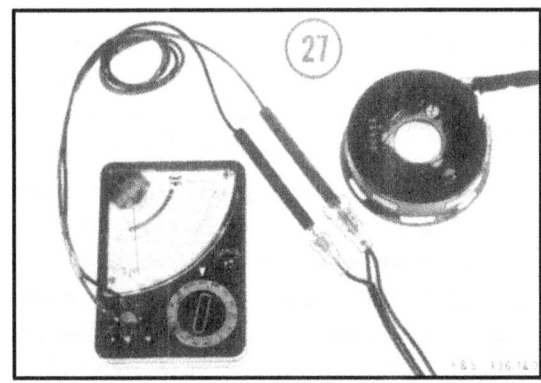

Timing

1. Rotate the flywheel to line up the "M" mark with the mark on the crankcase. Insert a timing pin (a bicycle spoke makes a good pin) into the timing hole in the flywheel (**Figure 28**). If the timing is correct, the pin should also enter the hole in the stator.

2. If the pin will not engage the hole in the stator, remove the flywheel and loosen the 3 screws (1) which hold the stator in place (see **Figure 29**).

3. Reinstall the flywheel on the shaft, put the timing pin into the hole in the flywheel and rotate it until the pin engages the hole in the stator. Rotate the flywheel and stator to line up the "M" mark with the crankcase mark.

4. Remove the flywheel without disturbing the position of the stator. Tighten the stator screws to 2.9-4.3 ft.-lb. (0.4-0.6 mkg) and reinstall the flywheel. Tighten the flywheel nut to 39-43 ft.-lb. (5.5-6.0 mkg) and recheck the timing with the pin as described in Step 1.

Establishing Timing Marks

If a new Motoplat ignition is being installed, either to replace an electronic unit that has failed or to update an engine previously equipped with a contact breaker ignition, the timing must be checked and set with the timing gauge as described for the contact breaker ignition and new timing marks established.

The firing point is the same for the electronic ignition as it is for the contact breaker type— 0.098-0.1118 in. (2.5-3.0mm) before TDC.

Install the Motoplat stator, leaving the 3 screws loose enough so the stator can be turned. Install the flywheel and line it up and lock with the stator with the timing pin. Then proceed to to time the ignition with the use of the timing gauge as described earlier and make a chisel mark on the crankcase to correspond with the "M" mark on the flywheel when the timing is correct.

MOTOPLAT IGNITION SYSTEM - INSTALLATION or REPLACEMENT

The technical conception of these breakerless magneto-generators, as compared with the conventional types provides a considerable improvement of the functioning and the reliability of the ignition system of the engine, since there are no wearing parts in it, such as breaker points, lubricating felt etc. Moreover, this new magneto with its ignition coil fitted outside of the engine is less sensitive to the effects of humidity and dust and does not require any maintenance or servicing.

Trouble shooting

We are listing various faults that are liable to occur, likewise as on the conventional magneto-generators, also on the electronically controlled magneto generators.

Check the electric connections and terminals.

Take care of bare, pinched, oxydized or wrongly connected cables.

Both electronic cables coming from the stator plate – blue and black – must on no account be cut for easing the removal or the installation and for connecting them afterwards with a terminal block.

This would create the risk that through dirt and humidity on the exposed terminals short-circuits occur and destroy the electronics.

The fitting strap of the ignition coil must be well grounded to the frame. The contact faces should be bright (watch for paint and rost).

When the spark plug is brought into ground contact and the starter activated, a spark must flash across the electrodes.

The electrode gap of the spark plug must be 0.4 + 0.1 mm (0.016 + 0.0039 in.).

The electronic magneto-generator must never be checked with conventional testing devices. Such attempts result in destroying the system.

Testing the electronic magneto-generator can only be carried out with a resistance testing device (Ohmmeter) with a testing capacity of 0 ... 10 000 Ω (Ω = Ohm).

Exchange and subsequent fitting of the MOTOPLAT ignition set

The electronic, breakerless MOTOPLAT magneto generator can also subsequently be fitted into previously sold SACHS engines 1001/1251.

For proceeding to such an exchange, take care of the following:
New ignition sets do not have marks. The top dead center and the firing point must be measured and marked anew.

Attention!

Replacement ignition sets have both marks "O" and "M" on the magneto flywheel.

The chisel mark on the crankcase, however, must in any case be measured and marked anew, using the spark advance timing gauge.

Delete the previous mark on the crankcase.

Short-circuiting button

On motorcycles with the conventional contact breaker ignition set, the engines had been short-circuited by the ignition-and lighting switch (B_1, see wiring diagram).

On introduction of the electronic ignition set, Messrs NHW (Nürnberger Hercules-Werke) have moved, for technical reasons, the short-circuiting device out of the head lamp to a short-circuiting button (B_9, see wiring diagram) at the handlebar.

When subsequently fitting an electronic magneto-generator, a short-circuiting button must on principle be fitted at the handlebar. The corresponding parts (short-circuiting button, clamp, cable etc,) are available from NHW/ZU under kit No. 927 380 30 02.

Instructions for fitting the rubber sliding piece

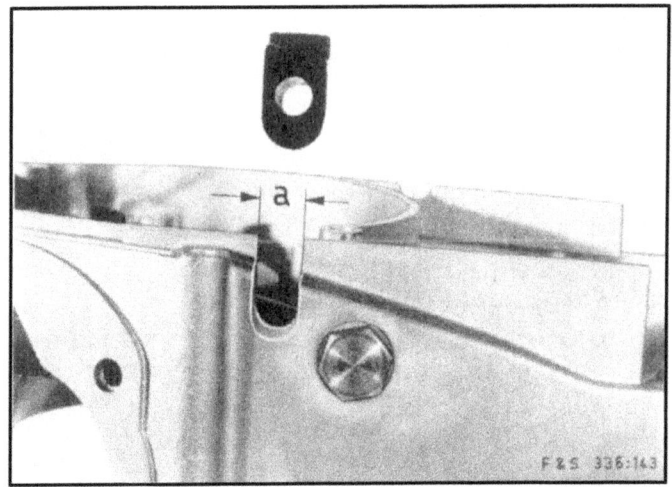

Engines that have previously been sold are provided with a round rubber grommet.

Fitting the set of cables can widely be eased by machining the crankcase as illustrated.

Dimension "a"
= 12 ± 0.1 mm
= 0.472 ± 0.0039 in.

instead of the round rubber grommet 0665 119 001, fit the sliding rubber unit 0665 124 000, as illustrated.

INSTRUCTIONS AND WIRING DIAGRAM FOR MAGNETO GENERATOR

version BOSCH (controlled by contact breaker)

6 Volt 35 Watt with 5 Watt tail light and 18 Watt stop light armature and ignition coil fitted outside of the engine

Terminals:
On generating armature C_2 (yellow cable with red stripes)
   Head light 6 Volt 35 Watt
On tail light armature (inductive) C_5 (grey cable)
   direct connection without switch to the tail light 6 Volt 5 Watt
On stop light armature C_1 (green cable with red stripes)
One rectifier 15 Volt, 1 Amp (for example BOSCH-LIWI 4 Z 2 Z No. 3 107 320 011) for charging a battery 6 Volt 12 Ah, for connecting:
   1 stop light 6 Volt 18 Watt
   1 direct current signal horn 6 Volt
   1 directional signal 6 Volt 18 Watt on each side
On ignition armature (primary) C_6 (blue cable)
   ignition coil terminal 1

Switch positions

0   Off (ignition short-circuited)
I   Daylight driving
II Driving lights on

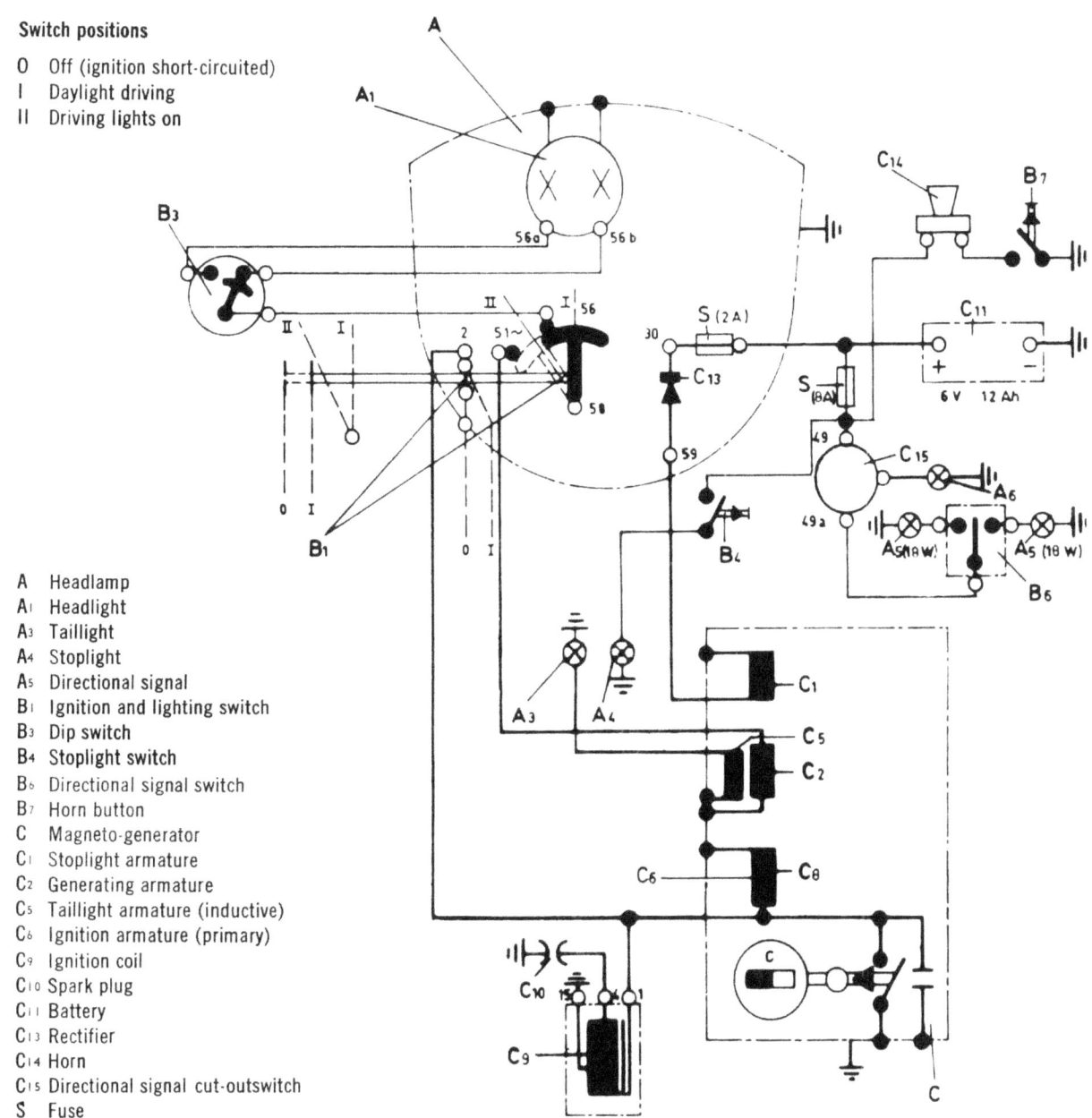

A   Headlamp
A_1 Headlight
A_3 Taillight
A_4 Stoplight
A_5 Directional signal
B_1 Ignition and lighting switch
B_3 Dip switch
B_4 Stoplight switch
B_6 Directional signal switch
B_7 Horn button
C   Magneto-generator
C_1 Stoplight armature
C_2 Generating armature
C_5 Taillight armature (inductive)
C_6 Ignition armature (primary)
C_9 Ignition coil
C_{10} Spark plug
C_{11} Battery
C_{13} Rectifier
C_{14} Horn
C_{15} Directional signal cut-outswitch
S   Fuse

INSTRUCTIONS AND WIRING DIAGRAM FOR MAGNETO GENERATOR
version **MOTOPLAT** (breakerless, electronic control)

6 Volt 35 - 5 - 18 Watt and ignition coil fitted outside of the engine

Terminals:

Lighting cable (yellow)
Head light 6 Volt 35 Watt
Tail light cable (red) direct connection without switch to the tail light 6 Volt 5 Watt
Stop light cable (green)
One rectifier for 15 Volt, 1 Amp (for example BOSCH-LIWI 4 Z 2 Z No. 3 107 320 011)
for charging a battery 6 Volt 12 Ah, for connecting:
1 stop light 6 Volt 18 Watt –1 direct current signal horn 6 Volt – 1 directional signal 6 Volt 21 Watt (each side)
Electronic cable (black) small terminal of the ignition coil
Electronic cable (blue) large terminal of the ignition coil

Attention!

The blue short-circuiting cable coming off the large terminal must be installed direct
(without intermediate connecting blocks) to the short-circuiting button B_9 at the handlebar

Switch positions

- 0 Off (ignition short-circuited)
- I Daylight driving
- II Driving lights on

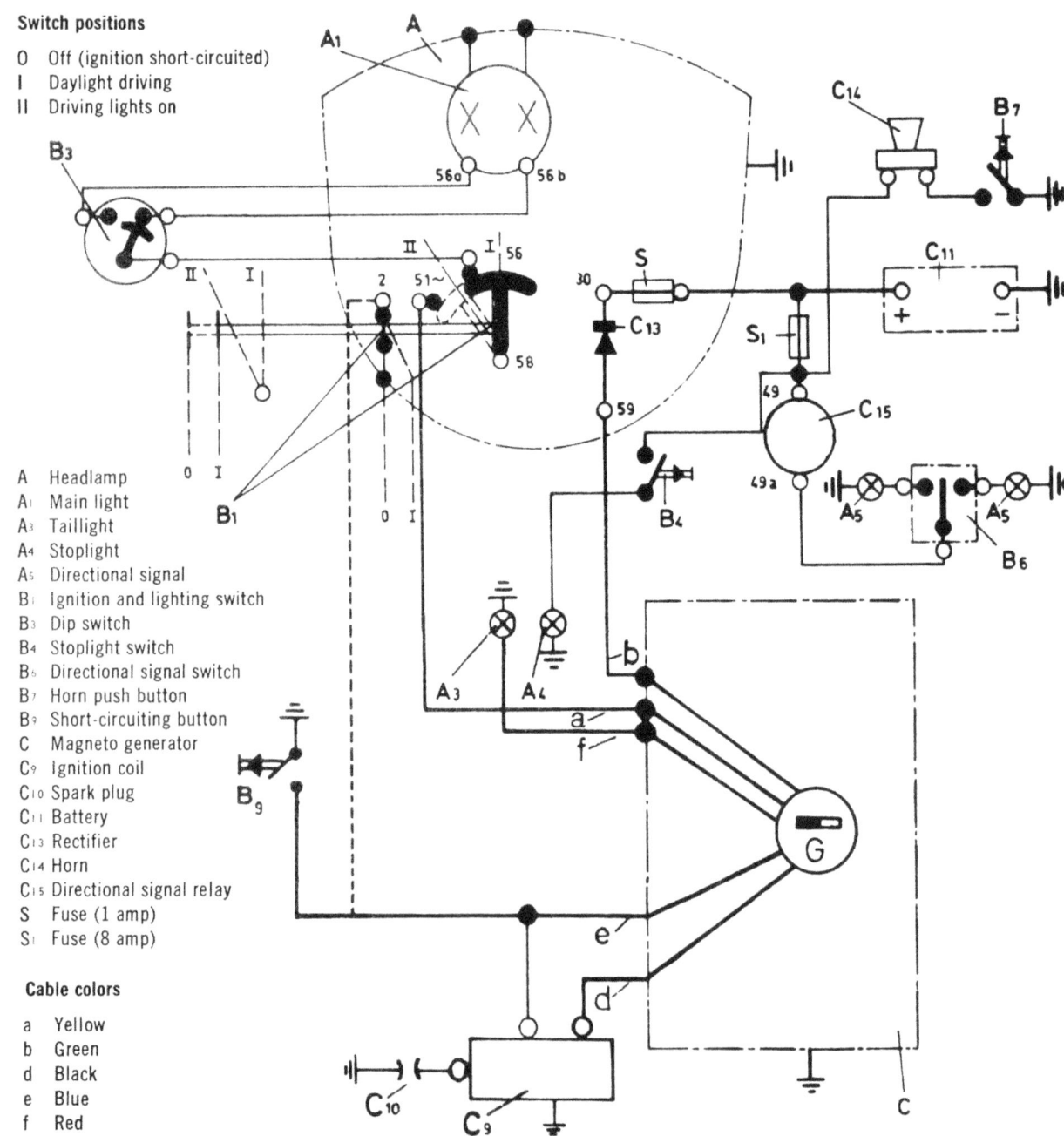

- A   Headlamp
- A_1 Main light
- A_3 Taillight
- A_4 Stoplight
- A_5 Directional signal
- B_1 Ignition and lighting switch
- B_3 Dip switch
- B_4 Stoplight switch
- B_5 Directional signal switch
- B_7 Horn push button
- B_9 Short-circuiting button
- C   Magneto generator
- C_9 Ignition coil
- C_{10} Spark plug
- C_{11} Battery
- C_{13} Rectifier
- C_{14} Horn
- C_{15} Directional signal relay
- S   Fuse (1 amp)
- S_1 Fuse (8 amp)

Cable colors

- a Yellow
- b Green
- d Black
- e Blue
- f Red

TROUBLESHOOTING
LOSS OF POWER

Cause	Things to check
Poor compression	Piston rings and cylinders Head gaskets Crankcase leaks
Overheated engine	Lubricating oil supply Clogged cooling fins Ignition timing Slipping clutch Carbon in combustion chamber

Cause	Things to check
Improper mixture	Dirty air cleaner Restricted fuel flow Gas cap vent hole
Miscellaneous	Dragging brakes Tight wheel bearings Defective chain Clogged exhaust system

GEARSHIFTING DIFFICULTIES

Cause	Things to check
Clutch	Adjustment Springs Friction plates Steel plates Oil quantity
Transmission	Oil quantity

Cause	Things to check
Transmission (contd.)	Oil grade Return spring or pin Change lever or spring Drum position plate Change drum Change forks

STEERING PROBLEMS

Problem	Things to check
Hard steering	Tire pressure Steering damper adjustment Steering stem head Steering head bearings
Pulls to one side	Unbalanced shock absorbers Drive chain adjustment Front/rear wheel alignment Unbalanced tires

Problem	Things to check
Pulls to one side (contd.)	Defective swinging arm Defective steering head
Shimmy	Drive chain adjustment Loose or missing spokes Deformed rims Worn wheel bearings Wheel balance

BRAKE TROUBLES

Problem	Things to check
Poor brakes	Brake adjustment Oil or water on brake linings Loose linkage or cables
Noisy brakes	Worn or scratched lining Scratched brake drums Dirt in brakes

Problem	Things to check
Unadjustable brakes	Worn linings Worn drums Worn brake cams

CHAPTER EIGHT

SPECIFICATIONS

> This chapter contains specifications for the various Sachs engines and related components covered by this manual.
>
> However, since there are differences between the various models, be sure to consult the correct table for the engine in question.

SPECIFICATIONS — MODEL 1251/5 A
(Cast-iron cylinder, vertical-finned head)

Displacement	122cc (7.444 cu. in.)
Bore	2.126 in. (54mm)
Stroke	2.126 in. (54mm)
Compression ratio	9 to 1
Output	12.5 hp (DIN) at 7,300 rpm
Engine lubrication	Oil/gasoline mix 1:25
Primary reduction (engine/transmission)	2.10:1
Transmission ratios	
1st	4.60:1
2nd	2.73:1
3rd	1.95:1
4th	1.50:1
5th	1.24:1
Transmission lubrication	1.3 pints (600cc) SAE 80
Clutch	Multiple disc, oil bath
Ignition	
Bosch	Magneto-generator, contact breaker
Motoplat	Magneto-generator, electronic
Ignition timing	0.098-0.118 in. (2.5-3.0mm) BTDC
Contact breaker gap (Bosch ignition)	0.014-0.018 in. (0.35-0.45mm)
Pole shoe separation (Bosch ignition)	0.866-0.984 in. (22-25mm)
Spark plug	Bosch W 260 T1
Gap	0.016-0.020 in. (0.4-0.5mm)
Carburetor	Bing No. 1/24/153
Venturi diameter	0.945 in. (24mm)
Main jet	100
Needle jet	2.73
Needle	5
Idle jet	40
Idle adjustment screw	
Cold weather	½ turn open
Warm weather	¾ turn open
Air filter	Micronic paper element
Head pipe diameter	1.496 in. (38mm) inside diameter
Head pipe length	15.75 in. (400mm)

SPECIFICATIONS — MODEL 1001/5A
(Cast-iron cylinder, vertical-finned head)

Displacement	97cc (5.9 cu. in.)
Bore	1.89 in. (48mm)
Stroke	2.126 in. (54mm)
Compression ratio	9 to 1
Output	10 hp (DIN) at 7,300 rpm
Engine lubrication	Oil/gasoline mix 1:25
Primary reduction (engine/transmission)	2.10 to 1
Transmission ratios	
1st	4.60:1
2nd	2.73:1
3rd	1.95:1
4th	1.50:1
5th	1.24:1
Transmission lubrication	1.3 pints (600cc) SAE 80
Clutch	Multiple disc, oil bath
Ignition	
Bosch	Magneto-generator, contact breaker
Motoplat	Magneto-generator, electronic
Ignition timing	0.098-0.118 in. (2.5-3.0mm) BTDC
Contact breaker gap (Bosch ignition)	0.014-0.018 in. (0.35-0.45mm)
Pole shoe separation (Bosch ignition)	0.866-0.984 in. (22-25mm)
Spark plug	Bosch W 260 T1
Gap	0.016-0.020 in. (0.4-0.5mm)
Carburetor	Bing No. 1/24/158
Venturi diameter	0.945 in. (24mm)
Main jet	95
Needle jet	2.73
Needle	5
Idle jet	40
Idle adjustment screw	
Cold weather	½ turn open
Warm weather	¾ turn open
Air filter	Micronic paper element
Head pipe diameter	1.496 in. (38mm) inside diameter
Head pipe length	15.75 in. (400mm)

SPECIFICATIONS — MODEL 1001/5 A
(Aluminum cylinder, sunburst head)

Displacement	97cc (5.9 cu. in.)
Bore	1.89 in. (48mm)
Stroke	2.126 in. (54mm)
Compression ratio	10.8 to 1
Output	12 hp (DIN) at 7,400 rpm
Engine lubrication	Oil/gasoline mix 1:25
Primary reduction (engine/transmission)	2.10:1
Transmissioin ratios	
1st	4.60:1
2nd	2.73:1
3rd	1.95:1
4th	1.50:1
5th	1.24:1
Transmission lubrication	1.3 pints (600cc) SAE 80
Clutch	Multiple disc, oil bath
Ignition	
Bosch	Magneto-generator, contact breaker
Motoplat	Magneto-generator, electronic
Ignition timing	0.098-0.118 in. (2.5-3.0mm) BTDC
Contact breaker gap (Bosch ignition)	0.014-0.018 in. (0.35-0.45mm)
Pole shoe separation (Bosch ignition)	0.866-0.984 in. (22-25mm)
Spark plug	Bosch W 260 T1
Gap	0.016-0.020 in. (0.4-0.5mm)
Carburetor	Bing No. 1/26/115
Venturi diameter	1.024 in. (26mm)
Main jet	105
Needle jet	2.73
Needle	5
Idle jet	40
Idle adjusting screw	½ to 1 turn open
Air filter	Micronic paper element
Head pipe diameter	1.496 in. (38mm) inside diameter
Head pipe length	15.75 in. (400mm)

SPECIFICATIONS — MODEL 1251/5 A
(Aluminum cylinder, sunburst head)

Displacement	122cc (7.444 cu. in.)
Bore	2.126 in. (54mm)
Stroke	2.126 in. (54mm)
Compression ratio	10.8 to 1
Output	15 hp (DIN) at 7,400 rpm
Engine lubrication	Oil/gasoline mix 1:25
Primary reduction (engine/transmission)	2.10:1
Transmission ratios	
1st	4.60:1
2nd	2.73:1
3rd	1.95:1
4th	1.50:1
5th	1.24:1
Transmission lubrication	1.3 pints (600cc) SAE 80
Clutch	Multiple disc, oil bath
Ignition	
Bosch	Magneto-generator, contact breaker
Motoplat	Magneto-generator, electronic
Ignition timing	0.098-0.118 in. (2.5-3.0mm) BTDC
Contact breaker gap (Bosch ignition)	0.014-0.018 in. (0.35-0.45mm)
Pole shoe separation (Bosch ignition)	0.866-0.984 in. (22-25mm)
Spark plug	Bosch W 260 T1
Gap	0.016-0.020 in. (0.4-0.5mm)
Carburetor	Bing No. 1/26/115
Venturi diameter	1.024 in. (26mm)
Main jet	105
Needle jet	2.73
Needle	5
Idle jet	40
Idle adjustment screw	½ to 1 turn open
Air filter	Micronic paper element
Head pipe diameter	1.496 in. (38mm) inside diameter
Head pipe length	15.75 in. (400mm)

SPECIFICATIONS — MODEL 1001/6 A
(Aluminum cylinder, sunburst head)

Displacement	97cc (5.919 cu. in.)
Bore	1.89 in. (48mm)
Stroke	2.126 in. (54mm)
Compression ratio	10.8 to 1
Output	12 hp (DIN) at 7,400 rpm
Engine lubrication	Oil/gasoline mix 1:25
Primary reduction (engine/transmission)	2.10:1
Transmission ratios	
1st	4.60:1
2nd	2.93:1
3rd	2.16:1
4th	1.72:1
5th	1.43:1
6th	1.24:1
Transmission lubrication	1.3 pints (600cc) SAE 80
Clutch	Multiple disc, oil bath
Ignition	
Bosch	Magneto-generator, contact breaker
Motoplat	Magneto-generator, electronic
Ignition timing	0.098-0.118 in. (2.5-3.0mm) BTDC
Contact breaker gap (Bosch ignition)	0.014-0.018 in. (0.35-0.45mm)
Pole shoe separation (Bosch ignition)	0.866-0.984 in. (22-25mm)
Spark plug	Bosch W 260 T1
Gap	0.016-0.020 in. (0.4-0.5mm)
Carburetor	Bing No. 1/26/115
Venturi diameter	1.024 in. (26mm)
Main jet	105
Needle jet	2.73
Needle	5
Idle jet	40
Idle adjustment screw	½ to 1 turn open
Air filter	Micronic paper element
Head pipe diameter	1.496 in. (38mm) inside diameter
Head pipe length	15.75 in. (400mm)

SPECIFICATIONS — MODEL 1251/6 A
(Aluminum cylinder, sunburst head)

Displacement	122cc (7.444 cu. in.)
Bore	2.126 in. (54mm)
Stroke	2.126 in. (54mm)
Compression ratio	10.8 to 1
Output	15 hp (DIN) at 7,400 rpm
Engine lubrication	Oil/gasoline mix 1:25
Primary reduction (engine/transmission)	2.10:1
Transmission ratios	
1st	4.60:1
2nd	2.93:1
3rd	2.16:1
4th	1.72:1
5th	1.43:1
6th	1.24:1
Transmission lubrication	1.3 pints (600cc) SAE 80
Clutch	Multiple disc, oil bath
Ignition	
Bosch	Magneto-generator, contact breaker
Motoplat	Magneto-generator, electronic
Ignition timing	0.098-0.118 in. (2.5-3.0mm) BTDC
Contact breaker gap (Bosch ignition)	0.014-0.018 in. (0.35-0.45mm)
Pole shoe separation (Bosch ignition)	0.866-0.984 in. (22-25mm)
Spark plug	Bosch W 260 T1
Gap	0.016-0.020 in. (0.4-0.5mm)
Carburetor	Bing No. 1/26/115
Venturi diameter	1.024 in. (25mm)
Main jet	105
Needle jet	2.73
Needle	5
Idle jet	40
Idle adjustment screw	½ to 1 turn open
Air filter	Micronic paper element
Head pipe diameter	1.496 in. (38mm) inside diameter
Head pipe length	15.75 in. (400mm)

SPECIFICATIONS — MODEL 1001/6 B
(Aluminum cylinder, sunburst head)

Displacement	97cc (5.919 cu. in.)
Bore	1.890 in. (48mm)
Stroke	2.126 in. (54mm)
Compression ratio	10.8 to 1
Output	14 hp (DIN) at 8,500 rpm
Engine lubrication	Oil/gasoline mix 1:25
Primary reduction (engine/transmission)	2.10:1
Transmission ratios	
1st	4.60:1
2nd	2.93:1
3rd	2.16:1
4th	1.72:1
5th	1.43:1
6th	1.24:1
Transmission lubrication	1.3 pints (600cc) SAE 80
Clutch	Multiple disc, oil bath
Ignition	Motoplat, magneto-generator, electronic
Timing	0.098-0.118 in. (2.5-3.0mm) BTDC
Spark plug	Bosch W 260 T1
	Bosch W 290 T16 (for competition)
Gap	0.016-0.020 in. (0.4-0.5mm)
Carburetor	
NHW	Bing No. 1/27/26
Venturi diameter	1.064 in. (27mm)
Main jet	135
Needle jet	2.73
Needle	4
Idle jet	45
Idle adjustment screw	1 turn open
KTM	Bing No. 1/27/21
Venturi diameter	1.064 in. (27mm)
Main jet	130
Needle jet	2.73
Needle	4
Idle jet	45
Idle adjustment screw	1 turn open
Monark	Bing No. 1/27/23
Venturi diameter	1.064 in. (27mm)
Main jet	115
Needle jet	2.73
Needle	4
Idle jet	45
Idle adjustment screw	1 turn open
Air filter	Micronic paper element
Head pipe diameter	1.496 in. (38mm) inside diameter
Head pipe length	14.57 in. (370mm)

SPECIFICATIONS — MODEL 1251/6 B
(Aluminum cylinder, sunburst head)

Displacement	122cc (7.444 cu. in.)
Bore	2.126 in. (54mm)
Stroke	2.126 in. (54mm)
Compression ratio	12 to 1
Output	18 hp (DIN) at 8,500 rpm
Engine lubrication	Oil/gasoline mix 1:25
Primary reduction (engine/transmission)	2.10:1
Transmission ratios	
1st	4.60:1
2nd	2.93:1
3rd	2.16:1
4th	1.72:1
5th	1.43:1
6th	1.24:1
Transmission lubrication	1.3 pints (600cc) SAE 80
Clutch	Multiple disc, oil bath
Ignition	Motoplat, magneto-generator, electronic
Timing	0.098-0.118 in. (2.5-3.0mm) BTDC
Spark plug	Bosch W 260 T1
	Bosch W 290 T16 (for competition)
Gap	0.016-0.020 in. (0.4-0.5mm)
Carburetor	
NHW	Bing No. 1/27/19
Venturi diameter	1.064 in. (27mm)
Main jet	140
Needle jet	2.73
Needle	4
Idle jet	45
Idle adjustment screw	1 turn open
KTM	Bing No. 1/27/20
Venturi diameter	1.064 in. (27mm)
Main jet	140
Needle jet	2.70
Needle	4
Idle jet	45
Idle adjustment screw	1 turn open
Monark	Bing No. 1/27/22
Venturi diameter	1.064 in. (27mm)
Main jet	120
Needle jet	2.73
Needle	4
Idle jet	45
Idle adjustment screw	1 turn open
Air filter	Micronic paper element
Head pipe diameter	1.496 in. (38mm) inside diameter
Head pipe length	14.57 in. (370mm)

SPECIFICATIONS — MODEL 1251/6 C
(Aluminum cylinder, sunburst head)

Displacement	122cc (7.444 cu. in.)
Bore	2.126 in. (54mm)
Stroke	2.126 in. (54mm)
Compression ratio	11.8 to 1
Output	17 hp (DIN) at 7,500 rpm
Engine lubrication	Oil/gasoline mix 1:25
Primary reduction (engine/transmission)	2.10:1
Tranmission ratios	
1st	4.60:1
2nd	2.93:1
3rd	2.16:1
4th	1.72:1
5th	1.43:1
6th	1.24:1
Transmission lubrication	1.3 pints (600cc) SAE 80
Clutch	Multiple disc, oil bath
Ignition	Motoplat, magneto-generator, electronic
Timing	0.098-0.118 in. (2.5-3.0mm) BTDC
Spark plug	Bosch W 280 M1
Gap	0.016-0.020 in. (0.4-0.5mm)
Carburetor	Bing No. 1/27/25
Venturi diameter	1.064 in. (27mm)
Main jet	110
Needle jet	2.70
Needle	4
Idle jet	45
Idle adjustment screw	1 turn open
Air filter	Micronic paper element
Head pipe diameter	1.496 in. (38mm) inside diameter
Head pipe length	14.96 in. (380mm)

CHAPTER NINE

USEFUL FORMULAS AND TABLES

> It is often necessary to convert metric to American dimensions or vice versa. This chapter contains formulas for doing so, with typical examples worked out. Also in this chapter are other useful tables and formulas.

CONVERSIONS

Multiply	by	To obtain
Volume		
Cubic centimeters	0.061	Cubic inches
Cubic inches	16.387	Cubic centimeters
Liters	0.264	Gallons
Gallons	3.785	Liters
Liters	1.057	Quarts
Quarts	0.946	Liters
Cubic centimeters	0.0339	Fluid ounces
Fluid ounces	29.57	Cubic centimeters
Length		
Millimeters	0.03937	Inches
Inches	25.4	Millimeters
Centimeters	0.3937	Inches
Inches	2.54	Centimeters
Kilometers	0.6214	Miles
Miles	1.609	Kilometers
Meters	3.281	Feet
Feet	0.3048	Meters
Millimeters	0.10	Centimeters
Centimeters	10.0	Millimeters
Weight		
Kilograms	2.205	Pounds
Pounds	0.4536	Kilograms
Grams	0.03527	Ounces
Ounces	28.35	Grams
Other		
Metric horsepower	1.014	Brake horsepower
Brake horsepower	0.9859	Metric horsepower
Kilogram-meters	7.235	Foot-pounds
Foot-pounds	0.1383	Kilogram-meters
Kilometers per liter	2.352	Miles per gallon
Miles per gallon	0.4252	Kilometers per liter
Square millimeters	0.00155	Square inches
Square inches	645.2	Square millimeters
Square inches	6.452	Square centimeters
Square centimeters	0.155	Square inches
Kilometers per hour	0.6214	Miles per hour
Miles per hour	1.609	Kilometers per hour
Foot-pounds	0.1383	Kilogram-meters
Kilogram-meters	7.233	Foot-pounds
Pounds per square inch	0.0703	Kilograms per square centimeter
Kilograms per square centimeter	14.22	Pounds per square inch
Miles per hour	88	Feet per minute
Feet per minute	0.01136	Miles per hour
Miles per hour	1.467	Feet per second

Table 1 FUEL AND OIL MIXTURES

Fuel U.S. Gallons	SAE 40 Motor Oil		Two-Stroke Oil	
	Oz.	(cc)	Oz.	(cc)
0.1	0.6	18	0.5	15
0.2	1.3	39	1.1	33
0.3	1.9	57	1.6	48
0.4	2.6	78	2.1	63
0.5	3.2	96	2.6	78
0.6	3.9	117	3.2	96
0.7	4.5	135	3.7	111
0.8	5.2	156	4.2	126
0.9	5.8	174	4.8	144
1.0	6.4	192	5.3	159
1.1	7.0	210	5.8	192
1.2	7.7	231	6.4	174
1.3	8.3	249	6.9	207
1.4	9.0	270	7.4	222
1.5	9.6	288	7.9	237
1.6	10.3	309	8.5	255
1.7	10.9	327	9.0	270
1.8	11.6	348	9.5	285
1.9	12.2	366	10.6	303
2.0	12.8	384	11.1	318
2.1	13.5	405	11.3	333
2.2	14.1	423	11.6	348
2.3	14.8	444	12.1	363
2.4	15.4	480	12.6	378
2.5	16.0	462	13.1	393
2.6	16.7	501	13.7	411
2.7	17.3	519	14.2	426
2.8	17.9	537	14.7	441

LUBRICANTS AND SEALANTS

required for rebuilding the engines

Lubricant or sealant	Suppliers/addresses
Molykote-Paste	DOW CORNING GmbH D-8000 München 54 Pelkoven Str. 152
Sealant No. 40 F & S Part No. 0999 107 000)	FICHTEL & SACHS AG D-8720 Schweinfurt
Sealant "Diamant" Typ OW	Schleifmittelwerk Kahl Artur GLÖCKLER D-8756 Kahl a. M. Postfach 80
Loctite AAV	LOCTITIE TECHNIK D-8000 München Arabella Str. 5
Alvania 3 (High melting point grease)	SHELL D-8500 Nürnberg Postfach 567
BOSCH grease Ft 1 v 4 Ft 1 v 8	Robert BOSCH GmbH D-7022 Leinfelden/Stuttgart Max-Lang-Str. 40–46 BOSCH agents

TIGHTENING TORQUES FOR BOLTS AND NUTS

Bolts

F&S Part No.	Qty.	used for	Dimension	Tightening torque kpm	Tightening torque ft lb
0940 119 102	6	Crankcase	M 6 x 60	0,8 ... 1,0	5.78 ... 7.23
0940 128 202	4	Crankcase	M 6 x 75	0,8 ... 1,0	5.78 ... 7.23
0640 005 005	1	Crankcase (kickstarter stop)	M 12	2,5 ... 3,0	18.08 ... 21.70
0240 100 000	1	Crankcase (oil drain)	M 10 x 1	1,3 ... 1,5	9.40 ... 10.85
0240 133 100	1	Selector lever	M 12 x 1	1,5	10.85
0240 106 100	3	Stator plate (version BOSCH)	M 4 x 14	0,4 ... 0,6	2.89 ... 4.34
0241 028 001	3	Base plate	M 4 x 12	0,4 ... 0,6	2.89 ... 4.34
2840 002 001	3	Stator plate (version MOTOPLAT)	M 4 x 20	0,4 ... 0,6	2.89 ... 4.34
1940 108 000	2	Selector adjusting plate	M 6 x 20	1,2 ... 1,5	8.68 ... 10.85
1940 114 000	2	Selector adjusting plate with stop bushes	M 6 x 25	1,2 ... 1,5	8.68 ... 10.85
0640 011 102	4	Crankcase cover, clutch side	M 6 x 65	0,8 ... 1,0	5.78 ... 7.23
0241 040 001	2	Crankcase cover, clutch side	M 6 x 38	0,8 ... 1,0	5.78 ... 7.23
0240 120 002	1	Crankcase cover, clutch side	M 6 x 52	0,8 ... 1,0	5.78 ... 7.23
0940 119 102	4	Crankcase cover, magneto side	M 6 x 60	0,8 ... 1,0	5.78 ... 7.23
2740 024 000	3	Clutch case on layshaft wheel	M 6 x 15	1,1 ... 1,2	7.95 ... 8.68
0941 049 006	4	Cylinder head on cast iron cylinder	M 8 x 40	3,0 ... 3,2	21.70 ... 23.15

Nuts

F&S Part No.	Qty.	used for	Dimension	Tightening torque kpm	Tightening torque ft lb
0642 105 001	1	Crankshaft, drive side	M 14 x 1,5	7,0 ... 7,5	50.63 ... 54.25
0242 106 005	1	Clutch hub	M 18 x 1	8,0 ... 9,0	57.86 ... 65.10
0942 067 100	4	Cast iron cylinder and aluminium cylinder on SACHS 1251/5 B	M 8	2,4 ... 2,6	17.36 ... 18.80
2842 003 004	4	Cylinder head on SACHS 1251/5 B	M 8	3,0 ... 3,2	21.70 ... 23.15
0942 072 110	1	Crankshaft, magneto-side (BOSCH magneto flywheel)	M 10 x 1 L	3,8 ... 4,0	27.48 ... 28.93
0942 072 110	1	Crankshaft, magneto-side (MOTOPLAT magneto flyhweel)	M 10 x 1 L	5,5 ... 6,0	39.78 ... 43.40
0642 103 001	1	Sprocket	M 20 x 1 L	7,0 ... 7,5	50.63 ... 54.25
0642 107 001	4	Cylinder and cylinder head (alu)	M 8 x 45	2,5 ... 3,0	18.08 ... 21.70
0316 057 003	3	Clutch case on layshaft wheel	M 6	0,5 ... 0,6	3.62 ... 4.34

Ersatzteile-Liste Nr. 336.6 D-E-F
List of Spares
Liste des Pièces de Rechange

SACHS 1001/5A
1001/6A
1001/6B
1001/6C

1251/5A
1251/5A L
1251/5B

1251/6A
1251/6B
1251/6C
1251/6D

Ausgabe   November 1974
Edition   November/Novembre 1974

FICHTEL & SACHS AG · D-8720 SCHWEINFURT

INHALTSVERZEICHNIS	CONTENTS	TABLE DES MATIERES	Seite / Page
Gehäuse, Kurbelwelle, Kolben, Zylinder	Crankcase, Crankshaft, Piston, Cylinder	Carter, Vilebrequin, Piston, Cylindre	1
Schalthebel, Hauptwelle, Getriebe für SACHS 1001/5 A bis Motor-Nr. 5692 842 für SACHS 1251/5 A und 1251/5 A L bis Motor-Nr. 6318 754	Gear-changing lever, Main shaft, Gearbox for SACHS 1001/5 A up to engine No. 5692 842 for SACHS 1251/5 A and 1251/5 A L up to engine No. 6318 754	Levier de changement de vitesse, Arbre primaire, Boîte de vitesses pour SACHS 1001/5 A jusqu'à moteur No. 5692 842 pour SACHS 1251/5 A et 1251/5 A L jusqu'à moteur No. 6318 754	5
Schalthebel, Hauptwelle, Getriebe für SACHS 1001/5 A ab Motor-Nr. 5692 843 für SACHS 1251/5 A und 1251/5 A L ab Motor-Nr. 6318 755	Gear-changing lever, Main shaft, Gearbox for SACHS 1001/5 A from engine No. 5692 843 for SACHS 1251/5 A and 1251/5 A L from engine No. 6318 755	Levier de changement de vitesse, Arbre primaire, Boîte de vitesses pour SACHS 1001/5 A à partir de moteur No. 5692 843 pour SACHS 1251/5 A et 1251/5 A L à partir de moteur No. 6318 755	6
Schalthebel, Hauptwelle, Getriebe für SACHS 1001/6 A ab Motor-Nr. 5692 843 für SACHS 1251/6 A ab Motor-Nr. 6320 501	Gear-changing lever, Main shaft, Gearbox for SACHS 1001/6 A from engine No. 5692 843 for SACHS 1251/6 A from engine No. 6320 501	Levier de changement de vitesse, Arbre primaire, Boîte de vitesses pour SACHS 1001/6 A à partir de moteur No. 5692 843 pour SACHS 1251/6 A à partir de moteur No. 6320 501	7
Starteinrichtung, Schaltung ohne und mit Schaltverrastung für SACHS 1001/5 A, 1251/5 A u. 1251/5 A L bis Motor-Nr. 6318 754	Starting device, Gear change mechanism without and with gear lock for SACHS 1001/5 A, 1251/5 A and 1251/5 A L up to engine No. 6318 754	Dispositif de démarrage, Changement de vitesse sans et avec verrouillage du changement de vitesse pour SACHS 1001/5 A, 1251/5 A et 1251/5 A L jusqu'à moteur No. 6318 754	8
Starteinrichtung, Schaltung für SACHS 1001/5 A, 1001/6 A u. 1251/6 A ab Motor-Nr. 5692 843 für SACHS 1001/6 B, 1001/6 C, 1251/6 C und 1251/6 D ab Motor-Nr. 6887 264 für SACHS 1251/5 A und 1251/5 A L ab Motor-Nr. 6318 543 für SACHS 1251/5 B ab Motor-Nr. 6319 316 für SACHS 1251/6 B ab Motor-Nr. 7103 005	Starting device, Gear change mechanism for SACHS 1001/5 A, 1001/6 A and 1251/6 A from engine No. 5692 843 for SACHS 1001/6 B, 1001/6 C, 1251/6 C and 1251/6 D from engine No. 6887 264 for SACHS 1251/5 A and 1251/5 A L from engine No. 6318 543 for SACHS 1251/5 B from engine No. 6319 316 for SACHS 1251/6 B from engine No. 7103 005	Dispositif de démarrage, Changement de vitesse pour SACHS 1001/5 A, 1001/6 A et 1251/6 A à partir de moteur No. 5692 843 pour SACHS 1001/6 B, 1001/6 C, 1251/6 C et 1251/6 D à partir de moteur No. 6887 264 pour SACHS 1251/5 A et 1251/5 A L à partir de moteur No. 6318 543 pour SACHS 1251/5 B à partir de moteur No. 6319 316 pour SACHS 1251/6 B à partir de moteur No. 7103 005	9
Magnetzünder-Generator (BOSCH) Magnetzünder-Generator (MOTOPLAT)	Magneto-generator (BOSCH) Magneto-generator (MOTOPLAT)	Magnéto-génératrice (BOSCH) Magnéto-génératrice (MOTOPLAT)	10
Deckel-Magnetseite, Tacho-Antrieb	Magneto side crankcase cover, Speedometer drive	Couvercle côté magnéto, Entraînement du compteur	12
Deckel-Kupplungsseite, Kupplung, Vorgelegewelle	Clutch side crankcase cover, Clutch, Layshaft	Couvercle côté embrayage, Embrayage, Arbre secondaire	13
Vergaser 1/24/..., 1/26/..., 1/27/..., Ansauggeräuschdämpfer	Carburettor 1/24/..., 1/26/..., 1/27/..., Intake silencer	Carburateur 1/24/..., 1/26/..., 1/27/..., Silencieux d'aspiration	15
Vergaser 2/28/..., Ansaugstutzen	Carburettor 2/28/..., Intake pipe	Carburateur 2/28/..., Pipe d'aspiration	17
Vergaser 1/18/24	Carburettor 1/18/24	Carburateur 1/18/24	18
Vergaser 2/26/...	Carburettor 2/26/...	Carburateur 2/26/...	19
Lüfterhaube, Lüfter, Auspufftopf	Fan housing, Fan, Muffler	Capot de ventilateur, Ventilateur, Pot d'échappement	21
Zylinderkopf, Zylinder	Cylinder head, Cylinder	Culasse, Cylindre	22
Vergasertabelle	Table for carburettors	Tableau des carburateurs	25
SACHS-Schmiermittel Dichtungssatz-Motor (ohne Abb.) Werkzeug (ohne Abb.)	SACHS lubricants Set of gaskets for the engine (without illustrations) Tools (without illustration)	Lubrifiants SACHS Jeu de joints du moteur (sans ill.) Outillage (sans ill.)	26
Scheiben-Abmessungen	Dimensions of shims	Dimensions des rondelles	27
Typschilder	Type plates	Plaques du moteur	28

Ersatzteile sind stets über unsere F & S-Vertretungen zu beziehen.
Sie erhalten dort SACHS-Original-Ersatzteile. Diese bieten Gewähr für richtige Materialauswahl und Maßhaltigkeit.
Bei Verwendung von nicht originalen Ersatzteilen erlischt jeder Anspruch in Fällen der Garantie.
Geben Sie bei jeder Ersatzteile-Bestellung unbedingt Teile-Nummer und Teile-Benennung an.
In Zweifelsfällen bitte Muster an die Vertretung einsenden.

Spares are always to be obtained by our F & S representatives.
There you will obtain SACHS genuine spare parts. These warrant for proper material choice and dimensional accuracy.
When using spares which are not genuine, each claim expires in cases of guaranty.
Quote part numbers and nomenclature always when ordering spares.
In cases of doubt please send samples to the agency.

Dans tous les cas, les pièces de rechange doivent être procurées par l'intermédiaire de notre Agence F & S.
Vous y trouverez les pièces d'origine SACHS. Les Stations-Services SACHS garantissent le choix du matériel correct et l'exactitude des mesures.
En cas d'utilisation de pièces de rechange non originales, aucune garantie ne pourra plus être accordée.
En cas de commande, veuillez indiquer le numéro et la désignation de la pièce de rechange.
En cas de doute, prière d'envoyer des échantillons à l'Agence F & S.

Zeichenerklärung:
● = Diese Teile-Nr. erscheinen in dieser Ersatzteile-Liste erstmalig.
Die Teile sind mit den bisherigen austauschbar, wenn nicht zusätzlich die Motor-Nr. angegeben ist.

Explanation of symbols:
● = These part numbers are shown for the first time in this list.
These parts are interchangeable with the previous ones, if the engine No. is not quoted additionally.

Légende:
● = Ces No. des pièces apparaissent pour la première fois dans la liste des pièces de rechange.
Les pièces sont interchangeables avec les pièces utilisées antérieurement, si le No. de moteur n'est pas indiqué en supplément.

Gehäuse, Kurbelwelle, Kolben, Zylinder
Crankcase, Crankshaft, Piston, Cylinder
Carter, Vilebrequin, Piston, Cylindre

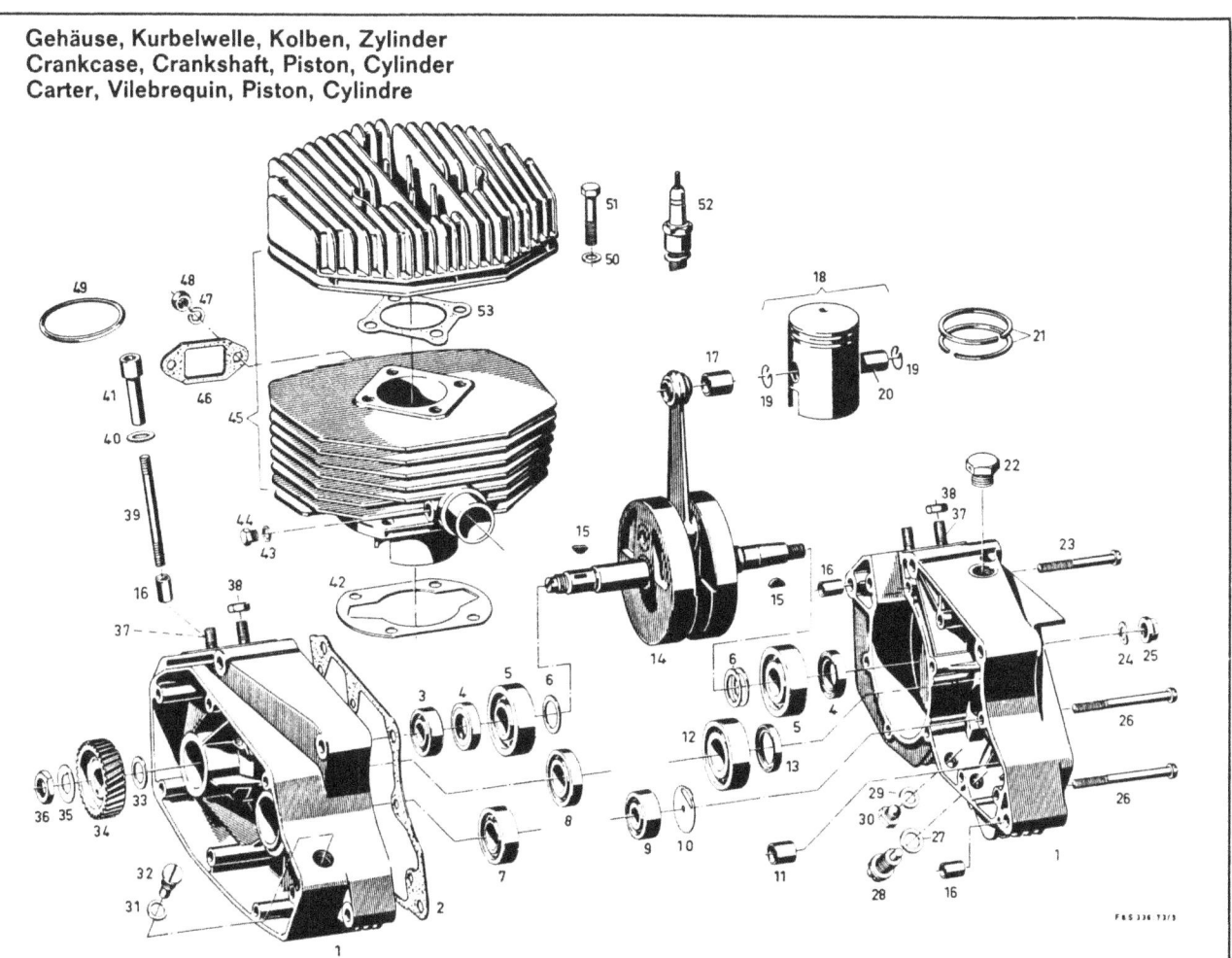

Bild-Nr. Ill. No.	Bestell-Nr. Part-No. Réf. No.	Benennung	Description	Désignation	1001/5 A	1001/6 A	1001/6 B	1001/6 C	1251/5 A	1251/5 A1	1251/5 B	1251/6 A	1251/6 B	1251/6 C	1251/6 D
1	0687 107 101	+Zsb. Gehäuse für BOSCH-Magnetzünder bis Motor-Nr. 5692 842 6318 754	+Crankcase ass'y for BOSCH-magneto-generator up to engine-No. 5692 842 6318 754	+Carter cpl. pour magnéto BOSCH jusqu'à moteur No. 5692 842 6318 754	1				1	1					
	0687 107 401	+Zsb. Gehäuse für BOSCH-Magnetzünder ab Motor-Nr. 5692 843 6318 755	+Crankcase ass'y for BOSCH-magneto-generator from engine-No. 5692 843 6318 755	+Carter cpl. pour magnéto BOSCH à part. de mot. No. 5692 843 6318 755	1				1	1					
		+Zsb. Gehäuse für MOTOPLAT-Magnetzünder ab Motor-Nr. 5693 736 6773 953	+Crankcase ass'y for MOTOPLAT-magneto-generator from engine-No. 5693 736 6773 953	+Carter cpl. pour magnéto MOTOPLAT à part. de mot. No. 5693 736 6773 953	1				1						
	●0687 107 613	+Zsb. Gehäuse für MOTOPLAT-Magnetzünder 0683 006 004 bis Motor-Nr.	+Crankcase ass'y for MOTOPLAT-magneto-generator 0683 006 004 up to engine-No.	+Carter cpl. pour magnéto MOTOPLAT 0683 006 004 jusqu'à moteur No.	1				1						
		+Zsb. Gehäuse für MOTOPLAT-Magnetzünder 0683 006 204	+Crankcase ass'y for MOTOPLAT-magneto-generator 0683 006 204	+Carter cpl. pour magnéto MOTOPLAT 0683 006 204	1				1						
		+=Zsb. Gehäuse mit Stiftschrauben, Paßhülsen und Dichtung, für Ausf. Grauguß-Zylinder	+=Crankcase ass'y with studs, dowel sleeves and seal, for type grey-cast cylinder	+=Carter cpl. avec goujons filetés, douilles d'ajustage et joint, pour version cylindre fonte grise											
	0687 107 205	*Zsb. Gehäuse für BOSCH-Magnetzünder bis Motor-Nr. 5692 842 6318 754	*Crankcase ass'y for BOSCH-magneto-generator up to engine-No. 5692 842 6318 754	*Carter cpl. pour magnéto BOSCH jusqu'à moteur No. 5692 842 6318 754	1						1				
	●0687 107 605	*Zsb. Gehäuse für MOTOPLAT-Magnetzünder 0683 006 004	*Crankcase ass'y for MOTOPLAT-magneto-generator 0683 006 004	*Carter cpl. pour magnéto MOTOPLAT 0683 006 004	1	1			1			1			

Bild-Nr. Ill. No.	Bestell-Nr. Part-No. Réf. No.	Benennung	Description	Désignation	1001/5 A	1001/6 A	1001/6 B	1001/6 C	1251/5 A	1251/5 AL	1251/5 B	1251/6 A	1251/6 B	1251/6 C	1251/6 D
		*Zsb. Gehäuse für MOTOPLAT-Magnetzünder 0683 006 204	*Crankcase ass'y for MOTOPLAT-magneto-generator 0683 006 204	*Carter cpl. pour magnéto MOTOPLAT 0683 006 204	1	1			1			1			
	●0687 107 609	*Zsb. Gehäuse für MOTOPLAT-Magnetzünder 0683 006 004	*Crankcase ass'y for MOTOPLAT-magneto-generator 0683 006 004	*Carter cpl. pour magnéto MOTOPLAT 0683 006 004			1	1					1	1	1
		*Zsb. Gehäuse für MOTOPLAT-Magnetzünder 0683 006 204	*Crankcase ass'y for MOTOPLAT-magneto-generator 0683 006 204	*Carter cpl. pour magnéto MOTOPLAT 0683 006 204			1	1					1	1	1
	●0687 107 611	*Zsb. Gehäuse für MOTOPLAT-Magnetzünder 0683 006 004 (DKW – NHW)	*Crankcase ass'y for MOTOPLAT-magneto-generator 0683 006 004 (DKW – NHW)	*Carter cpl. pour magnéto MOTOPLAT 0683 006 004 (DKW – NHW)					1				1	1	1
		*Zsb. Gehäuse für MOTOPLAT-Magnetzünder 0683 006 204 (DKW – NHW)	*Crankcase ass'y for MOTOPLAT-magneto-generator 0683 006 204 (DKW – NHW)	*Carter cpl. pour magnéto MOTOPLAT 0683 006 204 (DKW – NHW)					1				1	1	1
	0687 107 407	*Zsb. Gehäuse (NHW – Military)	*Crankcase ass'y (NHW – Military)	*Carter cpl. (NHW – Military)							1				
		* = Zsb. Gehäuse mit Stiftschrauben, Paßhülsen und Dichtung, für Ausf. Alu-Zylinder	* = Crankcase ass'y with studs, dowel sleeves and gasket, for type alu cylinder	* = Carter cpl. avec goujons filetés, douilles d'ajustage et joint, pour version cylindre aluminium											
2	0650 105 100	Dichtung Ø 110 (Kurbelraum)	Gasket Ø 110 (Crank space)	Joint Ø 110 (espace de manivelle)	1	1			1	1	1	1			
	0650 105 101	Dichtung Ø 94 (Kurbelraum)	Gasket Ø 94 (Crank space)	Joint Ø 94 (espace de manivelle)			1	1					1	1	1
3	0232 120 001	Rillenkugellager 6202 C3 DIN 625 (15 x 35 x 11)	Grooved ball bearing 6202 C3 DIN 625 (15 x 35 x 11)	Roulement rainuré à billes 6202 C3 DIN 625 (15 x 35 x 11)	1	1	1	1	1	1	1	1	1	1	1
4	0230 002 000	Wellendichtring 18,6 x 35 x 8	Oil sealing ring 18.6 x 35 x 8	Joint de retenu d'huile 18,6 x 35 x 8	2	2	2	2	2	2	2	2	2	2	2
5	0932 063 001	Schulterkugellager M 20 DIN 615 (20 x 52 x 15)	Magneto ball bearing M 20 DIN 615 (20 x 52 x 15)	Roulement à billes démontable et à épaulement M 20 DIN 615 (20 x 52 x 15)	2	2	2	2	2	2	2	2	2	2	2
6	0944 046 000	Scheibe 20,5 x 28,5, Seite 27	Shim 20.5 x 28.5, page 27	Rondelle 20,5 x 28,5, Page 27	x	x	x	x	x	x	x	x	x	x	x
	0644 117 000	Scheibe 20,5 x 28,5 x 1,0	Shim 20.5 x 28.5 x 1.0	Rondelle 20,5 x 28,5 x 1,0			2	2					2	2	2
		1 x Kurbelwange Kupplungsseite	1 x crank web clutch side	1 x flasque de manivelle côté embrayage											
		1 x Kurbelwange Magnetseite	1 x crank web magneto side	1 x flasque de manivelle côté magnéto											
7	0232 126 001	Rillenkugellager 6004 C3 DIN 625 für Vorgelegewelle	Grooved ball bearing 6004 C3 DIN 625 for layshaft	Roulement rainuré à billes 6004 C3 DIN 625	1	1	1	1	1	1	1	1	1	1	1
8	0232 130 001	Rillenkugellager 16004 DIN 625 (20 x 42 x 8) für Hauptwelle bis Motor-Nr. 6318 754	Grooved ball bearing 16004 DIN 625 (20 x 42 x 8) for mainshaft up to engine-No. 6318 754	Roulement rainuré à billes 16004 DIN 625 (20 x 42 x 8) pour arbre primaire jusqu'à moteur No. 6318 754	1		1	1							
	2732 006 000	Rillenkugellager 16005 DIN 625 (25 x 47 x 8) für Hauptwelle ab Motor-Nr. 6318 755	Grooved ball bearing 16005 DIN 625 (25 x 47 x 8) for mainshaft from engine-No. 6318 755	Roulement rainuré à billes 16005 DIN 625 (25 x 47 x 8) pour arbre primaire à partir de moteur No. 6318 755		1	1	1	1	1	1	1	1	1	1
9	0632 110 001	Rillenkugellager 6301 C3 DIN 625 für Vorgelegewelle	Grooved ball bearing 6301 C3 DIN 625 for layshaft	Roulement rainuré à billes 6301 C3 DIN 625 pour arbre secondaire	1	1	1	1	1	1	1	1	1	1	1
10	0644 109 100	Profilscheibe	Profile washer	Rondelle profilée	1	1	1	1	1	1	1	1	1	1	1
11	0232 129 000	Buchse 12 x 16 x 14,5	Bush 12 x 16 x 14.5	Douille 12 x 16 x 14,5	1	1	1	1	1	1	1	1	1	1	1
12	0632 017 201	Zylinderrollenlager NJ 205 E C3 ZS DIN 5412 für Hauptwelle	Cylindrical roller bearing NJ 205 E C3 ZS DIN 5412 for mainshaft	Roulement à rouleaux cylindriques J 205 E C3 ZS DIN 5412 pour arbre primaire	1	1	1	1	1	1	1	1	1	1	1
13	0630 001 000	Wellendichtring 23,4 x 34 x 5	Oil sealing ring 23.4 x 34 x 5	Joint de retenu d'huile 23,4 x 34 x 5	1	1	1	1	1	1	1	1	1	1	1
14	0688 005 100	Kurbelwelle (Alu-Pleuel)	Crankshaft (alu con-rod)	Vilebrequin (bielle aluminium)	1	1			1	1	1	1			
	0688 005 001	Kurbelwelle (Stahl-Pleuel) Kurbelwange Ø 107	Crankshaft (steel con-rod) Crank web Ø 107	Vilebrequin (bielle d'acier) flasque de manivelle Ø 107	1	1			1						
	0688 005 003	Kurbelwelle (Stahl-Pleuel) Kurbelwange Ø 90,2	Crankshaft (stell con-rod) Crank web Ø 90.2	Vilebrequin (bielle d'acier) flasque de manivelle Ø 90,2			1	1					1	1	1
15	0246 005 000	Scheibenfeder 3 x 3,7	Woodrift key 3 x 3.7	Clavette 3 x 3,7	2	2	2	2	2	2	2	2	2	2	2
16	0249 120 000	Paßhülse 10 x 15 zur Gehäusezentrierung	Dowel sleeve 10 x 15 for crankcase centering	Douille d'ajustage 10 x 15 pour la fixation du centre du carter	2	2	1	1	2	2	2	2	1	1	1
		zur Zylinderbefestigung	for cylinder fitting	pour la fixation du cylindre	2	2	2	2	2	2	2	2	2	2	2
	1949 011 000	Paßhülse 12 x 22 zur Gehäusezentrierung vorne bei Ausf. mit verstärkter Motoraufhängung	Dowel sleeve 12 x 22 for crankcase centering in front, when type with reinforced engine suspension	Douille d'ajustage 12 x 22 pour la fixation du centre du carter devant, en cas de version avec suspension du moteur renforcé	1	1	1	1	1	1	1	1	1	1	1
17	0932 061 005	Buchse 15 x 18,9 x 17 (für Alu-Pleuel)	Bush 15 x 18.9 x 17 (for alu con-rod)	Douille 15 x 18,9 x 17 (pour bielle d'aluminium)	1	1			1	1	1	1			
	0632 111 000	Nadelkäfig K 15 x 19 x 20 (für Stahl-Pleuel)	Needle cage K 15 x 19 x 20 (for steel con-rod)	Cage de palier à aiguilles K 15 x 19 x 20 (pour bielle d'acier)	1	1	1	1					1	1	1
		x = nach Bedarf	x = as required	x = suivant besoin											

Seite / Page: 2

Bild-Nr. III. No.	Bestell-Nr. Part-No. Réf. No.	Benennung	Description	Désignation	1001/5 A	1001/6 A	1001/6 B	1001/6 C	1251/5 A	1251/5 AL	1251/5 B	1251/6 A	1251/6 B	1251/6 C	1251/6 D
18		für Grauguß-Zylinder	for grey-cast cylinder	pour cylindre fonte grise											
	0686 208 005	Zsb. Kolben Ø 48,0	Piston ass'y. Ø 48,0	Piston cpl. Ø 48,0	1										
	0686 208 006	Zsb. Kolben Ø 48,5	Piston ass'y. Ø 48,5	Piston cpl. Ø 48,5	1										
	0686 208 007	Zsb. Kolben Ø 49,0	Piston ass'y. Ø 49,0	Piston cpl. Ø 49,0	1										
	0686 208 008	Zsb. Kolben Ø 49,5	Piston ass'y. Ø 49,5	Piston cpl. Ø 49,5	1										
	0686 207 005	Zsb. Kolben Ø 54,0	Piston ass'y. Ø 54,0	Piston cpl. Ø 54,0					1		1				
	0686 207 006	Zsb. Kolben Ø 54,5	Piston ass'y. Ø 54,5	Piston cpl. Ø 54,5					1		1				
	0686 207 007	Zsb. Kolben Ø 55,0	Piston ass'y. Ø 55,0	Piston cpl. Ø 55,0					1		1				
	0686 207 008	Zsb. Kolben Ø 55,5	Piston ass'y. Ø 55,5	Piston cpl. Ø 55,5					1		1				
		für Alu-Zylinder (NHW – Military)	for alu-cylinder (NHW – Military)	pour cylindre aluminium (NHW – Military)											
	0686 207 015	Zsb. Kolben Ø 54,0	Piston ass'y. Ø 54,0	Piston cpl. Ø 54,0						1					
	0686 207 016	Zsb. Kolben Ø 54,5	Piston ass'y. Ø 54,5	Piston cpl. Ø 54,5						1					
	0686 207 017	Zsb. Kolben Ø 55,0	Piston ass'y. Ø 55,0	Piston cpl. Ø 55,0						1					
	0686 207 018	Zsb. Kolben Ø 55,5	Piston ass'y. Ø 55,5	Piston cpl. Ø 55,5						1					
		für Alu-Zylinder	for alu-cylinder	pour cylindre aluminium											
	0686 208 115	Zsb. Kolben Ø 48,0	Piston ass'y. Ø 48,0	Piston cpl. Ø 48,0	1	1	1	1							
	0686 208 116	Zsb. Kolben Ø 48,5	Piston ass'y. Ø 48,5	Piston cpl. Ø 48,5	1	1	1	1							
	0686 208 117	Zsb. Kolben Ø 49,0	Piston ass'y. Ø 49,0	Piston cpl. Ø 49,0	1	1	1	1							
	0686 208 118	Zsb. Kolben Ø 49,5	Piston ass'y. Ø 49,5	Piston cpl. Ø 49,5	1	1	1	1							
	0686 207 025	Zsb. Kolben Ø 54,0	Piston ass'y. Ø 54,0	Piston cpl. Ø 54,0								1	1	1	1
	0686 207 026	Zsb. Kolben Ø 54,5	Piston ass'y. Ø 54,5	Piston cpl. Ø 54,5								1	1	1	1
	0686 207 027	Zsb. Kolben Ø 55,0	Piston ass'y. Ø 55,0	Piston cpl. Ø 55,0								1	1	1	1
	0686 207 028	Zsb. Kolben Ø 55,5	Piston ass'y. Ø 55,5	Piston cpl. Ø 55,5								1	1	1	1
19	0945 063 000	Drahtsprengring	Wire circlip	Sûreté	2	2	2	2	2	2	2	2	2	2	2
20	●0616 101 100	Kolbenbolzen 9 x 15 x 41	Gudgeon pin 9 x 15 x 41	Axe de piston 9 x 15 x 41	1	1	1	1							
	0616 100 000	Kolbenbolzen 9 x 15 x 46	Gudgeon pin 9 x 15 x 46	Axe de piston 9 x 15 x 46					1	1	1	1	1	1	1
21		für Grauguß-Zylinder	for grey-cast cylinder	pour cylindre fonte grise											
	0615 102 000	L-Profilkolbenring Ø 48,0	L-Profile piston ring Ø 48,0	L-profil segm. de pist. Ø 48,0	1										
	0615 102 001	L-Profilkolbenring Ø 48,5	L-Profile piston ring Ø 48,5	L-profil segm. de pist. Ø 48,5	1										
	0615 102 002	L-Profilkolbenring Ø 49,0	L-Profile piston ring Ø 49,0	L-profil segm. de pist. Ø 49,0	1										
	0615 102 003	L-Profilkolbenring Ø 49,5	L-Profile piston ring Ø 49,5	L-profil segm. de pist. Ø 49,5	1										
	0615 104 000	Rechteckring Ø 48,0	Rectangular ring Ø 48,0	Anneau rectangulaire Ø 48,0	1										
	0615 104 001	Rechteckring Ø 48,5	Rectangular ring Ø 48,5	Anneau rectangulaire Ø 48,5	1										
	0615 104 002	Rechteckring Ø 49,0	Rectangular ring Ø 49,0	Anneau rectangulaire Ø 49,0	1										
	0615 104 003	Rechteckring Ø 49,5	Rectangular ring Ø 49,5	Anneau rectangulaire Ø 49,5	1										
	0615 103 000	L-Profilkolbenring Ø 54,0	L-Profile piston ring Ø 54,0	L-profil segm. de pist. Ø 54,0					1		1				
	0615 103 001	L-Profilkolbenring Ø 54,5	L-Profile piston ring Ø 54,5	L-profil segm. de pist. Ø 54,5					1		1				
	0615 103 002	L-Profilkolbenring Ø 55,0	L-Profile piston ring Ø 55,0	L-profil segm. de pist. Ø 55,0					1		1				
	0615 103 003	L-Profilkolbenring Ø 55,5	L-Profile piston ring Ø 55,5	L-profil segm. de pist. Ø 55,5					1		1				
	0615 101 000	Rechteckring Ø 54,0	Rectangular ring Ø 54,0	Anneau rectangulaire Ø 54,0					1		1				
	0615 101 001	Rechteckring Ø 54,5	Rectangular ring Ø 54,5	Anneau rectangulaire Ø 54,5					1		1				
	0615 101 002	Rechteckring Ø 55,0	Rectangular ring Ø 55,0	Anneau rectangulaire Ø 55,0					1		1				
	0615 101 003	Rechteckring Ø 55,5	Rectangular ring Ø 55,5	Anneau rectangulaire Ø 55,5					1		1				
		für Alu-Zylinder	for alu-cylinder	pour cylindre aluminium											
	0615 103 005	L-Profilkolbenring Ø 54,0	L-Profile piston ring Ø 54,0	L-profil segm. de pist. Ø 54,0						1		1	1	1	1
	0615 103 006	L-Profilkolbenring Ø 54,5	L-Profile piston ring Ø 54,5	L-profil segm. de pist. Ø 54,5						1		1	1	1	1
	0615 103 007	L-Profilkolbenring Ø 55,0	L-Profile piston ring Ø 55,0	L-profil segm. de pist. Ø 55,0						1		1	1	1	1
	0615 103 008	L-Profilkolbenring Ø 55,5	L-Profile piston ring Ø 55,5	L-profil segm. de pist. Ø 55,5						1		1	1	1	1
	0615 101 005	Rechteckring Ø 54,0	Rectangular ring Ø 54,0	Anneau rectangulaire Ø 54,0						1		1	1	1	1
	0615 101 006	Rechteckring Ø 54,5	Rectangular ring Ø 54,5	Anneau rectangulaire Ø 54,5						1		1	1	1	1
	0615 101 007	Rechteckring Ø 55,0	Rectangular ring Ø 55,0	Anneau rectangulaire Ø 55,0						1		1	1	1	1
	0615 101 008	Rechteckring Ø 55,5	Rectangular ring Ø 55,5	Anneau rectangulaire Ø 55,5						1		1	1	1	1
		1. Ausführung	1st construction	1ère version											
	*0615 102 005	L-Profilkolbenring Ø 48,0	L-Profile piston ring Ø 48,0	L-profil segm. de pist. Ø 48,0	1	1									
	*0615 102 006	L-Profilkolbenring Ø 48,5	L-Profile piston ring Ø 48,5	L-profil segm. de pist. Ø 48,5	1	1									
	*0615 102 007	L-Profilkolbenring Ø 49,0	L-Profile piston ring Ø 49,0	L-profil segm. de pist. Ø 49,0	1	1									
	*0615 102 008	L-Profilkolbenring Ø 49,5	L-Profile piston ring Ø 49,5	L-profil segm. de pist. Ø 49,5	1	1									
		2. Ausführung	2nd construction	2ème version											
	+0615 102 105	L-Profilkolbenring Ø 48,0	L-Profile piston ring Ø 48,0	L-profil segm. de pist. Ø 48,0	1	1	1	1							
	+0615 102 106	L-Profilkolbenring Ø 48,5	L-Profile piston ring Ø 48,5	L-profil segm. de pist. Ø 48,5	1	1	1	1							
	+0615 102 107	L-Profilkolbenring Ø 49,0	L-Profile piston ring Ø 49,0	L-profil segm. de pist. Ø 49,0	1	1	1	1							
	+0615 102 108	L-Profilkolbenring Ø 49,5	L-Profile piston ring Ø 49,5	L-profil segm. de pist. Ø 49,5	1	1	1	1							
		*Profildicke 2,2 mm nicht austauschbar +Profildicke 1,9 mm	*Profile thickness 2,2 mm not interchangeable +Profile thickness 1,9 mm	*=épaisseur du profil 2,2 mm pas échangeable +=épaisseur du profil 1,9 mm											
		Zsb. Kolben besteht aus: Kolben, -ringen, -bolzen und Drahtsprengringen	Piston ass'y, consists of: Piston, piston rings, gudgeon pins and wire circlips	Piston cpl. comprenant: Piston, segments de piston, axe de piston et sûretés											
22	0241 048 000	Verschlußschraube M 16 x 1,25 x 6	Plug screw M 16 x 1.25 x 6	Vis de fermeture M 16 x 1,25 x 6	1	1	1	1	1	1	1	1	1	1	1
23	0940 119 112	Zylinderschraube M 6 x 60	Fillister head screw M 6 x 60	Vis à tête cylindrique M 6 x 60	6	6	6	6	6	6	6	6	6	6	6
24	0245 022 000	Federscheibe für M 10	Spring washer for M 10	Rondelle élastique pour M 10	1	1	1	1	1	1	1	1	1	1	1
25	0942 072 110	Bundmutter M 10 x 1 (Linksgewinde)	Collar nut M 10 x 1 (left-hand thread)	Ecrou à bride M 10 x 1 (filet à gauche)	1	1	1	1	1	1	1	1	1	1	1

Bild-Nr. / Ill. No.	Bestell-Nr. / Part-No. / Réf. No.	Benennung	Description	Désignation	1001/5 A	1001/6 A	1001/6 B	1001/6 C	1251/5 A	1251/5 AL	1251/5 B	1251/6 A	1251/6 B	1251/6 C	1251/6 D
26	0940 128 202	Zylinderschraube M 6 x 75	Fillister head screw M 6 x 75	Vis à tête cylindrique M 6 x 75	4	4	4	4	4	4	4	4	4	4	4
27	0650 004 000	Dichtring 12,2 x 20 x 1	Sealing ring 12.2 x 20 x 1	Anneau d'étanchéité 12,2 x 20 x 1	1	1	1	1	1	1	1	1	1	1	1
28	0640 005 005	Anschlagschraube M 12	Stop screw M 12	Vis d'arrêt M 12	1	1	1	1	1	1	1	1	1	1	1
29	1950 023 000	Dichtring 10,2 x 15,9 x 1	Sealing ring 10.2 x 15.9 x 1	Anneau d'étanchéité 10,2 x 15,9 x 1	1	1	1	1	1	1	1	1	1	1	1
30	0240 100 000	Ölablaßschraube M 10 x 1	Oil drain plug M 10 x 1	Bouchon de vidange M 10 x 1	1	1	1	1	1	1	1	1	1	1	1
	0241 029 005	Ölablaßschraube M 12 x 1 für Reparatur	Oil drain plug M 12 x 1 for repair	Bouchon de vidange M 12 x 1 pour réparations											
31	0250 118 000	Dichtring 12,2 x 15,4 x 1,5	Sealing ring 12.2 x 15.4 x 1.5	Anneau d'étanchéité 12,2 x 15,4 x 1,5	1	1	1	1	1	1	1	1	1	1	1
32	0240 133 100	Lagerschraube M 12 x 1	Pivot screw M 12 x 1	Vis de support M 12 x 1	1	1	1	1	1	1	1	1	1	1	1
33	0246 009 006	Scheibe 15,2 x 20,3 x 1,5	Washer 15.2 x 20.3 x 1.5	Rondelle 15,2 x 20,3 x 1,5	1	1	1	1	1	1	1	1	1	1	1
34	0634 112 000	Antriebszahnrad	Driving pinion	Pignon d'attaque	1	1	1	1	1	1	1	1	1	1	1
35	0645 102 000	Sicherungsscheibe	Tab washer	Rondelle de sûreté	1	1	1	1	1	1	1	1	1	1	1
36	0642 105 001	Sechskantmutter M 14 x 1,5 (Höhe 6 mm)	Hexagon nut M 14 x 1.5 (Height 6 mm)	Ecrou à six pans M 14 x 1,5 (hauteur 6 mm)	1	1			1	1	1	1			
	0942 020 100	Sechskantmutter M 14 x 1,5 (Höhe 8 mm)	Hexagon nut M 14 x 1.5 (Height 8 mm)	Ecrou à six pans M 14 x 1,5 (hauteur 8 mm)			1	2					1	1	1
37	•0240 029 201	Stiftschraube M 8 x 25	Stud M 8 x 25	Goujon fileté M 8 x 25						4					
	0940 017 101	Stiftschraube M 8 x 20 } *	Stud M 8 x 20 } *	Goujon fileté M 8 x 20 } *	4				4	4					
38	0942 067 100	Sechskantmutter M 8 }	Hexagon nut M 8 }	Ecrou à six pans M 8 }	4				4	4					
		* Befestigung für Grauguß-Zylinder an Gehäuse	* for fitting the grey-cast cylinder at the crankcase	* Fixation pour cylindre fonte grise au carter											
39	0640 108 001	Stiftschraube M 8 x 90 } *	Stud M 8 x 90 } *	Goujon fileté M 8 x 90 } *		4	4	4				4	4	4	4
40	0244 075 008	Scheibe 13,2 x 20 x 1,7 } *	Washer 13.2 x 20 x 1.7 } *	Rondelle 13,2 x 20 x 1,7 } *		4	4	4				4	4	4	4
41	0642 107 001	Halsmutter M 8 }	Collar nut M 8 }	Ecrou à col M 8 }		4	4	4				4	4	4	4
		* Befestigung für Alu-Zylinder und -Zylinderkopf an Gehäuse	* for fitting the alu cylinder and alu cylinder head at the crankcase	* Fixation pour cylindre aluminium et culasse aluminium au carter											
	0944 003 005	Scheibe 8,4 x 14 x 1,5 } *	Washer 8.4 x 14 x 1.5 } *	Rondelle 8,4 x 14 x 1,5 } *							4				
	0942 067 100	Sechskantmutter M 8 }	Hexagon nut M 8 }	Ecrou à six pans M 8 }							4				
		* Befestigung für Alu-Zylinder an Gehäuse	* for fitting the alu cylinder at the crankcase	* Fixation pour cylindre aluminium au carter											
42	0650 107 200	Dichtung	Gasket	Joint	1	1	1	1	1	1	1	1	1	1	1
43	1950 024 000	Dichtring 8,4 x 11,5 x 10	Sealing ring 8.4 x 11.5 x 10	Anneau d'étanchéité 8,4 x 11,5 x 10						1	1				
44	2015 008 000	Verschlußschraube M 8 x 1	Plug screw M 8 x 1	Vis de fermeture M 8 x 1						1	1				
45		Zylinderkopf und Zylinder, Seite 22	Cylinder head and cylinder, page 22	Culasse et cylindre, Page 22											
46	0650 108 000	Dichtung	Gasket	Joint	1				1	1					
47	0245 023 003	Federring für M 8 } *	Spring ring for M 8 } *	Anneau ressort pour M 8 } *	2				2	2					
48	0642 104 101	Sechskantmutter M 8 Höhe 36 mm }	Hexagon nut M 8 Height 36 mm }	Ecrou à six pans M 8 hauteur 36 mm }	2				2	2					
		* Befestigung für Auspufftopf an Grauguß-Zylinder	* for fitting the muffler at grey-cast cylinder	* Fixation pour pot d'échappement au cylindre fonte grise											
49	0650 112 000	Dichtring 40 x 47 x 2,5	Sealing ring 40 x 47 x 2.5	Anneau d'étanchéité 40 x 47 x 2,5		1	1	1				1	1	1	1
		(Befestigung für Auspuff an Alu-Zylinder)	(for fitting the muffler at alu cylinder)	(Fixation pour échappement au cylindre aluminium)											
50	0244 124 001	Scheibe 8,4 x 17 x 2 }	Washer 8.4 x 17 x 2 }	Rondelle 8,4 x 17 x 2 }	4				4	4	4				
51	0941 049 006	Sechskantschraube M 8 x 40 } *	Hexagon head screw M 8 x 40 } *	Vis à six pans M 8 x 40 } *	4				4	4	4				
	2842 003 004	Sechskantmutter M 8 }	Hexagon nut M 8 }	Ecrou à six pans M 8 }							4				
		* Befestigung für Zylinderkopf auf Zylinder	* for fitting the cylinder head on cylinder	* Fixation pour culasse sur cylindre											
52	0298 087 011	Zündkerze W 260 T 1	Spark plug W 260 T 1	Bougie d'allumage W 260 T 1	1	1			1		1	1	1		
	0298 087 009	Zündkerze W 225 T 1	Spark plug W 225 T 1	Bougie d'allumage W 225 T 1						1					
	0665 120 100	Zündkerze W 290 R 16	Spark plug W 290 R 16	Bougie d'allumage W 290 R 16											1
	3665 013 002	Zündkerze W 280 MZ 1	Spark plug W 280 MZ 1	Bougie d'allumage W 280 MZ 1			1	1						1	
	0665 120 001	Zündkerze W 290 T 16 für Ausf. CROSS-COUNTRY	Spark plug W 290 T 16 for type CROSS-COUNTRY	Bougie d'allumage W 290 T 16 pour version CROSS-COUNTRY											
53	0650 113 000	Dichtung Ø 48	Gasket Ø 48	Joint Ø 48	1	1	1								
	0650 114 000	Dichtung Ø 54	Gasket Ø 54	Joint Ø 54								1	1	1	1

Schalthebel, Hauptwelle, Getriebe
für SACHS 1001/5 A bis Motor-Nr. 5692 842
für SACHS 1251/5 A und 1251/5 AL bis Motor-Nr. 6318 754

Gear changing lever, Main shaft, Gearbox
for SACHS 1001/5 A up to engine-No. 5692 842
for SACHS 1251/5 A and 1251/5 AL up to engine-No. 6318 754

Levier de changement de vitesse, Arbre primaire, Boite de vitesses
pour SACHS 1001/5 A jusqu'à moteur No. 5692 842
pour SACHS 1251/5 A et 1251/5 AL jusqu'à moteur No. 6318 754

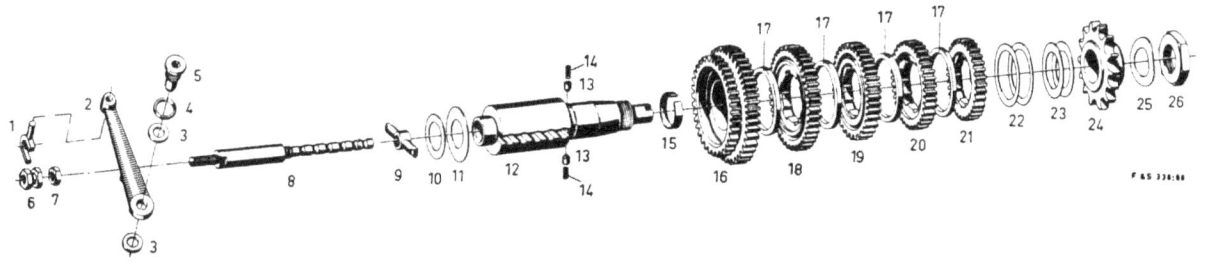

Bild-Nr. Ill. No.	Bestell-Nr. Part-No. Réf. No.	Benennung	Description	Désignation	1001/5 A	1001/6 A	1001/6 B	1001/6 C	1251/5 A	1251/5 AL	1251/5 B	1251/6 A	1251/6 B	1251/6 C	1251/6 D
1	0248 135 100	Schaltschuh	Selector fork	Sabot de changement de vitesse	1				1	1					
2	0248 131 100	Schalthebel	Selector lever	Levier de changement de vitesse	1				1	1					
3	0944 003 000	Scheibe 8,4 x 14, Seite 27	Shim 8.4 x 14, page 27	Rondelle 8,4 x 14, Page 27	x				x	x					
4	0250 118 000	Dichtring 12,2 x 15,4 x 1,5	Sealing ring 12.2 x 15.4 x 1.5	Anneau d'étanchéité 12,2 x 15,4 x 1,5	1				1	1					
5	0240 133 100	Lagerschraube M 12 x 1 mit Schlitz	Pivot screw M 12 x 1 with groove	Vis de support M 12 x 1 avec fente	1				1	1					
6	0242 103 100	Nutmutter M 6	Nut M 6	Ecrou cannelé M 6	1				1	1					
7	0242 109 000	Sechskantmutter M 6	Hexagon nut M 6	Ecrou à six pans M 6	1				1	1					
8	0237 120 200	Schaltstange M 8 x 1	Selector rod M 8 x 1	Bielle d'attaque M 8 x 1	1				1	1					
9	0619 001 100	Schaltkeil M 8 x 1	Selector key M 8 x 1	Cale de changement de vitesse M 8 x 1	1				1	1					
10	0244 118 001	Scheibe 20,2 x 32 x 0,8	Washer 20.2 x 32 x 0.8	Rondelle 20,2 x 32 x 0,8	1				1	1					
11	0644 103 000	Scheibe 20,2 x 39 x 1,0	Washer 20.2 x 39 x 1.0	Rondelle 20,2 x 39 x 1,0	1				1	1					
12	0637 102 000	Hauptwelle	Main shaft	Arbre primaire	1				1	1					
	0685 102 000	Zsb. Hauptwelle besteht aus: Bild 8, 9, 12...15	Main shaft ass'y. consists of: Ill. 8, 9, 12...15	Arbre primaire cpl. comprenant: ill. 8, 9, 12...15	1				1	1					
	0649 105 000	Napf für Index	Cup for index	Ecuelle pour index	2				2	2					
14	0639 100 100	Druckfeder	Pressure spring	Ressort de pression	2				2	2					
15	0639 101 000	Ringfeder	Spring ring	Ressort annulaire	1				1	1					
16	●0634 106 200	Schaltrad 1. Gang 46 und 34 Zähne	Selector gear 1st speed (46 and 34 teeth)	Roue de commande 1ère vitesse 46 et 34 dents	1				1	1					
17	0647 101 000	Ring 42 x 49 x 3	Ring 42 x 49 x 3	Anneau 42 x 49 x 3	4				4	4					
18	0634 107 000	Schaltrad 2. Gang 41 Zähne	Selector gear 2nd speed 41 teeth	Roue de commande 2ème vitesse 41 dents	1				1	1					
19	0634 108 000	Schaltrad 3. Gang 37 Zähne	Selector gear 3rd speed 37 teeth	Roue de commande 3ème vitesse 37 dents	1				1	1					
20	0634 109 000	Schaltrad 4. Gang 33 Zähne	Selector gear 4th speed 33 teeth	Roue de commande 4ème vitesse 33 dents	1				1	1					
21	0634 110 000	Schaltrad 5. Gang 31 Zähne	Selector gear 5th speed 31 teeth	Roue de commande 5ème vitesse 31 dents	1				1	1					
22	0644 104 000	Scheibe 35,2 x 44, Seite 27	Shim 35.2 x 44, page 27	Rondelle 35,2 x 44, Page 27	x				x	x					
23	0644 105 000	Scheibe 25,2 x 39, Seite 27	Shim 25.2 x 39, page 27	Rondelle 25,2 x 39, Page 27	x				x	x					
24	0636 106 000	Kettenrad 14 Zähne	Sprocket 14 teeth	Pignon à chaine 14 dents					1	1					
	0636 107 000	Kettenrad 13 Zähne	Sprocket 13 teeth	Pignon à chaine 13 dents	1										
25	0944 019 000	Federscheibe für Ø 20	Spring washer for Ø 20	Rondelle élastique pour Ø 20	1				1	1					
26	0642 103 001	Sechskantmutter M 20 x 1 (Linksgewinde)	Hexagon nut M 20 x 1 (left-hand thread)	Ecrou à six pans M 20 x 1 (filet à gauche)	1				1	1					

Schalthebel, Hauptwelle, Getriebe
für SACHS 1001/5 A ab Motor-Nr. 5692 843
für SACHS 1251/5 A und 1251/5 AL ab Motor-Nr. 6318 755

Gear changing lever, Main shaft, Gearbox
for SACHS 1001/5 A from engine-No. 5692 843
for SACHS 1251/5 A and 1251/5 AL from engine-No. 6318 755

Levier de changement de vitesse, Arbre primaire, Boite de vitesses
pour SACHS 1001/5 A à partir de moteur No. 5692 843
pour SACHS 1251/5 A et 1251/5 AL à partir de moteur No. 6318 755

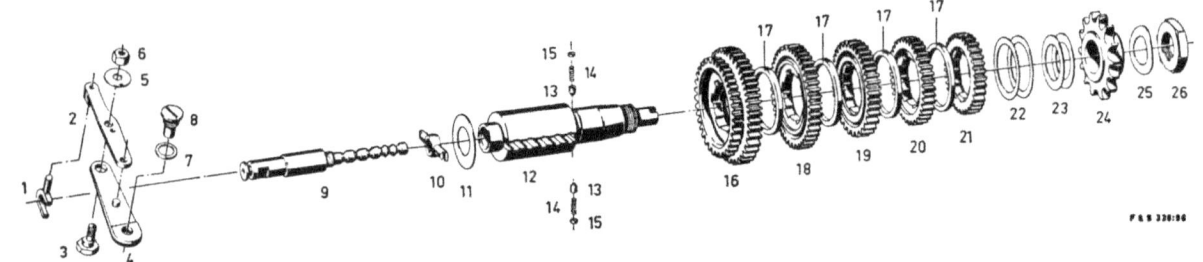

Bild-Nr. Ill. No.	Bestell-Nr. Part-No. Réf. No.	Benennung	Description	Désignation	1001/5 A	1001/6 A	1001/6 B	1001/6 C	1251/5 A	1251/5 AL	1251/6 A	1251/6 B	1251/6 C	1251/6 D
1	0248 135 100	Schaltschuh	Selector fork	Sabot de changement de vitesse	1				1	1	1			
2	0648 106 000	Schalthebel-Oberteil	Selector lever, upper part	Levier de changement de vitesse, partie supérieure	1				1	1	1			
3	0640 110 000	Exzenterschraube M 6	Eccentric screw M 6	Vis d'excentrique M 6	1				1	1	1			
4	0648 105 100	Schalthebel-Unterteil	Selector lever, lower part	Levier de changement de vitesse, partie inférieure	1				1	1	1			
5	1445 017 000	Sicherungsblech mit Innennase	Locking plate with inner tab	Tôle de sûreté avec ergot intérieur	1				1	1	1			
6	0642 108 000	Sechskantmutter M 6	Hexagon nut M 6	Ecrou à six pans M 6	1				1	1	1			
7	0250 118 000	Dichtring 12,2 x 15,4 x 1,5	Sealing ring 12.2 x 15.4 x 1.5	Anneau d'étanchéité 12,2 x 15,4 x 1,5	1				1	1	1			
8	0240 133 100	Lagerschraube M 12 x 1	Pivot screw M 12 x 1	Vis de support M 12 x 1	1				1	1	1			
9	0619 004 000	Schaltstange M 10 x 1	Selector rod M 10 x 1	Bielle d'attaque M 10 x 1	1				1	1	1			
10	0619 001 100	Schaltkeil M 10 x 1	Selector key M 10 x 1	Cale de changement de vitesse M 10 x 1	1				1	1	1			
11	0644 105 104	Scheibe 25,2 x 39 x 1	Washer 25.2 x 39 x 1	Rondelle 25,2 x 39 x 1	1				1	1	1			
12	0637 102 100	Hauptwelle	Main shaft	Arbre primaire	1				1	1	1			
	0685 102 100	Zsb. Hauptwelle besteht aus: Bild 9, 10, 12...15	Main shaft ass'y. consists of: Ill. 9, 10, 12...15	Arbre primaire cpl. comprenant: ill. 9, 10, 12...15	1				1	1	1			
13	0649 105 000	Napf für Index	Cup for index	Ecuelle pour index	2				2	2	2			
14	0639 100 100	Druckfeder	Pressure spring	Ressort de pression	2				2	2	2			
15	0663 002 000	Verschlußstopfen	Plug	Bouchon à visser	2				2	2	2			
16	●0634 106 200	Schaltrad 1. Gang 46 und 34 Zähne	Selector gear, 1st speed 46 and 34 teeth	Roue de commande 1ère vitesse 46 et 34 dents	1				1	1	1			
17	0647 101 000	Ring 42 x 49 x 3	Ring 42 x 49 x 3	Anneau 42 x 49 x 3	4				4	4	4			
18	0634 107 000	Schaltrad 2. Gang 41 Zähne	Selector gear, 2nd speed 41 teeth	Roue de commande 2ème vitesse 41 dents	1				1	1	1			
19	0634 108 000	Schaltrad Ø 69,35 3. Gang 37 Zähne	Selector gear Ø 69.35 3rd speed 37 teeth	Roue de commande Ø 69,35 3ème vitesse 37 dents	1				1	1				
	0634 108 003	Schaltrad Ø 68,2 3. Gang 37 Zähne	Selector gear Ø 68.2 3rd speed 37 teeth	Roue de commande Ø 68,2 3ème vitesse 37 dents									1	
20	0634 109 000	Schaltrad 4. Gang 33 Zähne	Selector gear 4th speed 33 teeth	Roue de commande 4ème vitesse 33 dents	1				1	1				
	0634 109 002	Schaltrad 4. Gang 32 Zähne	Selector gear 4th speed 32 teeth	Roue de commande 4ème vitesse 32 dents									1	
21	0634 110 000	Schaltrad 5. Gang 31 Zähne	Selector gear 5th speed 31 teeth	Roue de commande 5ème vitesse 31 dents	1				1	1				
	0634 110 002	Schaltrad 5. Gang 30 Zähne	Selector gear 5th speed 30 teeth	Roue de commande 5ème vitesse 30 dents									1	
22	0644 104 000	Scheibe 35,2 x 44, Seite 27	Shim 35.2 x 44, page 27	Rondelle 35,2 x 44, Page 27	x				x	x	x			
23	0644 105 000	Scheibe 25,2 x 39, Seite 27	Shim 25.2 x 39, page 27	Rondelle 25,2 x 39, Page 27	x				x	x	x			
24	0636 106 000	Kettenrad 14 Zähne	Sprocket 14 teeth	Pignon à chaîne 14 dents					1	1				
	0636 107 000	Kettenrad 13 Zähne	Sprocket 13 teeth	Pignon à chaîne 13 dents	1						1			
25	0944 019 000	Federscheibe für Ø 20	Spring washer for Ø 20	Rondelle élastique pour Ø 20	1				1	1	1			
26	0642 103 001	Sechskantmutter M 20 x 1 (Linksgewinde)	Hexagon nut M 20 x 1 (left-hand thread)	Ecrou à six pans M 20 x 1 (filet à gauche)	1				1	1	1			
	0644 114 100	Schutzkappe für Bild 12 (für Ausf. ohne Tachometer)	Protecting cap for Ill. 12 (for type without speedometer)	Capuchon protecteur pour ill. 12 (pour version sans compteur)	1				1	1	1			
		x = nach Bedarf	x = as required	x = suivant besoin										

Seite / Page: 6

Schalthebel, Hauptwelle, Getriebe
für SACHS 1001/6 A ab Motor-Nr. 5692 843
für SACHS 1251/6 A ab Motor-Nr. 6320 501

Gear changing lever, Main shaft, Gearbox
for SACHS 1001/6 A from engine-No. 5692 843
for SACHS 1251/6 A from engine-No. 6320 501

Levier de changement de vitesse, Arbre primaire, Boite de vitesses
pour SACHS 1001/6 A à partir de moteur No. 5692 843
pour SACHS 1251/6 A à partir de moteur No. 6320 501

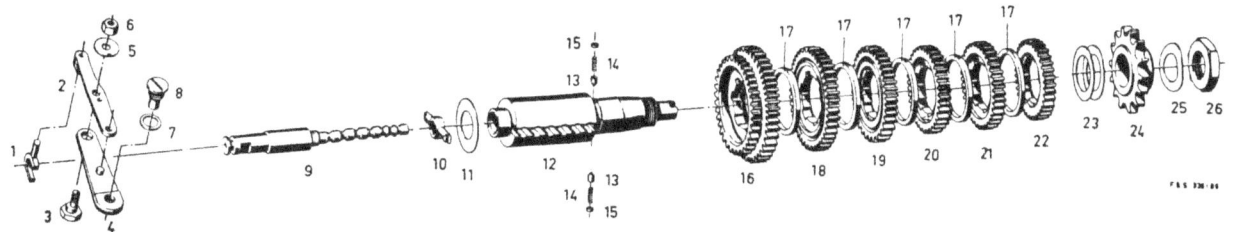

Bild-Nr. Ill. No.	Bestell-Nr. Part-No. Réf. No.	Benennung	Description	Désignation	1001/5 A	1001/6 A	1001/6 B	1001/6 C	1251/5 A	1251/5 AL	1251/5 B	1251/6 A	1251/6 B	1251/6 C	1251/6 D
1	0248 135 100	Schaltschuh	Selector fork	Sabot de changement de vitesse		1	1	1				1	1	1	1
2	0648 106 000	Schalthebel-Oberteil	Selector lever, upper part	Levier de changement de vitesse, partie supérieure		1	1	1				1	1	1	1
3	0640 110 000	Exzenterschraube M 6	Eccentric screw M 6	Vis d'excentrique M 6		1	1	1				1	1	1	1
4	0648 105 100	Schalthebel-Unterteil	Selector lever, lower part	Levier de changement de vitesse, partie inférieure		1	1	1				1	1	1	1
5	1445 017 000	Sicherungsblech mit Innennase	Locking plate with inner tab	Tôle de sûreté avec ergot intérieur		1	1	1				1	1	1	1
6	0642 108 000	Sechskantmutter M 6	Hexagon nut M 6	Ecrou à six pans M 6		1	1	1				1	1	1	1
7	0250 118 000	Dichtring 12,2 x 15,4 x 1,5	Sealing ring 12.2 x 15.4 x 1.5	Anneau d'étanchéité 12,2 x 15,4 x 1,5		1	1	1				1	1	1	1
8	0240 133 100	Lagerschraube M 12 x 1	Pivot screw M 12 x 1	Vis de support M 12 x 1		1	1	1				1	1	1	1
9	0619 004 001	Schaltstange M 10 x 1	Selector rod M 10 x 1	Bielle d'attaque M 10 x 1		1	1	1				1	1	1	1
10	0619 001 100	Schaltkeil M 10 x 1	Selector key M 10 x 1	Cale de changement de vitesse M 10 x 1		1	1	1				1	1	1	1
11	0644 105 104	Scheibe 25,2 x 39 x 1	Washer 25.2 x 39 x 1	Rondelle 25,2 x 39 x 1		1	1	1				1	1	1	1
12	0637 102 101	Hauptwelle	Main shaft	Arbre primaire		1	1	1				1	1	1	1
	0685 102 101	Zsb. Hauptwelle besteht aus: Bild 9, 10, 12...15	Main shaft ass'y. consists of: Ill. 9, 10, 12...15	Arbre primaire cpl. comprenant: ill. 9, 10, 12...15		1	1	1				1	1	1	1
13	0649 105 000	Napf für Index	Cup for index	Ecuelle pour index		2	2	2				2	2	2	2
14	0639 100 100	Druckfeder	Pressure spring	Ressort de pression		2	2	2				2	2	2	2
15	0663 002 000	Verschlußstopfen	Plug	Bouchon à visser		2	2	2				2	2	2	2
16	0634 106 201	Schaltrad 1. Gang 46 und 34 Zähne	Selector gear, 1st speed 46 and 34 teeth	Roue de commande 1ère vitesse 46 et 34 dents		1	1	1				1	1	1	1
17	0647 101 001	Ring 42 x 49 x 2,7	Ring 42 x 49 x 2.7	Anneau 42 x 49 x 2,7		x	x	x				x	x	x	x
	0647 101 002	Ring 42 x 49 x 2,6	Ring 42 x 49 x 2.6	Anneau 42 x 49 x 2,6		x	x	x				x	x	x	x
	0647 101 003	Ring 42 x 49 x 2,5	Ring 42 x 49 x 2.5	Anneau 42 x 49 x 2,5		x	x	x				x	x	x	x
18	0634 107 001	Schaltrad 2. Gang 41 Zähne	Selector gear 2nd speed 41 teeth	Roue de commande 2ème vitesse 41 dents		1	1	1				1	1	1	1
19	0634 108 001	Schaltrad 3. Gang 39 Zähne	Selector gear, 3rd speed 39 teeth	Roue de commande 3ème vitesse 39 dents		1	1	1				1	1	1	1
20	0634 108 002	Schaltrad 4. Gang 36 Zähne	Selector gear, 4th speed 36 teeth	Roue de commande 4ème vitesse 36 dents		1	1	1				1	1	1	1
21	0634 109 001	Schaltrad 5. Gang 33 Zähne	Selector gear, 5th speed 33 teeth	Roue de commande 5ème vitesse 33 dents		1	1	1				1	1	1	1
22	0634 110 001	Schaltrad 6. Gang 31 Zähne	Selector gear, 6th speed 31 teeth	Roue de commande 6ème vitesse 31 dents		1	1	1				1	1	1	1
23	0644 105 000	Scheibe 25,2 x 39, Seite 27	Shim 25.2 x 39, page 27	Rondelle 25,2 x 39, Page 27		x	x	x				x	x	x	x
24	0636 106 000	Kettenrad 14 Zähne	Sprocket 14 teeth	Pignon à chaîne 14 dents								1	1	1	1
	0636 107 000	Kettenrad 13 Zähne	Sprocket 13 teeth	Pignon à chaîne 13 dents		1	1	1							
25	0944 019 000	Federscheibe für Ø 20	Spring washer for Ø 20	Rondelle élastique pour Ø 20		1	1	1				1	1	1	1
26	0642 103 001	Sechskantmutter M 20 x 1 (Linksgewinde)	Hexagon nut M 20 x 1 (left-hand thread)	Ecrou à six pans M 20 x 1 (filet à gauche)		1	1	1				1	1	1	1

Starteinrichtung, Schaltung ohne und mit Schaltverrastung
für SACHS 1001/5 A, 1251/5 A und 1251/5 AL bis Motor-Nr. 6318 754

Starting device, Gear change mechanism without and with gear lock for
SACHS 1001/5 A, 1251/5 A and 1251/5 AL up to engine-No. 6318 754

Dispositif de démarrage, Changement de vitesse sans et avec verrouillage du changement de vitesse
pour SACHS 1001/5 A, 1251/5 A et 1251/5 AL jusqu'à moteur No. 6318 754

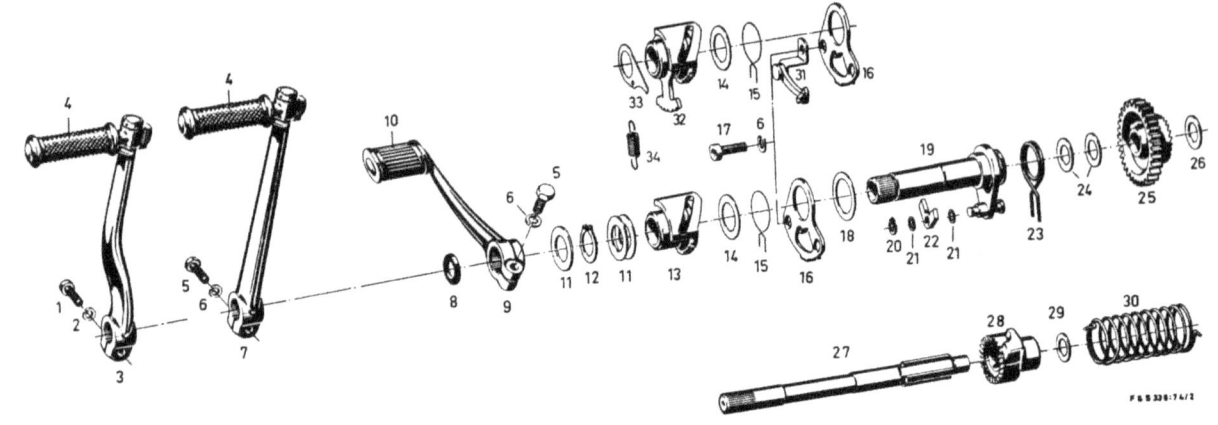

Bild-Nr. Ill. No.	Bestell-Nr. Part-No. Réf. No.	Benennung	Description	Désignation	1001/5 A	1001/6 A	1001/6 B	1001/6 C	1251/5 A	1251/5 AL	1251/5 B	1251/6 A	1251/6 B	1251/6 C	1251/6 D
1	1940 106 101	Innensechskantschraube M 8 x 22	Hexagon socket head screw M 8 x 22	Vis à tête à six pans M 8 x 22	1				1	1					
2	0245 023 003	Federring für M 8	Spring ring for M 8	Anneau ressort pour M 8	1				1	1					
3	0670 105 000	Zsb. Kickstarterschwenkkurbel 198 mm lang (gekröpft) mit Bild 1, 2 u. 4	Kickstarter crank ass'y. 198 mm long (bent at right angles) with ill. 1, 2 and 4	Manivelle de pédalier cpl. 198 mm de long (coudé) avec ill. 1, 2 et 4	1				1	1					
	●0270 130 004	Zsb. Kickstarterschwenkkurbel 151 mm lang (gekröpft) mit Bild 4, 5 u. 6	Kickstarter crank ass'y. 151 mm long (bent at right angles) with ill. 4, 5 and 6	Manivelle de pédalier cpl. 151 mm de long (coudé) avec ill. 4, 5 et 6	1										
4	0260 017 000	Gummimuffe	Rubber sleeve	Manchon en caoutchouc	1				1	1					
5	0240 005 000	Sechskantschraube M 6 x 20	Hexagon head screw M 6 x 20	Vis à six pans M 6 x 20	1				1	1					
6	0245 023 002	Federring für M 6	Spring ring for M 6	Anneau ressort pour M 6	1				1	1					
7	0289 028 001	Zsb. Kickstarterschwenkkurbel 151 mm lang (gerade) mit Bild 4, 5 und 6	Kickstarter crank ass'y. 151 mm long (straight) with ill. 4, 5 and 6	Manivelle de pédalier cpl. 151 mm de long (droit) avec ill. 4, 5 et 6											
8	0250 148 000	Runddichtring 11,3 x 2,4	Round sealing ring 11.3 x 2.4	Anneau d'étanchéité rond 11,3 x 2,4	1				1	1					
9	0290 124 000	Zsb. Fußschalthebel mit Bild 5, 6 u. 10	Selector pedal	Levier de changement à pédale	1				1	1					
10	0660 000 000	Gummimuffe	Rubber sleeve	Manchon en caoutchouc	1				1	1					
11	0944 046 000	Scheibe 20,5 x 28,4, Seite 27	Shim 20.5 x 28.4, page 27	Rondelle 20,5 x 28,4, Page 27	x				x	x					
12	0945 064 000	Sicherungsring	Circlip	Anneau de sûreté	1				1	1					
13	0286 317 000	Schaltnabe	Selector boss	Moyeu de changement de vitesse	1				1	1					
14	0244 118 000	Scheibe 20,2 x 32, Seite 27	Shim 20.2 x 32, page 27	Rondelle 20,2 x 32, Page 27	x				x	x					
15	0239 119 000	Klinkenfeder	Pawl spring	Ressort à cliquet	1				1	1					
16	0248 133 001	Aufnahmeplatte	Adjusting plate	Plaque de pose	1				1	1					
17	1940 114 000	Innensechskantschraube M 6 x 25	Hexagon socket head screw M 6 x 25	Vis à tête à six pans M 6 x 25	2				2	2					
18	0246 008 001	Scheibe 25,3 x 34 x 0,5 für Sperrhebel 5,8 mm dick	Washer 25.3 x 34 x 0.5 for locking lever 5.8 mm thick	Rondelle 25,3 x 34 x 0,5 pour levier d'arrêt 5,8 mm d'épais	1				1	1					
	0246 008 000	Scheibe 25,3 x 34 x 1,0 für Sperrhebel 4,5 mm dick	Washer 25.3 x 34 x 1.0 for locking lever 4.5 mm thick	Rondelle 25,3 x 34 x 1,0 pour levier d'arrêt 4,5 mm d'épais	1				1	1					
19	0290 106 211	Zsb. Schaltwelle mit Sperrhebel mit Bild 20...22	Selector shaft ass'y. with locking lever with ill. 20...22	Arbre de changement de vitesse cpl. avec levier d'arrêt, avec ill. 20...22	1				1	1					
20	0945 105 000	Sicherungsring	Circlip	Anneau de sûreté	1				1	1					
21	0244 100 000	Scheibe 6,2 x 10, Seite 27	Shim 6.2 x 10, page 27	Rondelle 6,2 x 10, Page 27	x				x	x					
22	0248 136 000	Schaltklinke	Selector pawl	Cliquet	1				1	1					
23	0239 120 000	Drehfeder	Torsion spring	Barre de torsion	1				1	1					
24	0244 055 000	Scheibe 14,5 x 24, Seite 27	Shim 14.5 x 24, page 27	Rondelle 14,5 x 24, Page 27	x				x	x					
25	0634 111 000	Starterrad	Starter gear	Roue de lanceur	1				1	1					
26	0244 055 002	Scheibe 14,5 x 24 x 1,0	Washer 14.5 x 24 x 1.0	Rondelle 14,5 x 24 x 1,0	1				1	1					
27	0237 122 200	Starterachse (in Verbindung mit Bild 8 montieren)	Starter shaft (to be fitted in connection with Ill. 8)	Arbre de lanceur (monter en liaison avec ill. 8)	1				1	1					
28	0634 005 001	Sperrad	Ratchet wheel	Roue d'arrêt	1				1	1					
29	0244 102 102	Scheibe 12,1 x 18,5 x 1,0	Washer 12.1 x 18.5 x 1.0	Rondelle 12,1 x 18,5 x 1,0	1				1	1					
30	0239 122 000	Drehfeder	Torsion spring	Barre de torsion	1				1	1					
31	0686 211 000	Winkel für Rastenklinke	Angle for notched pawl	Angle pour loquet à cran	1				1	1					
32	0286 317 020	Schaltnabe für Schaltverrastung	Selector boss for gear lock	Moyeu de changement de vitesse pour verrouillage du changement de vitesse	1				1	1					
33	0644 112 000	Einhängeblech	Inset sheet	Tôle d'accrochage	1				1	1					
34	0639 003 000	Zugfeder	Tension spring	Ressort de traction	1				1	1					
		x = nach Bedarf	x = as required	x = suivant besoin											

Bild-Nr. Ill. No.	Bestell-Nr. Part-No. Réf. No.	Benennung	Description	Désignation	1001/5 A	1001/6 A	1001/6 B	1001/6 C	1251/5 A	1251/5 AL	1251/5 B	1251/6 A	1251/6 B	1251/6 C	1251/6 D
	0290 112 101	**Zsb.** Schaltung mit Bild 11...16 und 18...23 für Ausf. ohne Schaltverrastung	Gear changing device ass'y. with ill. 11...16 and 18...23 for type without gear lock	Changement de vitesse cpl. avec ill. 11...16 et 18...23 pour version sans verrouillage du changement de vitesse	1				1	1					
	0290 112 107	**Zsb.** Schaltung mit Bild 11, 12, 14...16, 18...23 und 32, für Ausf. mit Schaltverrastung	Gear changing device ass'y. with ill. 11, 12, 14...16, 18...23 and 32, for type with gear lock	Changement de vitesse cpl. avec ill. 11, 12, 14...16, 18...23 et 32, pour version avec verrouillage du changement de vitesse	1				1	1					

Starteinrichtung, Schaltung
für SACHS 1001/5 A, 1001/6 A u. 1251/6 A   ab Motor-Nr. 5692 843
für SACHS 1001/6 B, 1001/6 C, 1251/6 C u. 1251/6 D   ab Motor-Nr. 6887 264
für SACHS 1251/5 A u. 1251/5 AL   ab Motor-Nr. 6318 543
für SACHS 1251/5 B   ab Motor-Nr. 6319 316
für SACHS 1251/6 B   ab Motor-Nr. 7103 005

Starting device, Gear change mechanism
for SACHS 1001/5 A, 1001/6 A and 1251/6 A   from engine-No. 5692 843
for SACHS 1001/6 B, 1001/6 C, 1251/6 C and 1251/6 D from engine-No. 6887 264
for SACHS 1251/5 A and 1251/5 AL   from engine-No. 6318 543
for SACHS 1251/5 B   from engine-No. 6319 316
for SACHS 1251/6 B   from engine-No. 7103 005

Dispositif de démarrage, Changement de vitesse
pour SACHS 1001/5 A, 1001/6 A et 1251/6 A   à partir de moteur No. 5692 843
pour SACHS 1001/6 B, 1001/6 C, 1251/6 C et 1251/6 D à partir de moteur No. 6887 264
pour SACHS 1251/5 A et 1251/5 AL   à partir de moteur No. 6318 543
pour SACHS 1251/5 B   à partir de moteur No. 6319 316
pour SACHS 1251/6 B   à partir de moteur No. 7103 005

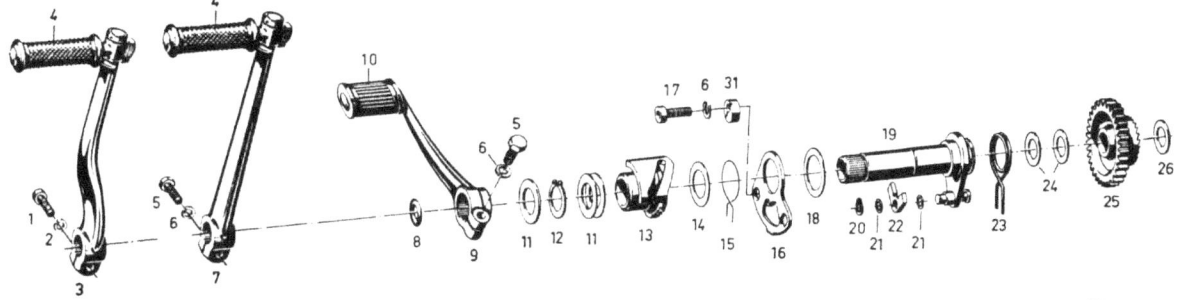
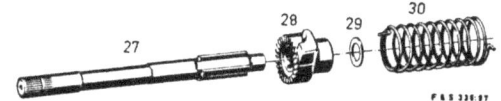

Bild-Nr.	Bestell-Nr.	Benennung	Description	Désignation	1001/5 A	1001/6 A	1001/6 B	1001/6 C	1251/5 A	1251/5 AL	1251/5 B	1251/6 A	1251/6 B	1251/6 C	1251/6 D
1	1940 106 101	Innensechskantschraube M 8 x 22	Hexagon socket head screw M 8 x 22	Vis à tête à six pans M 8 x 22	1	1	1	1	1	1		1	1	1	1
2	0245 023 003	Federring für M 8	Spring ring for M 8	Anneau ressort pour M 8	1	1	1	1	1	1		1	1	1	1
3	0670 105 000	**Zsb.** Kickstarterschwenkkurbel 198 mm lang (gekröpft) mit Bild 1, 2 u. 4	Kickstarter crank ass'y. 198 mm long (bent at right angles) with ill. 1, 2 and 4	Manivelle de pédalier cpl. 198 mm de long (coudé) avec ill. 1, 2 et 4	1	1	1	1	1	1		1	1	1	1
	●0270 130 004	**Zsb.** Kickstarterschwenkkurbel 151 mm lang (gekröpft) mit Bild 4, 5 u. 6	Kickstarter crank ass'y. 151 mm long (bent at right angles) with ill. 4, 5 and 6	Manivelle de pédalier cpl. 151 mm de long (coudé) avec ill. 4, 5 et 6	1				1						
4	0260 017 000	Gummimuffe	Rubber sleeve	Manchon en caoutchouc	1	1	1	1	1	1	1	1	1	1	1
5	0240 005 002	Sechskantschraube M 6 x 20	Hexagon head screw M 6 x 20	Vis à six pans M 6 x 20	1				1						
6	0245 023 002	Federring für M 6	Spring ring for M 6	Anneau ressort pour M 6	1				1						
7	0670 105 003	**Zsb.** Kickstarterschwenkkurbel 151 mm lang (gerade) mit Bild 4, 5 und 6 (gelboliv lackiert)	Kickstarter crank ass'y. 151 mm long (straight) with ill. 4, 5 and 6 (varnished yellow-olive)	Manivelle de pédalier cpl. 151 mm de long (droit) avec ill. 4, 5 et 6 vernie de laque jaune-olive	1				1						
	0289 028 001	**Zsb.** Kickstarterschwenkkurbel 151 mm lang (gerade) mit Bild 4, 5 und 6 (verchromt)	Kickstarter crank ass'y. 151 mm long (straight) with ill. 4, 5 and 6 (chromium-plated)	Manivelle de pédalier cpl. 151 mm de long (droit) avec ill. 4, 5 et 6 (chromée)							1				
8	0250 148 000	Runddichtring 11,3 x 2,4	Round sealing ring 11.3 x 2.4	Anneau d'étanchéité rond 11,3 x 2,4	1	1	1	1	1	1	1	1	1	1	1
9	0290 124 000	**Zsb.** Fußschalthebel (verchromt) mit Bild 5, 6 u. 10	Selector pedal (chromium-plated)	Levier du changement à pédale (chromé)	1	1			1	1		1	1	1	1

Seite / Page: 9

Bild-Nr. Ill. No.	Bestell-Nr. Part-No. Réf. No.	Benennung	Description	Désignation	1001/5 A	1001/6 A	1001/6 B	1001/6 C	1251/5 A	1251/5 Al	1251/5 B	1251/6 A	1251/6 B	1251/6 C	1251/6 D
	0290 124 002	Zsb. Fußschalthebel (gelboliv lackiert) mit Bild 5, 6 u. 10	Selector pedal (varnished yellow-olive)	Levier du changement à pédale (verni de laque jaune-olive)							1				
10	0660 000 0000	Gummimuffe	Rubber sleeve	Manchon en caoutchouc	1	1	1	1	1	1	1	1	1	1	1
11	0944 046 000	Scheibe 20,5 x 28,5, Seite 27	Shim 20.5 x 28.5, page 27	Rondelle 20,5 x 28,5, Page 27	x	x	x	x	x	x	x	x	x	x	x
12	0945 064 000	Sicherungsring	Circlip	Anneau de sûreté	1	1	1	1	1	1	1	1	1	1	1
13	0286 317 000	Schaltnabe	Selector boss	Moyeu du changement de vitesse	1				1	1	1				
	0286 317 021	Schaltnabe	Selector boss	Moyeu du changement de vitesse		1	1	1				1	1	1	1
14	0244 118 000	Scheibe 20,2 x 32, Seite 27	Shim 20.2 x 32, page 27	Rondelle 20,2 x 32, Page 27	x	x	x	x	x	x	x	x	x	x	x
15	0239 119 000	Klinkenfeder	Pawl spring	Ressort à cliquet	1	1	1	1	1	1	1	1	1	1	1
16	0248 133 001	Aufnahmeplatte	Adjusting plate	Plaque de pose	1	1	1	1	1	1	1	1	1	1	1
17	1940 114 000	Innensechskantschraube M 6 x 25	Hexagon socket head screw M 6 x 25	Vis à tête à six pans M 6 x 25	2	2	2	2	2	2	2	2	2	2	2
18	0246 008 001	Scheibe 25,3 x 34 x 0,5	Washer 25.3 x 34 x 0.5	Rondelle 25,3 x 34 x 0,5	1	1	1	1	1	1	1	1	1	1	1
19	0290 106 211	Zsb. Schaltwelle mit Sperrhebel, mit Bild 20, 21 und 22	Selector shaft ass'y. with locking lever with ill. 20, 21 and 22	Arbre du changement de vitesse cpl. avec levier d'arrêt avec ill. 20, 21 et 22	1	1	1	1	1	1	1	1	1	1	1
20	0945 105 000	Sicherungsring	Circlip	Anneau de sûreté	1	1	1	1	1	1	1	1	1	1	1
21	0244 100 000	Scheibe 6,2 x 10, Seite 27	Shim 6.2 x 10, page 27	Rondelle 6,2 x 10, Page 27	x	x	x	x	x	x	x	x	x	x	x
22	0248 136 000	Schaltklinke	Selector pawl	Cliquet	1	1	1	1	1	1	1	1	1	1	1
23	0239 120 000	Drehfeder	Torsion spring	Barre de torsion	1	1	1	1	1	1	1	1	1	1	1
24	0244 055 000	Scheibe 14,5 x 24, Seite 27	Shim 14.5 x 24, page 27	Rondelle 14,5 x 24, Page 27	x	x	x	x	x	x	x	x	x	x	x
25	0634 111 000	Starterrad	Starter gear	Roue de lanceur	1	1	1	1	1	1	1	1	1	1	1
26	0244 055 002	Scheibe 14,5 x 24 x 1,0	Washer 14.5 x 24 x 1.0	Rondelle 14,5 x 24 x 1,0	1	1	1	1	1	1	1	1	1	1	1
27	0237 122 200	Starterachse	Starter shaft	Arbre de lanceur	1	1	1	1	1	1	1	1	1	1	1
28	0634 005 001	Sperrad	Ratchet wheel	Roue d'arrêt	1	1	1	1	1	1	1	1	1	1	1
29	0244 102 102	Scheibe 12,1 x 18,5 x 1,0	Washer 12.1 x 18.5 x 1.0	Rondelle 12,1 x 18,5 x 1,0	1	1	1	1	1	1	1	1	1	1	1
30	0239 122 000	Drehfeder	Torsion spring	Barre de torsion	1	1	1	1	1	1	1	1	1	1	1
31	0647 103 100	Anschlagbuchse für Schaltverrastung	Stop bush for gear lock	Douille d'arrêt pour verrouillage du changement de vitesse	2	2	2	2	2	2	2	2	2	2	2
	0690 002 000	Zsb. Schaltung mit Bild 11...16 und 18...23	Gear changing device ass'y. with ill. 11...16 and 18...23	Changement de vitesse cpl. avec ill. 11...16 et 18...23	1				1	1	1				
	0690 002 001	Zsb. Schaltung mit Bild 11...16 und 18...23	Gear changing device ass'y. with ill. 11...16 and 18...23	Changement de vitesse cpl. avec ill. 11...16 et 18...23		1	1	1				1	1	1	1

x = nach Bedarf   x = as required   x = suivant besoin

Magnetzünder-Generator (BOSCH)
Magneto-Generator (BOSCH)
Magnéto-génératrice (BOSCH)

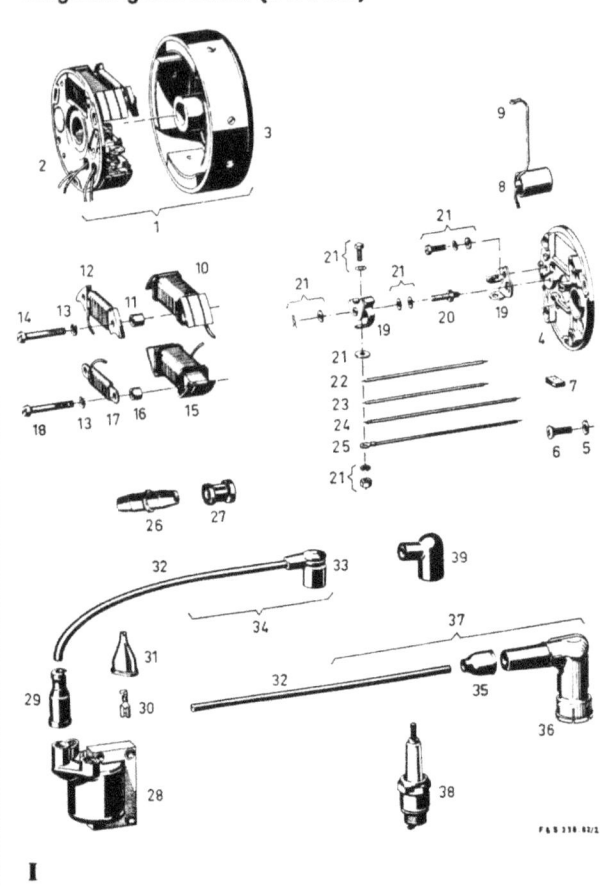

I

Magnetzünder-Generator (MOTOPLAT)
Magneto-Generator (MOTOPLAT)
Magnéto-génératrice (MOTOPLAT)

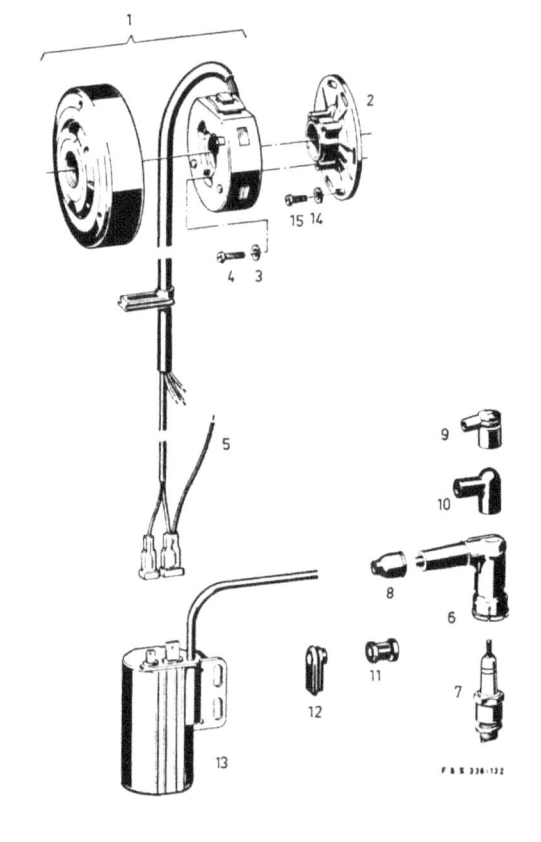

II

Seite / Page: 10

Bild-Nr. Ill. No.	Bestell-Nr. Part-No. Réf. No.	Benennung	Description	Désignation	1001/5 A	1001/6 A	1001/6 B	1001/6 C	1251/5 A	1251/5 AL	1251/5 B	1251/6 A	1251/6 B	1251/6 C	1251/6 D
I															
1	0283 100 402	**Zsb.** Magnetzünder-Generator 6 Volt 35-5/18 Watt (BOSCH: 0212 124 014)	Magneto-generator ass'y. 6 Volt 35-5/18 Watt (BOSCH: 0212 124 014)	Magnéto-génératrice cpl. 6 volts 35/5/18 watts (BOSCH: 0212 124 014)						1	1				
2	0283 105 017	**Zsb.** Ankerplatte	Armature base plate ass'y.	Socle d'allumage cpl.	1	1			1	1	1	1			
3	0283 108 018	Schwungrad	Flywheel	Volant						1	1				
	0283 108 023	Schwungrad mit verschweißter Nabe (BOSCH: 1215 254 402/S) nur unter Bild 2 lieferbar	Flywheel with welded hub (BOSCH: 1215 254 402/S) only available unter ill. 2	Volant avec moyeu soudé (BOSCH: 1215 254 402/S) uniquement livrable sous ill. 2	1	1			1			1			
4															
5	0244 108 000	Scheibe 4,1 x 9 x 1,2	Washer 4.1 x 9 x 1.2	Rondelle 4,1 x 9 x 1,2						3	3				
6	0240 106 100	Linsenschraube M 4 x 14	Oval head screw M 4 x 14	Vis à tête ovale M 4 x 14						3	3				
7	2865 008 000	Schmierfilz	Lubrication felt	Feutre de graissage	1	1			1	1	1	1			
8	0965 091 000	Kondensator	Condenser	Condensateur	1	1			1	1	1	1			
9	0265 077 001	Verbindungskabel zum Kondensator	Connecting cable to condenser	Câble du condensateur	1	1			1	1	1	1			
10	0265 139 012	Zündanker	Ignition armature	Bobine d'allumage	1	1			1	1	1	1			
11	0247 106 002	Buchse 4,2 x 8 x 8	Bush 4.2 x 8 x 8	Douille 4,2 x 8 x 8						2	2				
	0247 106 005	Buchse	Bush	Douille	1	1			1			1			
12	0265 139 014	Bremslichtanker	Stop light armature	Bobine de feu stop	1	1			1	1	1	1			
13	0245 023 000	Federring für M 4	Spring ring for M 4	Anneau ressort pour M 4	4	4			4	4	4	4			
14	0240 122 002	Zylinderschraube M 4 x 30	Fillister head screw M 4 x 30	Vis à tête cylindrique M 4 x 30	2	2			2	2	2	2			
15	0265 141 004	Generatoranker	Generating armature	Bobine génératrice	1	1			1	1	1	1			
16	0247 106 001	Buchse 4,2 x 8 x 7	Bush 4.2 x 8 x 7	Douille 4,2 x 8 x 7	2	2			2	2	2	2			
17	0265 139 013	Schlußlichtanker	Taillight armature	Bobine de feu arrière	1	1			1	1	1	1			
18	0240 153 000	Zylinderschraube M 4 x 32	Fillister head screw M 4 x 32	Vis à tête cylindrique M 4 x 32	2	2			2	2	2	2			
19	0283 101 100	Kontaktsatz	Contact breaker set	Rupteur cpl.	1	1			1	1	1	1			
20	0240 066 009	Lagerbolzen	Pivot pin	Pivot du rupteur	1	1			1	1	1	1			
21	0287 107 000	Kontakt-Teilesatz	Set of spares for contact breaker	Jeu de pièces rupteur	1	1			1	1	1	1			
22	0299 059 009	Lichtkabel	Lighting cable	Câble d'éclairage	1	1			1	1	1	1			
23	0299 059 016	Schlußlichtkabel — Länge angeben	Taillight cable — quote required length	Câble de feu arrière — indiquer la longueur	1	1			1	1	1	1			
24	0299 059 026	Bremslichtkabel	Brake light cable	Câble de feu stop	1	1			1	1	1	1			
25	0265 137 002	Generatorkabel	Generating cable	Câble de génératrice	1	1			1	1	1	1			
26	0265 073 000	Kabelklemme	Cable terminal	Borne de câble	2	2			2	2	2	2			
27	0665 119 000	Gummitülle (4 Bohrungen)	Rubber grommet (4 bores)	Passe-fil en caoutchouc (4 alésages)	1	1			1	1	1	1			
28	0283 109 000	Zündspule	Ignition coil	Bobine	1	1			1	1	1	1			
29	0265 150 000	Schutzkappe	Protective cap	Capuchon protecteur	1	1			1	1	1	1			
30	0265 152 000	Steckkabelschuh	Cable socket	Cosse-câble	2	2			2	2	2	2			
31	0265 151 000	Schutzkappe	Protective cap	Capuchon protecteur	2	2			2	2	2	2			
32	0665 016 101	Zündkabel Ø 7	Ignition cable Ø 7	Câble d'allumage Ø 7	1	1			1	1	1	1			
33	0288 091 000	Kerzenstecker, nicht geschirmt	Spark plug socket, not suppressed	Chapeau de bougie, non déparasité							1				
34	0283 110 006	**Zsb.** Zündkabel besteht aus: Bild 32 und 33	Ignition cable ass'y. consisting of: Ill. 32 and 33	Câble d'allumage cpl. comprenant: ill. 32 et 33							1				
35	0265 109 100	Regenschutzkappe	Protective rubber cap	Capuchon protecteur contre la pluie	1	1			1			1	1		
36	0265 100 100	Kerzenstecker, teilgeschirmt	Spark plug socket, partly suppressed	Chapeau de bougie, déparasité partiellement	1	1			1						
37	0283 110 005	**Zsb.** Zündkabel besteht aus: Bild 32, 35 und 36	Ignition cable ass'y. consisting of: Ill. 32, 35, 36	Câble d'allumage cpl. comprenant: ill. 32, 35 et 36	1	1			1						
38	0298 087 011	Zündkerze W 260 T 1	Spark plug W 260 T 1	Bougie d'allumage W 260 T 1						1			1	1	
	0298 087 009	Zündkerze W 225 T 1	Spark plug W 225 T 1	Bougie d'allumage W 225 T 1							1				
	0665 120 101	Zündkerze W 290 R 16 für Ausf. CROSS-COUNTRY	Spark plug W 290 R 16 for type CROSS-COUNTRY	Bougie d'allumage W 290 R 16 pour version CROSS-COUNTRY	1	1									
39	1465 011 001	Kerzenstecker (Gummi) mit Feder und Anschlußmutter, nicht geschirmt	Spark plug socket (rubber) with spring and terminal nut, not suppressed	Chapeau de bougie (caoutchouc) avec ressort et écrou de raccordement, non déparasité	1	1			1			1	1		
	0283 110 002	**Zsb.** Zündkabel mit Bild 39	Ignition cable ass'y. with ill. 39	Câble d'allumage cpl. avec ill. 39	1	1			1			1	1		
II															
1	0683 006 004	**Zsb.** Magnetzünder-Generator mit Bild 2, 3 u. 4 6 Volt 35/5/21 Watt mit Isolierkappen naturfarbig (MOTOPLAT: 9600 166) mit Diode, ohne Zündspule	Magneto-generator ass'y. with ill. 2, 3 and 4 6 Volt 35/5/21 Watt with insulating caps natural colour (MOTOPLAT: 9600 166) with diode, without ignition coil	Magnéto-génératrice cpl. avec ill. 2, 3 et 4 6 volts 35/5/21 watts avec capuchons isolants, qui ont des couleurs naturelles (MOTOPLAT: 9600 166) avec diode, sans bobine	1	1	1	1	1			1	1	1	1
	0665 125 000	Diode (nur für Generatoren mit aufgestempelten Kennzeichen: GK / GL)	Diode (only for generators with stamped-on markings: GK / GL)	Diode (uniquement pour génératrices avec tampon de marque distinctive: GK / GL)	1	1	1	1	1			1	1	1	1
	●0683 006 204	**Zsb.** Magnetzünder-Generator 6 Volt 35/5/21 Watt mit Isolierkappen rot (MOTOPLAT: 9600 166-1) ohne Diode, ohne Zündspule	Magneto-generator ass'y. with ill. 2, 3 and 4 6 Volt 35/5/21 Watt with insulating caps red (MOTOPLAT: 9600 166-1) without diode, without ignition coil	Magnéto-génératrice cpl. avec ill. 2, 3 et 4 6 volts 35/5/21 watts avec capuchons isolants rouges (MOTOPLAT: 9600 166-1) sans diode, sans bobine	1	1	1	1	1			1	1	1	1
2	0265 163 000	Grundplatte	Base plate	Plaque de pose	1	1	1	1	1			1	1	1	1
3	0644 031 000	Scheibe 4,3 x 8 x 0,5	Washer 4.3 x 8 x 0.5	Rondelle 4,3 x 8 x 0,5	3	3	3	3	3			3	3	3	3

Bild-Nr. Ill. No.	Bestell-Nr. Part-No. Réf. No.	Benennung	Description	Désignation	1001/5 A	1001/6 A	1001/6 B	1001/6 C	1251/5 A	1251/5 AL	1251/5 B	1251/6 A	1251/6 B	1251/6 C	1251/6 D
4	2840 002 001	Zylinderschraube M 4 x 20	Fillister head screw M 4 x 20	Vis à tête cylindrique M 4 x 20	3	3	3	3	3			3	3	3	3
5	0965 108 001	Kurzschlußkabel (Länge angeben)	Short-circuit cable (quote length)	Câble de court-circuit (indiquer la longueur)	1	1	1	1	1			1	1	1	1
	0665 123 000	Zubehör-Teilesatz besteht aus: 1 x großer Kabelschuh 1 x kleiner Kabelschuh 1 x große Isolierkappe 1 x kleine Isolierkappe	Set of accessories consisting of: 1 x large cable socket 1 x small cable socket 1 x large insulating cap 1 x small insulating cap	Jeu de pièces d'accessoires comprenant: 1 x grande cosse de câble 1 x petite cosse de câble 1 x grand capuchon isolant 1 x petit capuchon isolant	1			1							
	0265 167 000	Zubehör-Teilesatz besteht aus: 1 x Gummischieber Nr. 0260 020 016 1 x großer Kabelschuh 1 x kleiner Kabelschuh 1 x große Isolierkappe 1 x kleine Isolierkappe für Bild 1	Set of accessories consisting of: 1 x rubber slide No. 0260 020 016 1 x large cable socket 1 x small cable socket 1 x large insulating cap 1 x small insulating cap for ill. 1	Jeu de pièces d'accessoires comprenant: 1 x boisseau en caoutchouc No. 0260 020 016 1 x grande cosse de câble 1 x petite cosse de câble 1 x grand capuchon isolant 1 x petit capuchon isolant pour ill. 1	1	1	1	1	1			1	1	1	1
	●0265 167 100	Zubehör-Teilesatz besteht aus: 1 x Gummischieber Nr. 0260 020 016 1 x großer Kabelschuh 1 x kleiner Kabelschuh 1 x große Isolierkappe (rot) 1 x kleine Isolierkappe (rot) für 0683 006 204	Set of accessories consisting of: 1 x rubber slide No. 0260 020 016 1 x large cable socket 1 x small cable socket 1 x large insulating cap (red) 1 x small insulating cap (red) for 0683 006 204	Jeu de pièces d'accessoires comprenant: 1 x boisseau en caoutchouc No. 0260 020 016 1 x grande cosse de câble 1 x petite cosse de câble 1 x grand capuchon isolant (rouge) 1 x petit capuchon isolant (rouge) pour 0683 006 204	1	1	1	1	1			1	1	1	1
6	0265 100 100	Zündkerzenstecker, teilgeschirmt	Spark plug socket, partly suppressed	Chapeau de bougie, déparasité partiellement	1	1	1	1	1			1	1	1	1
7	0298 087 011	Zündkerze W 260 T 1	Spark plug W 260 T 1	Bougie d'allumage W 260 T 1	1	1			1			1	1		
	0665 120 101	Zündkerze W 290 R 16 für Ausf. CROSS-COUNTRY	Spark plug W 290 R 16 for type CROSS-COUNTRY	Bougie d'allumage W 290 R 16 pour version CROSS-COUNTRY			1	1						1	1
	3665 013 003	Zündkerze W 280 MZ 1	Spark plug W 280 MZ 1	Bougie d'allumage W 280 MZ 1			1	1						1	1
8	0265 109 100	Regenschutzkappe	Protective rubber cap	Capuchon protecteur contre la pluie	1	1			1			1	1		
9	0288 091 000	Zündkerzenstecker (Kunststoff) nicht geschirmt	Spark plug socket (synthetic) not suppressed	Chapeau de bougie (matière artificielle) non déparasité	1	1			1			1	1		
10	1465 011 001	Zündkerzenstecker (Gummi) mit Feder und Anschlußmutter, nicht geschirmt	Spark plug socket (rubber) with spring and terminal nut, not suppressed	Chapeau de bougie (caoutchouc) avec ressort et écrou de raccordement non déparasité	1	1			1			1	1		
11	0665 119 001	Gummitülle (Bohrung Ø 9 mm)	Rubber grommet (bore Ø 9 mm)	Passe-fil en caoutchouc alésage Ø 9 mm	1	1			1			1	1		
12	0665 124 000	Gummischieber Dicke 25 mm f. Magnetzünder 0683 006 004	Rubber slide, thickn. 25 mm for magneto 0683 006 004	Boisseau en caoutchouc épaisseur 25 mm pour magnéto 0683 006 004	1										
	0260 020 016	Gummischieber Dicke 13 mm f. Magnetzünder 0683 006 204	Rubber slide, thickn. 13 mm for magneto 0683 006 204	Boisseau en caoutchouc épaisseur 13 mm pour magnéto 0683 006 204	1	1	1	1	1			1	1	1	1
13	0283 124 000	Zündspule (Zündkabel schwarz) ohne Diode (nur für Bild 1) nach Aufbrauch ersetzt durch 0283 124 100	Ignition coil (ignition cable black) without diode (only for ill. 1) after consumation replaced by 0283 124 100	Bobine (câble d'allumage noir) sans diode (uniquement pour ill. 1) après consommation remplacée par 0283 124 100	1	1	1	1	1			1	1	1	1
	0283 124 100	Zündspule (Zündkabel rot) mit Diode (für 0683 006 004/204)	Ignition coil (ignition cable red) with diode (for 0683 006 004/204)	Bobine (câble d'allumage rouge) avec diode (pour 0683 006 004/204)	1	1	1	1	1			1	1	1	1
14	0244 108 000	Scheibe 4,1 x 9 x 1,2	Washer 4.1 x 9 x 1.2	Rondelle 4,1 x 9 x 1,2 Vis à tête cylindrique	3	3	3	3	3			3	3	3	3
15	0241 028 001	Zylinderschraube M 4 x 12	Fillister head screw M 4 x 12	M 4 x 12	3	3	3	3	3			3	3	3	3

Deckel-Magnetseite, Tacho-Antrieb
Magneto side cover, Speedometer drive
Couvercle de carter côté magnéto, Entrainement de compteur

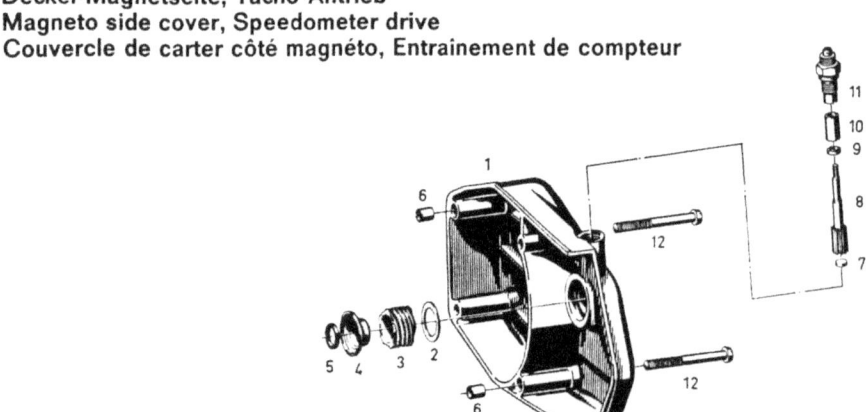

Seite / Page: 12

Bild-Nr. Ill. No.	Bestell-Nr. Part-No. Réf. No.	Benennung	Description	Désignation	1001/5 A	1001/6 A	1001/6 B	1001/6 C	1251/5 A	1251/5 Al	1251/5 B	1251/6 A	1251/6 B	1251/6 C	1251/6 D
1	0611 113 200	Deckel-Magnetseite (SACHS)	Magneto side cover (SACHS)	Couvercle côté magnéto (SACHS)	1	1	1	1	1			1	1	1	1
	0611 113 204	Deckel-Magnetseite (SACHS) Ausführung gekürzt	Magneto side cover (SACHS) type shortened	Couvercle côté magnéto (SACHS) vers. réduite						1					
	0677 002 002	**Zsb.** Deckel-Magnetseite (SACHS) mit Tacho-Antrieb i=7:12 besteht aus: Bild 1...5, 7...11	Magneto side cover ass'y. (SACHS) with speedometer drive i = 7:12 consisting of: ill. 1...5, 7...11	Couvercle côté magnéto cpl. (SACHS) avec entrainement de compteur i = 7:12 comprenant ill.1...5,7...11						1					
	0677 002 000	**Zsb.** Deckel-Magnetseite (SACHS) mit Tacho-Antrieb i = 7:12 besteht aus: Bild 1...5, 7...11	Magneto side cover ass'y. (SACHS) with speedometer drive i = 7:12 consisting of: Ill. 1...5, 7...11	Couvercle côté magnéto cpl. (SACHS) avec entrainement de compteur i = 7:12 comprenant: ill. 1...5, 7...11	1	1	1	1	1			1	1	1	1
	0677 002 003	**Zsb.** Deckel-Magnetseite (SACHS) mit Tacho-Antrieb i = 7:11 besteht aus: Bild 1...5, 7, 9...11 und 0234 070 110 Ausf. HERCULES	Magneto side cover ass'y. (SACHS) with speedometer drive i = 7:11 consisting of: Ill. 1...5, 7, 9...11 and 0234 070 110 Type HERCULES	Couvercle côté magnéto cpl. (SACHS) avec entrainement de compteur i = 7:11 comprenant: ill. 1...5, 7, 9...11 et 0234 070 110 version HERCULES							1				
	0611 113 202	Deckel-Magnetseite (DKW)	Magneto side cover (DKW)	Couvercle côté magnéto (DKW)	1				1						
	0677 002 001	**Zsb.** Deckel-Magnetseite (DKW) mit Tacho-Antrieb i = 7:12	Magneto side cover ass'y. (DKW) with speedometer drive i = 7:12	Couvercle côté magnéto cpl. (DKW) avec entrainement de compteur i = 7:12	1				1						
	0611 113 206	Deckel-Magnetseite (DKW) Ausführung gekürzt	Magneto side cover (DKW) type shortened	Couvercle côté magnéto (DKW) vers. réduite		1				1					
	0677 002 105	**Zsb.** Deckel-Magnetseite (DKW) mit Tacho-Antrieb i = 7:12	Magneto side cover ass'y. (DKW) with speedometer drive i = 7:12	Couvercle côté magnéto cpl. (DKW) avec entrainement de compteur i = 7:12		1				1					
	●1440 026 000	Nippel M 6 für Entlüftung	Nipple M 6 for ventilation	Nipple M 6 pour aération						1					
	●0650 115 000	Dichtung (Abil 0,25 mm dick)	Gasket (Abil 0.25 mm thick)	Joint (Abil 0,25 mm d'épais)						1					
2	0244 082 002	Scheibe 15,7 x 24,8 x 0,5	Washer 15.7 x 24.8 x 0.5	Rondelle 15,7 x 24,8 x 0,5	1	1	1	1	1		1	1	1	1	1
3	0234 071 000	Schraubenrad	Spiral gear	Pignon à vis	1	1	1	1	1		1	1	1	1	1
4	0246 052 000	Lagernapf	Bearing cup	Buselure	1	1	1	1	1		1	1	1	1	1
5	0650 017 000	Dichtring 12,6 x 19 x 2,5	Sealing ring 12.6 x 19 x 2.5	Anneau d'étanchéité 12,6 x 19 x 2,5	1	1	1	1	1		1	1	1	1	1
6	0949 090 000	Paßhülse 8,5 x 10	Dowel sleeve 8.5 x 10	Douille d'ajustage 8,5 x 10	2	2	2	2	2		2	2	2	2	2
7	0644 017 000	Scheibe 8,8 x 2	Shim 8.8 x 2	Rondelle 8,8 x 2	1	1	1	1	1		1	1	1	1	1
8	0234 070 111	Schraubenritzel 12 Zähne	Spiral pinion 12 teeth	Pignon hélicoïdal 12 dents	1	1	1	1	1			1	1	1	1
	0234 070 110	Schraubenritzel 11 Zähne	Spiral pinion 11 teeth	Pignon hélicoïdal 11 dents							1				
9	0246 047 000	Scheibe 6 x 9 x 1	Washer 6 x 9 x 1	Rondelle 6 x 9 x 1	1	1	1	1	1		1	1	1	1	1
10	0232 151 000	Buchse	Bush	Douille	1	1	1	1	1		1	1	1	1	1
11	0241 049 100	Anschlußschraube M 12 x 1	Connecting screw M 12 x 1	Vis de raccordement M 12 x 1	1	1	1	1	1		1	1	1	1	1
	0260 041 000	Gummikappe	Rubber cap	Capuchon en caoutchouc	1	1	1	1	1		1	1	1	1	1
	0240 095 105	Verschlußschraube M 12 x 1 (für Ausf. ohne Tacho-Antrieb)	Screw plug M 12 x 1 (for type without speedometer drive)	Vis de fermeture M 12 x 1 (pour version sans entrainement de compteur)	1	1	1	1	1		1	1	1	1	1
12	0940 119 102	Zylinderschraube M 6 x 60	Fillister head screw M 6 x 60	Vis à tête cylindrique M 6 x 60	4	4	4	4	4		4	4	4	4	4

Deckel-Kupplungsseite, Kupplung, Vorgelegewelle
Clutch side crankcase cover, Clutch, Layshaft
Couvercle côté embrayage, Embrayage, Arbre secondaire

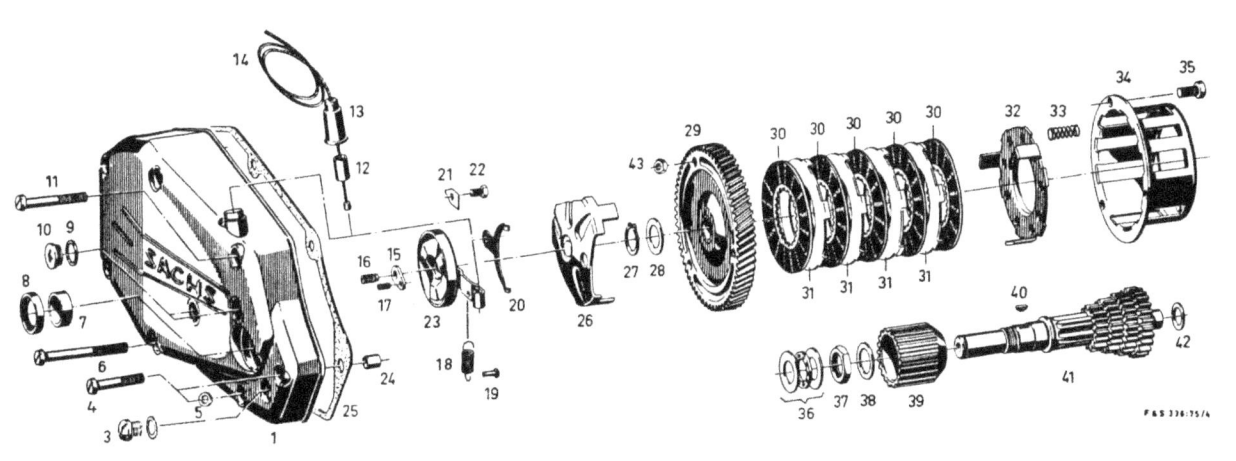

Bild-Nr. Ill. No.	Bestell-Nr. Part-No. Réf. No.	Benennung	Description	Désignation	1001/5 A	1001/6 A	1001/6 B	1001/6 C	1251/5 A	1251/5 AL	1251/6 A	1251/6 B	1251/6 C	1251/6 D
1	0611 114 100	Deckel-Kupplungsseite (SACHS) bis Motor-Nr. 6318 754 in Verbindung mit Bild 33, 34 und 0684 003 000	Cover – clutch side (SACHS) up to engine-No. 6318 754 to be used together with Ill. 33, 34 and 0684 003 000	Couvercle côté embrayage (SACHS) jusqu'à liaison avec No. 6318 754 en liaison avec ill. 33, 34 et 0684 003 000	1	1	1	1	1	1	1	1	1	1
	0677 001 100	Zsb. Deckel-Kupplungsseite (SACHS) besteht aus: Bild 1, 5, 7...10, 12...23	Cover ass'y. – clutch side (SACHS) consisting of: Ill. 1, 5, 7...10, 12...23	Couvercle côté embrayage cpl. (SACHS) comprenant: ill. 1, 5, 7...10, 12...23	1	1	1	1	1	1	1	1	1	1
	0611 114 104	Deckel-Kupplungsseite (DKW)	Cover – clutch side (DKW)	Couvercle côté embrayage (DKW)	1		1		1			1		
	0677 001 102	Zsb. Deckel-Kupplungsseite (DKW)	Cover ass'y. – clutch side (DKW)	Couvercle côté embrayage cpl. (DKW)	1		1		1			1		
2	0230 015 000	Dichtring 10 x 14 x 1,5	Sealing ring 10 x 14 x 1.5	Anneau d'étanchéité 10 x 14 x 1,5	1	1	1	1	1	1	1	1	1	1
3	0241 053 100	Linsenschraube M 10 x 10	Oval head screw M 10 x 10	Vis à tête ovale M 10 x 10	1	1	1	1	1	1	1	1	1	1
4	0241 040 001	Zylinderschraube M 6 x 38	Fillister head screw M 6 x 38	Vis à tête cylindrique M 6 x 38	2	2	2	2	2	2	2	2	2	2
5	0250 112 100	Dichtring 6,5 x 11 x 1	Sealing ring 6.5 x 11 x 1	Anneau d'étanchéité 6,5 x 11 x 1	1	1	1	1	1	1	1	1	1	1
6	0640 011 102	Zylinderschraube M 6 x 65	Fillister head screw M 6 x 65	Vis à tête cylindrique M 6 x 65	4	4	4	4	4	4	4	4	4	4
7	0232 131 000	Buchse 20 x 24 x 9	Bush 20 x 24 x 9	Douille 20 x 24 x 9	1	1	1	1	1	1	1	1	1	1
8	0250 128 000	Wellendichtring 19 x 28 x 4	Oil sealing ring 19 x 28 x 4	Joint de retenu d'huile 19 x 28 x 4	1	1	1	1	1	1	1	1	1	1
9	0250 131 000	Dichtring 14,1 x 17,2 x 0,5	Sealing ring 14.1 x 17.2 x 0.5	Anneau d'étanchéité 14,1 x 17,2 x 0,5	2	2	2	2	2	2	2	2	2	2
10	●0240 140 107	Verschlußschraube M 14 x 1	Screw plug M 14 x 1	Vis de fermeture M 14 x 1	2	2	2	2	2	2	2	2	2	2
11	0240 120 002	Zylinderschraube M 6 x 52	Fillister head screw M 6 x 52	Vis à tête cylindrique M 6 x 52	1	1	1	1	1	1	1	1	1	1
12	0299 141 000	Abstütznippel 14,5 x 15	Support nipple 14.5 x 15	Nipple de support 14,5 x 15	1	1	1	1	1	1	1	1	1	1
13	0260 125 000	Schutzkappe	Protective cap	Capuchon protecteur	1	1	1	1	1	1	1	1	1	1
14	0291 007 000	Seil mit Lötnippel	Wire with solder nipple	Câble avec embout soudé	1	1	1	1	1	1	1	1	1	1
15	0251 107 001	Sicherungslasche	Locking strap	Eclisse de sûreté	1	1	1	1	1	1	1	1	1	1
16	0640 107 100	Stellschraube M 8 x 1 x 13,5	Adjusting screw M 8 x 1 x 13.5	Vis de réglage M 8 x 1 x 13,5	1	1	1	1	1	1	1	1	1	1
17	0240 139 000	Gewindestift M 4 x 6	Grub screw M 4 x 6	Goupille filetée M 4 x 6	1	1	1	1	1	1	1	1	1	1
18	0239 123 000	Zugfeder	Tension spring	Ressort de traction	1	1	1	1	1	1	1	1	1	1
19	0949 003 002	Halbrundkerbnagel 3 x 8	Half-round grooved pin 3 x 8	Clou cannelé demi-rond 3 x 8	1	1	1	1	1	1	1	1	1	1
20	0239 126 000	Gabelfeder	Fork spring	Ressort à fourche	1	1	1	1	1	1	1	1	1	1
21	0245 112 000	Sicherungsblech	Locking plate	Tôle de sûreté	1	1	1	1	1	1	1	1	1	1
22	0941 087 000	Sechskantschraube M 5 x 10	Hexagon head screw M 5 x 10	Vis à six pans M 5 x 10	1	1	1	1	1	1	1	1	1	1
23	0286 324 201	Kurvennapf mit Gewinde M 8 x 1 bis Motor-Nr. 6318 754 nur in Verbindung mit Bild 15 (Kurvenhöhe 8,5 mm)	Cam cup with thread M 8 x 1 up to engine-No. 6318 754 only to be used together with Ill. 15 (Cam height 8.5 mm)	Ecuelle à bossages avec filetage M 8 x 1 jusqu'à moteur No. 6318 754 uniquement en liaison avec ill. 15 (hauteur de courbe 8,5 mm)	1		1		1			1		
	0684 003 000	Kurvennapf mit Gewinde M 8 x 1 ab Motor-Nr. 6318 755 (Kurvenhöhe 10 mm)	Cam cup with thread M 8 x 1 from engine-No. 6318 755 (Cam height 10 mm)	Ecuelle à bossages avec filetage M 8 x 1 à partir de moteur No. 6318 755 (hauteur de courbe 10 mm)	1	1	1	1	1	1	1	1	1	1
24	0949 090 000	Paßhülse 8,5 x 10	Dowel sleeve 8.5 x 10	Douille d'ajustage 8,5 x 10	2	2	2	2	2	2	2	2	2	2
25	0650 106 000	Dichtung	Gasket	Joint	1	1	1	1	1	1	1	1	1	1
26	0684 002 000	Druckteller	Thrust plate	Plateau de pression	1	1	1	1	1	1	1	1	1	1
27	0245 020 005	Sicherungsring	Circlip	Anneau de sûreté	1	1	1	1	1	1	1	1	1	1
28	0246 015 000	Scheibe 16,3 x 25,8, Seite 27	Shim 16.3 x 25.8, page 27	Rondelle 16,3 x 25,8, Page 27	x	x	x	x	x	x	x	x	x	x
29	0685 100 101	Vorgelegerad mit Buchse 0632 113 100	Layshaft wheel with bush 0632 113 100	Roue secondaire avec douille 0632 113 100	1	1	1	1	1	1	1	1	1	1
30	0284 007 000	Innenlamelle	Inner plate	Lame intérieure	5	5	5	5	5	5	5	5	5	5
31	0259 109 000	Außenlamelle	Outer plate	Lame extérieure	4	4	4	4	4	4	4	4	4	4
32	0658 003 000	Drucklamelle	Thrust plate	Lame de pression	1	1	1	1	1	1	1	1	1	1
33	0639 106 000	Druckfeder	Pressure spring	Ressort de pression	9	9	9	9	9	9	9	9	9	9
34	0658 002 100	Kupplungskorb	Clutch case	Cage d'embrayage	1	1	1	1	1	1	1	1	1	1
	0684 001 200	Zsb. Kupplung besteht aus: Bild 29...35 und 43	Clutch ass'y., consisting of: Ill. 29...35 and 43	Embrayage cpl. comprenant: ill. 29...35 et 43	1	1	1	1	1	1	1	1	1	1
35	2740 024 000	Innensechskantschraube M 6 x 16	Hexagon socket head screw M 6 x 16	Ecrou à tête à six pans M 6 x 16	3	3	3	3	3	3	3	3	3	3
36	0686 209 000	Kugelhalter mit 2 Scheiben	Ball cage with 2 washers	Retenue de billes avec 2 rondelles	1	1	1	1	1	1	1	1	1	1
37	0242 106 005	Sechskantmutter M 18 x 1	Hexagon nut M 18 x 1	Ecrou à six pans M 18 x 1	1	1	1	1	1	1	1	1	1	1
38	0644 106 000	Scheibe 18,3 x 27 x 2	Washer 18.3 x 27 x 2	Rondelle 18,3 x 27 x 2	1	1	1	1	1	1	1	1	1	1
39	0658 001 000	Kupplungsnabe	Clutch hub	Moyeu d'embrayage	1	1	1	1	1	1	1	1	1	1
40	0246 005 000	Scheibenfeder 3 x 3,7	Woodrift key 3 x 3.7	Cavette 3 x 3,7	1	1	1	1	1	1	1	1	1	1
41	0685 101 100	Vorgelegewelle	Layshaft	Arbre secondaire	1				1					
	0685 101 001	Vorgelegewelle	Layshaft	Arbre secondaire		1	1	1		1		1	1	1
	0685 101 102	Vorgelegewelle	Layshaft	Arbre secondaire							1			
42	0244 102 000	Scheibe 12,1 x 18,5, Seite 27	Shim 12.1 x 18.5, page 27	Rondelle 12,1 x 18,5, Page 27	x	x	x	x	x	x	x	x	x	x
43	●0316 057 003	Sechskantmutter M 6	Hexagon nut M 6	Ecrou à six pans M 6	3	3	3	3	3	3	3	3	3	3

x = nach Bedarf   x = as required   x = suivant besoin

Vergaser 1/24/..., 1/26/..., 1/27/..., Ansauggeräuschdämpfer
Carburettor 1/24/..., 1/26/..., 1/27/..., Intake silencer
Carburateur 1/24/..., 1/26/..., 1/27/..., Silencieux d'aspiration

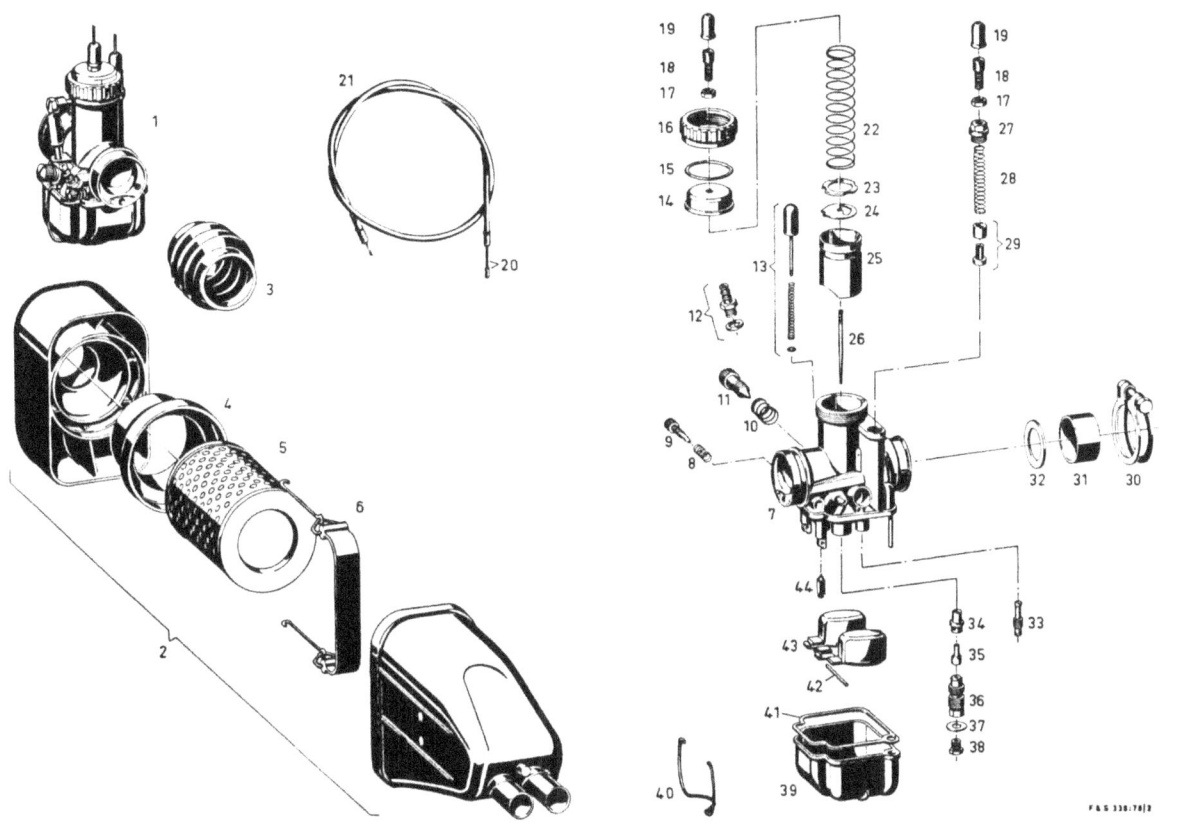

Bild-Nr. Ill. No.	Bestell-Nr. Part-No. Réf. No.	Benennung	Description	Désignation	1001/5 A	1001/6 A	1001/6 B	1001/6 C	1251/5 A	1251/5 AL	1251/5 B	1251/6 A	1251/6 B	1251/6 C	1251/6 D
1		**Zsb.** Vergaser, Seite 25	Carburettor ass'y., page 25	Carburateur cpl., Page 25											
2	0282 100 207	Zsb. Ansauggeräuschdämpfer ohne Bild 4 und 6 jedoch Micronicfilter mit Feder	Intake silencer ass'y. without ill. 4 and 6, however Micronic filter with spring	Silencieux d'aspiration cpl. sans ill. 4 et 6, mais filtre Micronic avec ressort						1					
3	0667 103 000	Faltenbalg	Bellows	Soufflet	1	1	1	1	1	1	1	1	1	1	1
4	0247 123 000	Zwischenring nur für Ersatz bei Ausf. Micronicfilter ohne Feder	Intermediate ring only for replacement when Micronic filter without spring	Anneau de raccord uniquement pour rechange en cas de version filtre Micronic sans ressort						1					
5	●0225 002 100	Micronicfilter mit Feder	Micronic filter with spring	Filtre Micronic avec ressort						1					
6	0263 007 000	Filterbandage nur für Ersatz bei Ausf. Micronicfilter ohne Feder	Filter bandage only for replacement when Micronic filter without spring	Bandage filtrant uniquement pour rechange en cas de version filtre Micronic sans ressort						1					
7		Vergasergehäuse nur unter Zsb. Vergaser lieferbar	Carburettor body only available under carburettor ass'y.	Corps de carburateur uniquement livrable sous carburateur cpl.											
8	0961 067 000	Feder	Spring	Ressort	1	1	1	1	1	1	1	1	1	1	1
9	0640 105 000	Luftregulierschraube	Air adjusting screw	Vis de réglage d'air	1	1	1	1	1	1	1	1	1	1	1
10	0639 103 000	Feder	Spring	Ressort	1	1	1	1	1	1	1	1	1	1	1
11	0640 106 000	Stellschraube	Adjusting screw	Vis de réglage	1	1	1	1	1	1	1	1	1	1	1
12	0986 432 000	Schlauchtülle	Hose fitting	Raccord de tuyau	1	1	1	1	1	1	1	1	1	1	1
13	0661 110 000	Tupfer	Tickler	Titillateur	1	1	1	1	1	1	1	1	1	1	1
14	0661 119 000	Deckelplatte	Cover plate	Couvercle	1	1	1	1	1	1	1	1	1	1	1
15	0650 111 000	Dichtring	Sealing ring	Anneau d'étanchéité	1	1	1	1	1	1	1	1	1	1	1
16	0642 106 000	Deckelverschraubung	Cover, to be screwed	Couvercle à visser	1	1	1	1	1	1	1	1	1	1	1
17	0961 018 001	Sechskantmutter	Hexagon nut	Ecrou à six pans	2	2	2	2	2	2	2	2	2	2	2
18	0961 081 000	Stellschraube	Adjusting screw	Vis de réglage	2	2	2	2	2	2	2	2	2	2	2
19	0260 024 001	Gummikappe	Rubber cap	Capuchon en caoutchouc	2	2	2	2	2	2	2	2	2	2	
19	0260 130 000	Gummikappe	Rubber cap	Capuchon en caoutchouc											2

Bild-Nr. III. No.	Bestell-Nr. Part-No. Réf. No.	Benennung	Description	Désignation	1001/5 A	1001/6 A	1001/6 B	1001/6 C	1251/5 A	1251/5 AL	1251/5 B	1251/6 A	1251/6 B	1251/6 C	1251/6 D
20	0291 004 000	Seil mit Lötnippel Nr. 0291 003 000 für Start- u. Gaszug (Länge angeben)	Wire with solder nipple No. 0291 003 000 for starter and throttle control (quote length)	Câble avec embout soudé No. 0291 003 000 pour tirant de démarreur et d'accélérateur (indiquer la longueur)	2	2	2	2	2	2	2	2	2	2	
21	0291 024 001	Seilhülle, schwarz	Outer casing, black	Gaine de câble noir	2	2	2	2	2		2	2	2	2	2
	0291 024 011	Seilhülle, silberfarbig	Outer casing, silver colour	Gaine de câble couleur argentée	2	2	2	2	2		2	2	2	2	2
22	0639 105 000	Feder	Spring	Ressort	1	1	1	1	1	1	1	1	1	1	
23	0644 111 000	Scheibe	Washer	Rondelle	1	1	1	1	1	1	1	1	1	1	
24	0661 113 000	Halteplättchen	Retaining plate	Plaquette d'arrêt	1	1			1	1	1	1			
	0639 107 000	Klemmfeder für Vergaser 1/24/170, 1/27/19, 20, 21, 22, 23, 25	Clamping spring for carburettor 1/24/170, 1/27/19, 20, 21, 22, 23, 25	Ressort à serrage pour carburateur 1/24/170, 1/27/19, 20, 21, 22, 23, 25			1	1			1		1	1	
25	0661 120 000	Gasschieber für Vergaser 1/24/153, 158, 161, 166, 1/26/115, 117, 120, 127, 1/27/16, 17	Throttle slide for carburettor 1/24/153, 158, 161, 166, 1/26/115, 117, 120, 127, 1/27/16, 17	Boisseau des gaz pour carburateur 1/24/153, 158, 161, 166, 1/26/115, 117, 120, 127, 1/27/16, 17	1	1			1	1	1				
	0661 120 001	Gasschieber für Vergaser 1/24/170, 1/27/19, 20, 21, 22, 23, 25	Throttle slide for carburettor 1/24/170, 1/27/19, 20, 21, 22, 23, 25	Boisseau des gaz pour carburateur 1/24/170, 1/27/19, 20, 21, 22, 23, 25			1	1			1		1	1	
26	0661 114 000	Düsennadel für Vergaser 1/24/153, 158, 161, 166, 1/26/115, 117, 120, 127, 1/27/16, 17	Jet needle for carburettor 1/24/153, 158, 161, 166, 1/26/115, 117, 120, 127, 1/27/16, 17	Aiguille de gicleur pour carburateur 1/24/153, 158, 161, 166, 1/26/115, 117, 120, 127, 1/27/16, 17	1	1			1	1	1				
	0661 114 001	Düsennadel für Vergaser 1/24/170	Jet needle for carburettor 1/24/170	Aiguille de gicleur pour carburateur 1/24/170						1					
	0661 114 002	Düsennadel für Vergaser 1/27/19, 20, 21, 22, 23, 25	Jet needle for carburettor 1/27/19, 20, 21, 22, 23, 25	Aiguille de gicleur pour carburateur 1/27/19, 20, 21, 22, 23, 25			1	1					1	1	
27	0661 007 000	Verschlußschraube	Screw plug	Vis de fermeture	1	1	1	1	1	1	1	1	1	1	
28	0661 005 000	Feder	Spring	Ressort	1	1	1	1	1	1	1	1	1	1	
29	0686 100 000	Startkolben mit Hülse	Starter slide with sleeve	Piston de lanceur avec douille	1	1	1	1	1	1	1	1	1	1	
30	0651 102 000	Klemmring	Clamping ring	Bague de serrage	1	1			1	1	1				
31	0647 102 000	Isolierbuchse für Vergaser 1/24/153, 158, 161, 166, 170, 1/26/117, 127, 1/27/16	Insulating bush for carburettor 1/24/153, 158, 161, 166, 170, 1/26/117, 127, 1/27/16	Douille isolante pour carburateur 1/24/153, 158, 161, 166, 170, 1/26/117, 127, 1/27/16	1	1			1	1	1				
	0947 125 000	Isolierbuchse für Vergaser 1/26/115, 120, 1/27/17, 19, 20, 21, 22, 23, 25	Insulating bush for carburettor 1/26/115, 120, 1/27/17, 19, 20, 21, 22, 23, 25	Douille isolante pour carburateur 1/26/115, 120, 1/27/17, 19, 20, 21, 22, 23, 25			1	1				1	1	1	
32	0644 110 000	Isolierscheibe für Vergaser 1/24/153, 158, 161, 166, 170	Insulating washer for carburettor 1/24/153, 158, 161, 166, 170	Rondelle isolante pour carburateur 1/24/153, 158, 161, 166, 170	1	1			1	1	1				
	0644 110 001	Isolierscheibe für Vergaser 1/26/115, 117, 120, 127, 1/27/19	Insulating washer for carburettor 1/26/115, 117, 120, 127, 1/27/19	Rondelle isolante pour carburateur 1/26/115, 117, 120, 127, 1/27/19						1					
	0644 110 002	Isolierscheibe für Vergaser 1/27/16, 17, 19, 20, 21, 22, 23, 25	Insulating washer for carburettor 1/27/16, 17, 19, 20, 21, 22, 23, 25	Rondelle isolante pour carburateur 1/27/16, 17, 19, 20, 21, 22, 23, 25			1	1					1	1	
33	0661 118 000	Leerlaufdüse (Größe angeben)	Idle jet (quote required size)	Gicleur de ralenti (indiquer la grandeur)	1	1	1	1	1	1	1	1	1	1	
34	0661 115 000	Zerstäuber für Vergaser 1/24/153, 158, 161, 166, 170, 1/26/115, 117, 120, 127, 1/27/16, 17	Vaporizer for carburettor 1/24/153, 158, 161, 166, 170, 1/26/115, 117, 120, 127, 1/27/16, 17	Atomiseur pour carburateur 1/24/153, 158, 161, 166, 170, 1/26/115, 117, 120, 127, 1/27/16, 17	1	1			1	1	1				
	0661 115 001	Zerstäuber für Vergaser 1/27/19, 20, 21, 22, 23, 25	Vaporizer for carburettor 1/27/19, 20, 21, 22, 23, 25	Atomiseur pour carburateur 1/27/19, 20, 21, 22, 23, 25			1	1					1	1	
35	0661 116 000	Nadeldüse 2,73	Needle jet 2.73	Gicleur à aiguille 2,73	1	1	1	1	1	1		1	1	1	
	0661 116 001	Nadeldüse 2,76	Needle jet 2.76	Gicleur à aiguille 2,76							1				
	0661 116 002	Nadeldüse 2,70	Needle jet 2.70	Gicleur à aiguille 2,70											1
36	0661 117 000	Mischrohr	Mixing tube	Tuyau de mélange	1	1	1	1	1	1	1	1	1	1	
37	0962 083 000	Scheibe	Washer	Rondelle	1	1	1	1	1	1	1	1	1	1	
	0661 126 000	Siebhülse für Vergaser 1/27/19, 20, 21, 23, 25	Strainer for carburettor 1/27/19, 20, 21, 23, 25	Douille de filtrage pour carburateur 1/27/19, 20, 21, 23, 25			1	1					1	1	
38	0961 106 000	Hauptdüse (Größe angeben)	Main jet (quote required size)	Gicleur principal (indiquer la grandeur)	1	1	1	1	1	1	1	1	1	1	
39	0661 122 000	Schwimmergehäuse für Vergaser 1/24/153, 158, 161, 166, 170, 1/26/115, 117, 120, 127, 1/27/16, 17	Float chamber for carburettor 1/24/153, 158, 161, 166, 170, 1/26/115, 117, 120, 127, 1/27/16, 17	Carter du flotteur pour carburateur 1/24/153, 158, 161, 166, 170, 1/26/115, 117, 120, 127, 1/27/16, 17	1	1			1	1	1				
	0661 122 001	Schwimmergehäuse für Vergaser 1/27/19, 20, 21, 22, 23, 25	Float chamber for carburettor 1/27/19, 20, 21, 22, 23, 25	Carter du flotteur pour carburateur 1/27/19, 20, 21, 22, 23, 25			1	1					1	1	
	0661 122 002	Schwimmergehäuse für Vergaser 2/26/66, 67	Float chamber for carburettor 2/26/66, 67	Carter du flotteur pour carburateur 2/26/66, 67	1				1						
40	0639 104 000	Federbügel	Stirrup	Étrier de ressort	1	1	1	1	1	1	1	1	1	1	
41	0650 110 000	Dichtung	Gasket	Joint	1	1	1	1	1	1	1	1	1	1	
42	0649 103 000	Stift für Schwimmer	Pin for float	Goupille pour flotteur	1	1	1	1	1	1	1	1	1	1	
43	0661 121 000	Schwimmer	Float	Flotteur	1	1	1	1	1	1	1	1	1	1	
44	0661 112 000	Schwimmernadel	Float needle	Aiguille du flotteur	1	1	1	1	1	1	1	1	1	1	

Vergaser 2/28/...
Carburettor 2/28/...
Carburateur 2/28/...

Ansaugstutzen
Intake pipe
Pipe d'aspiration

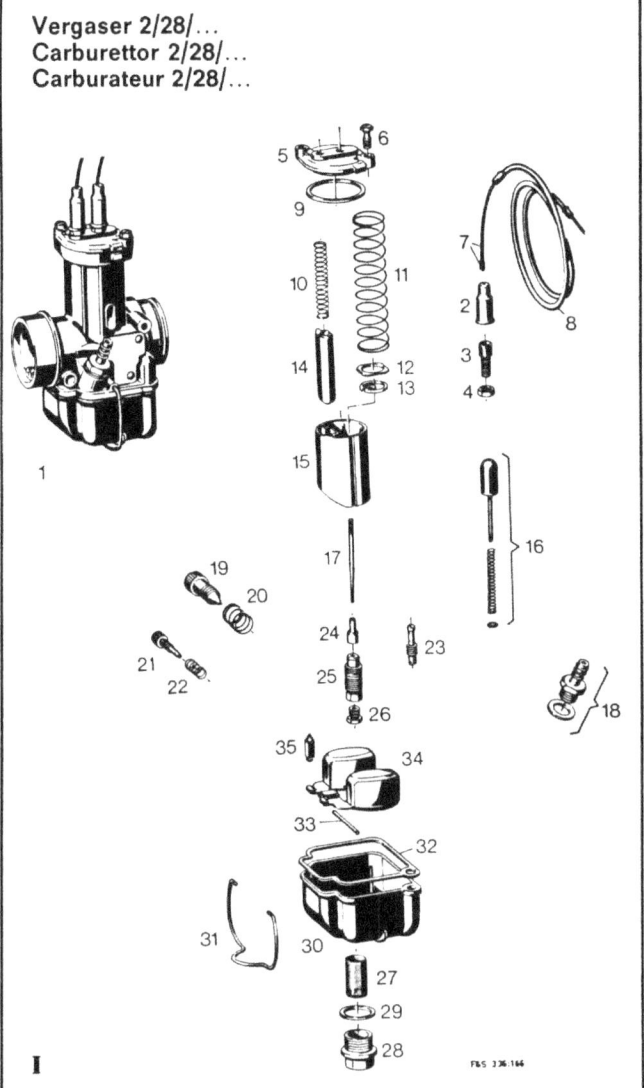

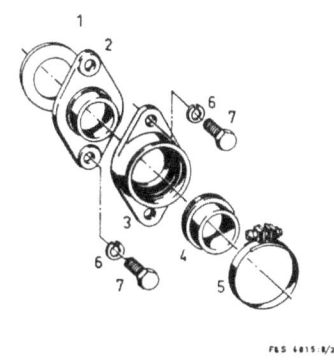

Bild-Nr. III. No.	Bestell-Nr. Part-No. Réf. No.	Benennung	Description	Désignation	1001/5 A	1001/6 A	1001/6 B	1001/6 C	1251/5 A	1251/5 AL	1251/6 A	1251/6 B	1251/6 C	1251/6 D
I														
1		Zsb. Vergaser, Seite 25	Carburettor ass'y., page 25	Carburateur cpl., Page 25										
2	0260 130 000	Gummikappe	Rubber cap	Capuchon en caoutchouc		2	2	2				2	2	2
3	0961 081 000	Stellschraube	Adjusting screw	Vis de réglage		2	2	2				2	2	2
4	0961 018 001	Sechskantmutter	Hexagon nut	Ecrou à six pans		2	2	2				2	2	2
5	●0661 131 000	Deckelplatte	Cover plate	Couvercle		1	1	1				1	1	1
6	0240 138 000	Sechskantschraube	Hexagon head screw	Vis à six pans		2	2	2				2	2	2
7	0298 090 005	Zsb. Seil mit Lötnippel Nr. 0299 002 002	Control wire ass'y. with solder nipple No. 0299 002 002	Câble cpl. avec embout soudé No. 0299 002 002		2	2	2				2	2	2
8	0291 024 001	Seilhülle, schwarz	Outer casing, black	Gaine de câble, noir		2	2	2				2	2	2
	0291 024 011	Seilhülle, silberfarbig	Outer casing, silver colour	Gaine de câble, couleur argentée		2	2	2				2	2	2
9	●0650 117 000	Dichtring	Sealing ring	Anneau d'étanchéité		1	1	1				1	1	1
10	●0639 108 000	Feder	Spring	Ressort		1	1	1				1	1	1
11	●0639 109 000	Feder	Spring	Ressort		1	1	1				1	1	1
12	●0644 118 000	Scheibe	Washer	Rondelle		1	1	1				1	1	1
13	●0661 136 000	Halteplättchen	Retaining plate	Plaquette d'arrêt		1	1	1				1	1	1
14	●0661 130 000	Luftschieber	Air slide	Boisseau d'air		1	1	1				1	1	1
15	●0661 134 000	Gasschieber	Throttle slide	Boisseau des gaz		1	1	1				1	1	1
16	0661 110 000	Zsb. Tupfer mit Feder und Splint	Tickler ass'y. with spring and split pin	Titillateur cpl. avec ressort et goupille fendue		1	1	1				1	1	1
17	●0661 135 000	Düsennadel	Jet needle	Aiguille de gicleur		1	1	1				1	1	1
18	1481 004 011	Zsb. Schlauchtülle mit Dichtring für Kraftstoffzuführung	Hose fitting ass'y. with sealing ring for fuel supply	Raccord de tuyau cpl. avec anneau d'étanchéité pour alimentation en carburant		1	1	1				1	1	1
19	0640 106 000	Stellschraube für Gasschieberstellung	Adjusting screw for throttle slide positioning	Vis de réglage pour position du boisseau des gaz		1	1	1				1	1	1
20	0639 103 000	Feder	Spring	Ressort		1	1	1				1	1	1

Bild-Nr. Ill. No.	Bestell-Nr. Part-No. Réf. No.	Benennung	Description	Désignation	1001/5 A	1001/6 A	1001/6 B	1001/6 C	1251/5 A	1251/5 AL	1251/5 B	1251/6 A	1251/6 B	1251/6 C	1251/6 D
21	0640 105 000	Luftregulierschraube	Air adjusting screw	Vis de réglage d'air		1	1	1					1	1	1
22	0961 067 000	Feder für Bild 21	Spring for ill. 21	Ressort pour ill. 21		1	1	1					1	1	1
23	0661 118 000	Leerlaufdüse	Idle jet	Gicleur de ralenti		1	1	1					1	1	1
24	●0661 129 000	Nadeldüse } Größe angeben	Needle jet } Quote required size	Gicleur à aiguille } indiquer la grandeur		1	1	1					1	1	1
25	0661 117 000	Mischrohr	Mixing tube	Tuyau de mélange		1	1	1					1	1	1
26	0961 106 000	Hauptdüse	Main jet	Gicleur principal		1	1	1					1	1	1
27	●0661 133 000	Siebhülse	Strainer bush	Douille de filtrage		1	1	1					1	1	1
28	●0640 111 002	Abschlußschraube	Terminal screw	Vis d'arrêt		1	1	1					1	1	1
29	0950 054 000	Dichtring	Sealing ring	Anneau d'étanchéité		1	1	1					1	1	1
30	●0661 132 000	Schwimmergehäuse	Float chamber	Carter du flotteur		1	1	1					1	1	1
31	0639 104 000	Federbügel	Stirrup	Etrier de ressort		1	1	1					1	1	1
32	0650 110 000	Dichtung	Gasket	Joint		1	1	1					1	1	1
33	0649 103 000	Stift für Schwimmerbefestigung	Pin for fastening float	Goupille pour fixation du flotteur		1	1	1					1	1	1
34	0661 121 000	Schwimmer	Float	Flotteur		1	1	1					1	1	1
35	0661 112 000	Schwimmernadel	Float needle	Aiguille du flotteur		1	1	1					1	1	1
II															
1	0650 116 100	Dichtring 31 x 42 x 2,6	Sealing ring 31 x 42 x 2.6	Anneau d'étanchéité 31 x 42 x 2,6		1	1	1					1	1	1
2	0667 109 000	Ansaugstutzen (starre Ausführung)	Intake pipe (rigid type)	Pipe d'aspiration (version inflexible)		1	1	1					1	1	1
3	0667 106 000	Ansaugstutzen (elastische Ausführung)	Intake pipe (elastic type)	Pipe d'aspiration (version élastique)		1	1						1	1	1
4	0667 108 000	Rohrstutzen	Pipe socket	Tubulure		1	1						1	1	1
5	0651 104 000	Schlauchschelle	Hose clip	Collier de serrage		1	1						1	1	1
6	0245 023 003	Federring für M 8	Spring ring for M 8	Anneau ressort pour M 8		2	2						2	2	2
7	0941 054 004	Sechskantschraube M 8 x 25	Hexagon head screw M 8 x 25	Vis à six pans M 8 x 25		2	2						2	2	2
	0651 104 000	Schlauchschelle } ohne Abb.	Hose clip } without illustration	Collier de serrage } sans ill.											1
	0647 104 000	Buchse	Bush	Douille											1
	0667 110 000	Schlauch	Hose	Tuyau flexible											1

Vergaser 1/18/24
Carburettor 1/18/24
Carburateur 1/18/24

1	0281 102 000	**Zsb.** Vergaser, Seite 25	Carburettor ass'y., page 25	Carburateur cpl., Page 25											
2	0651 102 000	**Zsb.** Klemmring Ø 32	Clamping ring ass'y. Ø 32	Bague de serrage cpl. Ø 32	1										
3	0250 130 000	Isolierscheibe	Insulating washer	Rondelle isolante	1										
4	0261 114 001	Isolierbuchse	Insulating bush	Douille isolante	1										
5	0667 105 000	Ansaugstutzen	Intake pipe	Pipe d'aspiration	1										
6	0651 102 000	**Zsb.** Klemmring Ø 38	Clamping ring ass'y. Ø 38	Bague de serrage cpl. Ø 38	1										

Seite / Page: 18

Vergaser 1/18/24
Carburettor 1/18/24
Carburateur 1/18/24

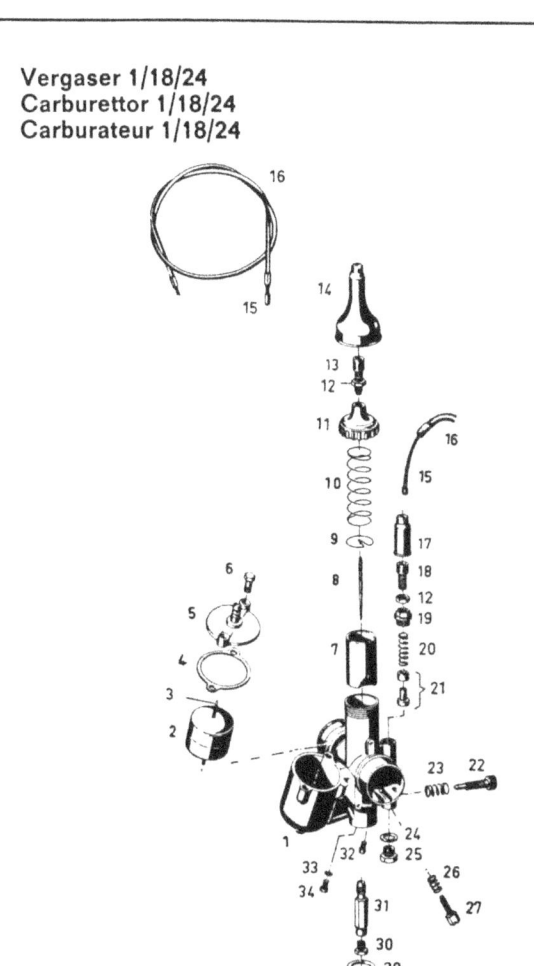

Vergaser 2/26/...
Carburettor 2/26/...
Carburateur 2/26/...

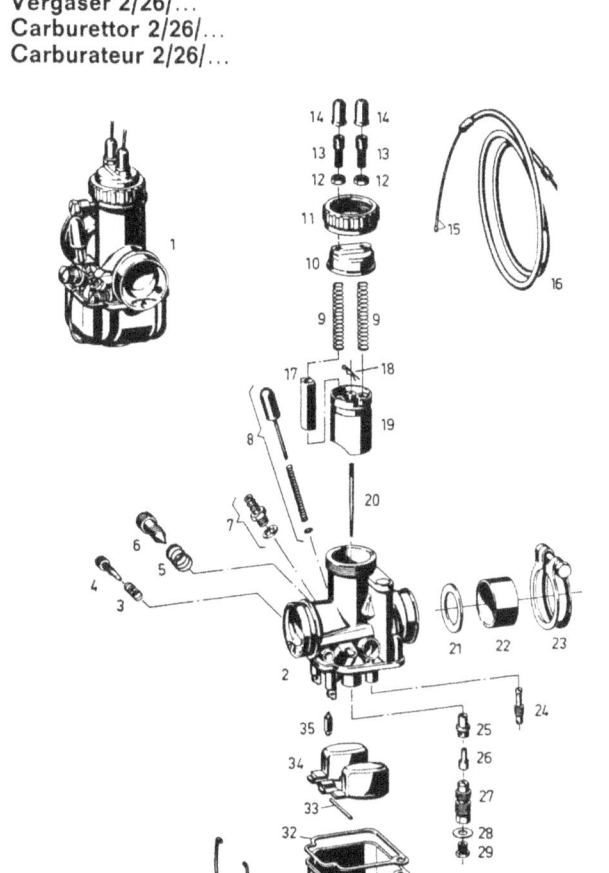

Bild-Nr. Ill. No.	Bestell-Nr. Part-No. Réf. No.	Benennung	Description	Désignation	1001/5 A	1001/6 A	1001/6 B	1001/6 C	1251/5 A	1251/5 AL	1251/5 B	1251/6 A	1251/6 B	1251/6 C	1251/6 D
I															
1		Vergasergehäuse nur unter **Zsb.** Vergaser, Seite 25, lieferbar	Carburettor body only available under carburettor ass'y., page 25	Corps du carburateur, uniquement livrable sous carburateur cpl., Page 25											
2	0261 117 000	Schwimmer	Float	Flotteur	1										
3	0261 116 000	Schwimmernadel	Float needle	Aiguille du flotteur	1										
4	0650 031 000	Dichtung	Gasket	Joint	1										
5	0261 118 000	Schwimmergehäusedeckel	Float chamber cover	Couvercle de la cuve du flotteur	1										
6	0240 138 000	Sechskantschraube	Hexagon head screw	Vis à six pans	2										
7	0261 119 001	Gasschieber	Throttle slide	Boisseau des gaz	1										
8	0968 086 001	Düsennadel	Jet needle	Aiguille du gicleur	1										
9	0261 041 000	Klemmfeder	Clamping spring	Ressort à serrage	1										
10	0261 044 000	Schieberfeder	Spring for throttle slide	Ressort de boisseau	1										
11	0261 040 000	Deckelverschraubung	Cover, to be screwed on	Couvercle à visser	1										
12	0961 018 001	Sechskantmutter M 6	Hexagon nut M 6	Ecrou à six pans M 6	2										
13	0961 081 000	Stellschraube	Adjusting screw	Vis de réglage	1										
14	0260 131 000	Gummikappe	Rubber cap	Capuchon en caoutchouc	1										
15	0291 004 000	Seil mit Lötnippel Nr. 0291 003 000	Control wire with solder nipple No. 0291 003 000 (quote required length)	Câble avec embout soudé No. 0291 003 000 (indiquer la longueur)	1										
16	0291 024 001	Seilhülle, schwarz	Outer casing, black	Gaine de câble, noir	x										
	0291 024 011	Seilhülle, silberfarbig	Outer casing, silver colour	Gaine de câble, couleur argentée	x										
17	0260 130 000	Gummikappe	Rubber cap	Capuchon en caoutchouc	1										
18	0962 071 000	Stellschraube M 6 x 19	Adjusting screw M 6 x 19	Vis de réglage M 6 x 19	1										
19	0240 135 000	Verschlußschraube	Screw plug	Vis de fermeture	1										
20	0239 127 000	Feder	Spring	Ressort	1										
21	0281 101 000	**Zsb.** Startkolben mit Hülse	Starter piston ass'y. with sleeve	Piston de lancement cpl. avec douille	1										
22	0240 134 000	Luftregulierschraube	Air adjusting screw	Vis de réglage d'air	1										
23	0961 067 000	Feder	Spring	Ressort	1										
24	0950 052 005	Dichtring	Sealing ring	Anneau d'étanchéité	1										
25	0240 136 000	Sechskantschraube	Hexagon head screw	Vis à six pans	1										
26	0962 090 000	Feder	Spring	Ressort	1										
		x = nach Bedarf	x = as required	x = suivant besoin											

Seite / Page: 19

Bild-Nr. III. No.	Bestell-Nr. Part-No. Réf. No.	Benennung	Description	Désignation	1001/5 A	1001/6 A	1001/6 B	1001/6 C	1251/5 A	1251/5 AL	1251/5 B	1251/6 A	1251/6 B	1251/6 C	1251/6 D
27	0240 137 000	Stellschraube	Adjusting screw	Vis de réglage	1										
28	0940 118 000	Abschlußschraube	Terminal screw	Vis d'arrêt	1										
29	0969 038 005	Dichtring	Sealing ring	Anneau d'étanchéité	1										
30	0961 106 000	Hauptdüse 90	Main jet 90	Gicleur principal 90	1										
31	0261 115 000	Nadeldüse 6247 A	Needle jet 6247 A	Gicleur à aiguille 6247 A	1										
32	0962 050 000	Leerlaufdüse 42	Idle jet 42	Gicleur de ralenti 42	1										
33	0250 133 000	Dichtung	Gasket	Joint	1										
34	0240 145 000	Zylinderschraube	Fillister head screw	Vis à tête cylindrique	1										
II															
1		Zsb. Vergaser, Seite 25	Carburettor ass'y., page 25	Carburateur cpl., Page 25											
2		Vergasergehäuse nur unter Zsb. Vergaser lieferbar	Carburettor body only available under carburettor ass'y.	Corps du carburateur, uniquement livrable sous carburateur cpl.											
3	0961 067 000	Feder	Spring	Ressort					1			1			
4	0640 105 000	Luftregulierschraube	Air adjusting screw	Vis de réglage d'air					1			1			
5	0639 103 000	Feder	Spring	Ressort					1			1			
6	0640 106 000	Stellschraube	Adjusting screw	Vis de réglage					1			1			
7	0986 432 000	Schlauchtülle	Hose fitting	Raccord de tuyau					1			1			
8	0661 110 000	Tupfer	Tickler	Titillateur					1			1			
9	0961 079 005	Feder	Spring	Ressort					1			1			
10	0961 074 008	Deckelplatte	Cover plate	Couvercle					1			1			
11	0961 027 005	Deckelverschraubung	Cover, to be screwed on	Couvercle à visser					1			1			
12	0961 018 001	Sechskantmutter M 6	Hexagon nut M 6	Ecrou à six pans M 6					1			1			
13	0961 081 000	Stellschraube	Adjusting screw	Vis de réglage					1			1			
14	0260 024 001	Gummikappe	Rubber cap	Capuchon en caoutchouc					1			1			
15	0291 004 000	Seil mit Lötnippel Nr. 0291 003 000 für Gaszug und Luftschieber (Länge angeben)	Cable with solder nipple No. 0291 003 000 for throttle slide and air slide (quote required length)	Câble avec embout soudé No. 0291 003 000 pour tirant d'accélérateur et boisseau des gaz (indiquer la longueur)					2			2			
16	0291 024 001	Seilhülle, schwarz	Outer casing, black	Gaine de câble, noir					2			2			
	0291 024 011	Seilhülle, silberfarbig	Outer casing, silver colour	Gaine de câble, couleur argentée					2			2			
17	0661 128 000	Luftschieber	Air slide	Boisseau d'air					1			1			
18	0961 089 000	Klemmbügel	Stirrup	Etrier de serrage					1			1			
19	0661 127 000	Gasschieber	Throttle slide	Boisseau des gaz					1			1			
20	0961 078 008	Düsennadel	Jet needle	Aiguille du gicleur					1			1			
21	0644 110 001	Isolierscheibe	Insulating washer	Rondelle isolante					1			1			
22	0647 102 000	Isolierbuchse	Insulating bush	Douille isolante					1			1			
23	0651 102 000	Klemmring	Clamping ring	Bague de serrage					1			1			
24	0661 118 000	Leerlaufdüse (Größe angeben)	Idle jet (quote required size)	Gicleur de ralenti (indiquer la grandeur)					1			1			
25	0661 115 000	Zerstäuber	Vaporizer	Atomiseur					1			1			
26	0661 116 000	Nadeldüse 2,73	Needle jet 2.73	Gicleur à aiguille 2,73					1			1			
	0661 116 001	Nadeldüse 2,76	Needle jet 2.76	Gicleur à aiguille 2,76					1			1			
27	0661 117 000	Mischrohr	Mixing tube	Tuyau de mélange					1			1			
28	0962 083 000	Scheibe	Washer	Rondelle					1			1			
29	0961 106 000	Hauptdüse (Größe angeben)	Main jet (quote required size)	Gicleur principal (indiquer la grandeur)					1			1			
30	0661 122 002	Schwimmergehäuse	Float chamber	Carter du flotteur					1			1			
31	0639 104 000	Federbügel	Stirrup	Etrier de ressort					1			1			
32	0650 110 000	Dichtung	Gasket	Joint					1			1			
33	0649 103 000	Stift für Schwimmer	Pin for float	Goupille pour flotteur					1			1			
34	0661 121 000	Schwimmer	Float	Flotteur					1			1			
35	0661 112 000	Schwimmernadel	Float needle	Aiguille du flotteur					1			1			

Seite / Page: 20

Lüfterhaube, Lüfter
Fan housing, Fan
Capot de ventilateur, Ventilateur

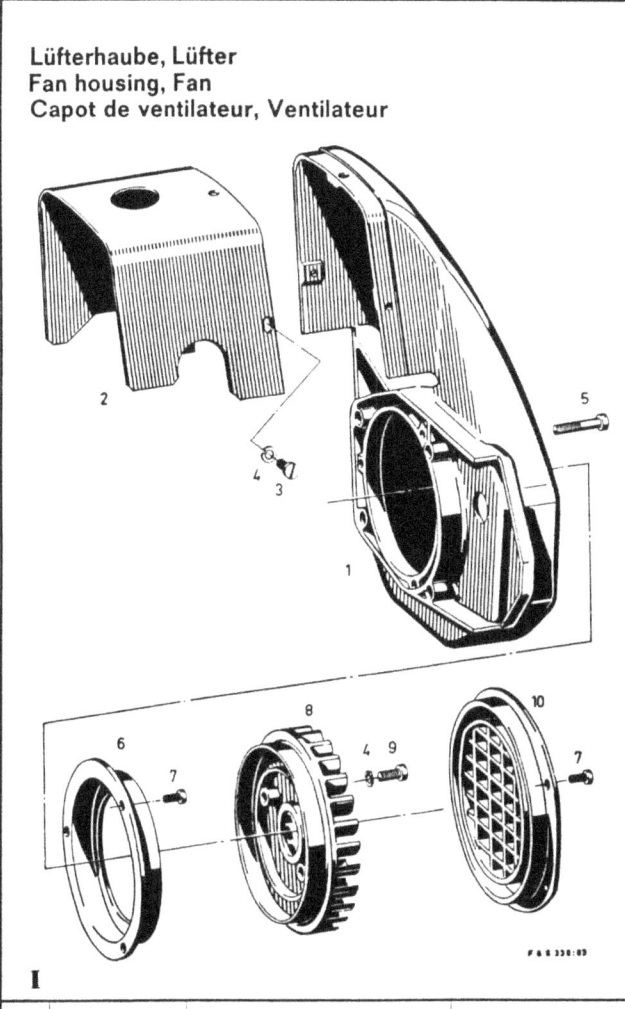

Auspufftopf
Muffler
Pot d'échappement

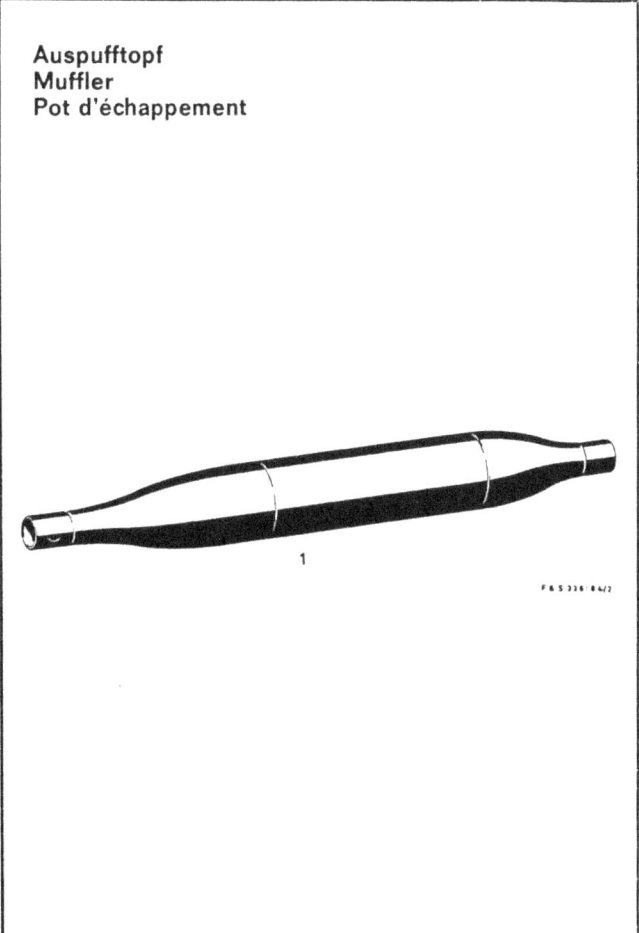

Bild-Nr. III. No.	Bestell-Nr. Part-No. Réf. No.	Benennung	Description	Désignation	1001/5 A	1001/6 A	1001/6 B	1001/6 C	1251/5 A	1251/5 AL	1251/5 B	1251/6 A	1251/6 B	1251/6 C	1251/6 D
I															
1	0611 115 000	Lüfterhaube	Fan housing	Capot de ventilateur						1					
2	0644 113 000	Leitkappe	Deflector cap	Coiffe rejet d'air						1					
3	0941 057 001	Zylinderschraube M 6 x 10	Fillister head screw M 6 x 10	Vis à tête cylindrique M 6 x 10						3					
4	0245 023 002	Federring für M 6	Spring ring M 6	Anneau ressort pour M 6						3					
5	0940 091 100	Zylinderschraube M 6 x 35	Fillister head screw M 6 x 35	Vis à tête cylindrique M 6 x 35						4					
6	0611 116 000	Abdeckung	Cover	Recouvrement						1					
7	0240 056 003	Zylinderschraube M 5 x 15	Fillister head screw M 5 x 15	Vis à tête cylindrique M 5 x 15						4					
8	0666 001 000	Lüfter	Fan	Ventilateur						1					
9	0940 008 003	Zylinderschraube	Fillister head screw	Vis à tête cylindrique						2					
10	0611 117 000	Deckel	Cover	Couvercle						1					
II															
1	0673 006 102	Auspufftopf Ø 90, Länge 861 mm, verchromt	Muffler Ø 90, Length 861 mm, chromium plated	Pot d'échappement Ø 90, longueur 861 mm, chromé	1	1			1	1			1	1	

Zylinderkopf, Zylinder
Cylinder head, Cylinder
Culasse, Cylindre

Bestell-Nr./Bemerkung	Part No./Remarks	Réf. No./Remarque	1001/5 A	1001/6 A	1001/6 B	1001/6 C	1251/5 A	1251/5 AL	1251/5 B	1251/6 A	1251/6 B	1251/6 C	1251/6 D
0613 109 000 Zylinderkopf	0613 109 000 Cylinder head	0613 109 000 Culasse	1										
0687 109 000 Zsb. Zylinder (Grauguß) Bohrung Ø 48 mit Stiftschrauben M 8 x 30	0687 109 000 Cylinder ass'y.(grey cast iron) Bore Ø 48 with studs M 8 x 30	0687 109 000 Cylindre cpl. (fonte grise) alésage Ø 48 avec goujons filetés M 8 x 30	1										
0613 106 000 Zylinderkopf	0613 106 000 Cylinder head	0613 106 000 Culasse					1						
0687 108 000 Zsb. Zylinder (Grauguß) Bohrung Ø 54 mit Stiftschrauben M 8 x 30	0687 108 000 Cylinder ass'y.(grey cast iron) Bore Ø 54 with studs M 8 x 30	0687 108 000 Cylindre cpl. (fonte grise) alésage Ø 54 avec goujons filetés M 8 x 30					1						
0613 106 005 Zylinderkopf	0613 106 005 Cylinder head	0613 106 005 Culasse							1				
0687 108 020 Zsb. Zylinder (Grauguß) Bohrung Ø 54 mit Stiftschrauben M 8 x 30	0687 108 020 Cylinder ass'y.(grey cast iron) Bore Ø 54 with studs M 8 x 30	0687 108 020 Cylindre cpl. (fonte grise) alésage Ø 54 avec goujons filetés M 8 x 30							1				
0613 109 002 Zylinderkopf	0613 109 002 Cylinder head	0613 109 002 Culasse	1										
0687 109 000 Zsb. Zylinder (Grauguß) Bohrung Ø 48 mit Stiftschrauben M 8 x 30 Ausf.: CROSS-COUNTRY	0687 109 000 Cylinder ass'y.(grey cast iron) Bore Ø 48 with studs M 8 x 30 Type: CROSS-COUNTRY	0687 109 000 Cylindre cpl. (fonte grise) alésage Ø 48 avec goujons filetés M 8 x 30 version: CROSS-COUNTRY	1										
0613 106 102 Zylinderkopf	0613 106 102 Cylinder head	0613 106 102 Culasse					1						
0687 108 000 Zsb. Zylinder (Grauguß) Bohrung Ø 54 mit Stiftschrauben M 8 x 30 Ausf.: CROSS-COUNTRY	0687 108 000 Cylinder ass'y.(grey cast iron) Bore Ø 54 with studs M 8 x 30 Type: CROSS-COUNTRY	0687 108 000 Cylindre cpl. (aluminium) alésage Ø 54 avec goujons filetés M 8 x 30 version: CROSS-COUNTRY					1						
0613 106 102 Zylinderkopf	0613 106 102 Cylinder head	0613 106 102 Culasse								1			
0687 108 035 Zsb. Zylinder (Alu) Bohrung Ø 54 mit Stiftschrauben M 8 x 30 und M 8 x 38	0687 108 035 Cylinder ass'y. (aluminium) Bore Ø 54 with studs M 8 x 30 and M 8 x 38	0687 108 035 Cylindre cpl. (aluminium) alésage Ø 54 avec goujons filetés M 8 x 30 et M 8 x 38								1			
0613 109 004 Zylinderkopf	0613 109 004 Cylinder head	0613 109 004 Culasse		1	1								
● 0687 109 130 Zsb. Zylinder (Alu) Bohrung Ø 48 mit Stiftschrauben M 8 x 30 Ausführung: USA 3 Rippen gekürzt und 18 Dämpfungsgummi Nr. 0960 000 100	0687 109 130 Cylinder ass'y. (aluminium) Bore Ø 48 with studs M 8 x 30 Type: USA, 3 fins shortened and 18 damping rubber No. 0960 000 100	0687 109 130 Cylindre cpl. (aluminium) alésage Ø 48 avec goujons filetés M 8 x 30 version: États-Unis 3 ailettes réduites et 18 caoutchoucs d'amortissement No. 0960 000 100		1	1								

Seite / Page: 22

	Bestell-Nr./Bemerkung	Part No./Remarks	Réf. No./Remarque	1001/5 A	1001/6 A	1001/6 B	1001/6 C	1251/5 A	1251/5 AL	1251/5 B	1251/6 A	1251/6 B	1251/6 C	1251/6 D
314	*0613 106 004 Zylinderkopf	*0613 106 004 Cylinder head	*0613 106 004 Culasse					1				1	1	
	0687 108 225 **Zsb.** Zylinder (Alu) Bohrung Ø 54 mit Stiftschrauben M 8 x 30 Ausführung: KTM u. Export	0687 108 225 Cylinder ass'y. (aluminium) Bore Ø 54 with studs M 8 x 30 Type: KTM and export	0687 108 225 Cylindre cpl. (aluminium) alésage Ø 54 avec goujons filetés M 8 x 30 version: KTM et Export					1				1	1	
	0613 106 004 Zylinderkopf	0613 106 004 Cylinder head	0613 106 004 Culasse					1			1	1	1	
	0687 108 227 **Zsb.** Zylinder (Alu) Bohrung Ø 54 mit Stiftschrauben M 8 x 30 Ausführung: Inland, mit 24 Dämpfergummi Nr. 0960 000 100 Ø 16,5 x 12	0687 108 227 Cylinder ass'y. (aluminium) Bore Ø 54 with studs M 8 x 30 Type: Inland, with 24 damping rubber No. 0960 000 100 Ø 16.5 x 12	0687 108 227 Cylindre cpl. (aluminium) alésage Ø 54 avec goujons filetés M 8 x 30 version: République Fédérale Allemande, avec 24 caoutchoucs d'amortissement No. 0960 000 100 Ø 16,5 x 12					1			1	1	1	
574	0613 109 004 Zylinderkopf Kennzeichen: roter Farbpunkt	0613 109 004 Cylinder head Mark: red colour dot up	0613 109 004 Culasse Repère: Point de couleur rouge	1	1	1	1							
	• 0687 109 215 +**Zsb.** Zylinder (Alu) Bohrung Ø 48 mit Stiftschrauben M 8 x 30 Ausführung: Export	• 0687 109 215 +Cylinder ass'y. (aluminium) Bore Ø 48 with studs M 8 x 30 Type: Export	• 0687 109 215 +Cylindre cpl. (aluminium) alésage Ø 48 avec goujons filetés M 8 x 30 version: Export	1	1	1	1							
	0613 106 004 Zylinderkopf	0613 106 004 Cylinder head	0613 106 004 Culasse					1				1	1	1
	• 0687 108 425 +**Zsb.** Zylinder (Alu) Bohrung Ø 54 mit Stiftschrauben M 8 x 30 Ausführung: Export	• 0687 108 425 +Cylinder ass'y. (aluminium) Bore Ø 54 with studs M 8 x 30 Type: Export	• 0687 108 425 +Cylindre cpl. (aluminium) alésage Ø 54 avec goujons filetés M 8 x 30 version: Export					1				1	1	1
	* anstelle dieses Zylinder- kopfes kann auch der Zylinderkopf Nr. 0613 106 006 mit einseitig kürzeren Rippen montiert werden.	* instead of this cylinder head, for this application can also be fitted the cylinder head 0613 106 006 with shorter fins on one side.	* au lieu de cette culasse, il est aussi possible de monter la culasse avec ailettes réduites d'un côté No. 0613 106 006											

	Bestell-Nr./Bemerkung	Part No./Remarks	Réf. No./Remarque	1001/5 A	1001/6 A	1001/6 B	1001/6 C	1251/5 A	1251/5 AL	1251/5 B	1251/6 A	1251/6 B	1251/6 C	1251/6 D
574	0613 106 004 Zylinderkopf ● 0687 108 431 +Zsb. Zylinder (Alu) Bohrung Ø 54 mit Stiftschrauben M 8 x 30 Ausführung: Inland, mit 20 Dämpfergummi Nr. 0663 005 100 Ø 16,5 x 13	0613 106 004 Cylinder head up to engine-No. ● 0687 108 431 +Cylinder ass'y. (aluminium) Bore Ø 54 with studs M 8 x 30 Type: Inland, with 20 damping rubber No. 0663 005 100 Ø 16.5 x 13	0613 106 004 Culasse jusqu'à moteur No. ● 0687 108 431 +Cylindre cpl. (aluminium) alésage Ø 54 avec goujons filetés M 8 x 30 version: République Fédérale Allemande, avec 20 caoutchoucs d'amortissement No. 0663 005 100 Ø 16,5 x 13					1 1				1 1	1 1	
575	0613 106 004 Zylinderkopf ● 0687 108 456 +Zsb. Zylinder (Alu) Bohrung Ø 54 mit Stiftschrauben M 8 x 30 Ausführung: USA, 3 Rippen gekürzt und 14 Dämpfergummi Nr. 0663 005 100 Ø 16,5 x 13	0613 106 004 Cylinder head ● 0687 108 456 +Cylinder ass'y. (aluminium) Bore Ø 54 with studs M 8 x 30 Type: USA, 3 fins shortened and 14 damping rubber No. 0663 005 100 Ø 16.5 x 13	0613 106 004 Culasse ● 0687 108 456 +Cylindre cpl. (aluminium) alésage Ø 54 avec goujons filetés M 8 x 30 version: États-Unis 3 ailettes réduites et 14 caoutchoucs d'amortissement No. 0663 005 100 Ø 16,5 x 13									1 1		
440	0613 109 004 Zylinderkopf Kennzeichen: roter Farbpunkt ● 0687 109 230 +Zsb. Zylinder (Alu) Bohrung Ø 48 mit Stiftschrauben M 8 x 30 Ausführung: USA, 3 Rippen gekürzt und 14 Dämpfergummi Nr. 0663 005 100 Ø 16,5 x 13	0613 109 004 Cylinder head Mark: red colour dot up to engine-No. ● 0687 109 230 +Cylinder ass'y. (aluminium) Bore Ø 48 with studs M 8 x 30 Type: USA, 3 fins shortened and 14 damping rubber No. 0663 005 100 Ø 16.5 x 13	0613 109 004 Culasse Repère: Point de couleur rouge jusqu'à moteur No. ● 0687 109 230 +Cylindre cpl. (aluminium) alésage Ø 48 avec goujons filetés M 8 x 30 version: États-Unis, 3 ailettes réduites et 14 caoutchoucs d'amortissement No. 0663 005 100 Ø 16,5 x 13					1 1	1 1					
	+ in Verbindung mit: 1 x 0650 116 000 Dichtung 1 x 0667 109 000 Ansaug- stutzen 2 x 0245 023 003 Federring 2 x 0941 054 004 Sechskant- schraube M 8 x 25	+ in connection with: 1 x 0650 116 000 gasket 1 x 0667 109 000 intake pipe 2 x 0245 023 003 spring ring 2 x 0941 054 004 hexagon head screw M 8 x 25	+ en liaison avec: 1 x 0650 116 000 joint 1 x 0667 109 000 pipe d'aspiration 2 x 0245 023 003 anneau ressort 2 x 0941 054 004 vis à six pans M 8 x 25											

Vergasertabelle / Table of carburettors / Tableau des carburateurs

Bestell-Nr. / Part-No. / Réf. No.	BING-Nr. / BING no. / BING-No.	Hauptdüse / Main jet / Gicleur principal	Nadeldüse / Needle jet / Gicleur à aiguille	Nadelposition / Needle position / Position de l'aiguille	Leerlaufdüse / Idle jet / Gicleur de ralenti	Leerlaufluftschraube Öffnung in Umdr. / Idle air adjustment screw ... turns open / Nombre des tours de l'ouverture de la vis de réglage d'air de ralenti	Schiebervergaser / Slide carburettor / Carburateur à boisseau	1001/5 A	1001/6 A	1001/6 B	1001/6 C	1251/5 A	1251/5 Al	1251/5 B	1251/6 A	1251/6 B	1251/6 C	1251/6 D
0281 100 108	1/18/24	90	6747 A	II	42	½	+ mit AGD / with AGD / avec SIL 0282 100 203 Ausführung / version / version ÖGLAEND	1										
0681 003 001	1/24/153	100	2,73	III	40	½	+ Ausführung / version / version BATAVUS, HERCULES, ÖGLAEND, SARAGEN, TAYLOR USA / États-Unis					1						
0681 003 003	1/24/161	120	2,73	III	40	½	+ Ausführung / version / version ENDURO					1						
0681 003 006	1/24/158	95	2,73	II	40	½	+ Ausführung / version / version ARMAKOLAS, HERCULES	1										
0681 003 008	1/24/166	120	2,76	II	40	½	+ Ausführung / version / version HERCULES	1										
0681 003 011	1/24/171	85	2,73	II	40	1	+ mit AGD / with AGD / avec SIL 0282 100 207 Ausführung / version / version AGHA, ARMAKOLAS, BITAR							1				
0681 003 013	1/24/170	125	2,76	III	45	½	*								1			
0681 004 001	2/26/67	120	2,73	III	40	½	+ mit Luftschieber / with throttle slide / avec boisseau d'air Ausführung / version / version CROSS-COUNTRY					1						
0681 004 005	2/26/66	125	2,76	II	40	½	+ mit Luftschieber / with throttle slide / avec boisseau d'air Ausführung / version / version CROSS-COUNTRY	1										
0681 005 105	1/27/16	120	2,76	II	45	1½	+ Ausführung / version / version KTM					1						
0681 005 001	1/26/115	105	2,73	III	40	½...1	* Ausführung / version / version COLEMANN USA / États-Unis, HERCULES, ROSSI, SARACEN, SPRITE	1	1		1				1	1		
0681 005 011	1/26/120	130	2,76	II	45	1	* Ausführung / version / version MONARK	1	1		1					1		
0681 005 109	1/27/17	140	2,76	III	45	1	* Ausführung / version / version NHW/USA / États-Unis, KTM	1	1		1					1		
0681 005 113	1/27/19	140	2,73	II	45	1	* Ausführung / version / version NHW/USA / États-Unis	1	1							1		
0681 005 115	1/27/20	140	2,70	II	45	1	* Ausführung / version / version KTM/USA / États-Unis	1			1					1		
0681 005 117	1/27/22	120	2,73	II	45	1	* Ausführung / version / version MONARK/USA / États-Unis									1		
• 0681 005 119	1/27/21	130	2,73	II	45	1	* Ausführung / version / version KTM		1	1								
• 0681 005 121	1/27/23	115	2,73	II	45	1	* Ausführung / version / version MONARK/USA / États-Unis		1									
• 0681 005 127	1/27/25	110	2,70	II	45	1	* Ausführung / version / version HERCULES										1	
• 0681 009 001	2/28/1001	135	2,76	II	35	1	* mit Luftschieber / with throttle slide / avec boisseau d'air Ausführung / version / version HERCULES, KTM, S.W.M.										1	1

Zeichenerklärung / Explanation of symbols / Abbréviations:

AGD = Ansauggeräuschdämpfer /
AGD = Intake silencer /
SIL = Silencieux d'aspiration
+ = Ausführung Grauguß-Zylinder /
+ = version grey cast cylinder /
+ = version: cylindre fonte grise
* = Ausführung Alu-Zylinder /
* = version aluminium cylinder /
* = version: cylindre aluminium

Alle aufgeführten Vergaser sind Ausführungen mit 2 Seilen. /
All indicated carburettors are versions with 2 wires. /
Tous les carburateurs spécifiés sont des versions avec 2 câbles.

SACHS-Schmiermittel
SACHS Lubricants
Lubrifiants SACHS

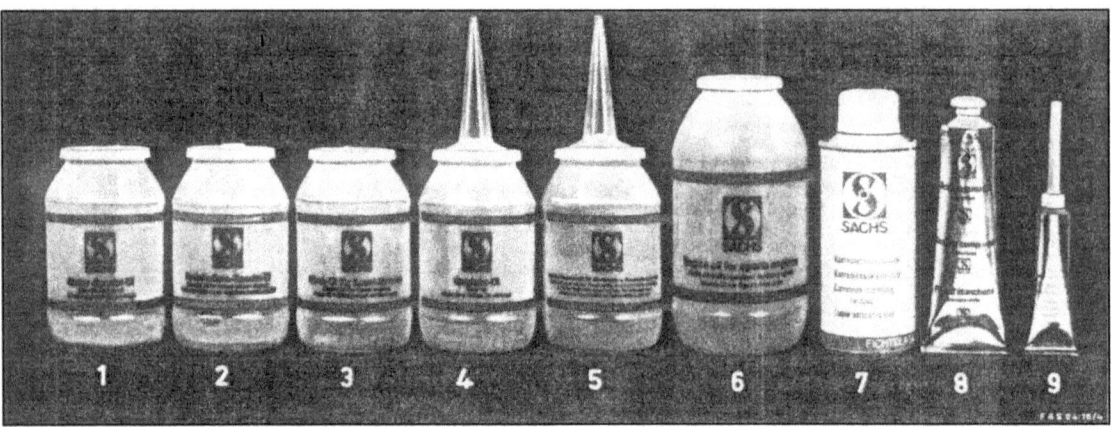

Bild-Nr. Ill. No.	Bestell-Nr. Part No. Réf. No.	Benennung	Description	Désignation
1	0263 005 100	250 cm³ SACHS-Motor-Spezialöl selbstmischend (Farbring blau)	250 ccm SACHS special engine oil, self-mixing (colour ring blue)	250 cm³ Huile spéciale de moteur SACHS, auto-mélange (anneau bleu)
2	2769 008 000	250 cm³ SACHS-Spezialöl für Kreiskolbenmotoren (Farbring gelb)	250 ccm SACHS special oil for rotary piston engines (colour ring yellow)	250 cm³ Huile spéciale SACHS pour moteurs à piston rotatif (anneau jaune)
3	0263 013 000	250 cm³ SACHS-Mischöl für Sport-Motoren (Farbring rot)	250 ccm SACHS mixing oil for sport engines (colour ring red)	250 cm³ Huile de mélange SACHS pour moteurs sport (anneau rouge)
4	0263 015 005	250 cm³ SACHS-Getriebeöl mit Ausgießer (Farbring braun)	250 ccm SACHS gear oil with spout (colour ring brown)	250 cm³ Huile spéciale SACHS pour boîte de vitesses avec bec verseur (anneau brun)
5	0263 014 002	250 cm³ SACHS-Spezial-Getriebeöl mit Ausgießer für Saxonette, Saxonette Automatic, SACHS 502/1, SACHS 503/..., SACHS 504/1 und SACHS 505/1 (Farbring grün)	250 ccm SACHS special gear oil with spout for Saxonette, Saxonette Automatic, SACHS 502/1, SACHS 503/..., SACHS 504/1 and SACHS 505/1 (colour ring green)	250 cm³ Huile spéciale SACHS pour boîte de vitesses avec bec verseur pour Saxonette, Saxonette Automatic, SACHS 502/1, SACHS 503/..., SACHS 504/1 et SACHS 505/1 (anneau vert)
6	0263 013 001	473 cm³ SACHS-Mischöl für Sport-Motoren (Farbring rot)	473 ccm SACHS mixing oil for sport engines (colour ring red)	473 cm³ Huile de mélange SACHS pour moteurs sport (anneau rouge)
7	0269 001 100	150 g Korrosionsschutzlack lufttrocknend	150 g Corrosion inhibiting laquer, air-drying	150 g Vernis de protection séchant à l'air
8	0999 107 000	100 g SACHS-Dichtungsmasse	100 g SACHS Sealing compound	100 g Pâte d'étanchéité SACHS
9	0699 002 000	17 cm³ SACHS-Tachometer-Fett	17 ccm SACHS speedometer grease	17 cm³ Graisse SACHS pour tachymètres
	0250 158 001	50 cm³ Loctite TL 270 (Flasche) ohne Abb.	50 ccm Loctite TL 270 (bottle) without ill.	50 cm³ Loctite TL 270 (bouteille), sans ill.
	0686 210 000	**Dichtungssatz-Motor ohne Abb.**	**Set of gaskets for the engine without ill.**	**Jeu de joints du moteur sans ill.**
		Werkzeug ohne Abb.	Tools without ill.	Outillage, sans ill.
	•2876 014 001	Steckschlüssel SW 21	Socket wrench SW 21	Clé à douille SW 21
	•2876 012 000	Drehstift	Torsion pin	Goujon de rotation

Scheiben-Abmessungen
Dimensions of shims
Dimensions des Rondelles

Bestell-Nr. Part No. Réf. No.	Maße Dimensions	Bestell-Nr. Part No. Réf. No.	Maße Dimensions
0244 055 000	14,5 × 24 × 0,2	0644 104 000	35,2 × 44 × 0,3
0244 055 001	14,5 × 24 × 0,5	0644 104 001	35,2 × 44 × 0,5
0244 055 002	14,5 × 24 × 1,0	0644 104 002	35,2 × 44 × 0,6
0244 055 003	14,5 × 24 × 0,3	0644 104 003	35,2 × 44 × 0,8
		0644 104 004	35,2 × 44 × 1,0
0244 100 000	6,2 × 10 × 0,2		
0244 100 001	6,2 × 10 × 0,3	0644 105 000	25,2 × 39 × 0,2
0244 100 002	6,2 × 10 × 0,5	0644 105 001	25,2 × 39 × 0,3
0244 100 003	6,2 × 10 × 1,0	0644 105 002	25,2 × 39 × 0,5
		0644 105 103	25,2 × 39 × 0,8
0244 102 000	12,1 × 18,5 × 0,2	0644 105 104	25,2 × 39 × 1,0
0244 102 001	12,1 × 18,5 × 0,5		
0244 102 102	12,1 × 18,5 × 1,0	0944 003 000	8,4 × 14 × 0,3
0244 102 003	12,1 × 18,5 × 1,5	0944 003 001	8,4 × 14 × 0,5
		0944 003 002	8,4 × 14 × 0,6
0244 118 000	20,2 × 32 × 1,0	0944 003 003	8,4 × 14 × 1,0
0244 118 001	20,2 × 32 × 0,8	0944 003 004	8,4 × 14 × 0,4
0244 118 002	20,2 × 32 × 0,5		
0244 118 003	20,2 × 32 × 0,3	0944 046 000	20,5 × 28,5 × 0,2
0244 118 004	20,2 × 32 × 0,15	0944 046 001	20,5 × 28,5 × 0,3
		0944 046 002	20,5 × 28,5 × 0,5
0246 008 000	25,3 × 34 × 1,0	0944 046 003	20,5 × 28,5 × 0,4
0246 008 001	25,3 × 34 × 0,5	0944 046 004	20,5 × 28,5 × 0,8
0246 008 002	25,3 × 34 × 0,3	0944 046 005	20,5 × 28,5 × 0,15
0246 008 003	25,3 × 34 × 0,2	0944 046 006	20,5 × 28,5 × 1,0
0246 015 000	16,3 × 25,8 × 0,3		
0246 015 001	16,3 × 25,8 × 0,5		
0246 015 002	16,3 × 25,8 × 1,0		
0246 015 003	16,3 × 25,8 × 0,15		

Typschilder
Engine plates
Plaques du moteur

Typschild-Bezeichnung / Description of engine plate / Désignation/Plaque du moteur	Motor-Bezeichnung / Engine model / Désignation du moteur	Typschild-Bezeichnung / Description of engine plate / Désignation/Plaque du moteur	Motor-Bezeichnung / Engine model / Désignation du moteur
TYP SACHS 1001/5A (316)	SACHS 1001/5 A	TYP SACHS 1251/5 AL 9PS (321)	SACHS 1251/5 A L
TYP SACHS 1001/5A Typz. 10 413 (317)	SACHS 1001/5 A	TYP SACHS 1251/5 AL 9 PS (374)	SACHS 1251/5 A L
TYP SACHS 1001/5A 10 PS (318)	SACHS 1001/5 A	TYP SACHS 1251/5 B (492)	SACHS 1251/5 B
TYP DKW 1001/5 A (554)	D K W 1001/5 A	TYP SACHS 1251/5 D (559)	SACHS 1251/5 D
TYP SACHS 1001/6A (438)	SACHS 1001/6 A	TYP SACHS 1251/6A (439)	SACHS 1251/6 A
TYP DKW 1001/6A (495)	D K W 1001/6 A	TYP DKW 1251/6A (496)	D K W 1251/6 A
TYP SACHS 1001/6 B (555)	SACHS 1001/6 B	TYP SACHS 1251/6 B (493)	SACHS 1251/6 B
TYP DKW 1001/6 B (556)	D K W 1001/6 B	TYP DKW 1251/6 B (560)	D K W 1251/6 B
TYP SACHS 1001/6 C (557)	SACHS 1001/6 C	TYP SACHS 1251/6 C (526)	SACHS 1251/6 C
TYP SACHS 1251/5A (319)	SACHS 1251/5 A	TYP SACHS 1251/6 D (561)	SACHS 1251/6 D
TYP SACHS 1251/5A Typz 10 412 (320)	SACHS 1251/5 A	TYP DKW 1251/6 D (562)	D K W 1251/6 D
TYP DKW 1251/5 A (558)	D K W 1251/5 A		

Seite / Page: 28

Sämtliche Abbildungen, Maße und Beschreibungen entsprechen dem Stand der jeweiligen Ausgabe.

Im Interesse der konstruktiven Weiterentwicklung bleiben Änderungen vorbehalten.

All illustrations, dimensions and descriptions correspond to the state of the edition concerned.

In the interest of technical progress, we reserve the right to introduce modifications.

Toutes les illustrations, les mesures et les descriptions répondent à l'état de l'édition respective.

Sous réserve de modifications dans l'intérêt de la mise au point technique ultérieure.

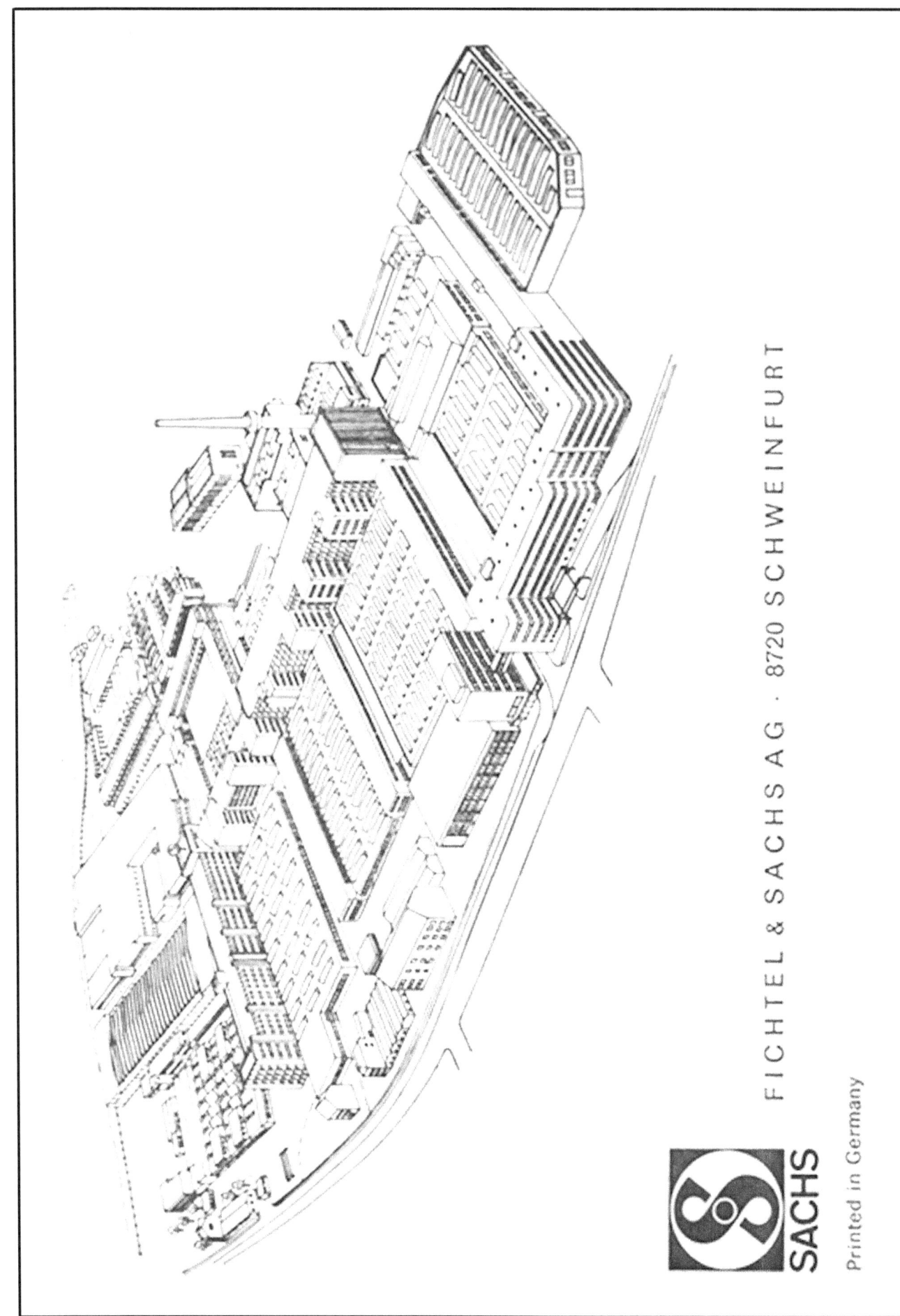

SACHS

SPARE PARTS LIST

FOR FRAME

MODEL

ENDURO	100/125 cc.
CROSS COUNTRY	100/125 cc.
MOTO CROSS	100/125 cc.

Changing-information No. 1 — Nov. 1968 —
Änderungsmitteilung Nr. 1 — Nov. 1968 —

Re.: **Spare parts list for the models ENDURO, CROSS-COUNTRY, MOTO-CROSS made in 1968**
Betr.: **Ersatzteilliste für die Modelle ENDURO, CROSS-COUNTRY, MOTO-CROSS — Baujahr 1968**

The order-No. for "steering set, complete" is changed. Please correct on page 4, picture 5-5e "steering set, complete" and insert the **new order-No.:** **417 100 97 02**

Die Bestellnummer für das Lenkungslager kpl. mußte geändert werden. Bitte berichtigen Sie deshalb auf Seite 4, Bild 5-5e „Lenkungslager kpl.". **Die neue Bestellnummer lautet:** **417 100 97 02**

In the following we inform you about some changes, which will be due within the next weeks, after the start of the series.

Nachstehend geben wir Ihnen einige Teile-Änderungen bekannt, die bei der Serienfertigung im Laufe der nächsten Wochen inkrafttreten.

Page	2	Ill.-No.	7- 7f	Foot rest left, complete, with foot rest rubber Fußraste links, kpl., mit Fußrastergummi	927 100 48 26
			7	Foot rest Fußraste	927 100 48 25
			—	Foot rest rubber Fußrastergummi	927 993 26 03
			7a	Bracket for foot rest, left Lasche, links	427 100 85 08
			8- 8f	Foot rest right, complete, with foot rest rubber Fußraste rechts, kpl., mit Fußrastergummi	927 100 48 27
			8	Foot rest Fußraste	927 100 48 25
			—	Foot rest rubber Fußrastergummi	927 993 26 03
			8a	Bracket for foot rest, right Lasche, rechts	427 100 85 09
Page	3	Ill.-No.	10-10c	Seat with hinge Sitzbank mit Scharnier	427 140 01 04
Page	10	Ill.-No.	1	Handlebar Lenker	427 156 09 01

These parts are interchangeable against the existing executions (footrest only in pairs) and can be delivered after the start of the series.

Diese Teile sind gegen die bisherigen Ausführungen voll austauschbar (bei Fußrasten jedoch nur paarweise) und werden nach Serienanlauf als Ersatz geliefert.

CONTENTS
INHALTSVERZEICHNIS

	Page
Frame, trussing of the frame, rear swingarm, rear shock absorber	1
Rahmen, Unterzug, Hinterradschwinge, hintere Federbeine	
Side stand, foot rests, footbrake arm	2
Seitenstütze, Fußrasten, Fußbremshebel	
Brake rod, seat, tool box	3
Bremstange, Sitzbank, Werkzeugdose	
Front fork, front swingarm, front shock absorber, steering yoke, steering set	4
Vorderradgabel, Vorderradschwinge, vordere Federbeine, Lenkjoch, Lenkungslager	
Steering demper, fuel tank, petrol cock	5
Lenkungsdämpfer, Kraftstoffbehälter, Kraftstoffhahn	
Aerosol tin, filter box	6
Lack-Sprühdosen, Filterkasten	
Front fender, rear fender, license plate bracket, chain guard, chain guide	7
Vorderradschutzblech, Hinterradschutzblech, Kennzeichenhalter, Kettenschutz, Kettenführung	
Exhaust system for „ENDURO"	8
Auspuffanlage für „ENDURO"	
Exhaust system for „CROSS-COUNTRY" and „MOTO-CROSS"	9
Auspuffanlage für „CROSS-COUNTRY" und „MOTO-CROSS"	
Handlebar, throttle twistgrip, brake lever, clutch lever, rubber grip	10
Lenker, Gasdrehgriff, Handbremshebel, Kupplungshebel, Festgriff	
Cables	11
Seilzüge	
Head lamp, head lamp bracket, switch, speedometer	12
Scheinwerfer, Scheinwerferhalter, Schalter, Geschwindigkeitsmesser	
Taillight, brake light switch, terminal, snare, ignition coil, cables, passengers foot rest	13
Schlußlicht, Bremslichtschalter, Leitungsverbinder, Schnarre, Zündspule, Kabel, Soziusfußrasten	
Tool kit	14
Werkzeugsatz	
Front wheel, front hub	15
Vorderrad, Vorderradnabe	
Tire for front wheel	16
Bereifung	
Rear wheel, rear hub, spocket	17
Hinterrad, Hinterradnabe, Kettenrad	
Rear hub, chain tensioner, chain, tire for rear wheel	18
Hinterradnabe, Kettenspanner, Kette, Bereifung für Hinterrad	
Wiring diagrams	19
Schaltpläne	

Frame, trussing of the frame, rear swingarm, rear shock absorber
Rahmen, Unterzug, Hinterradschwinge, hintere Federbeine

Ill. No.	Description			Order No.	Pcs.	Order	Price
1	Frame / Rahmen			427 100 01 05.088	1		
1a	Trussing of the frame / Unterzug			427 100 43 02.088	1		
1b	Hexagon screw / Sechskantschraube	M 8 x 145	DIN 931	08 025 00931 37	1		
1c	Spring washer / Federscheibe	B 8	DIN 137	08 015 00137 35	1		
1d	Nut / Sechskantmutter	M 8	DIN 985	08 008 00985 17	1		
1e	Bracket / Haltebügel			927 968 41 04	1		
1f	Hexagon screw / Sechskantschraube	M 8 x 15	DIN 933	08 005 00933 37	2		
1g	Spring washer / Federscheibe	B 8	DIN 137	08 015 00137 35	2		
1h	Nut / Sechskantmutter	M 8	DIN 985	08 008 00985 17	2		
2	Lubrication nipple / Schmiernippel	AM 6	DIN 3402	06 001 03402 07	1		
3	Hexagon screw / Sechskantschraube	M 8 x 100	DIN 931	08 019 00931 47	2		
3a	Hexagon screw / Sechskantschraube	M 8 x 150	DIN 931	08 026 00931 47	1		
3b	Loop / Öse			927 999 98 09	1		
3c	Washer / Scheibe	8,4	DIN 125	08 011 00125 07	1		
3d	Spring washer / Federscheibe	B 8	DIN 137	08 015 00137 35	3		
3e	Nut / Sechskantmutter	M 8	DIN 985	08 008 00985 17	3		
4	Rear swingarm / Hinterradschwinge			427 140 04 01.088	1		
4a-4f	Link bracket / Schwingenlagerung kpl.			698 990 42 01	1		
4a	Swing axle / Schwingenlagerachse			927 992 42 09	1		
4b	Swing axle screw / Schwingenlagerschraube			927 991 01 13	2		
4c	Spring washer / Federscheibe	B 14	DIN 137	14 019 00137 35	2		
4d	Washer / Scheibe			927 992 07 01	2		
4e	Gasket ring / Dichtring			927 993 38 04	2		
4f	Needle bearing / Nadellager			927 492 26 05	2		
5	Rear shock absorber / Hinteres Federbein			920 040 01 74	2		
5a	Spring for rear shock absorber / Feder für hinteres Federbein			920 049 14 07	2		
5b	Hexagon screw (left side) / Sechskantschraube	M 10 x 85	DIN 931	10 014 00931 37	1		
	Hexagon screw (right side, for CC, MC) / Sechskantschraube	M 10 x 85	DIN 931	10 014 00931 37	1		
	Hexagon screw (right side, for Enduro) / Sechskantschraube	M 10 x 100	DIN 931	10 016 00931 37	1		
5c	Washer (right side, for Enduro) / Scheibe	10		927 992 01 86	1		
5d	Hexagon nut (right side, for Enduro) / Sechskantmutter	M 10	DIN 934	10 011 00934 17	1		
5e	Washer / Scheibe			115 149 01 10	4		
5f	Spring washer / Federscheibe	B 10	DIN 137	10 017 00137 35	4		
5g	Hexagon nut / Sechskantmutter	M 10	DIN 985	10 010 00985 17	4		

Side stand, foot rests, footbrake arm
Seitenstütze, Fußrasten, Fußbremshebel

Ill. No.	Description			Order No.	Pcs.	Order	Price
6	Side stand / Seitenstütze			427 100 63 01.088	1		
6a	Return spring / Rückholfeder			927 994 05 08	1		
6b	Bolt / Lagerbolzen			927 992 42 19	1		
6c	Safety washer / Sicherungsscheibe	9	DIN 6799	09 012 06799 35	2		
7-7f	Foot rest left, complete / Fußraste links, kpl.			927 100 48 21.088	1		
7	Foot rest, left / Fußraste links			927 100 48 23.088	1		
7a	Bracket for foot rest, left / Lasche, links			427 100 85 05.088	1		
7b	Hexagonal screw / Sechskantschraube	M 8 x 40	DIN 931	08 006 00931 37	1		
7c	Nut / Sechskantmutter	M 8	DIN 985	08 008 00985 17	1		
7d	Return spring / Zugfeder			927 994 02 23	1		
7e	Pull chain / Zugkette			927 979 50 01	1		
7f	Loop / Öse			927 999 98 10	1		
8-8f	Foot rest right, complete / Fußraste rechts, kpl.			927 100 48 22.088	1		
8	Foot rest, right / Fußraste, rechts			927 100 48 24.088	1		
8a	Bracket for foot rest, right / Lasche, rechts			427 100 85 06.088	1		
8b	Hexagonal screw / Sechskantschraube	M 8 x 40	DIN 931	08 006 00931 37	1		
8c	Nut / Sechskantmutter	M 8	DIN 985	08 008 00985 17	1		
8d	Return spring / Zugfeder			927 994 02 23	1		
8e	Pull chain / Zugkette			927 979 50 01	1		
8f	Loop / Öse			927 999 98 10	1		
8g	Spring washer / Federscheibe	B 12	DIN 137	12 018 00137 35	2		
8h	Nut / Sechskantmutter	M 12	DIN 985	12 013 00985 17	2		
9	Footbrake arm / Fußbremshebel			685 210 30 01.910	1		
9a	Bushing / Bundbüchse			927 994 21 05	2		
9b	Brake lever / Bremshebel			698 170 12 03.910	1		
9c	Spring washer / Federscheibe	B 10	DIN 137	10 017 00137 35	1		
9d	Nut / Sechskantmutter	M 10	DIN 985	10 010 00985 17	1		
9e	Return spring / Rückholfeder			927 994 05 05	1		

Brake rod, seat, tool box
Bremsstange, Sitzbank, Werkzeugdose

III. No.	Description			Order No.	Pcs.	Order	Price
9f-9k	Brake rod, complete Bremsstange, kpl.			675 170 37 02	1		
9f	Brake rod Bremsstange			927 171 37 02	1		
9g	Washer Scheibe	6,4	DIN 125	06 009 00125 07	3		
9h	Cutter pin Splint	2 x 12	DIN 94	20 002 00094 04	1		
9i	Return spring Druckfeder			927 994 03 51	1		
9j	Locking clip Gebogene Scheibe			927 992 02 03	2		
9k	Knurled nut Rändelmutter			927 991 55 01	1		
10-10c	Seat with hinge Sitzbank mit Scharnier			427 140 01 02	1		
10a	Hinge Scharnier			927 970 56 03	1		
10b	Hexagonal screw Sechskantschraube	M 6 x 15	DIN 933	06 007 00933 37	2		
10c	Lock washer Zahnscheibe	6,4	DIN 6797	06 014 06797 35	2		
10d	Hexagonal screw Sechskantschraube	M 6 x 12	DIN 933	06 005 00933 37	2		
10e	Washer Scheibe			927 992 01 67	2		
10f	Spring washer Federscheibe	B 6	DIN 137	06 011 00137 35	2		
10g	Nut Sechskantmutter	M 6	DIN 985	06 006 00985 17	2		
10h	Hexagonal screw Sechskantschraube	M 8 x 145	DIN 931	08 025 00931 37	1		
10i	Spring washer Federscheibe	B 8	DIN 137	08 015 00137 35	1		
10j	Nut Sechskantmutter	M 8	DIN 985	08 008 00985 17	1		
11	Tool box Werkzeugdose			417 940 14 01.088	1		
11a	Round head screw, slotted Linsenzylinderschraube	AM 5 x 10	DIN 85	05 003 00085 17	2		
11b	Spring washer Federring	B 5	DIN 128	05 016 00128 35	2		

Front fork, front swingarm, front shock absorber, steering yoke, steering set
Vorderradgabel, Vorderradschwinge, vordere Federbeine, Lenkjoch, Lenkungslager

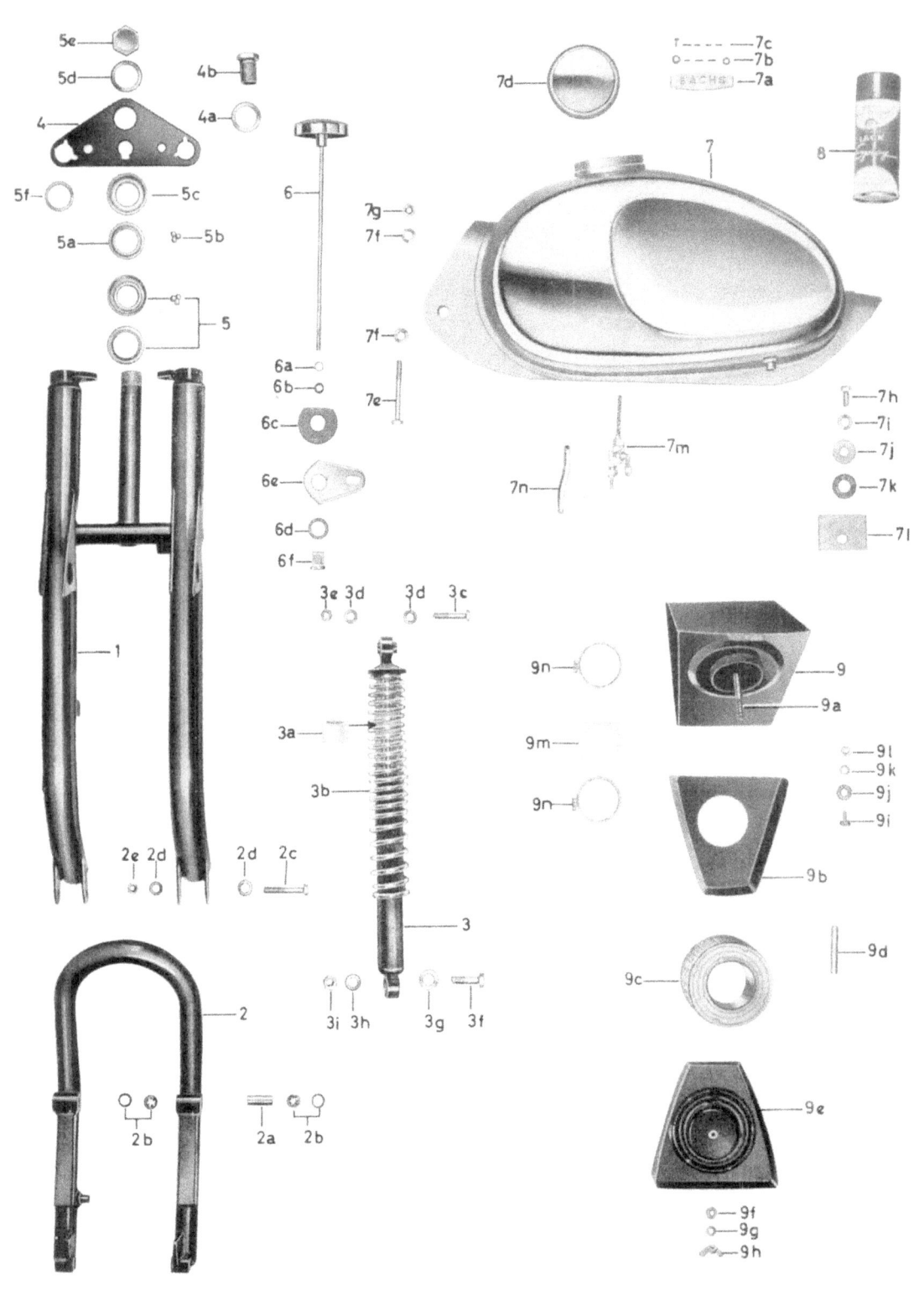

Ill. No.	Description			Order No.	Pcs.	Order	Price
1-6f	Front fork, complete Vorderradgabel, kpl.			921 150 02 83.088	1		
1	↑ Front fork Vorderradgabel			921 150 02 12.088	1		
2	Front swingarm Vorderradschwinge			922 150 05 04.088	1		
2a	Bushing Büchse			927 499 70 01	2		
2b	Needle bearing with gasket Nadellager mit Dichtring			927 492 26 07	4		
2c	Hexagonal screw Sechskantschraube	M 8 x 50	DIN 931	08 008 00931 37	2		
2d	Spring washer Federscheibe	B 8	DIN 137	08 015 00137 35	4		
2e	Nut Sechskantmutter	M 8	DIN 985	08 008 00985 17	2		
3	Front shock absorber Vorderes Federbein			920 040 01 24	2		
3a	↑ Rubber damper Anschlagpuffer			927 993 29 03	2		
3b	Spring for front shock absorber Feder für vorderes Federbein			920 049 14 06	2		
3c	Hexagonal screw Sechskantschraube	M 8 x 45	DIN 931	08 007 00931 37	2		
3d	Spring washer Federscheibe	B 8	DIN 137	08 015 00137 35	4		
3e	Nut Sechskantmutter	M 8	DIN 985	08 008 00985 17	2		
3f	Hexagonal screw Sechskantschraube	M 10 x 35	DIN 931	10 003 00931 37	2		
3g	Spring washer Federscheibe	B 10	DIN 137	10 017 00137 35	2		
3h	Washer Scheibe	10,5 x 25 x 1		115 149 01 10	2		
3i	Nut Sechskantmutter	M 10	DIN 985	10 010 00985 17	2		
4	Upper steering yoke Oberes Lenkjoch			921 154 25 15.088	1		
4a	Washer Scheibe			927 992 01 60	2		
4b	Short mounting bolt Kurze Gabelholmschraube			922 991 23 01	2		
5-5e	Steering set, complete Lenkungslager, kpl.			675 100 97 03	1 set		
5	↑ Lower steering set Unteres Lenkungslager, kpl.		DIN 71974	05 001 71974 40	1		
5a	Upper bearing race Obere Lagerschale			927 101 33 04	1		
5b	Ball Kugel	¼"	DIN 5401	19 003 05401 40	19		
5c	Frame cone Rahmenkonus			927 101 31 28	1		
5d	Washer Scheibe			927 101 36 01	1		
5e	Steering yoke nut Abschlußmutter			427 101 35 01	1		
5f	Washer Ausgleichscheibe			927 992 08 17	1-2		

Steering demper, fuel tank, petrol cock
Lenkungsdämpfer, Kraftstoffbehälter, Kraftstoffhahn

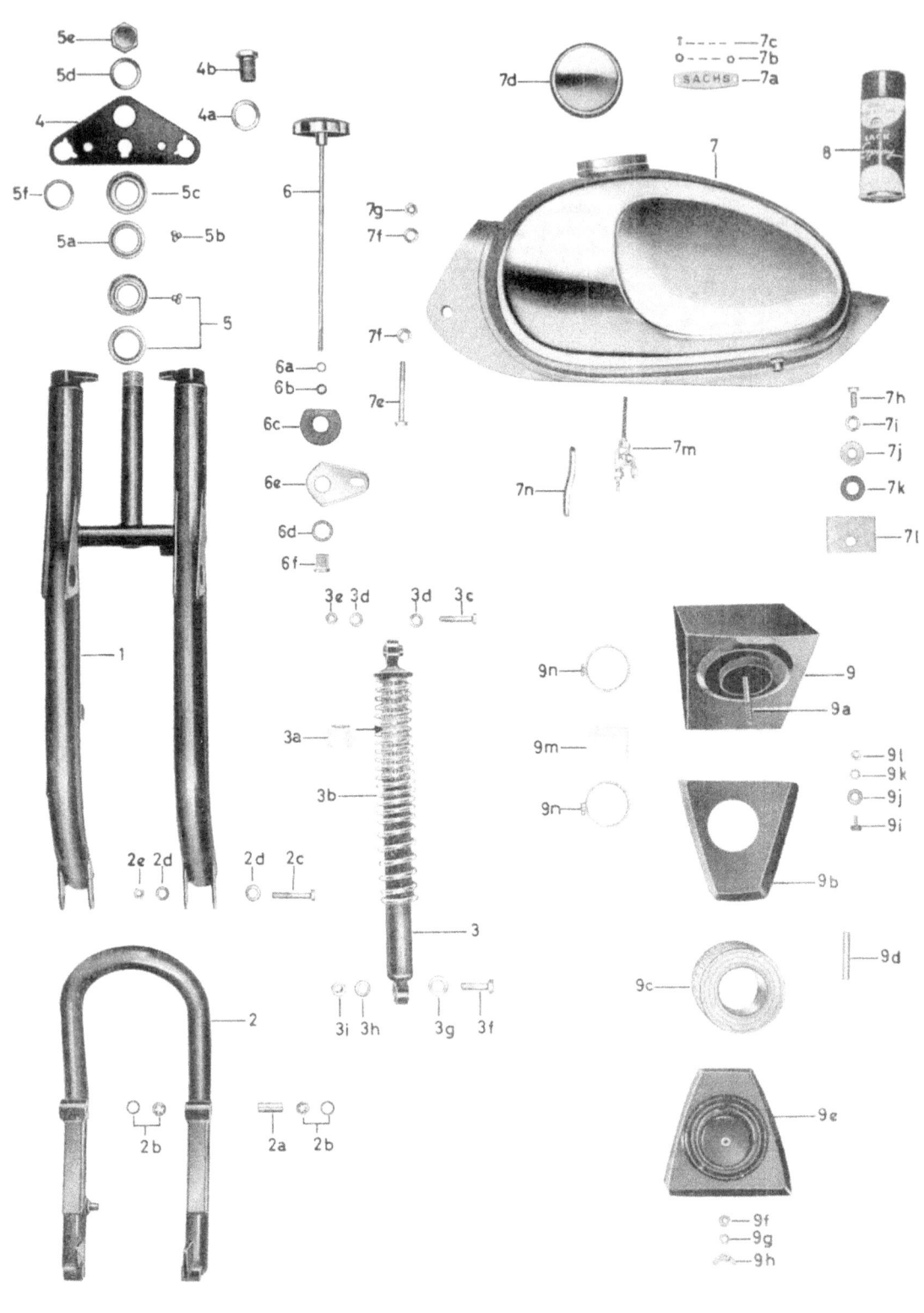

Ill. No.	Description			Order No.	Pcs.	Order	Price
6-6f	Steering demper / Lenkungsdämpfer			427 150 47 01	1		
6	Traction rod / Zugstange, kpl.			427 150 48 01	1		
6a	Spring washer / Federring			927 992 96 01	1		
6b	Washer / Scheibe	B 6,4	DIN 9021	06 012 09021 07	1		
6c	Friction disk / Reibscheibe			927 992 13 01	1		
6d	Washer / Scheibe			927 992 00 28	1		
6e	Clip / Lasche			927 971 85 88	1		
6f	Nut / Bundmutter			927 991 56 08	1		
7	Fuel tank, chrome plated and ground painted / Kraftstoffbehälter, verchromt und grundiert			417 180 05 03.103	1		
7a	Tank emblem „Sachs" / Plakette „Sachs"			927 947 02 21	2		
7b	Washer / Scheibe			136 189 01 00	4		
7c	Round head screw, slotted / Halbrund-Schneidschraube	CM 2,6 x 8	DIN 7513	26 011 07513 07	4		
—	Decal „Made in Western Germany" / Abziehbild			927 947 05 84	1		
—	Decal „Enduro 100 cc" / Abziehbild			927 947 05 76	1		
—	Decal „Enduro 125 cc" / Abziehbild			927 947 05 77	1		
—	Decal „Cross-Country 100 cc" / Abziehbild			927 947 05 78	1		
—	Decal „Cross-Country 125 cc" / Abziehbild			927 947 05 79	1		
—	Decal „Moto-Cross 100 cc" / Abziehbild			927 947 05 80	1		
—	Decal „Moto-Cross 125 cc" / Abziehbild			927 947 05 81	1		
7d	Fuel cap / Tankverschluß			60 002 73400 70	1		
7e	Hexagonal screw / Sechskantschraube	M 8 x 90	DIN 931	08 016 00931 37	1		
7f	Spring washer / Federscheibe	B 8	DIN 137	08 015 00137 35	2		
7g	Nut / Sechskantmutter	M 8	DIN 985	08 008 00985 17	1		
7h	Hexagonal screw / Sechskantschraube	M 8 x 20	DIN 933	08 007 00933 37	1		
7i	Spring washer / Federscheibe	B 8	DIN 137	08 015 00137 35	1		
7j	Curved washer / Gewölbte Scheibe			927 992 01 65	1		
7k	Rubber washer / Gummischeibe			927 993 32 01	1		
7l	Rubber pad / Gummiplatte			927 993 27 01	1		
7m	Petrol cock / Kraftstoffhdhn			675 180 03 01	1		
7n	Fuel hose / Kraftstoffschlauch	5x8x120 mm		927 993 72 00	meter		

Edition Nov. 68   Enduro, Cross-Country, Moto-Cross Model 1968

Aerosol tin, filter box
Sprühdosen, Filterkasten

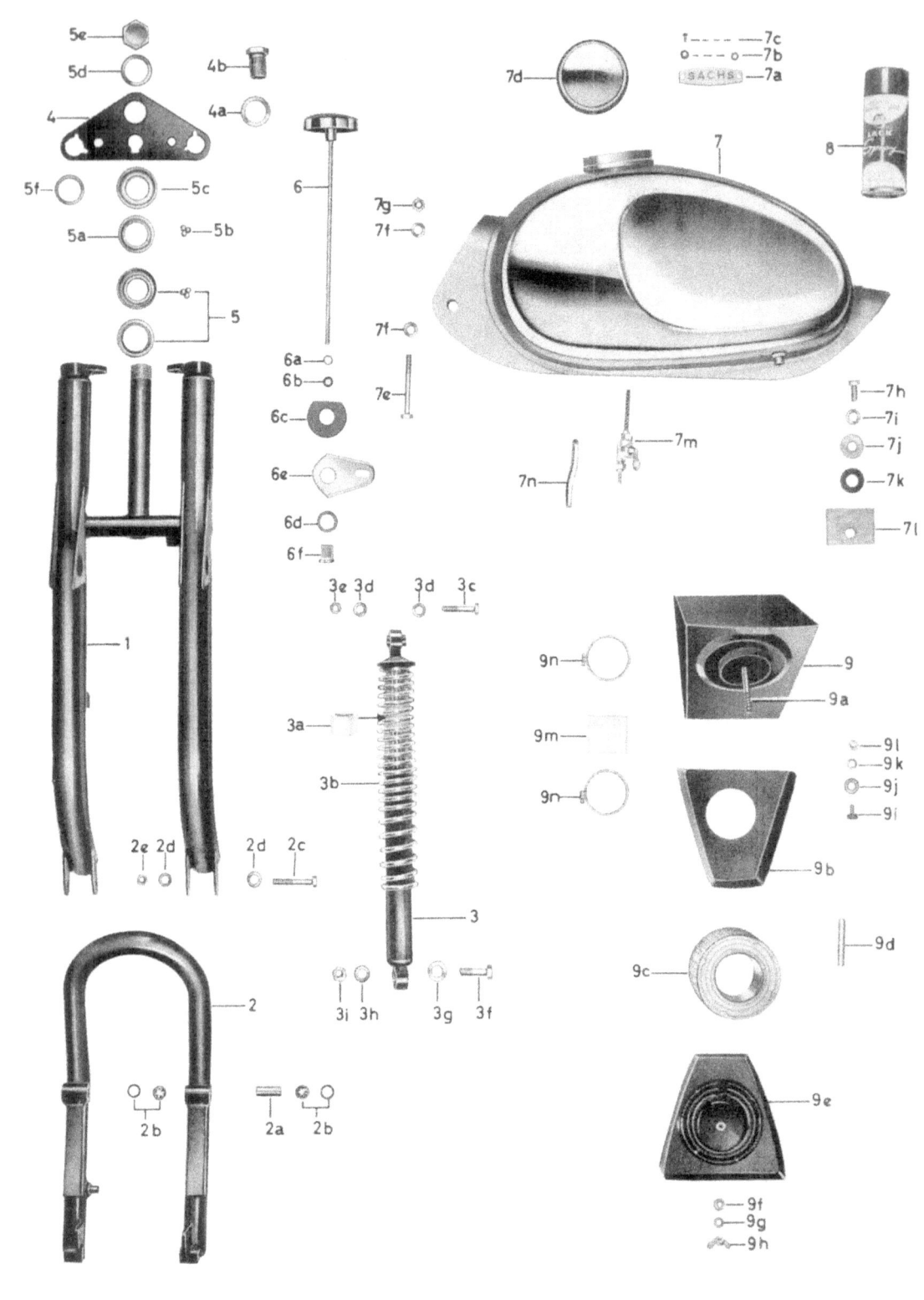

Edition Nov. 68 — Enduro, Cross Country, Moto-Cross Model 1968

Ill. No.	Description			Order No.	Pcs.	Order	Price
8	Aerosol tin „red" (fuel tank) Sprühdose „karminrot"			929 200 00 01.049	—		
	Aerosol tin „blue" (fuel tank) Sprühdose „petrolblau"			929 200 00 01.226	—		
	Aerosol tin „gold" (fuel tank) Sprühdose „gold"			929 200 00 01.625	—		
	Aerosol tin „black" (frame) Sprühdose „schwarz"			929 200 00 01.088	—		
9-9h	Filter box, complete Filterkasten, kpl.			427 460 10 02.088	1		
9	↑ Filter box Ansauggeräuschdämpfer			427 460 10 01.088	1		
9a	Bolt Stiftschraube	M 6 x 90	DIN 938	06 020 00938 37	1		
9b	Filter box, bottom part Filtergehäuse-Unterteil			698 460 15 02.088	1		
9c	Filter element Filterpatrone			927 463 01 01	1		
9d	Distance bushing Distanzrohr			927 996 01 27	1		
—	Feltring Filzring	72 x 60 x 3		927 993 76 01	1		
9e	Filter box, top part Filtergehäuse-Oberteil			698 460 15 01.088	1		
9f	Nylon washer Kunststoffscheibe			927 992 01 66	1		
9g	Spring washer Federscheibe	B 6	DIN 137	06 011 00137 35	1		
9h	Wing nut Flügelmutter	M 6	DIN 315	06 007 00315 05	1		
9i	Hexagonal screw Sechskantschraube	M 6 x 12	DIN 933	06 005 00933 37	1		
9j	Washer Scheibe			927 992 01 67	1		
9k	Spring washer Federscheibe	B 6	DIN 137	06 011 00137 35	1		
9l	Nut Sechskantmutter	M 6	DIN 985	06 006 00985 17	1		
—	Hexagonal screw Sechskantschraube	M 6 x 8	DIN 933	06 002 00933 37	1		
—	Gasket ring Dichtring	A 6 x 10	DIN 7603	06 003 07603 90	1		
9m	Bellow sleeve Plastikschlauch			927 993 73 01	1		
9n	Clamp Schlauchbinder			927 973 33 01	2		

Edition Nov. 68   Enduro, Cross-Country, Moto-Cross Model 1968

Front fender, rear fender, license plate bracket, chain guard, chain guide
Schutzbleche, Kennzeichenhalter, Kettenschutz, Kettenführung

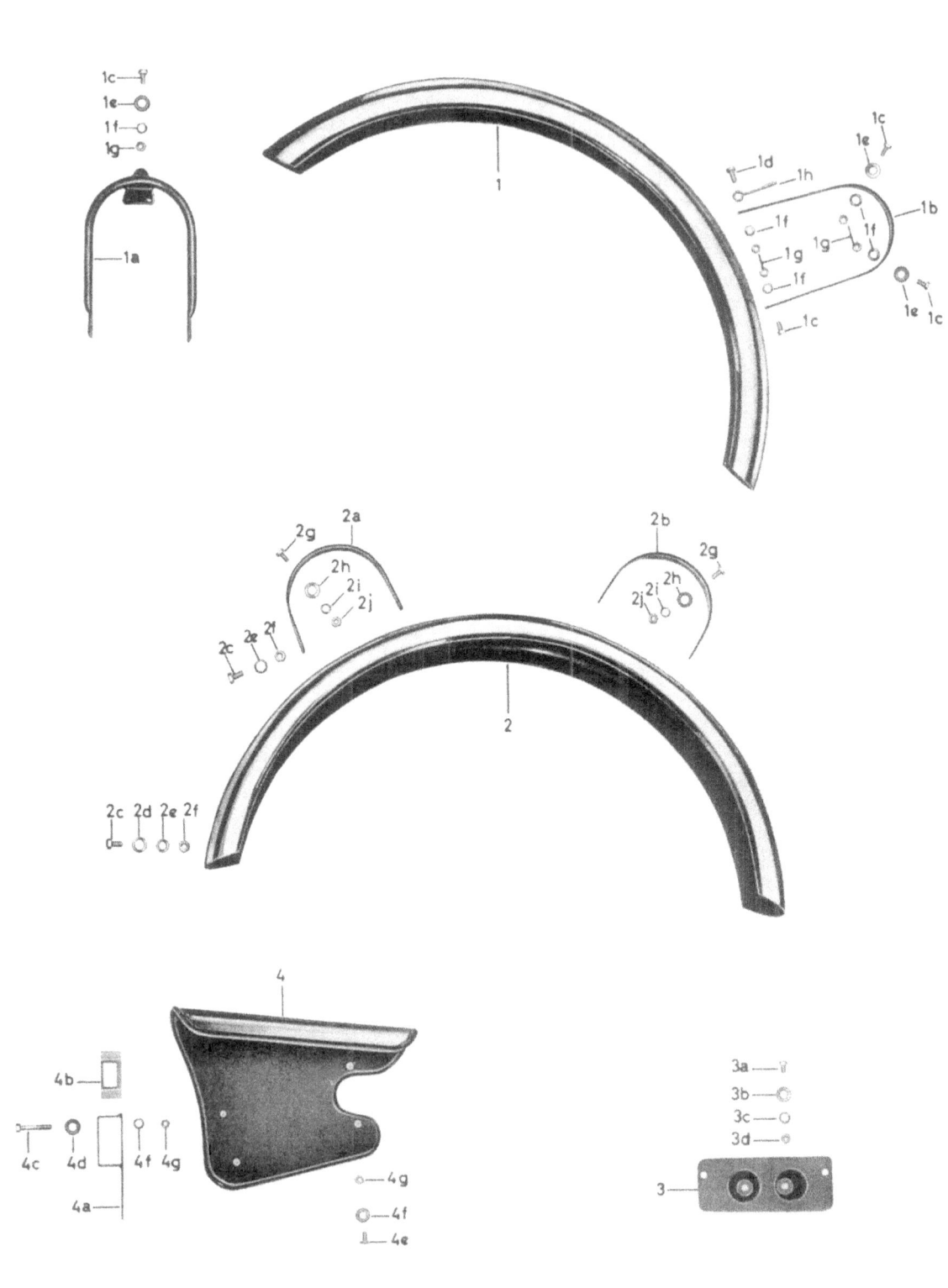

Ill. No.	Description			Order No.	Pcs.	Order	Price
1	Front fender Vorderradschutzblech, verchromt			427 116 01 01.098	1		
1a	Upper fender bracket for front fender Oberer Schutzblechbügel			927 110 06 05.088	1		
1b	Lower fender bracket for front fender Unterer Schutzblechbügel			927 962 90 13.088	1		
1c	Hexagonal screw Sechskantschraube	M 6 x 12	DIN 933	06 005 00933 37	6		
1d	Hexagonal screw Sechskantschraube	M 6 x 15	DIN 933	06 007 00933 37	1		
1e	Washer Scheibe			927 992 01 67	5		
1f	Spring washer Federscheibe	B 6	DIN 137	06 011 00137 35	7		
1g	Nut Sechskantmutter	M 6	DIN 985	06 006 00985 17	7		
1h	Brake cable guide Bremskabelhalter			927 968 46 09	1		
2	Rear fender Hinterradschutzblech, verchromt			427 117 11 04.098	1		
2a	Front bracket for rear fender Vorderer Schutzblechbügel			927 962 90 11.088	1		
2b	Rear bracket for rear fender Hinterer Schutzblechbügel			927 962 90 12.088	1		
2c	Hexagonal screw Sechskantschraube	M 8 x 15	DIN 933	08 005 00933 37	3		
2d	Washer Scheibe	8,4	DIN 125	08 011 00125 07	1		
2e	Spring washer Federscheibe	B 8	DIN 137	08 015 00137 35	3		
2f	Nut Sechskantmutter	M 8	DIN 985	08 008 00985 17	3		
2g	Hexagonal screw Sechskantschraube	M 6 x 12	DIN 933	06 005 00933 37	4		
2h	Washer Scheibe			927 992 01 67	4		
2i	Spring washer Federscheibe	B 6	DIN 137	06 011 00137 35	4		
2j	Nut Sechskantmutter	M 6	DIN 985	06 006 00985 17	4		
3	License plate bracket Nummernschildhalter			675 968 46 09.910	1		
3a	Hexagonal screw Sechskantschraube	M 6 x 10	DIN 933	06 004 00933 37	2		
3b	Washer Scheibe			927 992 01 67	2		
3c	Spring washer Federscheibe	B 6	DIN 137	06 011 00137 35	2		
3d	Nut Sechskantmutter	M 6	DIN 985	06 006 00985 17	2		
4	Chain guard Kettenschutz			050 147 00 02.088	1		
4a	Chain guide holder Halter für Kettenführung			050 100 78 02.088	1		
4b	Chain guide (plastic) Kettenführung			927 144 31 01	1		
4c	Hexagonal screw Sechskantschraube	M 6 x 40	DIN 931	06 008 00931 37	2		
4d	Washer Scheibe			927 992 01 67	5		
4e	Round head screw, slotted Linsensenkschraube	M 6 x 15	DIN 91	06 004 00091 17	2		
—	Hexagonal screw Sechskantschraube	M 6 x 15	DIN 933	06 007 00933 37	1		
4f	Spring washer Federscheibe	B 6	DIN 137	06 011 00137 35	5		
4g	Nut Sechskantmutter	M 6	DIN 985	06 006 00985 17	4		

Exhaust system for ENDURO
Auspuffanlage für ENDURO

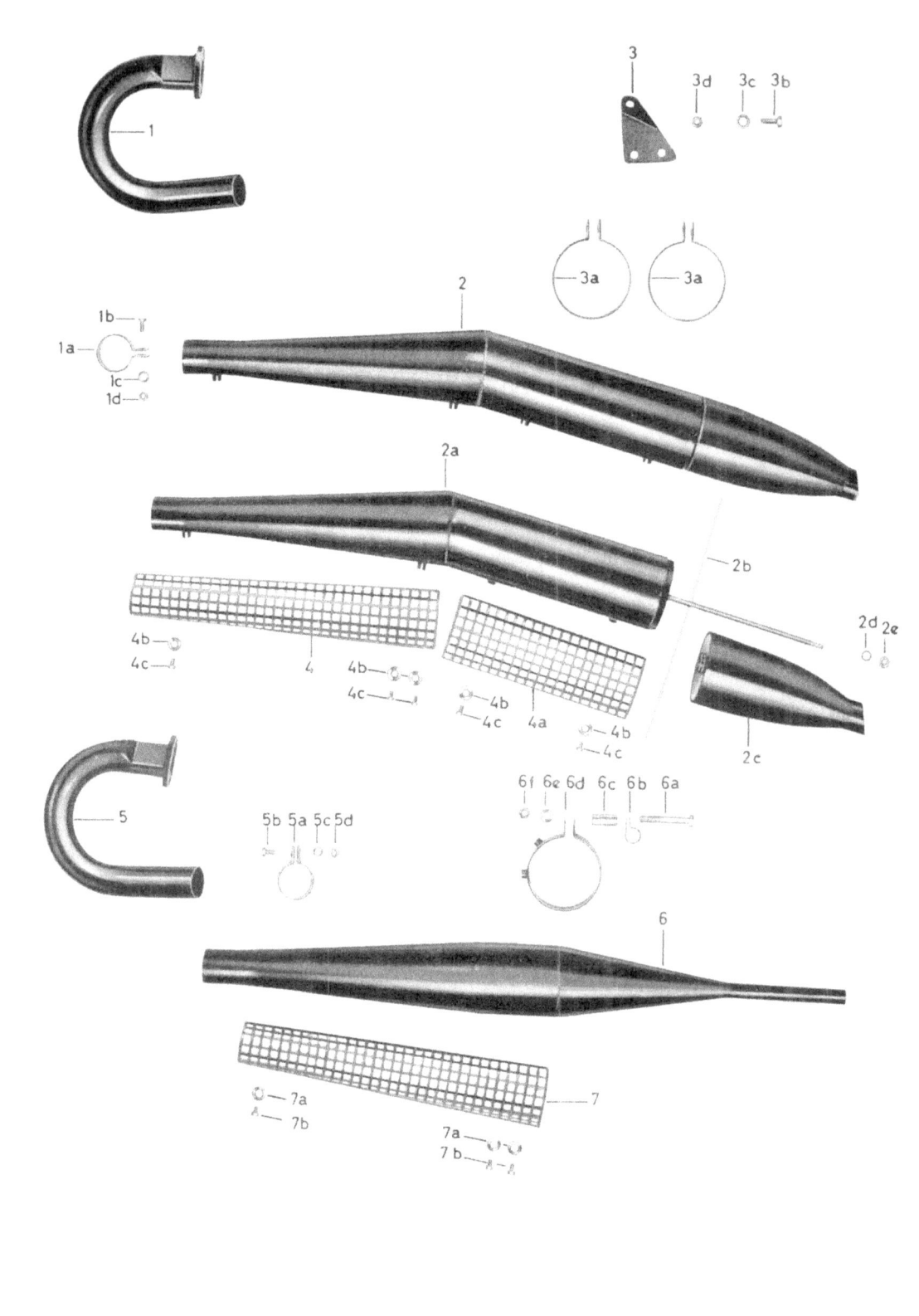

Ill. No.	Description			Order No.	Pcs.	Order	Price
	Exhaust system for „ENDURO" **Auspuffanlage für „ENDURO"**						
1	Exhaust pipe Auspuffrohr			427 190 01 01.606	1		
1a	Exhaust pipe clamp Auspuffrohrschelle			927 969 98 13	1		
1b	Hexagon screw Sechskantschraube	M 6 x 15	DIN 933	06 007 00933 37	1		
1c	Spring washer Federscheibe	B 6	DIN 137	06 011 00137 35	1		
1d	Hexagon nut Sechskantmutter	M 6	DIN 985	06 006 00985 17	1		
2	Muffler, complete Auspufftopf, kpl.			427 190 20 01.606	1		
2a	↑ Muffler front part Auspufftopf-Vorderteil			427 190 99 01.606	1		
2b	Asbestos gasket Asbestschnur	3 ∅ x 290 mm		927 198 97 01	meter		
2c	Muffler end-piece Auspufftopf-Endstück			927 190 97 07.606	1		
2d	Spring washer Federring	B 8	DIN 127	08 010 00127 31	1		
2e	Hexagon nut Sechskantmutter	M 8	DIN 934	08 009 00934 10	1		
3	Muffler mount bracket Lasche			927 971 85 10.088	1		
3a	Muffler mount clamp Auspufftopf-Klemmschelle			927 969 98 14.606	2		
3b	Hexagon screw Sechskantschraube	M 8 x 20	DIN 933	08 007 00933 37	2		
3c	Spring washer Federscheibe	B 8	DIN 137	08 015 00137 35	4		
3d	Hexagon nut Sechskantmutter	M 8	DIN 985	08 008 00985 17	2		
4	Heat shield Schutzgitter			427 771 26 01.098	1		
4a	Heat shield Schutzgitter			427 771 26 02.098	1		
4b	Washer Senkscheibe			927 992 17 01	5		
4c	Round head screw, slotted Linsensenkschraube	M 6 x 10	DIN 91	06 002 0091 17	5		

Exhaust system for CROSS-COUNTRY and MOTO-CROSS
Auspuffanlage für CROSS-COUNTRY und MOTO-CROSS

Ill. No.	Description			Order No.	Pcs.	Order	Price
	Exhaust system for „CROSS-COUNTRY" and „MOTO-CROSS" **Auspuffanlage für „CROSS-COUNTRY" und „MOTO-CROSS"**						
5	Exhaust pipe Auspuffrohr			417 190 01 02.606	1		
5a	Exhaust pipe clamp Auspuffrohrschelle			927 969 98 13	1		
5b	Hexagon screw Sechskantschraube	M 6 x 15	DIN 933	06 007 00933 37	1		
5c	Spring washer Federscheibe	B 6	DIN 137	06 011 00137 35	1		
5d	Hexagon nut Sechskantmutter	M 6	DIN 985	06 006 00985 17	1		
6	Muffler Auspufftopf			427 190 20 02.606	1		
6a	Hexagon screw Sechskantschraube	M 8 x 50	DIN 931	08 008 00931 37	1		
6b	Clamp Klemmschelle			927 969 98 33	1		
6c	Distance bushing Distanzrolle	26 mm lg.		927 996 00 03	1		
6d	Muffler mount clamp Auspufftopf-Klemmschelle			427 190 04 02.606	1		
6e	Spring washer Federring	B 8	DIN 128	08 022 00128 35	2		
6f	Hexagon nut Sechskantmutter	M 8	DIN 985	08 008 00985 17	1		
7	Heat shield Schutzgitter			427 771 26 01.098	1		
7a	Washer Senkscheibe			927 992 17 01	3		
7b	Round head screw, slotted Linsensenkschraube	M 6 x 10	DIN 91	06 002 00091 17	3		

Handlebar, throttle twistgrip, brake lever, clutch lever, rubber grip
Lenker, Gasdrehgriff, Handbremshebel, Kupplungshebel, Festgriff

Ill. No.	Description			Order No.	Pcs.	Order	Price
1	Handlebar Lenker			411 156 09 01	1		
1a	Hexagonal screw Sechskantschraube	M 10 x 50	DIN 931	10 006 00931 47	2		
1b	Washer Scheibe	10,5	DIN 125	10 012 00125 07	2		
1c	Number plate bracket Nummernschildhalter			675 968 46 06.088	1		
1d	Clamp Lenkerklemme			927 156 59 06	2		
1e	Distance bushing Distanzbüchse			927 996 00 15	2		
2	Throttle twistgrip, complete Gasdrehgriff kpl.			927 150 24 20	1		
2a	↑ Grip tube with twistgrip Griffrohr mit Drehgriffbezug			927 156 98 03	1		
2b	↑ Rubber grip Drehgriffbezug			159 156 99 04	1		
2c-2e	Housing with spring and screw Gehäuse mit Feder und Schraube			927 150 97 19	1		
2d	↑ Return spring Druckfeder			927 156 91 01	1		
2e	Adjustable screw Stellschraube			927 156 95 02	1		
2f	Sink screw Senkschraube	AM 4 x 15	DIN 63	04 007 00063 17	2		
3	Brake lever, complete Handbremshebel kpl.			159 156 94 01	1		
3a	↑ Mounting ass'y Gelenkstück			159 150 94 02	1		
3b	Round head screw, slotted Linsenzylinderschraube		DIN 85	06 204 00085 17	1		
3c	Brake lever only Bremshebel			159 156 94 03	1		
3d	Lever bolt Hebelschraube			159 156 93 01	1		
3e	Lock washer Zahnscheibe	J 6,4	DIN 6797	06 014 06797 35	1		
3f	Hexagonal nut Sechskantmutter	M 6	DIN 934	06 006 00934 17	1		
4	Clutch lever, complete Kupplungshebel kpl.			927 150 95 04	1		
4a	↑ Mounting ass'y Gelenkstück			927 150 94 08	1		
4b	Round head screw, slotted Linsenzylinderschraube			06 204 00085 17	1		
4c	Clutch lever only Kupplungshebel			159 156 90 02	1		
4d	Lever bolt Hebelschraube			159 156 93 01	1		
4e	Lock washer Zahnscheibe	J 6,4	DIN 6797	06 014 06797 35	1		
4f	Hexagonal nut Sechskantmutter	M 6	DIN 934	06 006 00934 17	1		
4g	Adjustable screw with nut Stellschraube			927 159 96 01	1		
5	Rubber grip Festgriff			927 156 87 03	1		
6	Starter lever for „ENDURO" Starthebel für „ENDURO"			159 156 82 01	1		
6a	Choke lever for „CROSS-COUNTRY" and „MOTO-CROSS" Luftregulierhebel für „CROSS-COUNTRY" und „MOTO-CROSS"			927 150 89 02	1		

Cable for throttle, starter, brake and clutch
Seilzüge

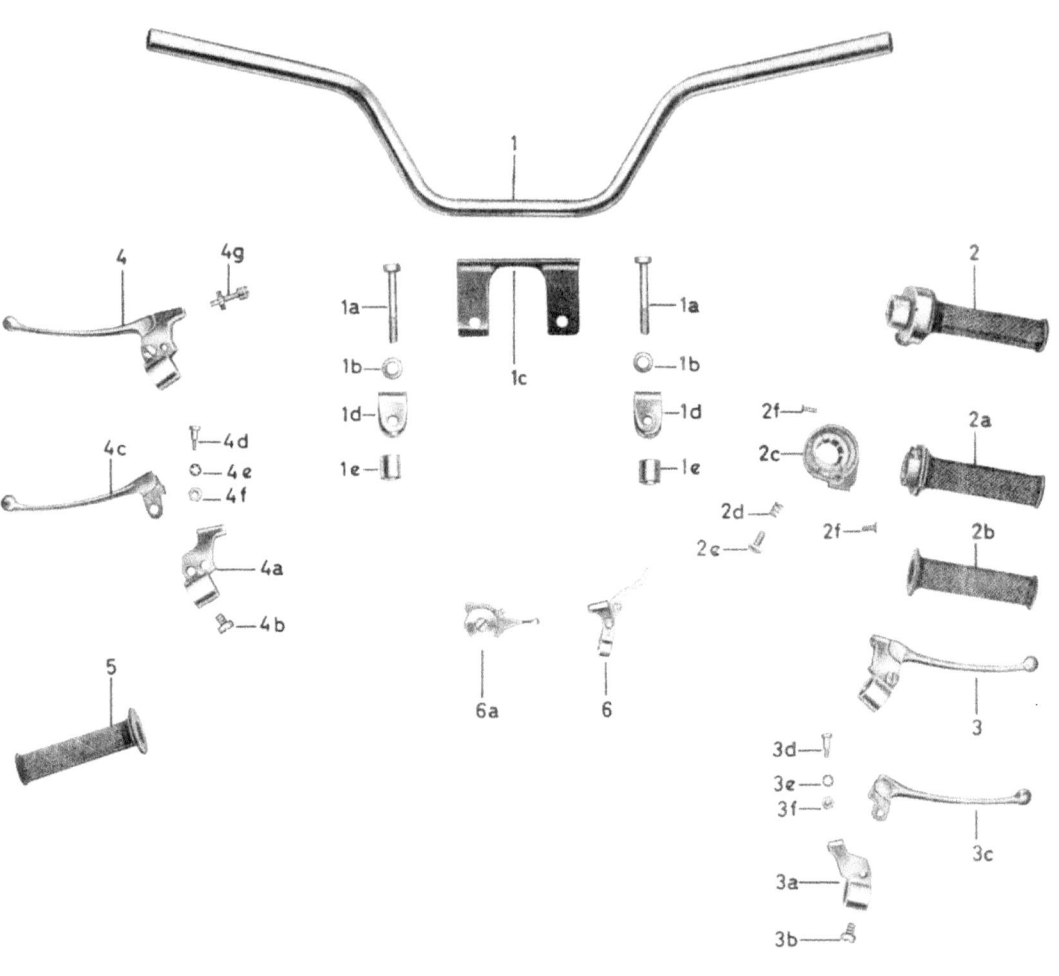

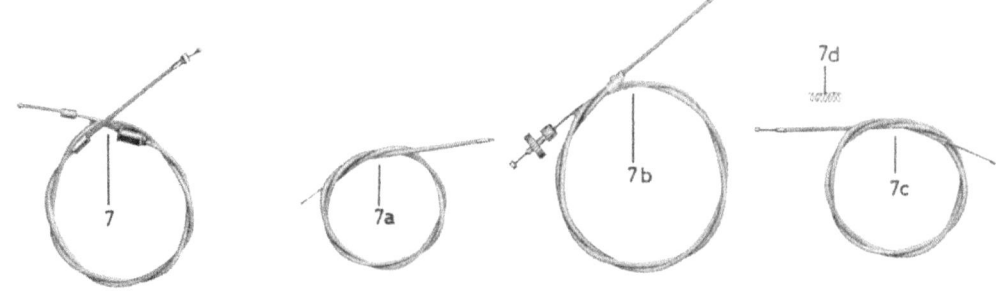

Ill. No.	Description	Order No.	Pcs.	Order	Price
7	Clutch cable Kupplungszug	927 170 73 43	1		
7a	Starter- and choke cable Starterzug	927 170 77 01	1		
7b	Brake cable Handbremszug	927 170 70 30	1		
7c	Throttle cable for „ENDURO" Gaszug	927 170 72 35	1		
	Throttle cable for „CROSS-COUNTRY" and „MOTO-CROSS" Gaszug	927 170 72 41	1		
7d	Spring for throttle cable Stützfeder für Gaszug	927 994 01 01	1		

Head lamp, head lamp bracket, switch, speedometer
Scheinwerfer, Scheinwerferhalter, Schalter, Geschwindigkeitsmesser

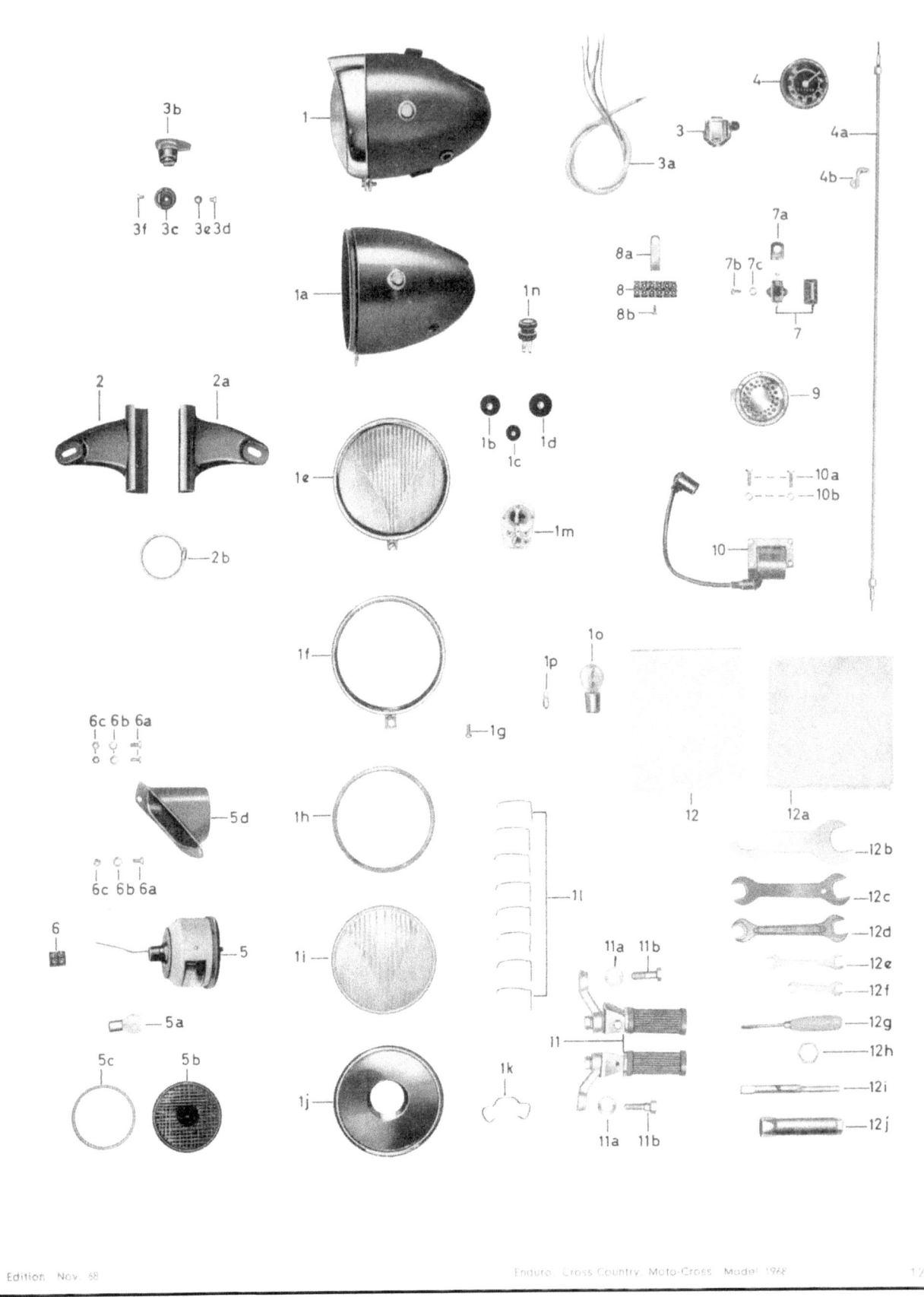

Ill. No.	Description			Order No.	Pcs.	Order	Price
1	Head lamp, complete Scheinwerfer kpl.			675 340 01 05.088	1		
1a	↑ Head lamp housing Scheinwerfergehäuse			675 341 01 01.088	1		
1b	Rubber grommet Gummitülle			927 993 21 06	1		
1c	Rubber grommet Gummitülle		DIN 72613	03 003 72613 90	1		
1d	Rubber grommet Gummitülle			927 993 21 05	1		
1e	Head lamp set Scheinwerfereinsatz			375 340 05 05	1		
1f-1g	↑ Headlight door Glashaltering			166 341 99 01	1		
1g	↑ Round slotted head screw Linsenzylinderkopfschraube		DIN 84	05 005 00084 14	1		
1h	Gasket for glass Dichtring			115 348 50 00	1		
1i	Head lamp glass Scheinwerferglas			675 341 95 01	1		
1j-1k	Reflector with spring Reflektor mit Federbügel			540 341 98 00	1		
1k	↑ Spring for Reflektor Federbügel			927 341 92 01	1		
1l	Spring for glass Glashaltefeder			166 341 88 01	8		
1m	Socket for bulb Lampenfassung			540 341 94 00	1		
1n	High beam indicator, complete Fernlichtkontrolle			675 340 20 05	1		
1o	Bilux-bulb B 6 V - 35/35 W Bilux-Lampe		DIN 72601	06 010 72601 90	1		
1p	Bulb for HBI J 6 V - 0,6 W Glühlampe für Fernlichtkontrolle		DIN 72601	06 001 72601 90	1		
2	Head lamp bracket, left Scheinwerferhalter links			921 150 39 14.088	1		
2a	Head lamp bracket, right Scheinwerferhalter rechts			921 150 39 15.088	1		
2b	Clamp Schlauchschelle			927 973 33 01	2		
3	Light switch for ENDURO Lichtschalter			685 380 31 02	1		
3a	Cable for light switch Kabelstrang für Lichtschalter			427 360 01 04	1		
3b	Connect- and snare switch for CROSS-COUNTRY and MOTO CROSS Kurzschluß- und Hornschalter			685 380 31 01	1		
3c-3f	Bracket for connect switch, complete Schalteraufnahme, kpl.			927 384 45 01	1		
3d	↑ Round head screw, slotted Linsenzylinderschraube	AM 5x6	DIN 85	05 001 00085 17	1		
3e	Lock washer Zahnscheibe	J 5,1	DIN 6797	05 011 06797 35	1		
3f	Round head screw, slotted Linsenschraube mit Zapfen	M 4x4x2,5	DIN 922	04 003 00922 17	1		
4	Speedometer 0-80 mph for ENDURO 100 cc Geschwindigkeitsmesser (Wegdrehzahl 1,9)			427 291 05 02	1		
	Speedometer 0-80 mph for ENDURO 125 cc Geschwindigkeitsmesser (Wegdrehzahl 1,77)			427 291 05 03	1		
4a	Speedometer drive shaft Antriebswelle	820 mm		698 297 01 01	1		
4b	Speedometer drive shaft bracket Halteöse für Antriebswelle			927 999 98 01	1		

Taillight, brake light switch, terminal, snare, ignition coil, cables, passengers foot rest
Schlußlicht, Bremslichtschalter, Leitungsverbinder, Schnarre, Zündspule, Kabel, Soziusfußrasten

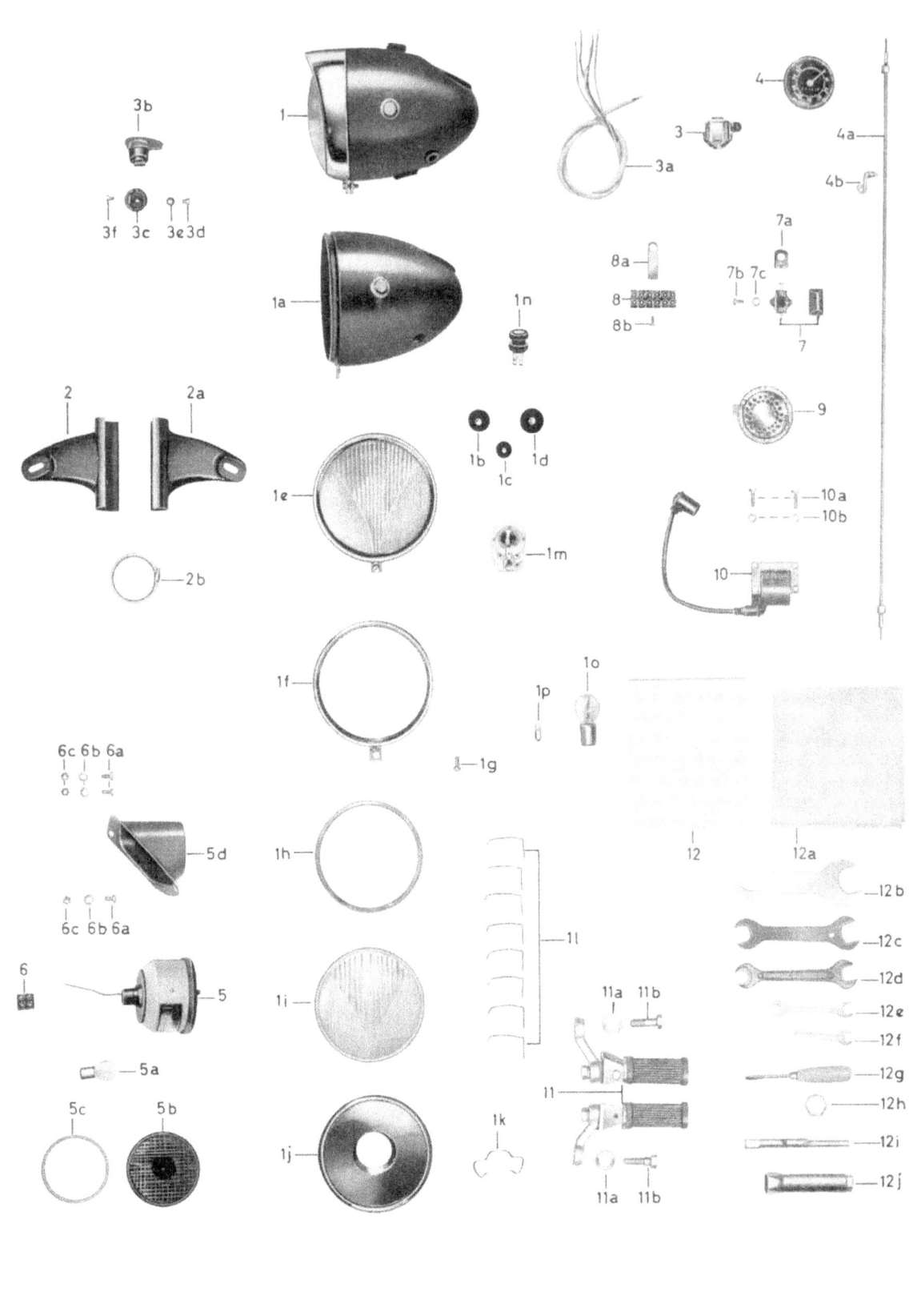

Ill. No.	Description			Order No.	Pcs.	Order	Price
5-5d	Taillight with mount, complete Schlußlicht mit Halter, kpl.			675 340 02 02.088	1		
5	Taillight, complete Schlußlicht, kpl.			675 340 02 01.088	1		
5a	Bulb S 6 V - 18/5 W Glühlampe			06 017 72601 90	1		
5b	Taillight lens Schlußlicht-Glas			927 344 09 01	1		
5c	Gasket Dichtung			927 993 38 07	1		
5d	Mount for taillight Halter für Schlußlicht			675 968 46 01.088	1		
6	Terminal Leitungsverbinder			927 995 62 02	1		
6a	Round head screw, slotted Linsenzylinderschraube	AM 6 x 10	DIN 85	06 002 00085 17	3		
6b	Spring washer Federring	B 6	DIN 128	06 018 00128 35	3		
6c	Nut Sechskantmutter	M 6	DIN 985	06 006 00985 17	3		
7	Brake light switch Bremslichtschalter			927 380 40 01	1		
7a	Bracket Anschlagwinkel			927 978 60 33	1		
7b	Round head screw Linsenzylinderschraube	AM 4 x 12	DIN 85	04 008 00085 17	2		
7c	Spring washer Federscheibe	A 4	DIN 137	04 006 00137 35	2		
8	Terminal Leitungsverbinder 4-polig			12 004 72586 90	4/12		
8a	Mounting bracket Lasche			927 971 85 16	1		
8b	Round slotted head screw Linsenzylinderschraube	AM 3 x 15	DIN 85	03 008 00085 17	1		
9	Snare (horn) Schnarre			166 393 20 00	1		
10	Ignition coil Zündspule			927 316 10 01	1		
10a	Hexagonal screw Sechskantschraube	M 5x20	DIN 933	05 011 00933 37	2		
10b	Spring washer Federring	B 5	DIN 128	05 016 00128 35	2		
—	Cable (terminal - head lamp) for ENDURO Kabelstrang Leitungsverbinder-Scheinwerfer)			427 360 01 06	1		
—	Cable (terminal-connect switch) for CC and MC Kabelstrang (Leitungsverbinder zum Kurzschlußschalter)			417 360 01 04	1		
—	Cable for taillight Kabelstrang für Schlußlicht			427 360 01 05	1		
—	Cable for ignition coil Massekabel für Zündspule			927 360 20 03	1		
—	Terminal for head lamp Leitungsverbinder im Scheinwerfer 3-polig			927 995 62 03	1		
11	Passengers foot rest Soziusfußraste			115 100 25 99	1 pair (1 Paar)		
11a	Spring washer Federring	B 12	DIN 128	12 026 00128 35	2		
11b	Hexagonal screw Sechskantschraube	M 12 x 30	DIN 931	12 002 00931 37	2		

13 Enduro, Cross-Country, Moto-Cross Model 1968 Edition Nov. 68

Tool kit
Werkzeugsatz

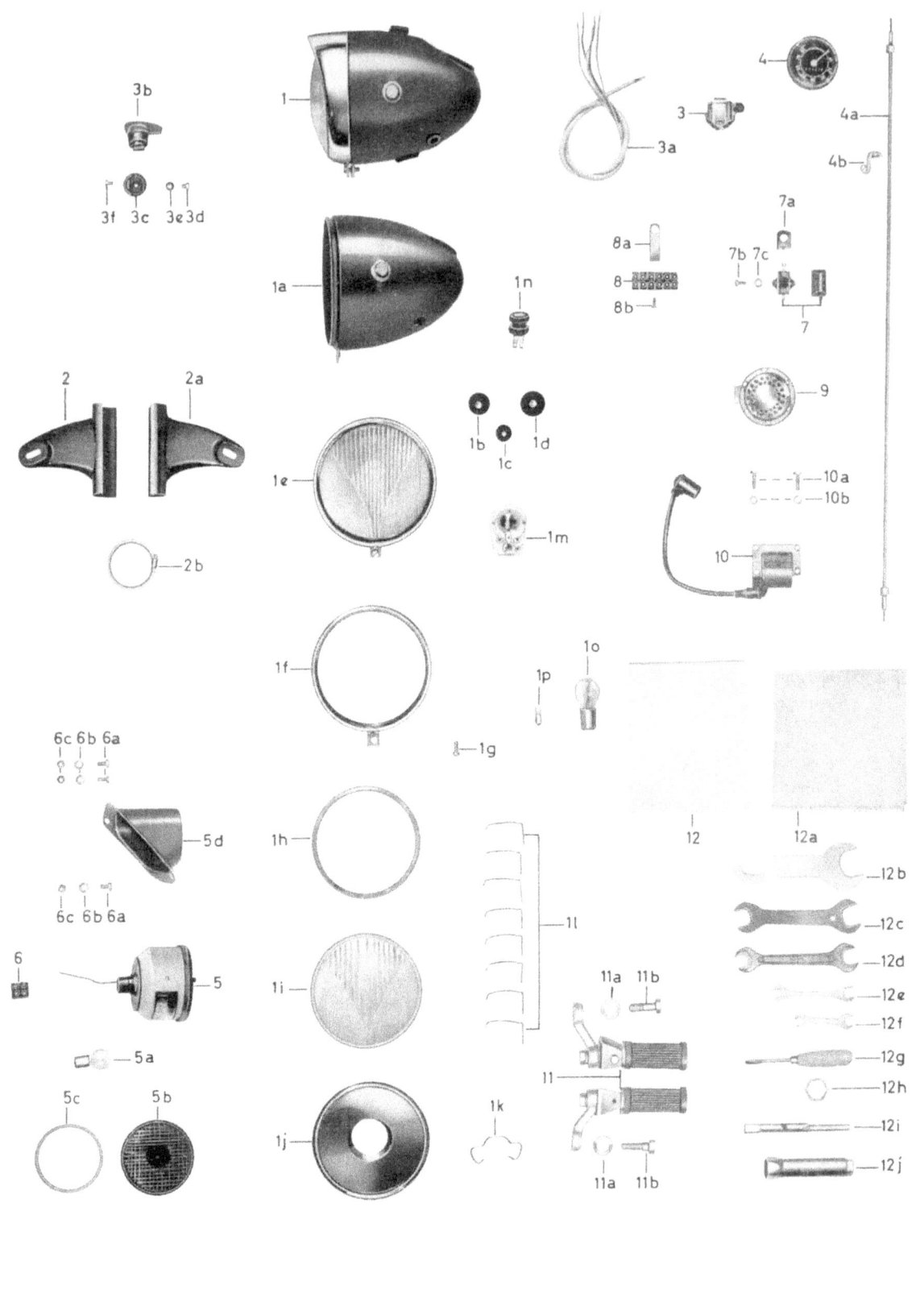

Ill. No.	Description		Order No.	Pcs.	Order	Price
12-12j	Tool kit, complete Werkzeugsatz, kpl.		676 940 06 03	1		
12	Plastic bag Plastikbeutel		927 959 62 03	1		
12a	Polishing rag Putztuch		925 943 90 02	1		
12b	Special wrench Spezialschlüssel		925 943 07 02	1		
12c	Open end wrench Doppelmaulschlüssel	19/22	925 943 03 04	1		
12d	Open end wrench Doppelmaulschlüssel	13/17	13 024 00895 47	1		
12e	Open end wrench Doppelmaulschlüssel	9/11	0276 111 000	1		
12f	Open end wrench Doppelmaulschlüssel	7/8	0977 016 200	1		
12g	Screw driver Schraubenzieher		08 004 05270 20	1		
12h	Hexagon adapter Reduzierhülse	26/24	927 968 80 03	1		
12i	Socket wrench Steckschlüssel	10/14	0976 005 100	1		
12j	Socket wrench Steckschlüssel	21/26	0976 004 100	1		
—	Master link Steckglied	½ × 5/16	06 084 08187 40	1		

Front wheel, front hub
Vorderrad, Vorderradnabe

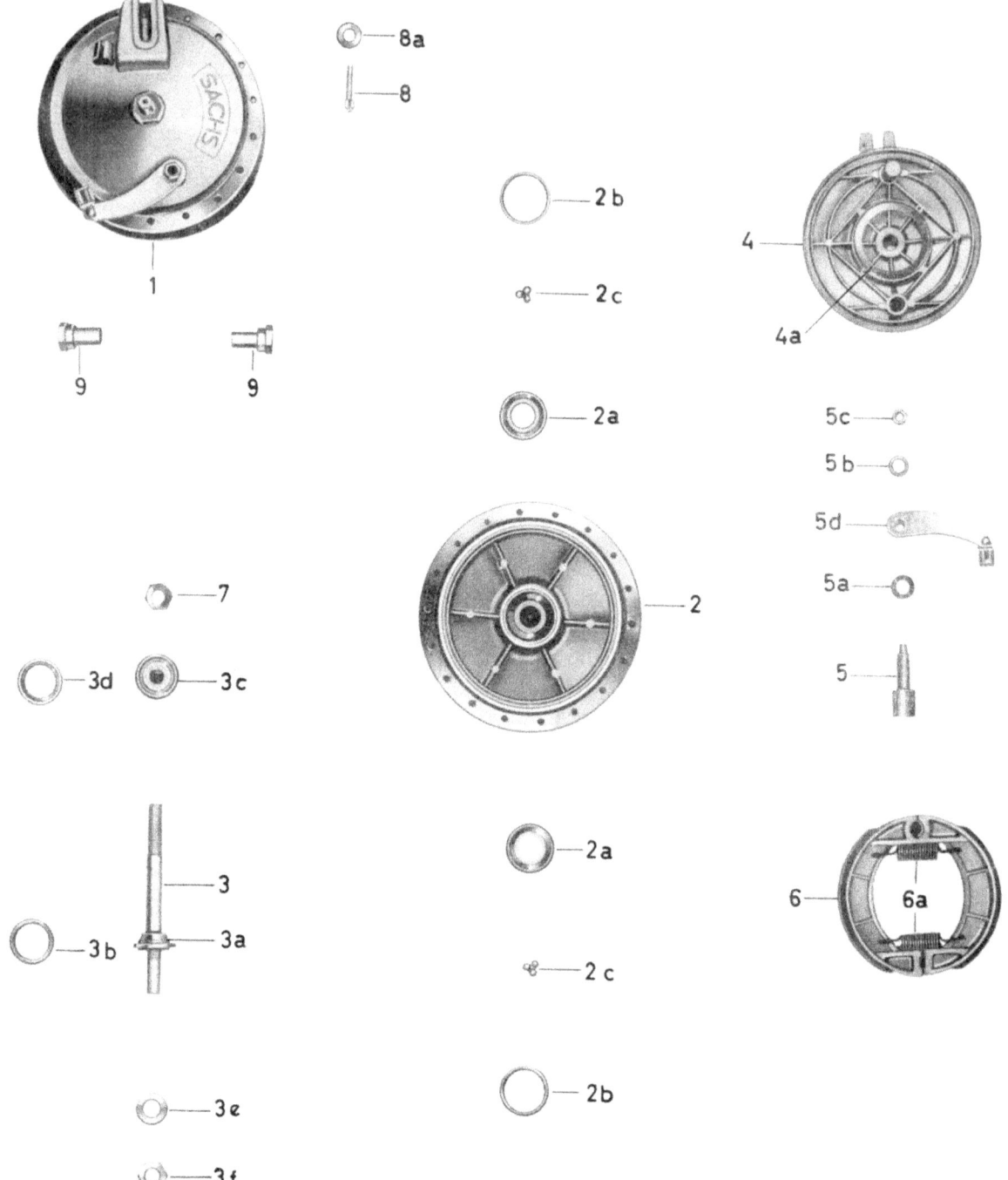

Ill. No.	Description		Order No.	Pcs.	Order	Price
—	Front wheel, complete, without tire (for CONTINENTAL-tire 3,00 - 21) Vorderrad kpl., ohne Bereifung		417 240 99 01	1		
—	Front wheel, complete, without tire (for METZELER-tire 2,50-21) Vorderrad kpl., ohne Bereifung		417 240 99 02	1		
—	Rim, chrome plated, (for CONTINENTAL-tire 3,00-21) Tiefbettfelge	1,85 B x 21	427 241 10 01	1		
—	Rim, chrome plated (for METZELER-tire 2,50-21) Tiefbettfelge		18 007 07816 09	1		
—	Spoke (Inside) Innenspeiche	M 3 x 225	30 024 74371 39	18		
—	Spoke (Outside) Außenspeiche	M 3 x 225	30 025 74371 39	18		
—	Nipple Speichennippel	M 3	30 091 74371 68	36		
1	Front hub, complete Vorderradnabe kpl.	SACHS V 1401	12 0800 001 001	1		
2-2b	Hub body with bearing races and U-cover Nabenkörper mit Lagerschalen u. U-Deckel		0870 152 000	1		
2a	Bearing race Lagerschale		0835 104 000	2		
2b	U-couver U-Deckel		0821 130 000	2		
2c	Ball 9/32" Kugel		0323 032 000	24		
3-3b	Axle with one cone Achse mit Stellkonus	145 mm	0871 135 000	1		
3a-3b	Cone with dust cover Stellkonus mit Staubdeckel	14 mm	0874 111 000	1		
3b	Dust cover Staubdeckel		0821 103 000	1		
3c-3d	Cone with dust cover Stellkonus mit Staubdeckel	14 mm	0874 111 000	1		
3d	Dust cover Staubdeckel		0821 103 000	1		
3e	Safety washer with flange Sicherungsscheibe mit Innennase		0817 102 000	1		
3f	Hexagonal nut Sechskantmutter	M 12 x 1,5	0816 105 001	1		
4-4a	Brake plate Bremsteller		0877 136 000	1		
5-5c	Brake cam with rubber gasket, washer and hexagonal nut Bremsnocken mit Gummiring, Federring und Sechskantmutter		0879 110 000	1		
5a	Rubber gasket Gummi-Dichtring		0822 104 000	1		
5b	Spring washer Federring	B 8 DIN 128	08 022 00128 35	1		
5c	Hexagonal nut Sechskantmutter	M 8 x 1 DIN 936	08 001 00936 17	1		
5d	Brake arm Bremshebel mit Nippelaufnahme		0878 113 000	1		
6-6a	Brake shoes complete, with springs Bremsbackensatz mit Federn		0873 103 000	1 set		
6a	Return spring Rückholfeder		0825 102 301	2		
7	Hexagonal nut Sechskantmutter	M 12 x 1	0816 105 001	1		
9	Axle nut Bundmutter		927 991 56 02	2		

15   Enduro, Cross-Country, Moto-Cross   Model 1968   Edition Nov. 68

Tire for front wheel
Bereifung für Vorderrad

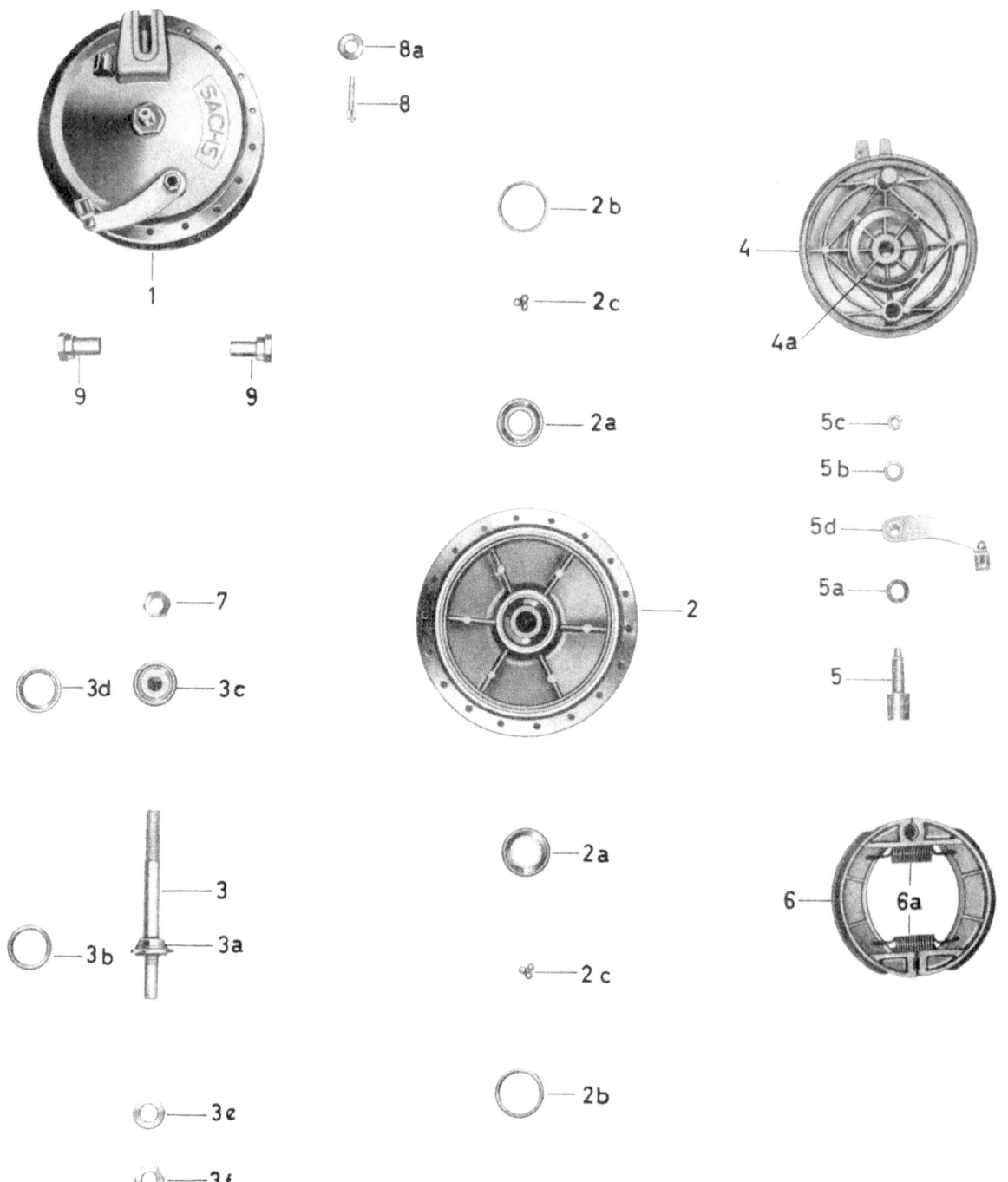

Ill. No.	Description		Order No.	Pos.	Order	Price
—	Tire „CONTINENTAL-GS 6" Reifen	3,00-21	30 411 07802 90	1		
—	Tire „METZELER-D" Reifen	2,50-21	25 404 07802 90	1		
—	Tube (for CONTINENTAL-tire) Schlauch	3,00-21	927 241 71 10	1		
—	Tube (for METZELER-tire) Schlauch	C 21	698 241 71 02	1		
—	Rim band Felgenband	19"/20	698 241 70 02	1		
—	Tire holder „DUNLOP MW 3" Reifenhalter		427 241 67 01	1		

Rear wheel, rear hub, sprocket
Hinterrad, Hinterradnabe, Kettenrad

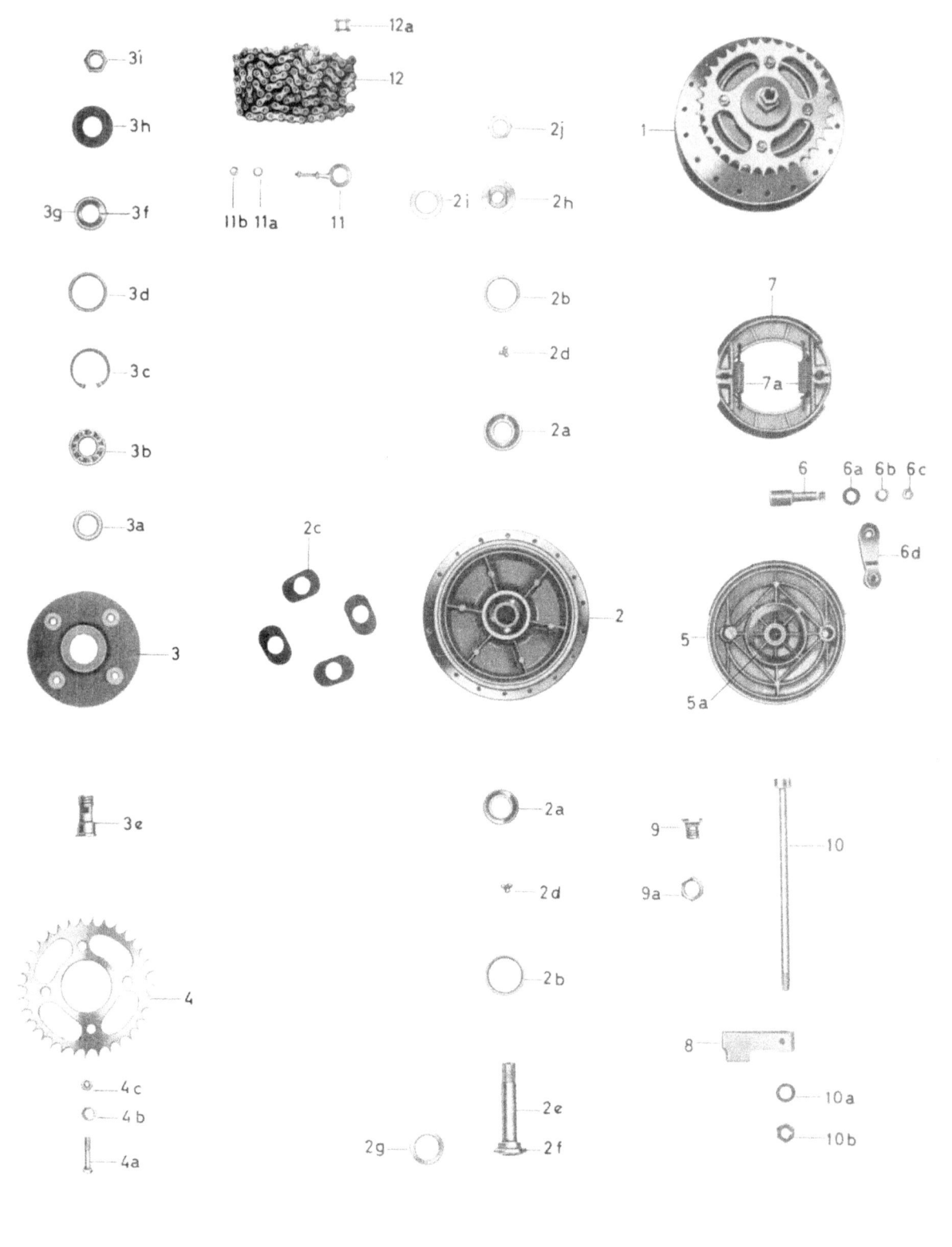

Ill. No.	Description		Order No.	Pcs.	Order	Price
—	Rear wheel, complete, **without sprocket** and tire Hinterrad kpl., **ohne Kettenrad** und Bereifung		417 240 98 01	1		
—	Rim, chrome plated Tiefbettfelge	1,85 B x 18	427 241 10 05	1		
—	Spoke (inside) Innenspeiche	M 3,5 x 190 DIN 74371	35 408 74371 39	18		
—	Spoke (outside) Außenspeiche	M 3,5 x 190 DIN 74371	35 407 74371 39	18		
—	Nipple Speichennippel	M 3,5 DIN 74371	35 092 74371 68	36		
1	Rear hub SACHS HS 1401 GS, **without sprocket and spring-stop-nuts** Hinterradnabe kpl., **ohne Kettenrad und Sechskantmuttern**		65 0800 001 002	1		
2-2c	Hub body with races and U-covers Nabenkörper mit Lagerschalen und U-Deckel		0870 154 002	1		
2a	Bearing race Lagerschale		0835 104 000	2		
2b	U-cover U-Deckel		0821 130 000	2		
2c	Rubber damper Dämpfergummi		0822 106 000	4		
2d	Ball 9/32" Kugel		0323 032 000	24		
2e-2g	Cone bushing with cone and U-cover Konusbüchse mit Stellkonus und U-Deckel		0874 112 000	1		
2f	Cone with U-cover Stellkonus mit U-Deckel	14 mm	0874 114 000	2		
2g	U-cover U-Deckel (Staubdeckel)		0821 103 000	2		
2h	Cone with U-cover Stellkonus mit U-Deckel		0874 114 000	2		
2i	U-cover U-Deckel (Staubdeckel)		0821 103 000	2		
2j	Hexagonal nut Sechskantmutter	M 17 x 1 x 3,5	0816 108 001	1		
3-3j	Clutch-piece complete Kupplungsstück kpl.		0872 120 000	1		
3	Clutch-piece only Kupplungsstück, leer		0841 109 000	1		
3a	Washer Scheibe	35 mm ⌀ - 0,5	0818 130 000	1		
3b	Bearing Kugellager	6004 C 3 DIN 625	60 049 00625 40	1		
3c	Circlip Sicherungsring		0812 107 000	1		
3d	U-cover U-Deckel		0821 122 001	1		
3e	Axle bushing Achsaufsatz		0842 112 000	1		
3f-3g	Spacer with U-cover Distanzbuchse mit U-Deckel		0874 115 000	1		
3g	U-cover Staubdeckel		0821 123 000	1		
3h	Washer Scheibe	50 mm ⌀ x 3	0818 124 001	1		
3i	Hexagonal nut Sechskantmutter	M 17 x 1 x 7,5	0816 106 001	1		
4	Sprocket, 48 teeth Kettenrad		901 035 02 48	1		
	Sprocket, 50 teeth Kettenrad (serienmäßige Ausrüstung)		901 035 02 50	1		
	Sprocket, 52 teeth Kettenrad		901 035 02 52	1		

Enduro, Cross-Country, Moto-Cross Model 1968   Edition Nov. 68

Rear hub, chain tensioner, chain, tire for rear wheel
Hinterradnabe, Kettenspanner, Kette, Bereifung für Hinterrad

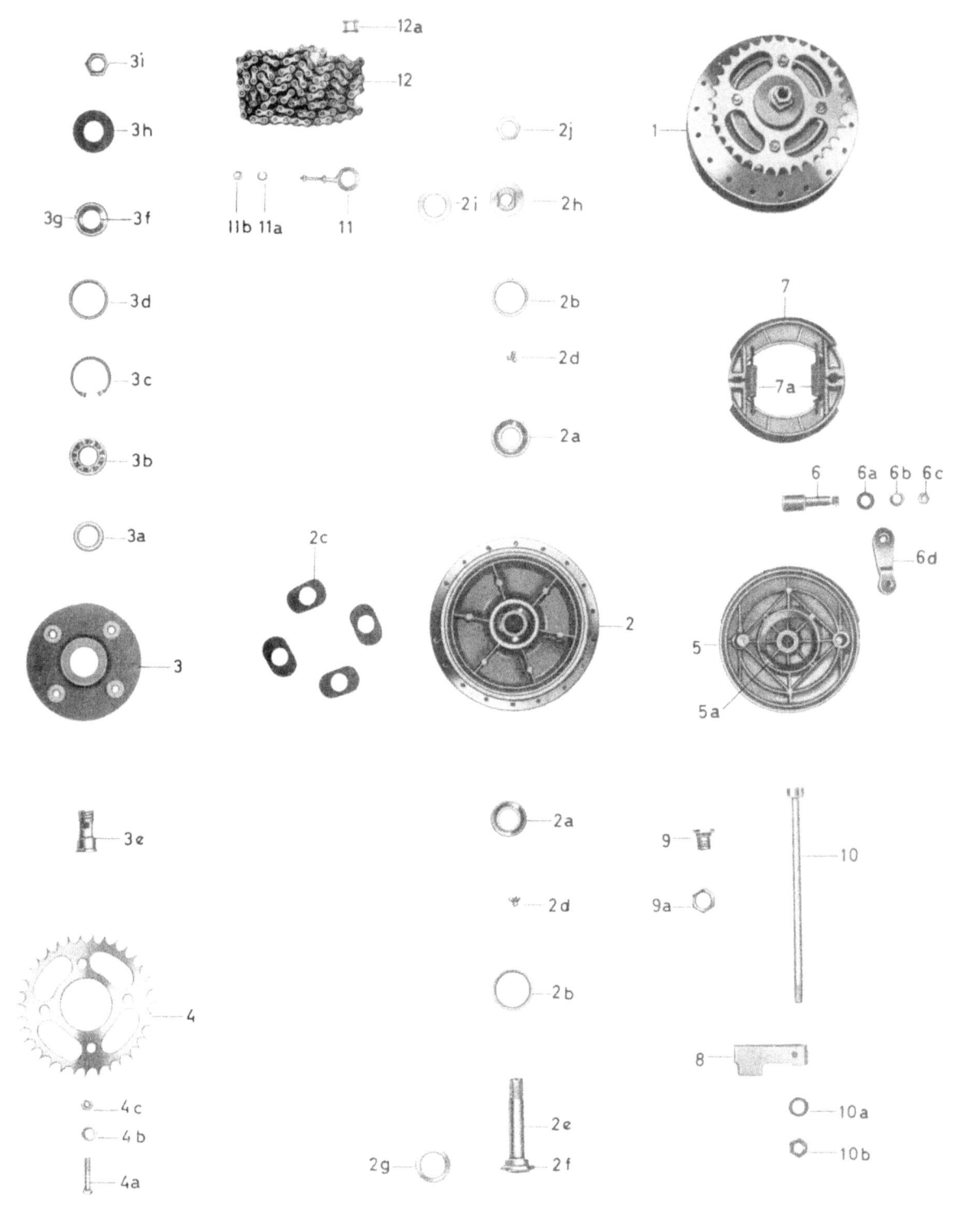

Ill. No.	Description			Order No.	Pcs.	Order	Price
4a	↑ Hexagonal screw Sechskantschraube	M 7 x 35	DIN 931	07 006 00931 47	4		
4b	| Spring washer | Federring	B 7	DIN 128	07 020 00128 35	4		
4c	Nut Sechskantmutter	M 7	DIN 985	07 007 00985 17	4		
5-5a	Brake plate Bremsteller			0877 137 000	1		
6-6c	Brake cam with rubber gasket, washer and hexagonal nut Bremsnocken mit Gummidichtring, Federring und Sechskantmutter			0879 110 000	1		
6a	↑ Rubber gasket Gummi-Dichtring			0822 104 000	1		
6b	| Spring washer | Federring	B 8	DIN 128	08 022 00128 35	1		
6c	| Hexagonal nut | Sechskantmutter	M 8 x 1	DIN 936	08 001 00936 17	1		
6d	Brake arm Bremshebel			0878 115 000	1		
7-7a	Brake shoes with springs Bremsbacken mit Rückholfedern			0873 103 000	1 set		
7a	↑ Return spring Rückholfeder			0825 102 301	2		
8	Brake plate holder Bremstellerhalter			0841 110 000	1		
9-9a	Axle bushing Achsaufsatz	22,5 mm		0871 136 000	1		
9a	↑ Hexagonal nut Sechskantmutter	17 x 1 x 7,5		0816 106 001	1		
10-10b	Axle, complete Steckachse kpl.	220,5 mm		0871 137 000	1		
10a	↑ Washer Scheibe	13	DIN 125	13 013 00125 07	1		
10b	| Hexagonal nut | Sechskantmutter	M 12 x 1,5	DIN 934	12 014 00934 17	1		
11	Chain tensioner Kettenspanner, leer			927 030 44 04	2		
11a	Washer Scheibe	6,4	DIN 125	06 009 00125 07	2		
11b	Nut Sechskantmutter	M 6	DIN 985	06 006 00985 17	2		
12	Chain with lock 1 x 12,7 x 7,75 x 116 Rollenkette		DIN 8187	06 012 08187 40	1		
12a	Master link 1E 12,7 x 7,75 Steckglied		DIN 8187	06 084 08187 40	1		
—	Tire „CONTINENTAL GS 6" Reifen	3,25/3,50-18	DIN 7802	30 417 07802 90	1		
—	Tire „METZELER D" Reifen	3,50/18	DIN 7802	35 017 07802 90	1		
—	Tube Schlauch	E 18		698 241 71 01	1		
—	Rim band Felgenband	18"/27		698 241 70 01	1		
—	Tire holder „DUNLOP WM 3" Reifenhalter			427 241 67 01	1		

Wiring diagram for ENDURO
Schaltplan für ENDURO

Edition Nov. 68 — Enduro, Cross-Country, Moto-Cross Model 1968

Wiring diagram for CROSS-COUNTRY and MOTO-CROSS
Schaltplan für CROSS-COUNTRY und MOTO-CROSS

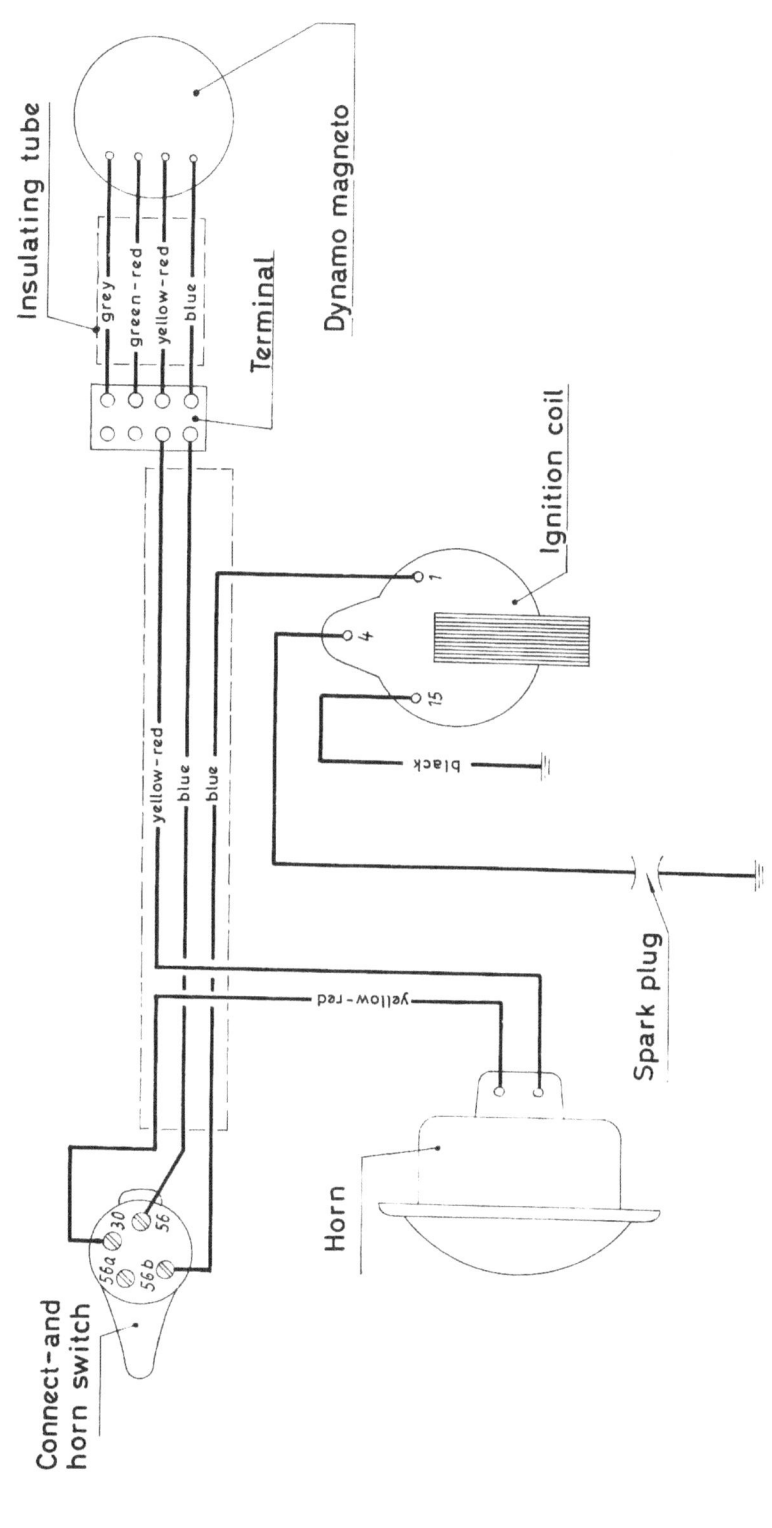

NOTES

CHAPTER TWELVE

DKW

Specific service procedures and illustrations presented in this chapter are confined to DKW motorcycles. However, the information is designed to serve also as a general guide for other makes. Specific problems relating to the wide variety of proprietary components (forks, rear suspension units, brakes) used on such makes as Penton, Dalesman, Monark, Wassell, and Tyran should be referred to the manufacturer or the dealer from whom the motorcycle was purchased.

In general, service on makes other than DKW will be similar. Careful attention to the order and relationship of components during disassembly, supplemented by information from your dealer, will help to ensure successful servicing and repair of chassis components.

FRAME

DKW frames, as well as most other manufacturers using Sachs engines, are made of welded steel tubing. Service is limited to inspection for bending of frame members and cracked welds. If the motorcycle has suffered a collision or hard spill, the frame should be examined carefully for damage and repaired by a competent frame specialist.

HANDLEBAR

A variety of handlebar types are used on Sachs-powered motorcycles. Handlebars and related components are shown in the parts list. Handlebars should be examined for cracks or bends following a collision or hard spill. Minor bends can be corrected by straightening the bars, but severe bending or cracks warrant replacement.

Clutch, throttle, choke, and front brake controls are mounted on the handlebar. On models equipped with lights and horn, the light beam control switch and horn button are also mounted on the handlebar, and on motocross models, the ignition kill button is near the throttle grip.

The tension or resistance of the throttle grip is controlled by a friction plate. Tension can be adjusted by turning the thumb screw (**Figure 1**) in or out to suit your liking. Throttle cable free-play is adjusted at the carburetor (**Figure 2**). With the throtttle closed, loosen the locknut on the top of the carburetor and turn the knurled adjuster in or out until the play in the cable sheath is about 0.039 in. (1mm). Hold the knurled adjuster to prevent it from turning and tighten the locknut.

Front brake control adjustment is largely a matter of personal preference, but the cable must never be adjusted so tightly that it causes the

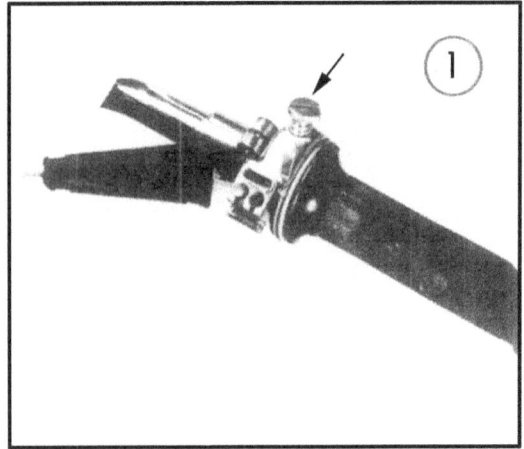

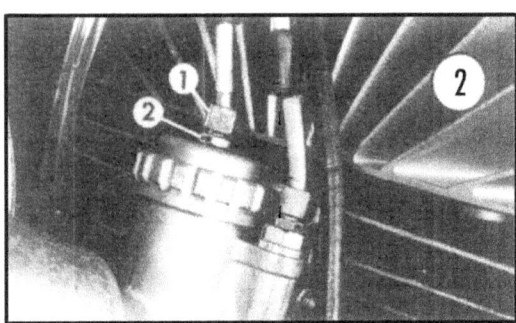

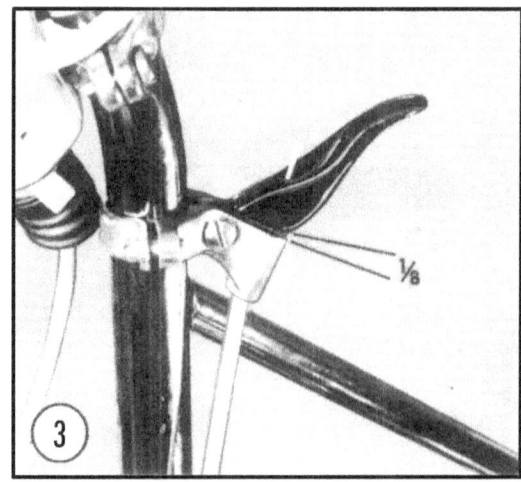

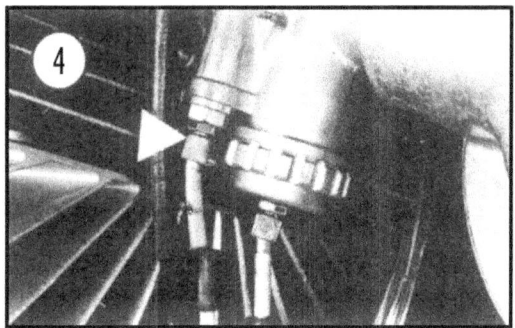

brake shoes to drag in the drum when the lever is in the relaxed position. When the brake lining wears and the cable stretches to a point where maximum braking effect is no longer attainable with cable adjustment, the brake arm must be removed and repositioned on the brake camshaft. Screw the cable adjuster about half way in and unscrew the nut from the end of the brake cam. Pull the brake arm off of the cam and rotate it one notch forward. Reinstall and tighten the nut on the cam and adjust the brake to suit your riding style.

The free-play in the clutch lever should be about ½ in. (12mm), measured at the end of the lever. If adjustment is not possible with the cable adjuster, refer to Chapter Five for the basic clutch adjustment.

The choke control lever (**Figure 3**) should have at least ⅛ in. (3mm) of free-play to ensure that the choke is fully disengaged when the lever is in the off position. The free-play is adjusted at the carburetor (**Figure 4**) by loosening the locknut and turning the knurled adjuster in or out until the play is correct at the lever. Then, hold the adjuster to prevent it from turning and tighten the locknut.

FRONT FORKS

Front forks on some DKW models are conventional oil-damped telescopic types with internal springs. Other DKW models have leading link front suspension with removal suspension units that are also oil damped but have external springs (see parts list).

Telescopic Forks

Damping characteristics can be altered by changing the viscosity of the damping oil in the fork legs. However, it's recommended that automatic transmission fluid be used in accordance with manufacturer's instructions. This oil offers the best all-round damping characteristics and is specially compounded to resist foaming during hard, sustained usage.

Changing Fork Oil

1. Place a drip pan beneath each fork leg, remove the drain plugs from the bottoms of the

legs, and allow the oil to drain for several minutes. Lock the front brake and depress the forks several times to expel all of the oil.

2. Reinstall and tighten the drain plugs.

3. Remove the cap nut from one upper fork tube at a time, fill it with 240cc (8 ounces) of the appropriate viscosity oil, and reinstall and tighten the nut. Repeat the procedure for the other fork tube.

Changing Fork Seals

The only service operation normally required for the front forks is replacement of the seals. The seals may be replaced without removing the upper fork tubes from the clamps. If oil seepage past the seals seems to indicate that they are worn or damaged, first check the breather valves on the tops of the fork tubes; if these valves are obstructed they can cause oil seepage through a good seal. If the valves are clear, however, and the seals continue to leak, they should be replaced.

1. Support the front end of the motorcycle so the wheel is clear of the ground. Remove the wheel and drain plugs from the fork legs.

2. After the oil has drained, remove axle pitch bolts from fork legs. Remove Allen bolts from bottom of fork legs.

3. Pull the lower fork legs down and off of the upper tubes. Remove the rubber dust seals from the legs.

4. Clamp one of the fork legs in a vise, using light pressure to prevent collapse or denting of the leg. Also, it's advisable to protect the finish of the leg by using soft vise jaw inserts or a clean shop rag wrapped around the leg.

5. Remove the circlip from the upper end of the leg and pry out the 2 seals with a screwdriver (**Figure 5**). It may be necessary to heat the fork leg, and care should be taken not to damage the opening or inner surfaces of the leg.

6. Clean the seal bore in the top of the leg and inspect the damper valve and bushings in both the lower leg and upper tube for galling. Severe galling warrants replacement. Inspect the dust covers and O-rings for damage and replace as necessary. Thoroughly clean and dry all the components.

7. Install new seals, making certain that they are seated and square in the leg. A large socket may be used as a seal driver. Oil the seals and reinstall the lower leg on the upper tube. Install the Allen bolt and tighten it securely. Repeat the procedure for the other fork leg.

8. Reassemble the rest of the components, reversing the order of disassembly. Fill the fork tubes with oil as described earlier.

Fork Removal

1. Drain the oil from the forks and remove the front wheel as described earlier.

2. Remove the cap nuts from the top of the forks and loosen the pinch bolts in both the upper and lower fork clamps.

3. Pull the fork legs down and out of the clamps.

Fork Installation

Fork installation is in reverse order of removal. On all makes, before tightening the opposing axle pinch bolt and the axle nut, place the motorcycle back on both wheels and while holding the front brake on, compress and extend the front suspension several times to align the front end components. Then tighten the opposing pinch bolt and the axle nut.

Steering Head

Periodically, the steering head should be disassembled and the bearings and races cleaned, inspected, and greased. The frequency of this service depends on use, but it should be carried out at least once a year. More frequently, the steering head should be checked for play and tightened if necessary.

1. Support the front of the motorcycle so the wheel is off the ground.
2. Grasp the lower fork legs and attempt to move them back and forth. If any movement can be felt, the steering head must be tightened.
3. Loosen the steering stem pinch bolt on the upper clamp. If the play is extreme, it may also be necessary to loosen the fork tube pinch bolts in the top clamp so that the clamps will remain parallel when the steering stem nut is tightened.
4. Tighten the top steering nut until play can no longer be felt when checked for as described above.

> NOTE: *Don't overtighten the steering stem. While there should be no apparent play in the steering head, neither should there be any resistance to turning of the head. Steering resistance in the unloaded condition will be compounded when the front end has weight on it, and handling will be adversely affected. Also, excessive pre-load on the bearings will result in damage to the races and balls.*

5. When the adjustment is satisfactory, tighten the pinch bolt.

REAR SUSPENSION

DKW motorcycles have hydraulically damped, spring-controlled rear suspension units (**Figure 6**). Those on some models have a fixed pre-load while those on other models are adjustable to 3 pre-load positions. Neither type is rebuildable; when they are found to be faulty they must be replaced.

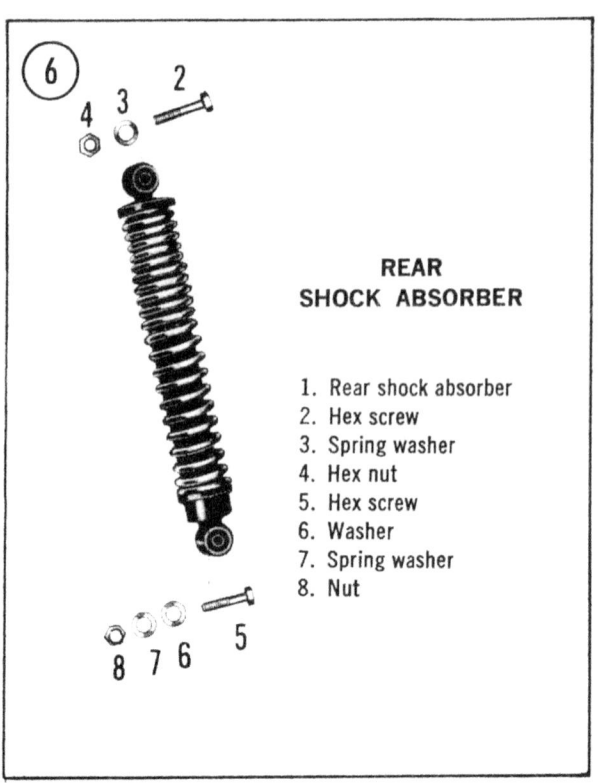

REAR SHOCK ABSORBER

1. Rear shock absorber
2. Hex screw
3. Spring washer
4. Hex nut
5. Hex screw
6. Washer
7. Spring washer
8. Nut

Removal and Disassembly

1. Support the motorcycle so there is no weight on the rear wheel.
2. Remove the bolt from the bottom eye of each spring-shock. On Penton models, note the location of the bolt in the hanger plate on the swinging arm for reference during reassembly.
3. Remove the bolts from the upper eyes and remove the units from the motorcycle.
4. Clamp the lower eye of the shock in a vise and compress the spring to release the keepers beneath the upper eye. On adjustable units, it is necessary to set the pre-load adjustment at its softest position before compressing the spring.
5. Lift the spring and cover (if fitted) off the shock.
6. Thoroughly clean and dry all parts.

Inspection

1. Check the condition of the rubber bumper on the plunger and if it's damaged or deteriorated, replace it with a new one. Before unscrewing the upper eye from the plunger, protect the plunger shaft with tape or a clean shop rag and then clamp it securely with Vise Grips.

2. Check the plunger to make sure it is straight and that there is no oil leakage where it enters the cylinder. Test the action of the shock absorber by compressing and extending the plunger. The resistance during an extension stroke should be noticeably greater than during a compression stroke. In both cases, the movement of the plunger must be smooth and even throughout the stroke. If resistance is very low or nil in both directions, if the plunger is bent, or if the movement of the plunger is erratic, the unit should be replaced. If at all possible, the units should be replaced as a set, particularly if they have been in service for a long time.

Reassembly and Reinstallation

1. When reassembling the spring-shocks, make certain that the rubber bumper is in place, the upper eye is screwed tightly on the plunger and that the keepers are correctly seated beneath the upper eye.

2. Prior to assembly, the contact surfaces should be lightly greased. This includes the plunger shaft, the inside of any covers, and the pre-load rings.

3. Installation of the spring shocks is reverse order of removal. Make certain all the mounting bolts are tight and the eye grommets are installed.

WHEELS AND TIRES

Tire and wheel size may vary on some models but generally DKW motorcycles are equipped with a 3.00 x 21 in. front tire and a 3.50 x 18 in. rear tire.

Rims

The rims should be checked periodically for roundness and runout, and for bends or dents following a collision or hard spill. Severe rim damage is difficult to repair successfully and it's generally wiser to replace the rim. The rubber rim band, which covers the spoke nipples and prevents them from chafing the inner tube, should be checked carefully each time the tire is dismounted. If the rubber rim band is torn, exposing a spoke, it should be replaced or repaired with tape.

Spokes

Spokes should be checked often for looseness and bending. A bent spoke should be replaced immediately. Loose spokes should be tightened until their tone, when struck, is similar to that of other spokes in the same wheel which are tight.

Wheel Balance

An imbalanced wheel, depending upon its degree of imbalance, can cause anything from a fatiguing vibration to a violent shimmy which can adversely affect handling. Imbalance can be corrected by applying weights to the light side of a wheel.

1. Before attempting to balance a wheel, make sure the bearings are in good condition and properly lubricated and that the brakes do not drag.

2. If you're balancing a rear wheel, remove the chain from the wheel sprocket.

3. Elevate the wheel being balanced so it is free to rotate.

4. Spin it slowly and allow it to come to rest.

5. Add a weight to the light, or high side, and spin the wheel again, adding weights to the light side until the wheel comes to rest at a different point each time it's spun.

Wheel Inspection

1. Support each axle in a lathe, V-blocks, or other suitable centering device as shown in **Figure 7**. Rotate the axle through a complete revolution and check its trueness with a dial indicator. Straighten or replace it if it is bent more than 0.028 in. (0.7mm).

2. Check the bearing races in the wheel for cracks, galling, or pitting. Rotate the bearings by hand and check them for roughness. Replace any bearings that are worn or damaged.

3. Check grease seals for wear and damage and replace any that are in questionable condition.

Wheel Runout

1. Support the axle as shown in **Figure 8** and check runout of the wheel with a dial indicator as the wheel is slowly rotated.

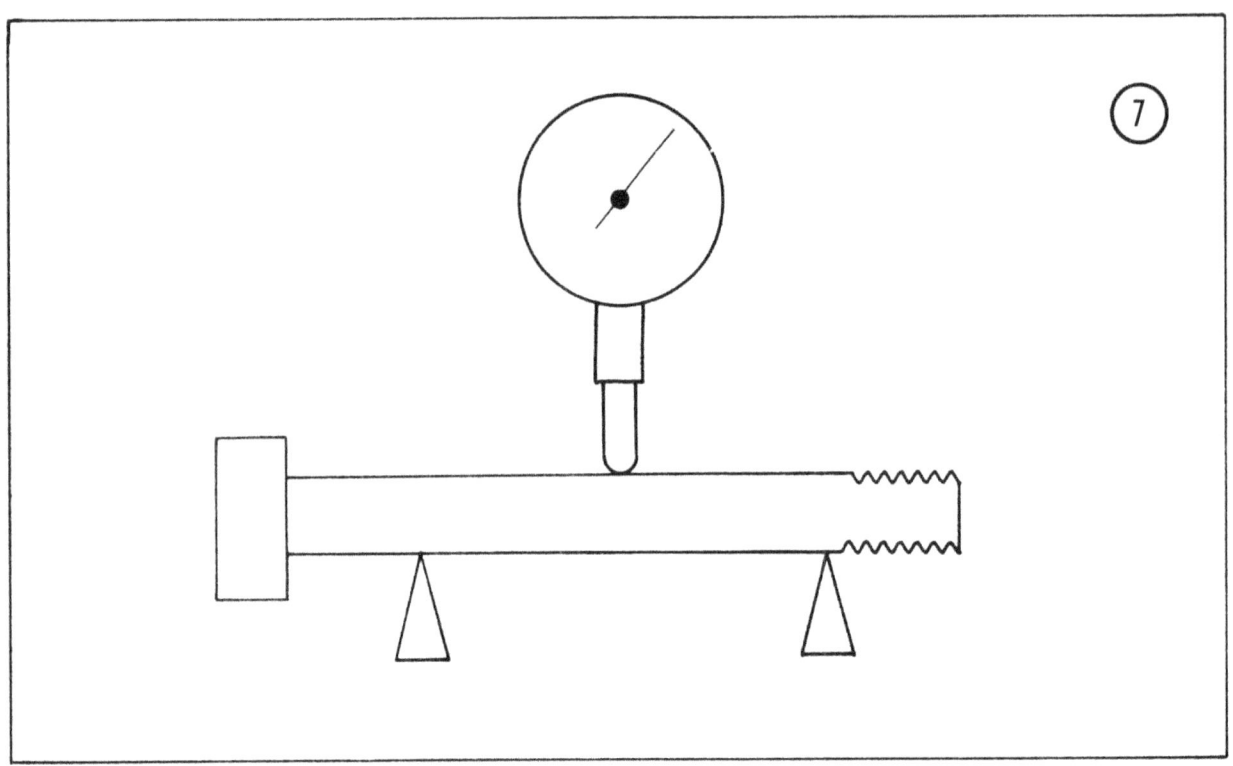

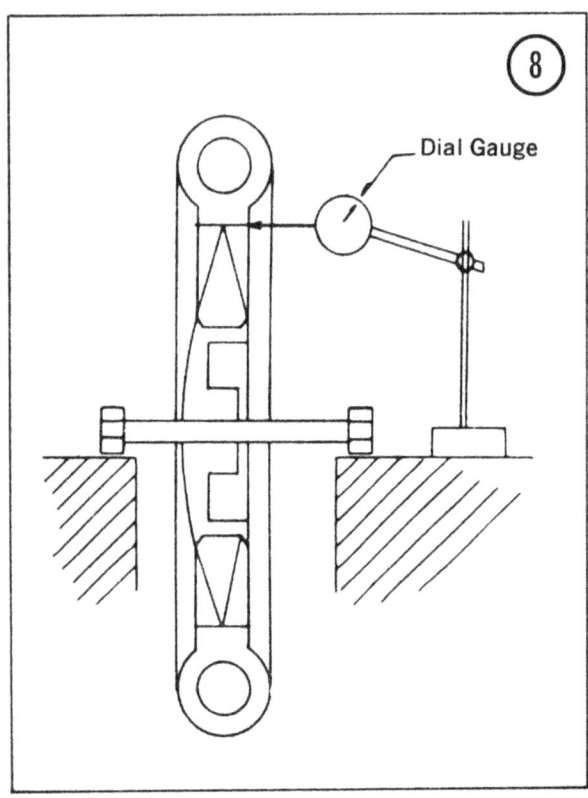

2. If runout exceeds 0.12 in. (3.0mm) correct it by loosening spokes in the area of and on the same side as the high spot, and tightening those in the area of but on the opposite side from the high spot.

3. Go slowly, checking the runout as you work. A careful, patient job can correct what may have appeared as a bent wheel. If a wheel rim is severely bent, however, it will probably not be correctable with runout adjustment and should be replaced.

BRAKES

Brake and hub assemblies for DKW motorcycles are shown in the parts list.

Removal

Front and rear hub and brake components are identical, with some external differences in the backing plate design. In addition, the rear hub is fitted to a sprocket carrier which may remain in the swinging arm when the rear wheel is removed.

1. Support the motorcycle to raise the wheel off the ground.

2. On the front wheel, unscrew the axle nut and loosen the axle pinch bolts.

3. Disconnect the brake cable from the brake backing plate and pull the axle out of the forks and wheel. Pull the brake out of the hub.

4. To remove the rear wheel, disconnect the brake rod at the backing plate, unscrew the axle

nut and pull out the axle. Note the location of the spacers for reference during reassembly.

5. With the spacers removed, the wheel can be moved to the left, off the sprocket carrier and out of the swinging arm.

Inspection

1. Inspect the inside diameter of the brake drum for wear and deep grooves. A groove that is deep enough to catch a fingernail is deep enough to impair braking efficiency. If any are present, the drum should be turned down by an experienced brake shop and new shoes arced to the contour of the drum.

2. Inspect the brake lining for oil, grease, or imbedded foreign matter. Dirt may be removed with a wire brush, but if oil or grease have soaked the lining material, it must be replaced. Measure the thickness of the lining at its thinnest point and if it is less than 1/16 in. (1.5mm) have the shoes relined or replace them with new ones. Again, the shoes must be arced to the contour of the drums.

3. Check the return springs for tension. They should be resilient enough to quickly withdraw the shoes from the drum. Replace them if they are weak or stretched.

Reassembly

Reassembly is in reverse order of disassembly.

When assembling the brake, apply a little bit of high-temperature grease to the shoe pivots and the cam.

Brake Adjustment

Adjustment of the front brake is presented earlier in this chapter. Adjustment of the rear brake is similar in principle in that it is largely a matter of personal preference. There should be about one inch of free-play in the pedal. If the brake is in good condition, this will ensure that the shoes do not drag and at the same time provide adequate brake effectiveness. The adjustment is made by turning the wing nut or thumbscrew on the end of the brake rod either in or out until the free-play is correct. If adjustment is not possible with the rod adjustment, the brake arm may be removed from the cam and rotated back one notch. When lining wear is excessive, however, the cam will simply go over center and remain in the full on position. If the arm has been rotated more than once, it's a good idea to remove the rear wheel and check for the likelihood of this condition.

Wheel Bearings

Wheel bearings should be cleaned, inspected, and greased periodically. The frequency of service depends upon use; for a motorcycle used as transportation, yearly service should be sufficient. At the extreme, for a motorcycle used in rigorous weekly competition, the wheel bearings should be serviced at least once a month and always after the motorcycle has been operated in deep mud or sand. Under these conditions, the rear sprocket carrier bearing should be serviced as well; sand and grit can find their way into the carrier and lock the bearing, causing its outer race to rotate in the carrier. This can damage a carrier to the extent that it must be replaced.

1. Remove the covers and seals from the ends of the wheel hubs.

2. Use the axle as a drift and knock out the brake-side bearing. The opposite bearing can then be drifted out from the inside.

3. Remove the circlip from the sprocket carrier and remove the carrier bearing. Check the condition of the bearings as described earlier.

4. Thoroughly clean and dry the bearings. Grease them liberally and install them, reversing the order in which they were removed. Make sure that each bearing is square in its bore and that it is driven all the way to the shoulder in the hub.

5. Clean and dry the seals and covers. If they show any signs of damage or wear, they should be replaced. Install any circlips which were removed, and then the seals and covers.

SWINGING ARM

Shimmy, wander, and wheel hop are common symptoms of worn swinging arm bushings or bearings. If they are suspected of wear or damage, check them in the following manner.

1. Remove the rear wheel and suspension units and make certain the swinging arm pivot bolts are tight.

2. Grab the swinging arm by the aft ends and try to move it from side to side in a horizontal arc. If any movement can be felt, the bushings or bearings must be replaced.

Replacement

1. Remove the pivot bolt, washers, and spacers, noting their locations for reference during reassembly.
2. Remove the bushings or bearings from the swinging arm and clean and dry all of the parts thoroughly. Grease the bearings and install them in the swinging arm.
3. Reassemble and reinstall the swinging arm in reverse order of disassembly and reinstall the suspension units and rear wheel. Check and adjust the free-play of the chain and the alignment of the rear wheel.

EXHAUST SYSTEM

Carbon deposits in the exhaust system can cause a decrease in engine efficiency and result in a loss of power. An easy way to remove carbon from an exhaust pipe is to run an old drive chain through it. As an alternate method, chuck a length of old control cable into an electric drill motor, fray end of cable to make a brush, and run cable through the length of the pipe several times with the drill motor running.

DRIVE CHAIN

Service and adjustment of the drive chain are discussed in Chapter Two.

FUEL TANK

Service of the fuel tank is described in Chapter Two.

SPARE PARTS

Model

ENDURO   125 cc
MOTO-CROSS   125 cc
HORNET   125 cc
BOONDOCKER   125 cc

1972

NOTES

CONTENTS

Frame   Page

Frame, rear swingarm, rear shock absorber, side stand, foot rest, foot brake arm, brake rod, seat	2— 5
Front fork for "Moto-Cross" and "Enduro"	6— 7
Front fork, front fender for "Hornet" and "Boondocker"	8—11
Fuel tank, filter box, side cover, mount for battery	12—15
Fenders, chain guard, exhaust system	16—17
Handlebar, throttle wist grip, brake lever, clutch lever, cables	18—19
Head lamp, head lamp bracket, switch, speedometer	20—21
Brake light switch, taillight, horn	22—23
Front wheel, front hub	24—25
Rear wheel, rear hub, chain tensioner, chain	26—27
Tool kit, number plate	28—29

Engine

Crankcase, crankshaft, cylinder	30—31
Gear-changing lever, main shaft, gearbox, starting device, gear changing	32—33
Clutch side crankcase cover, clutch, layshaft, magneto side crankcase	34—35
Magneto-generator	36—37
Carburettor	38—39
Dimensions of shims	39
Wiring diagram of the "Enduro" and "Boondocker"	40—41
Wiring diagram of the "Moto-Cross" and "Hornet"	42—43

Frame, rear swingarm, rear shock absorber, side stand, foot rest, foot brake arm, brake rod, seat

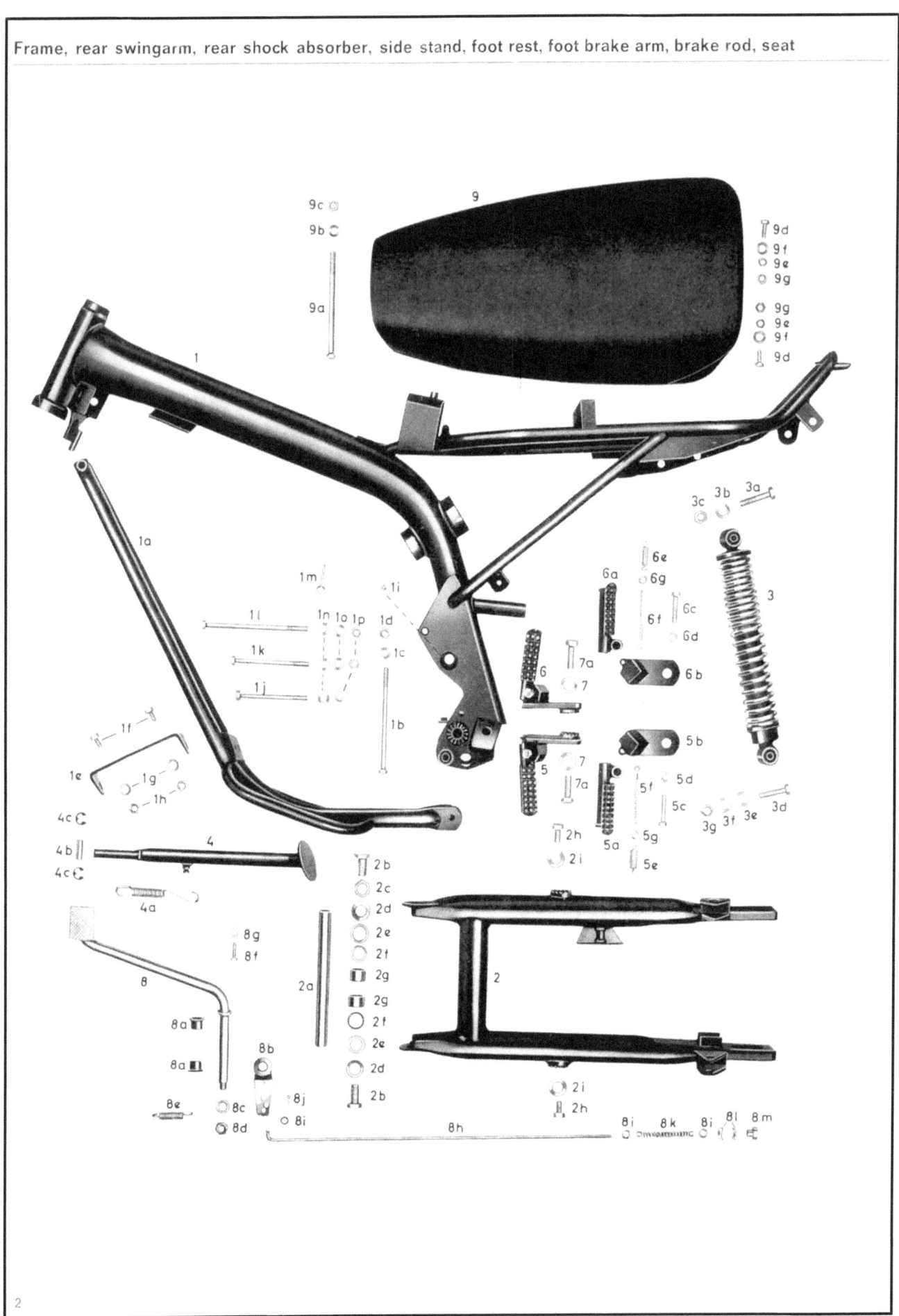

Ill. No.	Description			Order No.	Pcs.
1	Frame*			427 100 01 21.088	1
				428 100 43 01.088	1
1a	Trussing of the frame				
1b	Hexagon screw	M 8 x 145	DIN 931	08 025 00931 37	1
1c	Spring washer	B 8	DIN 137	08 015 00137 35	1
1d	Nut	M 8	DIN 985	08 708 00985 17	1
1e	Bracket			927 968 41 04.088	1
1f	Hexagon screw	M 8 x 16	DIN 933	08 005 00933 37	2
1g	Spring washer	B 8	DIN 137	08 015 00137 35	2
1h	Nut	M 8	DIN 985	08 708 00985 17	2
1i	Lubrication nipple	AM 6	DIN 3402	06 001 03402 07	1
1j	Hexagon screw (f. Moto-Cross/Hornet)	M 8 x 100	DIN 931	08 019 00931 47	2
1j	Hexagon screw (f. Enduro/Boondocker)	M 8 x 100	DIN 931	08 019 00931 47	1
1k	Hexagon screw (f. Enduro/Boondocker)	M 8 x 110	DIN 931	08 021 00931 47	1
1l	Hexagon screw	M 8 x 150	DIN 931	08 026 00931 47	1
1m	Loop			927 999 98 09	1
1n	Washer (f. Enduro/Boondocker)	A 8,4	DIN 125	08 011 00125 07	2
1n	Washer (f. Moto-Cross/Hornet)	A 8,4	DIN 125	08 011 00125 07	1
1o	Spring washer	B 8	DIN 137	08 015 00137 35	3
1p	Nut	M 8	DIN 985	08 708 00985 17	3
2	Rear swingarm			427 140 04 08.088	1
2a–2g	Link bracket			427 140 33 01	1
2a	↑Swing axle			927 992 42 09	1
2b	Swing axle screw			927 991 01 13	2
2c	Nut	M 14 x 1		927 991 51 02	1
2d	Spring washer	B 14	DIN 137	14 019 00137 35	2
2e	Washer			927 992 07 01	2
2f	Gasket ring			927 993 38 04	2
2g	Needle bearing			927 492 26 05	2
2h	Hexagon screw	M 12 x 20	DIN 933	12 005 00933 37	2
2i	Spring washer	B 12	DIN 128	12 026 00128 35	2
3	Rear shock absorber BOGE	V 1-02-2014-0		920 040 01 88	2
3a	Hexagon screw, left side	M 10 x 45	DIN 931	10 005 00931 37	1
	Hexagon screw, right side	M 10 x 50	DIN 931	10 006 00931 37	1
3b	Spring washer	B 10	DIN 137	10 017 00137 35	2
3c	Hexagon nut	BM 10	DIN 439	10 012 00439 17	2
3d	Hexagon screw	M 10 x 40	DIN 931	10 004 00931 37	2
3e	Washer	A 10,5	DIN 125	10 012 00125 07	2
3f	Spring washer	B 10	DIN 128	10 024 00128 35	2
3g	Nut	M 10	DIN 985	10 710 00985 17	2
4	Side stand			427 100 63 03.088	1
4a	Return spring			927 994 05 08	1
4b	Bolt			927 992 42 19	1
4c	Safety washer	9	DIN 6799	09 012 06799 35	2
5	Foot rest left, complete			927 100 48 35.088	1
5a	↑Foot rest, left			927 100 48 33.088	1
5b	Bracket for foot rest, left			427 100 85 14.088	1
5c	Hexagon screw	M 8 x 40	DIN 931	08 006 00931 37	1
5d	Nut	M 8	DIN 985	08 708 00985 17	1
5e	Return spring			927 994 02 23	1
5f	Pull chain			927 979 50 01	1
5g	Loop			927 999 98 10	1
6	Foot rest right, complete			927 100 48 36.088	1
6a	↑Foot rest, right			927 100 48 34.088	1
6b	Bracket for foot rest, right			427 100 85 15.088	1
6c	Hexagon screw	M 8 x 40	DIN 931	08 006 00931 37	1
6d	Nut	M 8	DIN 985	08 708 00985 17	1
6e	Return spring			927 994 02 23	1
6f	Pull chain			927 979 50 01	1
6g	Loop			927 999 98 10	1

* For replacement up to frame No. 428 000 581 the following parts must simultaneously be supplied:
Bellow 927 933 71 07
NORMA-Clip 927 973 33 60

Frame, rear swingarm, rear shock absorber, side stand, foot rest, foot brake arm, brake rod, seat

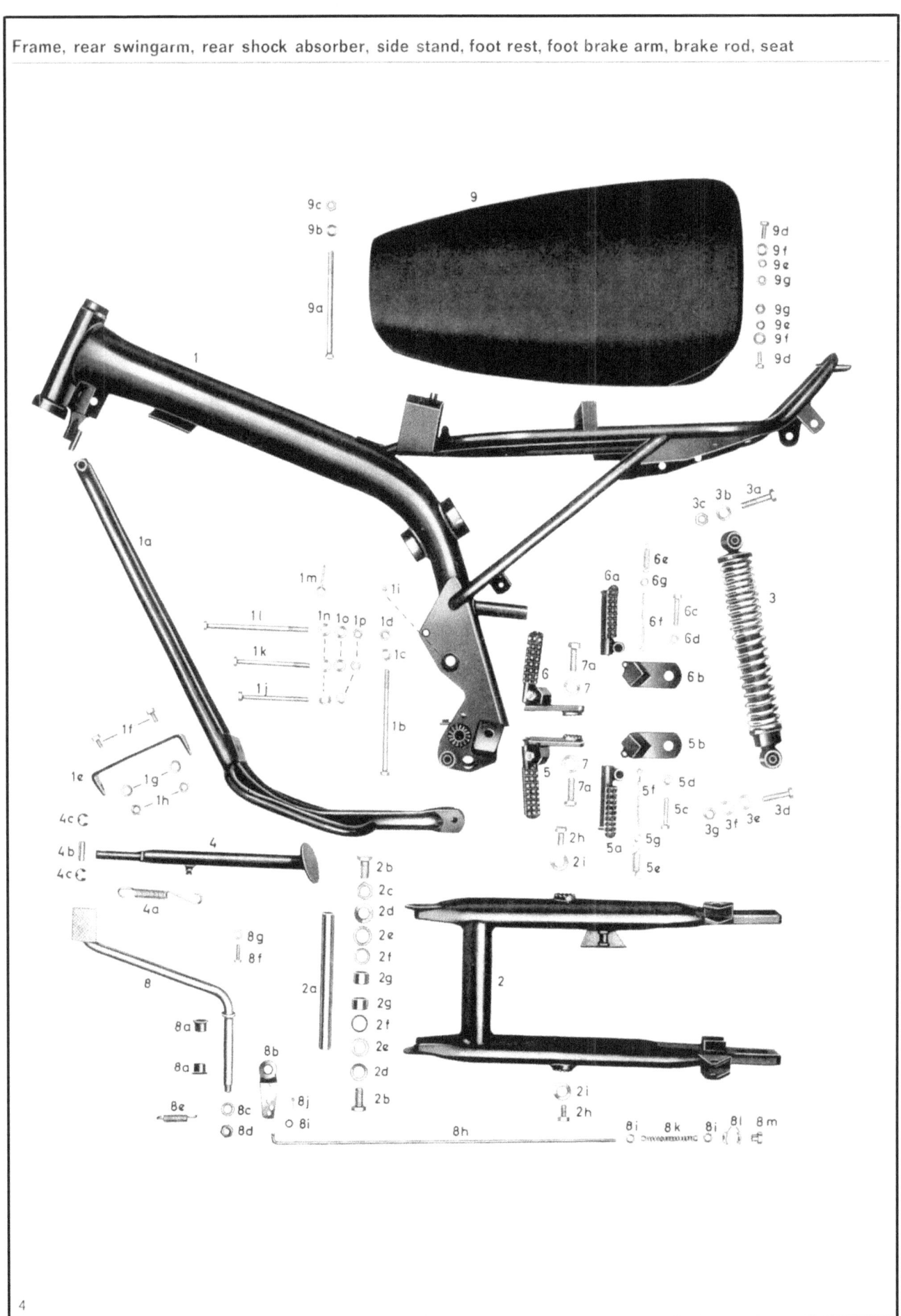

Ill. No.	Description			Order No.	Pcs.
7	Spring washer	B 12	DIN 137	12 018 00137 35	2
7a	Hexagon screw	M 12 x 40	DIN 933	12 010 00933 37	2
8	Footbrake arm			685 210 30 01.910	1
8a	Bushing			927 994 21 05	2
8b	Brake lever			698 170 12 01.910	1
8c	Spring washer	B 10	DIN 137	10 017 00137 35	1
8d	Nut	M 10	DIN 985	10 710 00985 17	1
8e	Return spring			927 994 05 05	1
8f	Hexagon screw	M 6 x 25	DIN 933	06 011 00933 37	1
8g	Nut	M 6	DIN 934	06 006 00934 17	1
8h-8m	Brake rod, complete			675 170 37 02	1
8h	↑Brake rod			927 171 37 02	1
8i	Washer	A 6,4	DIN 125	06 009 00125 07	3
8j	Cotter pin	2 x 12	DIN 94	20 002 00094 04	1
8k	Return spring			927 994 03 51	1
8l	Locking clip			927 992 02 03	2
8m	Knurled nut			927 991 55 01	1
9	Seat			417 140 01 06	1
9a	Hexagon screw	M 8 x 150	DIN 931	08 026 00931 37	1
9b	Washer	8,4 x 25 x 1		117 149 01 00	2
9c	Nut			927 991 70 59	1
9d	Hexagon screw	M 8 x 20	DIN 933	08 007 00933 37	2
9e	Distance bushing			927 996 00 11	2
9f	Spring washer	B 8	DIN 137	08 015 00137 35	2
9g	Nut	M 8	DIN 985	08 708 00985 17	2

Front fork for "Moto-Cross" and "Enduro"

Ill. No.	Description			Order No.	Pcs.
1–3f	Front fork, complete, for Moto-Cross and Enduro			921 150 02 72.088	1
1	↑Front fork			921 150 02 16.088	1
1a	│ Front swingarm			921 150 05 13.088	1
1b	│ Bushing			927 499 70 01	2
1c	│ Needle bearing with gasket			927 492 26 07	4
1d	│ Hexagonal screw	M 8 x 50	DIN 931	08 008 00931 37	2
1e	│ Spring washer	B 8	DIN 137	08 015 00137 35	4
1f	│ Nut	M 8	DIN 985	08 708 00985 17	2
1g	│ Front shock absorber BOGE	1-0230-22-782-0		920 040 01 27	2
1h	│ Hexagonal screw	M 8 x 50	DIN 931	08 008 00931 37	2
1i	│ Spring washer	B 8	DIN 137	08 015 00137 35	4
1j	│ Nut	M 8	DIN 985	08 708 00985 17	2
1k	│ Hexagonal screw	M 10 x 35	DIN 933	10 012 00933 37	2
1l	│ Spring washer	B 10	DIN 137	10 017 00137 35	2
1m	│ Nut	M 10	DIN 934	10 011 00934 17	2
1n	│ Upper steering yoke, for Moto-Cross			921 154 25 24.088	1
	│ Upper steering yoke, for Enduro			921 154 25 30.088	1
1o	│ Washer			927 992 01 60	2
1p	│ Short mounting bolt			922 991 23 01	2
2–2e	Steering set, complete			675 100 97 03	1 set
2	↑Lower steering set		DIN 71974	05 001 71974 40	1
2a	│ Upper bearing race			927 101 33 04	1
2b	│ Ball	¼"	DIN 5401	19 003 05401 40	19
2c	│ Frame cone			927 101 31 28	1
2d	│ Washer			927 101 36 01	1
2e	│ Steering yoke nut			427 101 35 01	1
2f	Washer			927 992 08 17	1–2
3–3f	Steering demper			427 150 47 02	1
3	↑Traction rod			427 150 48 01	1
3a	│ Spring washer			927 992 96 01	1
3b	│ Washer	A 6,4	DIN 9021	06 013 09021 07	1
3c	│ Friction disk			927 992 13 01	1
3d	│ Washer			927 992 00 28	1
3e	│ Clip			428 971 84 01	1
3f	│ Nut			927 991 56 08	1

Front fork, front fender for "Hornet" and "Boondocker"

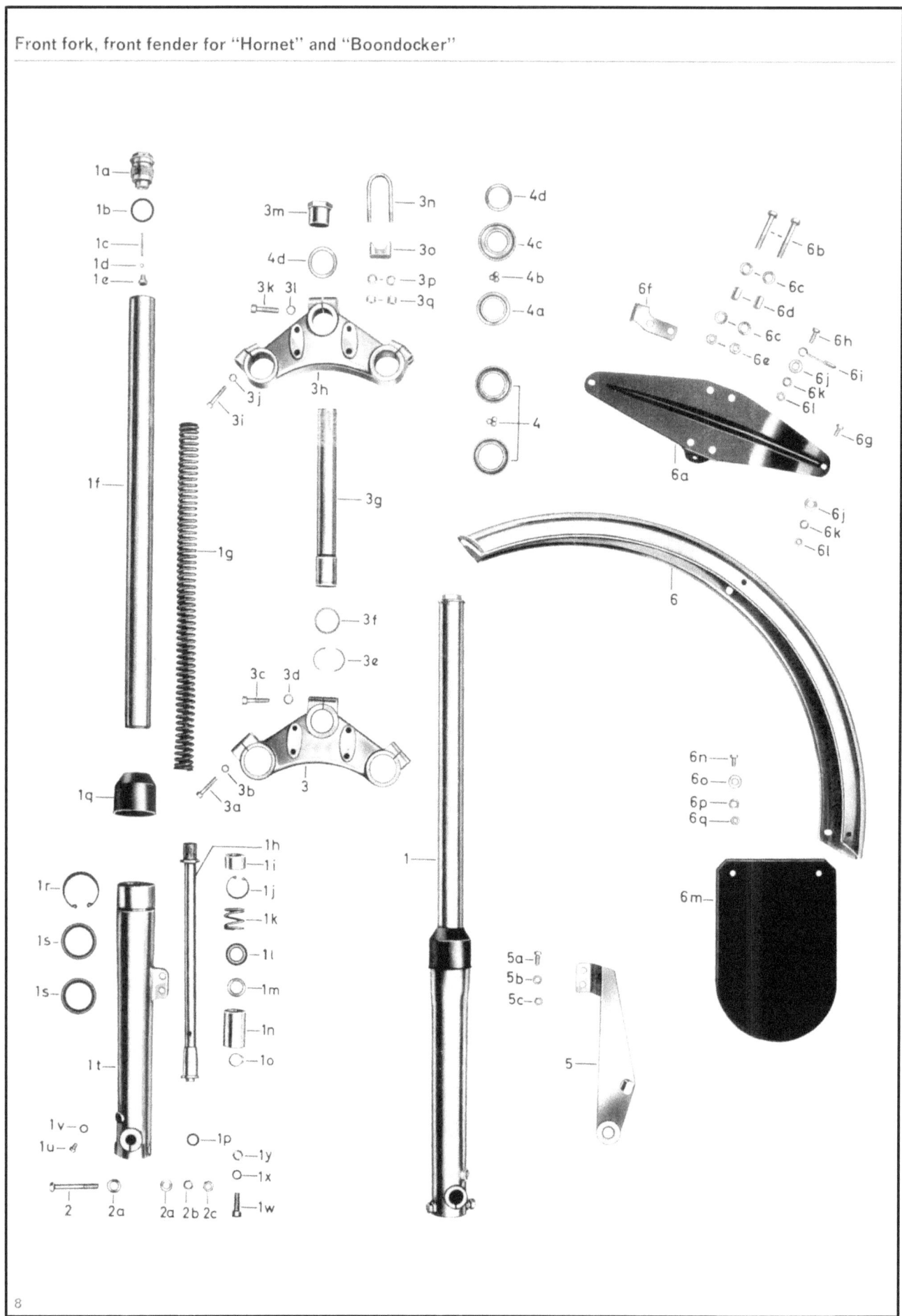

198

Ill. No.	Description			Order No.	Pcs.
—	Telescopic fork, complete			428 150 01 02	1
1	↑Leg assembly, left			921 150 14 73	1
1	│ Leg assembly, right			921 150 14 74	1
1a	│ ↑Tube cap			921 155 65 02	2
1b	│ │ Gum ring			927 993 32 04	2
1c	│ │ Spring			921 156 91 11	2
1d	│ │ Ball	3,5 mm	DIN 5401	10 003 05401 40	2
1e	│ │ Cap screw			927 991 01 44	2
1f	│ │ Tube			921 154 02 12	2
1g	│ │ Spring support			921 156 91 12	2
1h—1p	│ │ Valve assembly			921 150 64 02	2
1h	│ │ ↑Valve set			921 155 27 02	2
1i	│ │ │ Piston			921 155 20 03	2
1j	│ │ │ Safety ring	32 x 1,2	DIN 472	32 014 00472 31	2
1k	│ │ │ Retention spring			921 156 91 13	2
1l	│ │ │ Valve			921 155 34 01	2
1m	│ │ │ Valve washer			921 992 00 03	2
1n	│ │ │ Cylinder support			921 155 18 02	2
1o	│ │ │ Safety ring	16 x 1	DIN 471	16 013 00471 31	2
1p	│ │ │ Gum ring			927 993 32 05	2
1q	│ │ Dust cover			927 993 31 13	2
1r	│ │ Safety ring	50 x 2	DIN 472	50 025 00472 31	2
1s	│ │ Seal			921 993 38 08	4
1t	│ │ Tube, left			921 154 02 13	1
1t	│ │ Tube, right			921 154 02 14	1
1u	│ │ Drain plug	M 6 x 8	DIN 84	06 001 00084 17	2
1v	│ │ Washer			921 993 38 09	2
1w	│ │ Cylinder screw	M 8 x 25	DIN 912	08 009 00912 37	2
1x	│ │ Spring washer	B 8	DIN 127	08 010 00127 35	2
1y	│ │ Washer	A 8,4	DIN 125	08 011 00125 07	2
2	Hexagon screw	M 8 x 60	DIN 931	08 010 00931 37	2
2a	Washer	A 8,4	DIN 125	08 011 00125 07	4
2b	Spring washer	B 8	DIN 127	08 010 00127 35	2
2c	Nut	M 8	DIN 934	08 009 00934 17	2
3	Lower steering yoke			921 154 26 51	1
3a	Cylinder screw	M 6 x 30	DIN 912	06 009 00912 37	4
3b	Spring washer	6 x 9,5 x 1,5		927 992 96 15	4
3c	Cylinder screw	M 8 x 30	DIN 912	08 011 00912 37	1
3d	Spring washer	8 x 12,5 x 2		927 992 96 16	1
3e	Spindle safety ring			921 992 95 06	1
3f	Support washer			921 974 80 03	1
3g	Spindle			921 154 07 14	1
3h	Upper steering yoke			921 154 25 51	1
3i	Cylinder screw	M 6 x 30	DIN 912	06 009 00912 37	4
3j	Spring washer	6 x 9,5 x 1,5		927 992 96 15	4
3k	Cylinder screw	M 8 x 30	DIN 912	08 011 00912 37	1
3l	Spring washer	8 x 12,5 x 2		927 992 96 16	1
3m	Spindle nut			921 154 66 03	1
3n	Handle bar U-Bolt			927 969 97 05	2
3o	Base bar			927 968 46 26	2
3p	Spring washer	B 8	DIN 127	07 009 00127 35	4
3q	Bridle nut	M 7 x 10		927 991 51 30	4
4—4c	Steering set, complete			427 100 97 03	1
4	↑Lower steering set			05 001 71974 40	1
4a	│ Upper bearing race			927 101 33 04	1
4b	│ Ball	¼"		19 003 05401 40	19
4c	│ Frame cone			927 101 31 28	1
4d	Washer			927 992 08 17	1—3
5	Brake plate houlder			921 960 05 05	1
5a	Hexagon screw	M 6 x 20	DIN 933	06 009 00933 37	2
5b	Spring washer	B 6	DIN 128	06 018 00128 35	2
5c	Nut	M 6	DIN 985	06 706 00985 17	2

Front fork, front fender for "Hornet" and "Boondocker"

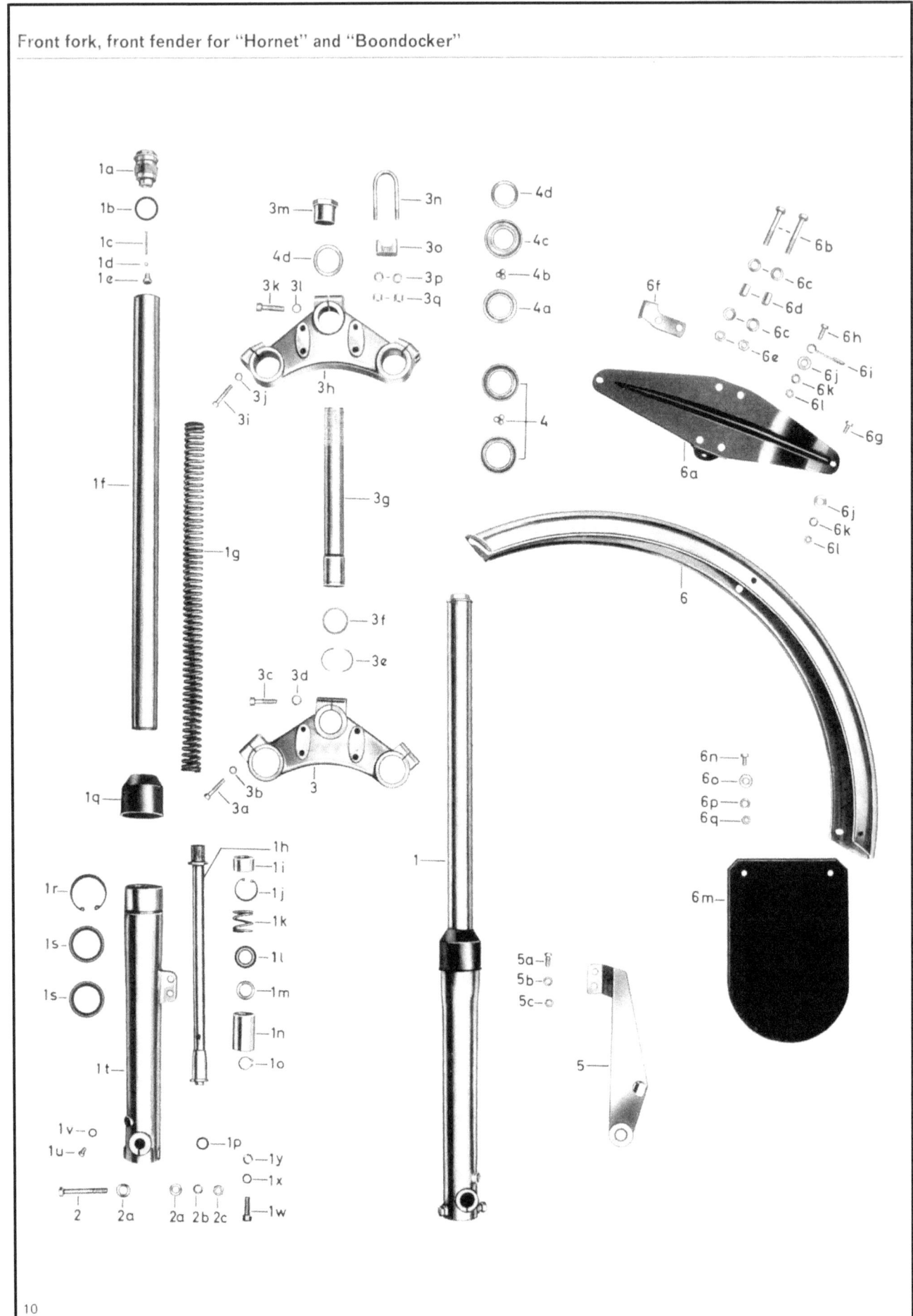

Ill. No.	Description			Order No.	Pcs.
6	Front fender for Boondocker and Hornet			427 116 01 06.098	1
6a	Fender bracket			428 110 82 01.088	1
6b	Hexagon screw	M 8 x 60	DIN 931	08 010 00931 37	4
6c	Spring washer	B 8	DIN 137	08 015 00137 35	8
6d	Bushing			927 994 20 49	4
6e	Nut	M 8	DIN 985	08 708 00985 17	4
6f	Bracket, left			927 961 60 32	1
6f	Bracket, right			927 961 60 33	1
6g	Hexagon screw	M 6 x 12	DIN 933	06 005 00933 37	3
6h	Hexagon screw	M 6 x 16	DIN 933	06 007 00933 37	1
6i	Brake cable guide			927 968 46 09	1
6j	Washer	A 6,4	DIN 9021	06 013 09021 07	4
6k	Spring washer	B 6	DIN 137	06 011 00137 35	4
6l	Nut	M 6	DIN 985	06 706 00985 17	4
6m	Dirt trap			427 771 24 01	1
6n	Hexagon screw	M 6 x 12	DIN 933	06 005 00933 37	2
6o	Washer	A 6,4	DIN 9021	06 013 09021 07	2
6p	Spring washer	B 6	DIN 137	06 011 00137 35	2
6q	Nut	M 6	DIN 985	06 706 00985 17	2

Fuel tank, filter box, side cover, mount for battery

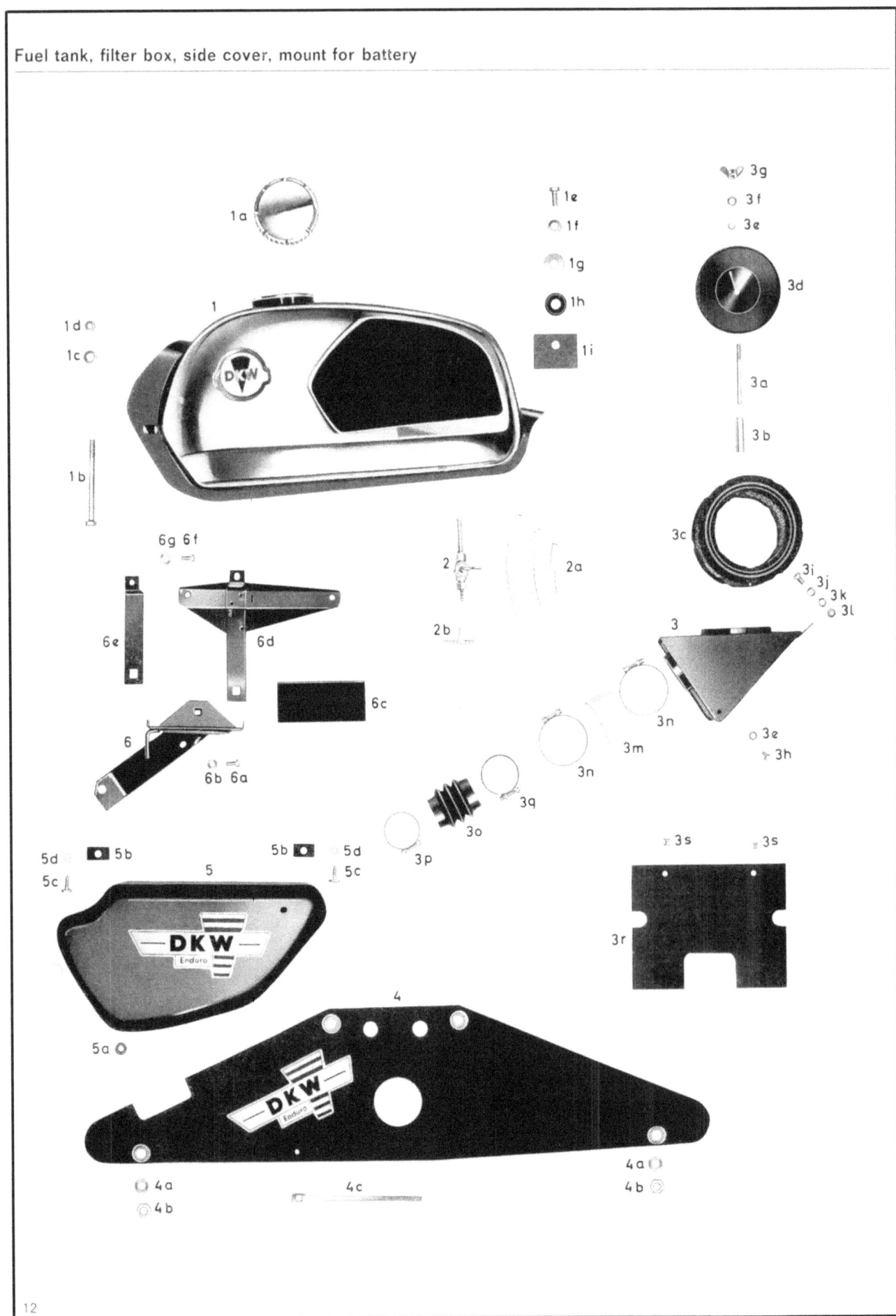

Ill. No.	Description			Order No.	Pcs.
1	Fuel tank (Moto-Cross)			4 417 180 05 17.627	1
1	Fuel tank (MC-Hornet)			4 427 180 05 22.444	1
1	Fuel tank (Enduro)			4 427 180 05 23.295	1
1	Fuel tank (Boondocker)			4 428 180 05 17.135	1
—	↑Tank emblem "DKW"			050 947 02 04	2
—	Decal "Made in Western Germany"			927 947 05 84	1
—	Decal "Moto-Cross 125 cc"			927 947 05 81	1
—	Decal "Moto-Cross-Hornet 125 cc"			937 947 05 46	1
—	Decal "Enduro 125 cc"			927 947 05 77	1
—	Decal "Boondocker 125 cc"			937 947 05 53	1
—	Knee pad guard, left			685 181 40 03	1
—	Knee pad guard, right			685 181 40 04	1
1a	Fuel cap	60	DIN 73400	60 002 73400 70	1
1b	Hexagon screw	M 10 x 100	DIN 931	10 016 00931 47	1
1c	Washer (f. Moto-Cross/Hornet)	10,3 x 22,5 x 1,25		927 992 01 80	2
1c	Washer (f. Enduro/Boondocker)	10,3 x 22,5 x 1,25		927 992 01 80	1
1d	Nut	M 10	DIN 985	10 710 00985 17	1
1e	Hexagonal screw	M 8 x 20	DIN 933	08 007 00933 37	1
1f	Spring washer	B 8	DIN 137	08 015 00137 35	1
1g	Curved washer			927 992 01 65	1
1h	Rubber washer			927 993 32 01	1
1i	Rubber pad			927 993 27 01	1
2	Petrol cock			675 180 03 01	2
2a	Fuel hose	1 = 5 x 8 x 165 mm		927 993 72 00	meter
		1 = 5 x 8 x 80 mm			
		1 = 5 x 8 x 40 mm			
2b	Tube connection piece			927 186 99 01	1
3-3h	Filter box, complete			427 460 10 09.088	1
3	↑Filter box			427 460 10 08.088	1
3a	Bolt	M 6 x 75	DIN 938	06 019 00938 37	1
3b	Distance bushing			927 996 01 27	1
3c	Filter element			427 463 06 01	1
3d	Cape			927 964 05 12	1
3e	Gasket ring	A 6 x 10	DIN 7603	06 003 07603 90	2
3f	Spring washer	B 6	DIN 137	06 011 00137 35	1
3g	Wring nut	M 6	DIN 315	06 007 00315 05	1
3h	Round head screw	AM 6 x 10	DIN 91	06 002 00091 17	1
3i	Hexagon screw	M 6 x 12	DIN 933	06 005 00933 37	1
3j	Washer	A 6,4	DIN 9021	06 013 09021 07	1
3k	Spring washer	B 6	DIN 137	06 011 00137 35	1
3l	Nut	M 6	DIN 985	06 706 00985 17	1
3m	Sleeve	55 x 65 x 35		927 973 93 05	1
3n	Clamp			927 973 33 63	2
3o	Bellow up to Frame No. 428 000 581			0260 127 000	1
	Bellow from Frame No. 428 000 582			927 993 71 07	1
3p	NORMA-Clip for bellow	S 44/9 Zy		116 158 33 00	1
3q	NORMA-Clip for bellow up to frame No. 428 000 581	S 49/9 Zy		927 973 33 49	1
	NORMA-Clip for bellow from frame No. 428 000 582	S 60/9 Zy		927 973 33 60	1
3r	Dirt trap, behind			427 771 24 02	1
3s	Rivet	A 5 x 10 x 9	DIN 7331	05 005 07331 02	2
4	Side cover for filter box, without Decal			427 100 20 03	1
4a	Washer	10,5 x 25 x 1		115 149 01 10	2
4b	Nut			927 991 70 60	2
4c	Cable ribbon			927 995 60 11	1
5-5b	Side cover for battery			427 200 75 01.088	1
5a	↑Rubber grommet			927 993 21 09	1
5b	Rubber pad			927 993 27 02	2

Fuel tank, filter box, side cover, mount for battery

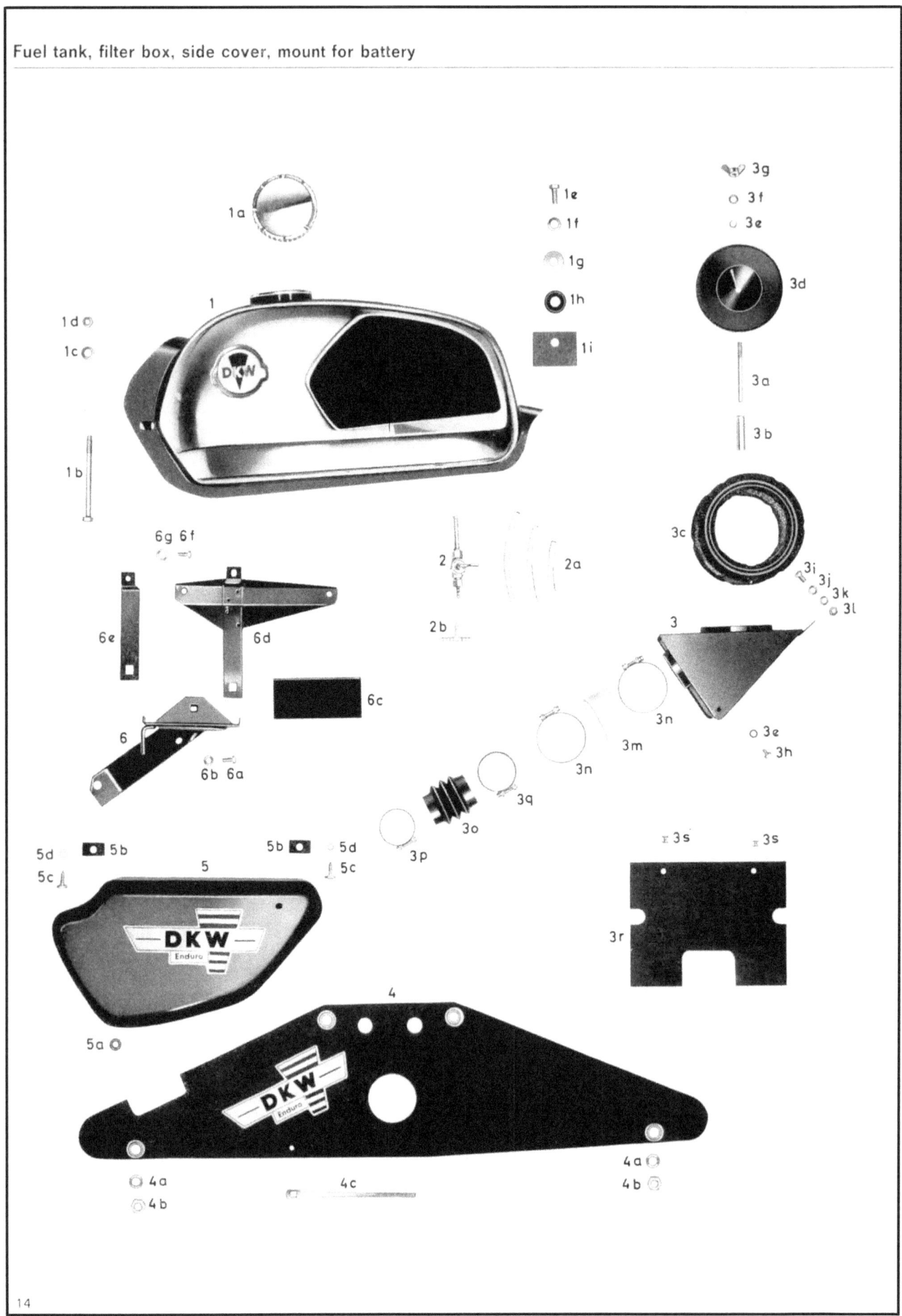

Ill. No.	Description			Order No.	Pcs.
5c–5d	Knurled screw, complete			927 110 52 01	2
5c	↑Knurled screw			927 991 07 01	2
5d	│Washer			927 992 01 66	2
—	Decal "DKW"			159 947 19 01	2
—	Decal "MC 125"			927 947 19 38	2
—	Decal "Hornet"			927 947 19 40	2
—	Decal „Enduro"			927 947 19 39	2
—	Decal „Boondocker"			927 947 19 45	2
6	Mount for battery			417 130 25 07.088	1
6a	Hexagon screw	M 6 x 16	DIN 933	06 007 00933 37	1
6b	Spring washer	B 6	DIN 128	06 018 00128 35	1
6c	Rubber pad			927 993 27 10	1
6d	Bracket			427 110 82 03.088	1
6e	Tightening strap			927 990 71 06.088	1
6f	Hexagon screw	M 6 x 20	DIN 933	06 017 00933 37	1
6g	Washer	A 6,4	DIN 125	06 009 00125 07	1

Fenders, chain guard, exhaust system

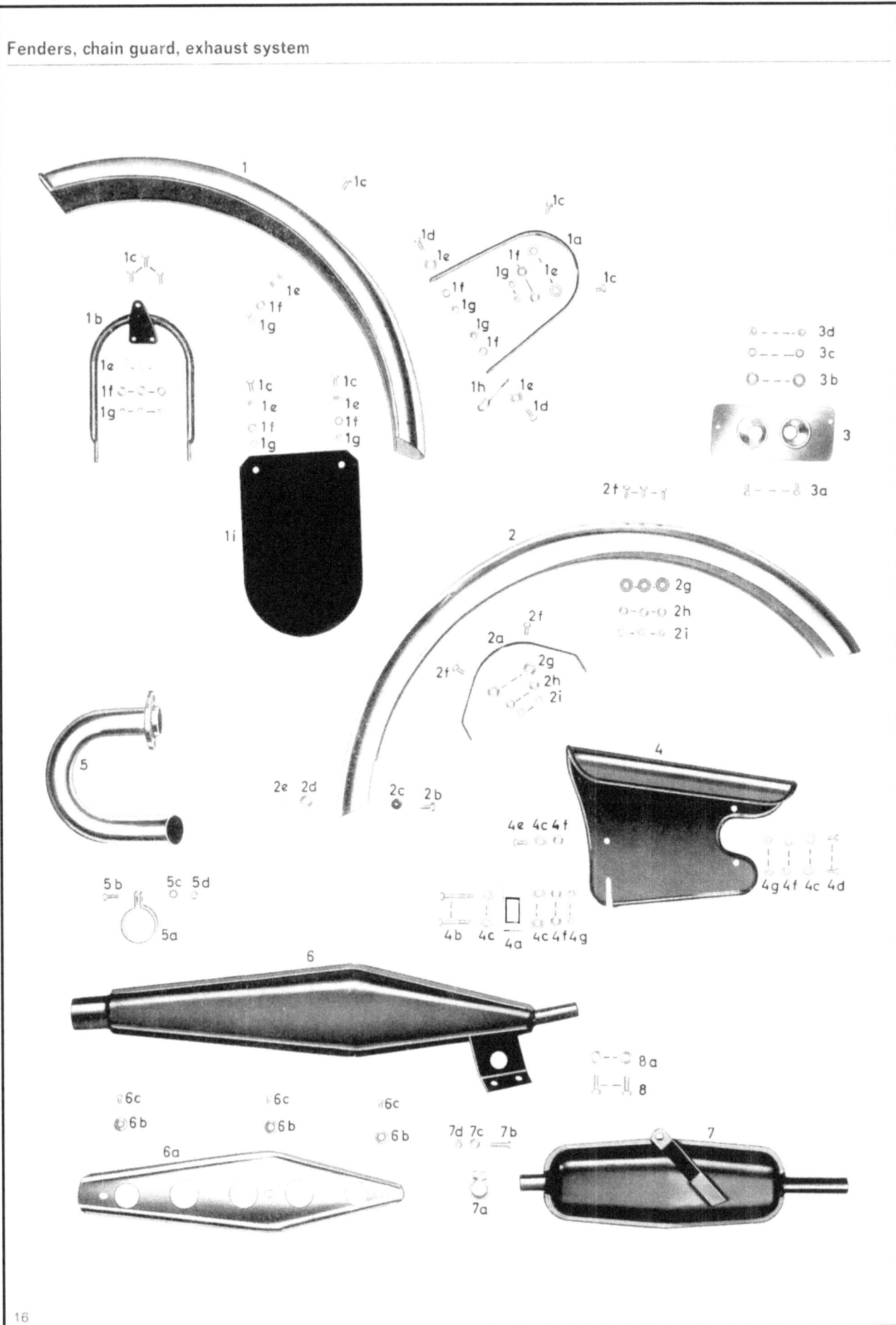

Ill. No.	Description			Order No.	Pcs.
1	Front fender for Moto-Cross and Enduro			427 116 01 05.098	1
1a	Upper fender bracket			927 110 06 05.088	1
1b	Lower fender bracket			927 962 90 13.088	1
1c	Hexagon screw	M 6 x 12	DIN 933	06 005 00933 37	8
1d	Hexagon screw	M 6 x 16	DIN 933	06 007 00933 37	2
1e	Washer	A 6,4	DIN 9021	06 013 09021 07	10
1f	Spring washer	B 6	DIN 137	06 011 00137 35	10
1g	Nut	M 6	DIN 985	06 706 00985 17	10
1h	Brake cable guide			927 968 46 09	1
1i	Dirt trap for front fender			427 771 24 01	1
2	Rear fender for Moto-Cross and Hornet			427 117 11 10.098	1
	Rear fender for Enduro and Boondocker			427 117 11 11.098	1
2a	Fender bracket			927 116 06 11.088	1
2b	Hexagon screw	M 8 x 16	DIN 933	08 005 00933 37	1
2c	Washer	A 8,4	DIN 125	08 011 00125 07	1
2d	Spring washer	B 8	DIN 137	08 015 00137 35	1
2e	Nut	M 8	DIN 985	08 708 00985 17	1
2f	Hexagon screw	M 6 x 12	DIN 933	06 005 00933 37	5
2g	Washer	A 6,4	DIN 9021	06 013 09021 07	5
2h	Spring washer	B 6	DIN 137	06 011 00137 35	5
2i	Nut	M 6	DIN 985	06 706 00985 17	5
3	License plate bracket			675 968 46 09.910	1
3a	Hexagon screw	M 6 x 12	DIN 933	06 005 00933 37	2
3b	Washer	A 6,4	DIN 9021	06 013 09021 07	2
3c	Spring washer	B 6	DIN 137	06 011 00137 35	2
3d	Nut	M 6	DIN 985	06 706 00985 17	2
4	Chain guard			417 147 00 03.088	1
4a	Chain guide (plastic)			927 144 31 01	1
4b	Hexagon screw	M 6 x 40	DIN 931	06 008 00931 37	2
4c	Washer	A 6,4	DIN 9021	06 013 09021 07	7
4d	Round head screw, slotted	M 6 x 15	DIN 91	06 004 00091 17	2
4e	Hexagonal screw	M 6 x 16	DIN 933	06 007 00933 37	1
4f	Spring washer	B 6	DIN 137	06 011 00137 35	5
4g	Nut	M 6	DIN 985	06 706 00985 17	4
5	Exhaust pipe			427 190 01 02.098	1
5a	Exhaust pipe clamp			927 190 20 01	1
5b	Hexagon screw	M 6 x 16	DIN 933	06 007 00933 37	1
5c	Spring washer	B 6	DIN 137	06 011 00137 35	1
5d	Nut	M 6	DIN 985	06 706 00985 17	1
6	Muffler			428 190 20 01.606	1
6a	Heat shield			428 193 70 01.098	1
6b	Washer			927 992 17 01	3
6c	Round head screw, slotted	AM 6 x 10	DIN 91	06 002 00091 17	3
7	Muffler			428 190 20 04.606	1
7a	Muffler clamp			927 190 04 03	1
7b	Hexagon screw	M 6 x 25	DIN 933	06 011 00933 37	1
7c	Spring washer	B 6	DIN 137	06 011 00137 35	1
7d	Nut	M 6	DIN 985	06 706 00985 17	1
8	Hexagon screw	M 8 x 16	DIN 933	08 005 00933 37	2
8a	Spring washer	B 8	DIN 137	08 015 00137 35	2

Handlebar, throttle twist grip, brake lever, clutch lever, cables

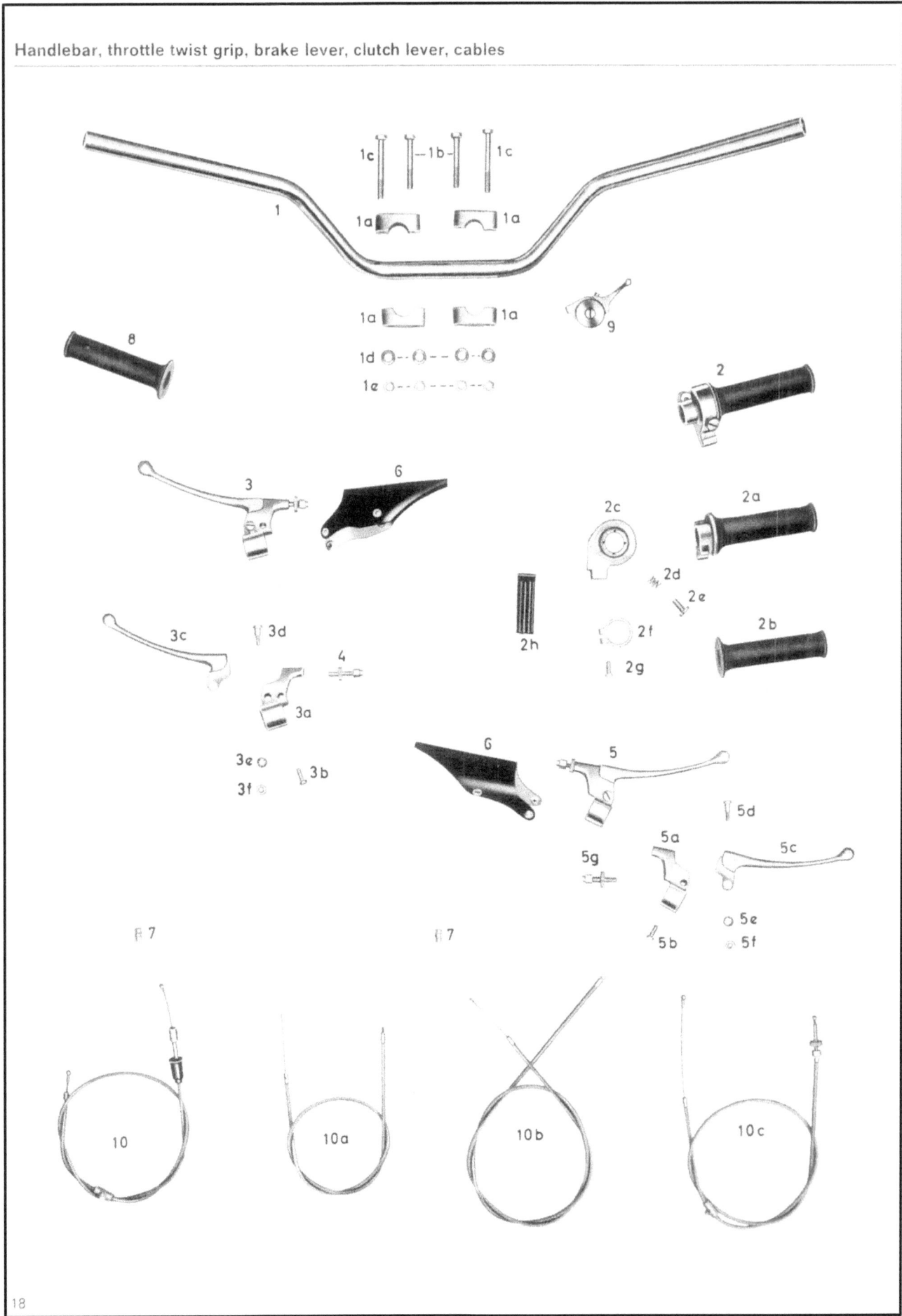

III. No.	Description			Order No.	Pcs.
1	Handlebar			427 156 09 01	1
1a	Handlebar clamp for Moto-Cross and Enduro			927 156 08 16	4
1b	Hexagon screw	M 8 x 60	DIN 931	08 010 00931 47	2
1c	Hexagon screw for Moto-Cross	M 8 x 65	DIN 931	08 011 00931 47	2
1c	Hexagon screw for Enduro	M 8 x 70	DIN 931	08 012 00931 47	2
1d	Spring washer	B 8	DIN 137	08 015 00137 35	4
1e	Nut	M 8	DIN 985	08 708 00985 17	4
2	Throttle twistgrip, complete			927 150 24 31	1
2a	↑Grip tube with twistgrip			927 150 97 30	1
2b	↑Rubber grip			159 156 99 04	1
2c	Housing with spring and screw			927 150 97 31	1
2d	↑Return spring			927 156 91 01	1
2e	Adjustable screw			927 156 95 02	1
2f	Clamp			927 156 73 02	1
2g	Round head screw	M 6 x 15	DIN 85	06 004 00085 17	1
2h	Cape			927 993 79 08	1
3	Brake lever, complete for Moto-Cross an Hornet			159 156 94 01	1
3	Brake lever, complete for Enduro and Boondocker			927 150 88 09	1
3a	↑Mounting ass'y, for Moto-Cross and Hornet			159 150 94 02	1
3a	Mounting ass'y, for Enduro and Boondocker			927 150 94 18	1
3b	Round head screw, slotted			06 204 00085 17	1
3c	Brake lever			159 156 94 03	1
3d	Lever bolt			159 156 93 01	1
3e	Lock washer	J 6,4	DIN 6797	06 014 06797 35	1
3f	Hexagon nut	M 6	DIN 934	06 006 00934 17	1
4	Adjustable screw with nut			927 159 96 01	1
5	Clutch lever, complete			927 150 95 04	1
5a	↑Mounting ass'y			927 150 94 08	1
5b	Round head screw, slotted			06 204 00085 17	1
5c	Clutch lever			159 156 90 02	1
5d	Lever bolt			159 156 93 01	1
5e	Lock washer	J 6,4	DIN 6797	06 014 06797 35	1
5f	Hexagon nut	M 6	DIN 934	06 006 00934 17	1
5g	Adjustable screw with nut			927 159 96 01	1
6	Spraying protection			427 771 25 01	2
7	Nipple for cable			927 179 53 05	2
8	Rubber grip			927 156 87 03	1
9	Choke lever			927 150 89 02	1
10	Clutch cable			927 170 73 43	1
10a	Starter cable			927 170 77 01	1
10b	Throttle cable			927 170 72 61	1
10c	Brake cable, for Moto-Cross and Enduro			927 170 70 30	1
10c	Brake cable, for Hornet and Boondocker			927 170 70 55	1

Head lamp, head lamp bracket, switch, speedometer

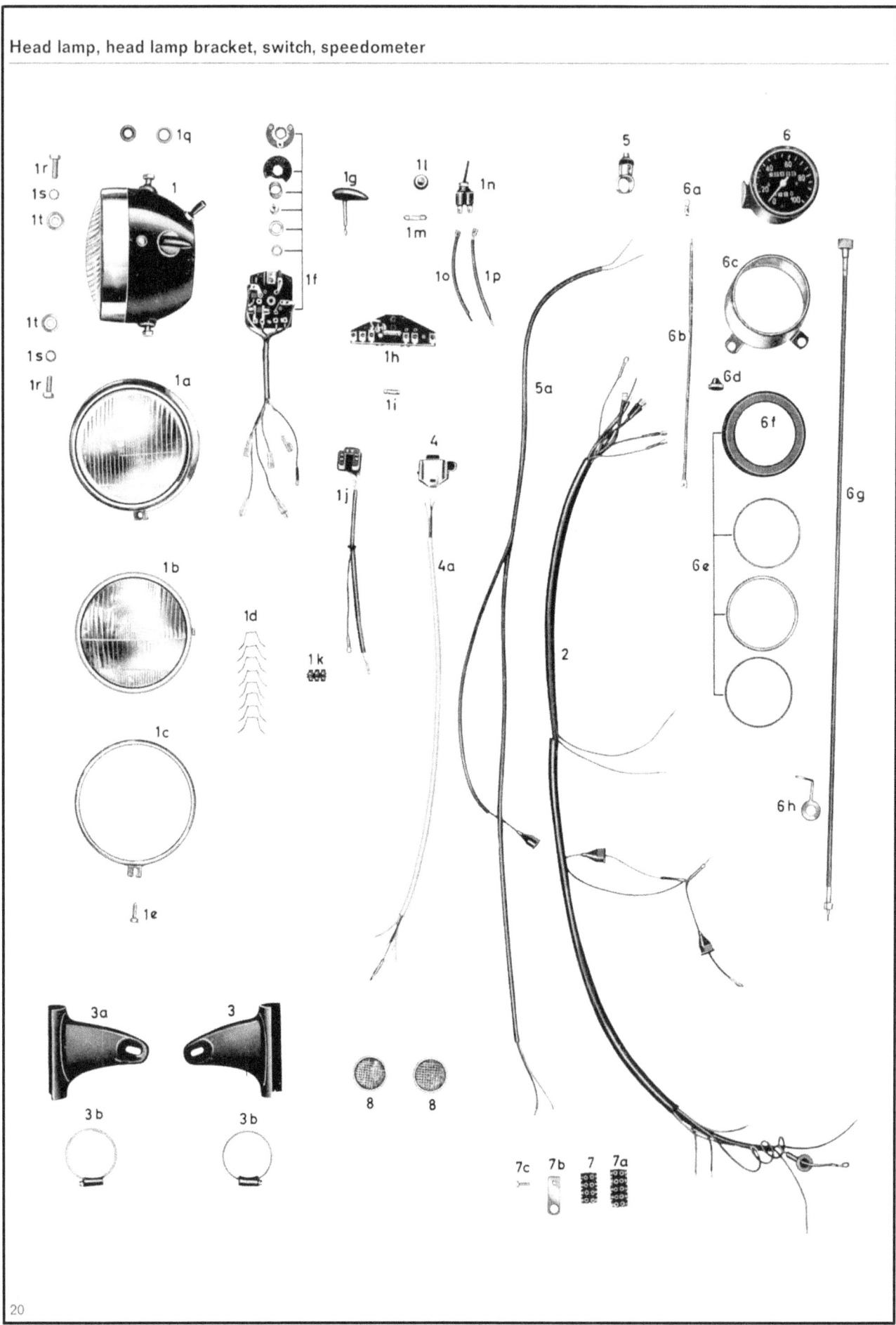

III. No.	Description			Order No.	Pcs.
1	Head lamp, complete			428 340 01 03.088	1
1a	↑Sealed beam, complete			927 340 05 10	1
1b	↑Sealed beam	6 V – 30/30 W		927 341 98 14	1
1c	Headlight door			417 341 99 01	1
1d	Spring for sealed beam			927 341 88 12	10
1e	Round head screw, slotted	BM 6 x 20	DIN 85	685 341 86 01	1
1f	Ingnition – and light switch with cable			927 380 97 01	1
1g	Ignition-key			927 382 10 01	1
1h	Connection plate with rectifying diode			927 380 96 01	1
1i	Fuse	F 15 A		927 362 60 01	1
1j	Plug with cable			927 360 11 01	1
1k	Terminal			927 380 62 01	1
1l	High beam indicator, complete			675 340 20 01	1
1m	Bulb of HBI	M 6 V – 0,6 W		06 506 72601 90	1
1n	Two-way-switch			927 380 34 01	1
1o	Cable, yellow-red			927 360 03 17	1
1p	Cable, white			927 360 03 16	1
1q	Rubber grommet			927 993 21 28	2
1r	Hexagon Screw	M 8 x 22	DIN 933	08 009 00933 37	2
1s	Lock washer	A 8,2	DIN 6797	08 019 06797 35	2
1t	Washer			927 992 00 58	2
2	Cable (terminal – head lamp) for Enduro and Boondocker, up to frame No. 428 000 581			427 360 01 14	1
	Cable (terminal – head lamp) for Enduro and Boondocker, from frame No. 428 000 582			428 360 01 02	1
3	Head lamp bracket, left, for Enduro			921 150 39 14.088	1
3	Head lamp bracket, left, for Boondocker			921 150 39 32.088	1
3a	Head lamp bracket, right, for Enduro			921 150 39 15.088	1
3a	Head lamp bracket, right, for Boondocker			921 150 39 33.088	1
3b	Clamp for Enduro			927 973 33 01	2
3b	Clamp for Boondocker			927 973 33 02	2
4	Light switch for Enduro and Boondocker			101 380 31 00	1
4a	Cable for light switch			427 360 01 15	1
5	Connect switch for Moto-Cross and Hornet			927 380 30 01	1
5a	Cable for connect-switch up to frame No. 428 000 581			428 360 01 01	1
6	Speedometer 0—100 mph for Enduro and Boondocker			428 291 05 01	1
6a	Bulb	J 6 V – 0,6 W		06 001 72601 90	1
6b	Cable			927 360 03 15	1
6c	Speedometer housing for Enduro			428 100 83 01	1
6c	Rubber grommet (for Boondocker)			428 100 83 02	1
6d	Speedometer housing for Boondocker			115 139 23 00	1
6e	Damping retaining, complete			428 290 05 01	1
6f	↑Rubber ring			428 993 20 01	1
6g	Speedometer drive shaft	820 mm		698 297 01 01	1
6h	Speedometer drive shaft bracket			428 990 98 01	1
7	Terminal for Moto-Cross and Hornet			12 004 72586 90	3/12
7a	Terminal for Enduro and Boondocker			12 004 72586 90	4/12
7b	Mounting bracket			927 971 85 16	1
7c	Round head screw, slotted	AM 3 x 15	DIN 85	03 008 00085 17	1
8	Rear reflector, yellow, front			927 340 09 02	2

Brake light switch, taillight, horn, ignition coil, battery

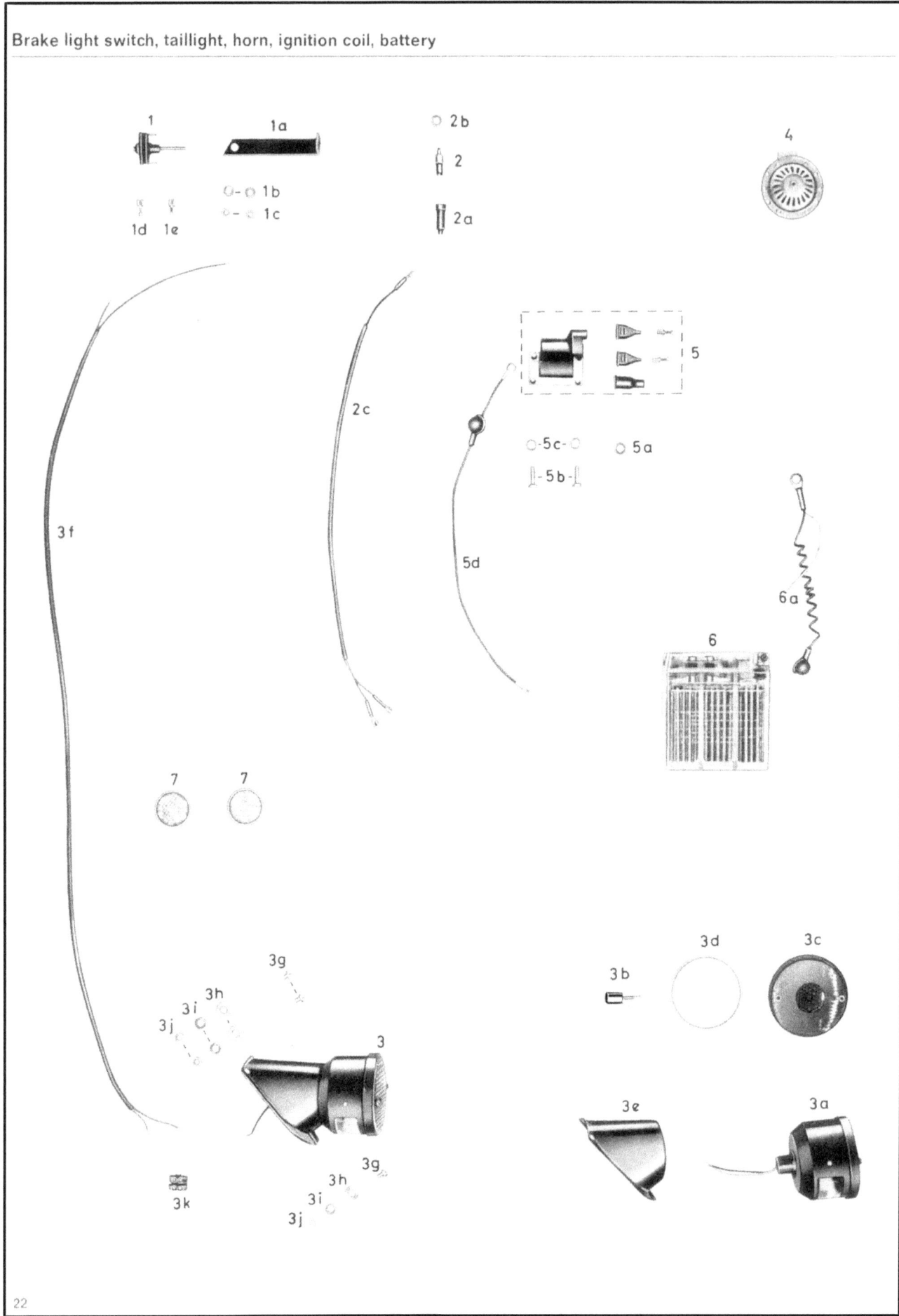

Ill. No.	Description			Order No.	Pcs.
1	Brake light switch for rear wheel			927 380 40 05	1
1a	Mounting bracket			927 968 40 45	1
1b	Spring washer	B 6	DIN 137	06 011 00137 35	2
1c	Nut	M 6	DIN 934	06 006 00934 17	2
1d	Connector socket	6,3 x 1	DIN 46247	06 005 46247 60	1
1e	Connector socket	6,3 x 2,5	DIN 46247	06 006 46247 60	1
2	Brake light switch for front wheel			927 380 40 07	1
2a	Rubber cape			927 993 21 31	1
2b	Washer	6,4	DIN 433	06 012 00433 07	1
2c	Cable for brake ligth switch (front wheel)			427 360 01 17	1
3	Taillight with mount, complete			675 340 02 02.088	1
3a	↑Taillight, complete			675 340 02 01.088	1
3b	↑Bulb	S 6 V – 18/5 W		06 017 72601 90	1
3c	Taillight lens			927 344 09 01	1
3d	Gasket			927 993 38 07	1
3e	Mount for taillight			675 968 46 01.088	1
3f	Cable for taillight			427 360 01 16	1
3g	Round head screw, slotted	AM 6 x 12	DIN 85	06 003 00085 17	3
3h	Washer	A 6,4	DIN 9021	06 013 09021 07	3
3i	Spring washer	B 6	DIN 137	06 011 00137 35	3
3j	Nut	M 6	DIN 985	06 706 00985 17	3
3k	Terminal			927 995 62 02	1
4	Horn PAGANI			927 393 20 05	1
—	Hexagon screw	M 6 x 12	DIN 933	06 005 00933 37	1
—	Spring washer	B 6	DIN 128	06 018 00128 35	1
—	Nut	M 6	DIN 985	06 706 00985 17	1
5	Ignition coil, complete up to frame No. 428 000 581			927 316 10 01	1
5a	Distance bushing (for Enduro and Boondocker)			927 996 01 07	1
5b	Hexagon screw	M 5 x 25	DIN 931	05 004 00931 37	2
5c	Spring washer	B 5	DIN 128	05 016 00128 35	2
5d	Cable for ignition coil up to frame No. 428 000 581			927 360 20 03	1
—	Cable for ignition coil from frame No. 428 000 582			927 360 20 06	1
—	Ignition coile from frame No. 428 000 582			see page 37 (from engine No. 9031 501)	1
—	Hexagon screw	M 6 x 20	DIN 933	06 009 00933 37	2
—	Washer	A 6,4	DIN 9021	06 013 09021 07	3
—	Spring washer	B 6	DIN 128	06 018 00128 35	2
—	Nut	M 6	DIN 985	06 706 00985 17	2
6	Battery (VARTA)	6 V – 12 Ah		927 391 20 01	1
6a	Cable for battery (—)			427 360 20 03	1
7	Rear reflector, red			927 340 09 03	2
—	Clamp for rear-reflector	20 mm ⌀		1626 112 003	2
—	Nut	M 5	DIN 934	05 005 00934 17	2

Front wheel, front hub

24

Ill. No.	Description			Order No.	Pcs.
—	Front wheel, complete without tire for Hornet and Boondocker			428 240 99 01	1
—	Front wheel, complete without tire for Moto-Cross and Enduro			417 240 99 11	1
—	↑Rim	1,85 B – 21		428 241 10 02	1
—	Spoke (inside)	M 4 x 224		40 411 74371 39	18
—	Spoke (outside)	M 4 x 224		40 410 74371 39	18
—	Nipple	M 4		40 093 74371 68	36
1	Front hub, complete, for Hornet and Boondocker	VS 1401		12 0800 001 021	1
1	Front hub, complete, for Moto-Cross and Enduro	VS 1401		12 0800 001 018	1
2	Hub body, complete			0870 174 002	1
2a	↑Hub body			0801 126 002	1
2b	Axle bushing			0842 113 000	1
2c	Bearing	40 x 17 x 12	6203 RS	62 034 00625 40	2
2d	U-cover			0821 103 002	2
2e	Distance bushing with U-cover			0874 115 003	2
2f	↑U-cover			0821 123 004	2
3	Brake plate			0877 136 003	1
3a–3d	Brake cam with rubber gasket, washer and nut			0879 110 003	1
3b	↑Rubber gasket			0822 104 000	1
3c	Spring washer	B 8	DIN 128	08 022 00128 35	1
3d	Nut	M 8 x 1	DIN 936	08 001 00936 17	1
3e	Brake arm			0878 113 000	1
3f–3g	Brake shoes complete, with springs			0873 104 000	1 set
3g	↑Return spring			0825 102 301	2
3h	Adjustable screw			0839 026 000	1
3i	Knurled nut			0816 111 000	1
4	Cover			0821 130 002	1
5	Axle for Moto-Cross and Enduro			0809 123 002	1
5	Axle for Hornet and Boondocker			0809 127 000	1
5a	Washer	B 13	DIN 125	13 014 00125 07	1
5b	Nut	M 12 x 1,5	DIN 934	12 014 00934 17	1
—	Tire "METZELER D"	3,00–21		30 412 07802 90	1
—	Tube	3,00–21		927 241 71 10	1
—	Rim band	19"/20		698 241 70 02	1
—	Tire holder "DUNLOP WM 3"			427 241 67 01	1

Rear wheel, rear hub, chain tensioner, chain

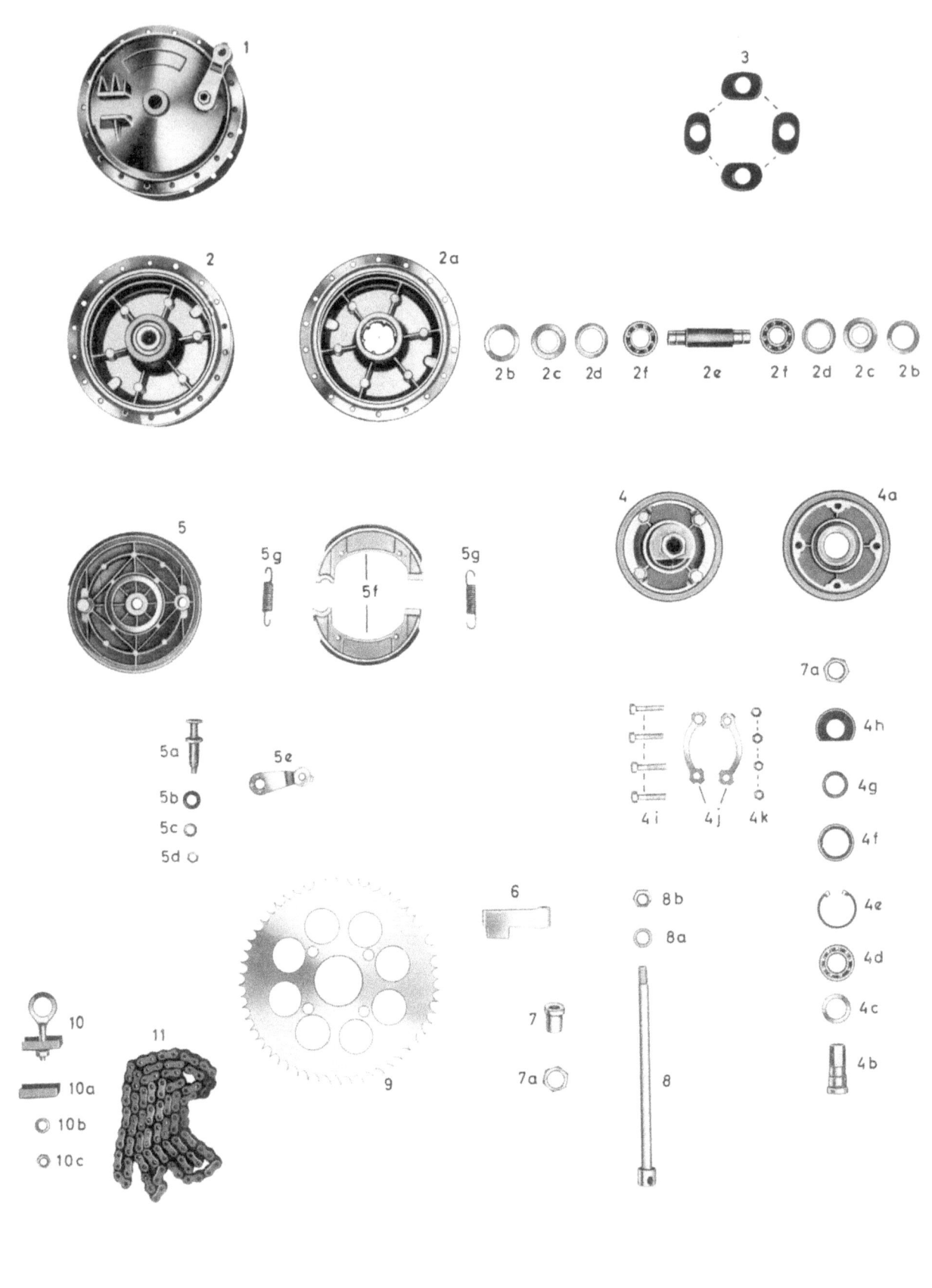

Ill. No.	Description			Order No.	Pcs.
—	Rear wheel, complete, without sprocket and tire			427 240 98 08	1
—	↑Rim	1.85 B-18		428 241 10 01	1
—	Spoke (inside)	M 4 x 189		40 409 74371 39	18
—	Spoke (outside)	M 4 x 189		40 408 74371 39	18
—	Nipple	M 4		40 093 74371 68	36
1	Rear hub, without sprocket		HS 1401	65 0800 001 018	1
2	Hub body, complete			0870 174 002	1
2a	↑Hub body			0801 126 002	1
2b	U-cover			0821 103 002	2
2c	Distance bushing, complete			0874 115 003	2
2d	↑U-cover			0821 123 004	2
2e	Axle bushing			0842 113 000	1
2f	Bearing	40 x 17 x 12	6203 RS	62 034 00625 40	2
3	Rubber damper			0822 106 000	4
4	Clutch piece, complete			0872 119 002	1
4a	↑Clutch piece			0841 109 002	1
4b	Axle bushing			0842 112 002	1
4c	Washer			0818 130 000	1
4d	Bearing	20 x 42 x 12	6004-2 RS	60 044 00625 40	1
4e	Circlip	42 x 1,75		42 021 00472 31	1
4f	Gasket	30 x 42 x 7		0822 055 001	1
4g	Distance bushing			0834 115 003	1
4h	Washer			0818 124 003	1
4i	Hexagon screw	M 8 x 35	DIN 931	08 005 00931 47	4
4j	Security bracket			0817 105 002	2
4k	Nut	M 8		0942 067 100	4
5	Brakeplate			0877 135 008	1
5a–5d	Brake cam with rubber-gasket, washer and nut			0879 110 003	1
5b	↑Rubber gasket			0822 104 000	1
5c	Spring washer	B 8	DIN 128	08 022 00128 35	1
5d	Nut	M 8 x 1	DIN 936	08 001 00936 17	1
5e	Brake arm			0878 115 000	1
5f–5g	Brake shoes with springs			0873 104 000	1 set
5g	↑Return spring			0825 102 301	2
6	Brake plate houlder			0841 110 003	1
7	Axle bushing			0842 111 002	1
7a	Nut			927 991 51 16	2
8	Axle			0809 122 002	1
8a	Washer	B 13	DIN 125	13 014 00125 07	1
8b	Nut	M 12 x 1,5	DIN 934	12 014 00934 17	1
9	Sprocket, 56 teeth			0833 154 001	1
10	Chain tensioner, complete			927 030 44 22.910	2
10a	↑Plate			927 973 70 18.088	2
10b	Washer	A 8,4	DIN 125	08 011 00125 07	2
10c	Nut	M 8	DIN 985	08 708 00985 17	2
11	Chain with lock (IWIS)	½ x 5/16"-120		915 998 05 35	1
—	↑Master link (IWIS)			915 998 15 01	1
—	Tire "METZELER D"	3,50–18		35 017 07802 90	1
—	Tube	E 18		698 241 71 01	1
—	Rim band	18"/27		698 241 70 01	1
—	Tire holder "DUNLOP WM 3"			427 241 67 01	1

Tool kit, number plate

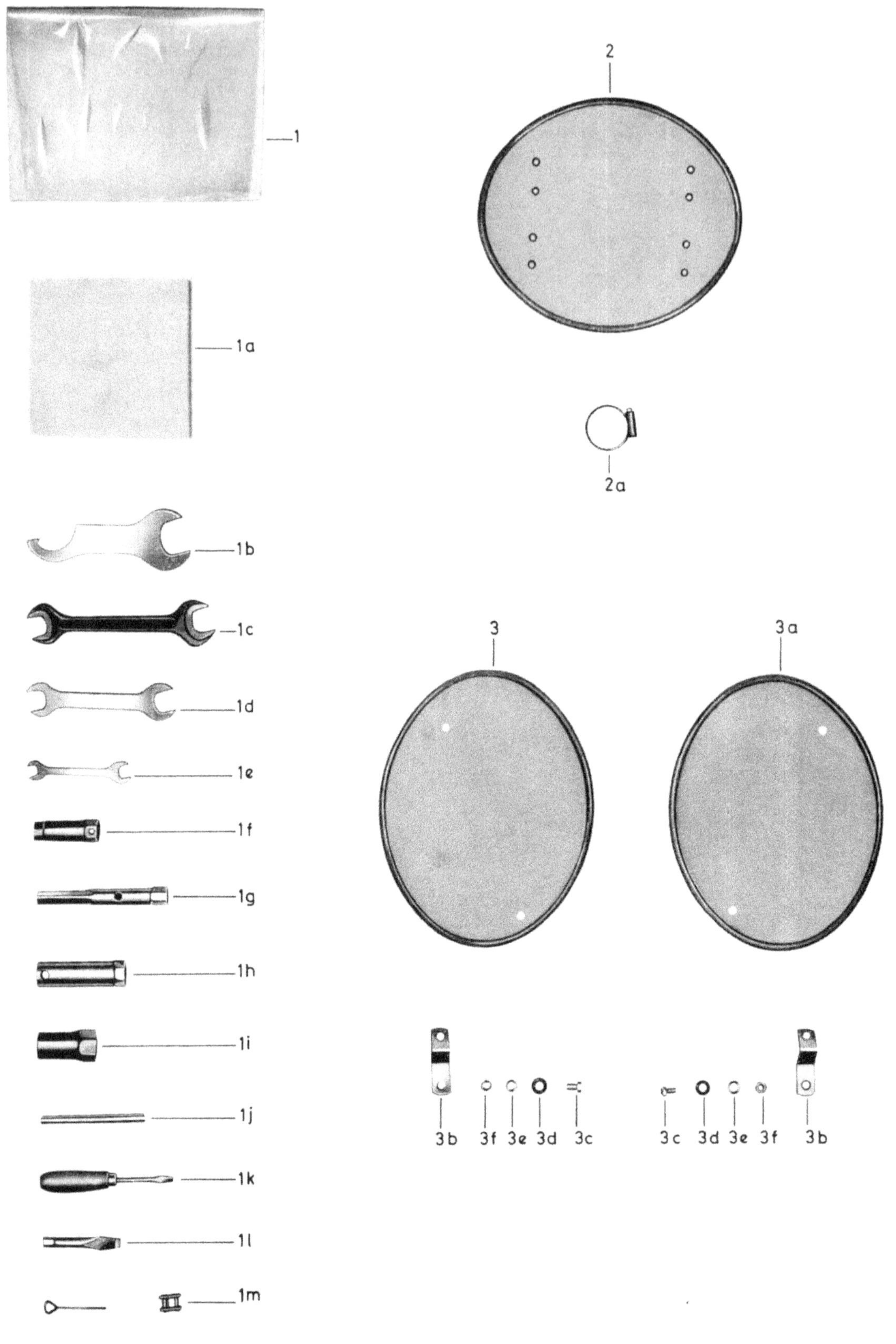

28

218

Ill. No.	Description			Order No.	Pcs.
1–1m	Tool kit, complete			676 940 06 03	1
1	Plastic bag			927 959 62 03	1
1a	Polishing rag			925 943 90 02	1
1b	Special wrench			925 943 07 02	1
1c	Open end wrench	19/22		19 018 00895 40	1
1d	Open end wrench	17/19		0976 084 001	1
1e	Open end wrench	9/11		0276 111 000	1
1f	Socket wrench	13/17		0976 009 102	1
1g	Socket wrench	10/14		0976 005 100	1
1h	Socket wrench	21		2876 014 001	1
1i	Socket wrench	24		925 943 01 32	1
1j	Rad for socket wrench			2876 012 000	1
1k	Screw driver	6 x 1		925 943 04 00	1
1l	Screw driver			0676 009 100	1
1m	Master link	$1/2 \times 5/16''$		06 084 08187 40	1
2	Number plate for Moto-Cross (front)			927 770 35 02.079	1
2	Number plate for Hornet (front)			927 770 35 03.079	1
2a	Clamp for Hornet			927 973 33 02	2
2a	Clamp for Moto-Cross			927 973 33 01	2
3	Number plate, left			427 771 35 04.079	1
3a	Number plate, right			427 771 35 05.079	1
3b	Number plate bracket			927 968 40 51	2
3c	Hexagon screw	M 6 x 12	DIN 933	06 005 00933 37	5
3d	Washer	A 6,4	DIN 9021	06 013 09021 07	7
3e	Spring washer	B 6	DIN 137	06 011 00137 35	6
3f	Nut	M 6	DIN 985	06 706 00985 17	6

Crankcase, Crankshaft, Cylinder

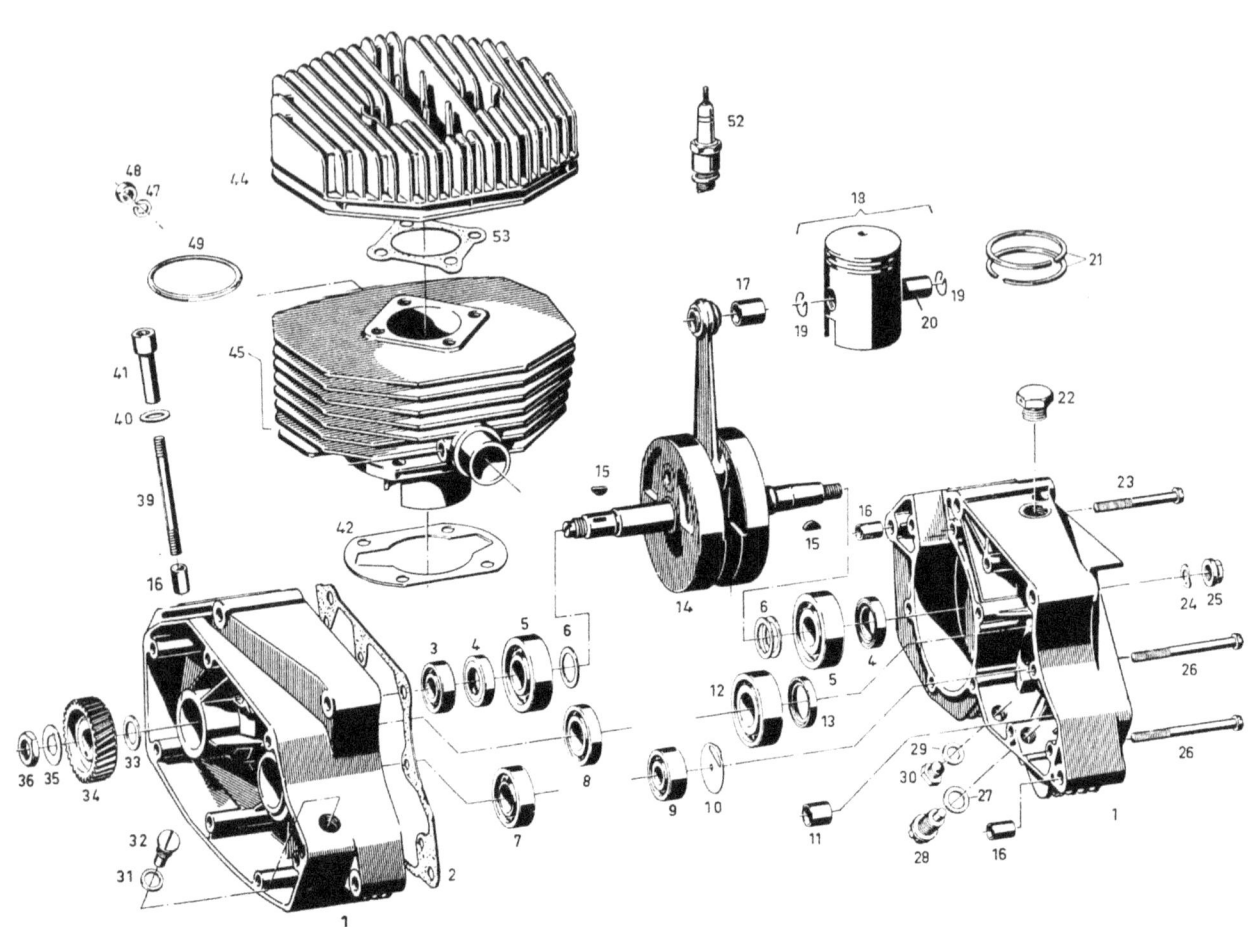

The illustration No. 44 (Cylinder head) and No. 45 (Cylinder) are only for information and do not conform with the specification of the models contained in the list.

Ill. No.	Description	Order No.	Pcs.
1	Crankcase ass'y. with 2 dowel sleeves, 1 crankcase gasket and 4 studs	0687 107 409	1
2	Gasket	0650 105 101	1
3	Deep groove ball bearing 6202 C3 DIN 625	0232 120 001	1
4	Oil seal 18.6 x 35 x 8	0230 002 000	1
5	Ball bearing M 20 DIN 615	0932 063 001	1
6	Shim 20.5 x 28.5, page 39	0944 046 000	x
7	Deep groove ball bearing 6004 C3 DIN 625 for layshaft	0232 126 001	1
8	Deep groove ball bearg. 16005 DIN 625, 25 x 47 x 8 for main shaft	2732 006 000	1
9	Deep groove ball bearing 6301 C3 DIN 625 for layshaft	0632 110 001	1
10	Profile washer	0644 109 100	1
11	Washer 12 x 16 x 14.5	0232 129 000	1
12	Cylindrical roller bearing NJ 205 E C3 ZS DIN 5423 for main shaft	0632 017 201	1
13	Oil seal 23.4 x 34 x 5	0630 001 000	1
14	Crankshaft	0688 005 001	1
15	Key 3 x 3.7	0246 005 000	1
16	Dowel sleeve	1949 111 000	4
17	Needle cage K 15 x 19 x 20	0632 111 000	1
18	Piston ass'y. ⌀ 54.0	0686 207 015	1
	Piston ass'y. ⌀ 54.5	0686 207 016	
	Piston ass'y. ⌀ 55.0	0686 207 017	
	Piston ass'y. ⌀ 55.5	0686 207 018	
19	Circlip	0945 063 000	2
20	Gudgeon pin 9 x 15 x 46	0616 100 000	1
21	Piston ring, L, ⌀ 54.0	0615 103 005	1
	Piston ring, L, ⌀ 54.5	0615 103 006	1
	Piston ring, L, ⌀ 55.0	0615 103 007	1
	Piston ring, L, ⌀ 55.5	0615 103 008	1
21	Piston ring, rect., ⌀ 54.0	0615 101 005	1
	Piston ring, rect., ⌀ 54.5	0615 101 006	1
	Piston ring, rect., ⌀ 55.0	0615 101 007	1
	Piston ring, rect., ⌀ 55.5	0615 101 008	1
22	Plug screw M 16 x 1.25 x 6	0241 048 000	1
23	Screw M 6 x 60	0940 119 102	6
24	Spring washer for M 10	0245 022 000	1
25	Collar nut M 10 x 1 (lefthand thread)	0942 072 110	1
26	Screw M 6 x 75	0940 128 202	4
27	Sealing washer 12.2 x 20 x 1	0650 004 000	1
28	Stop screw M 12 x 1	0640 005 005	1
29	Sealing washer 10.2 x 15.9 x 1	1950 023 000	1
30	Oil drain plug M 10 x 1	0240 100 000	1
	Oil drain plug M 12 x 1 (repair)	0241 029 005	1
31	Sealing washer 12.2 x 15.4 x 1.5	0250 118 000	1
32	Pivot screw M 12 x 1	0240 133 100	1
33	Washer 15.2 x 20.3 x 1.5	0246 009 006	1
34	Driving pinion	0634 112 000	1
35	Tab washer for ⌀ 14 with inner tab	0944 055 001	1
36	Nut M 14 x 1.5	0642 105 001	1
39	Stud M 8 x 90	0640 108 001	4
40	Washer 13.2 x 20 x 1.7	0244 075 008	4
41	Nut with shaft M 8 x 40	0642 107 001	4
42	Gasket	0650 107 200	1
44	Cylinder head	0613 106 004	1
45	Cylinder ass'y	0687 108 250	1
47	Spring washer for M 8	0245 023 003	2
48	Nut M 8 x 36	0642 104 101	2
49	Sealing ring 40 x 47 x 2.5	0650 112 000	1
52	Spark plug W 260 T 1	0298 087 011	1
53	Gasket ⌀ 54 mm	0650 114 000	1

Gear-changing lever, Main shaft, Gearbox

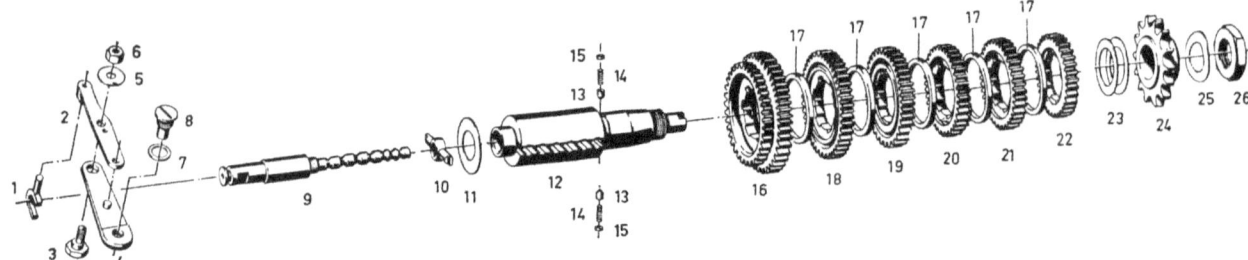

I

Starting device, Gear-changing

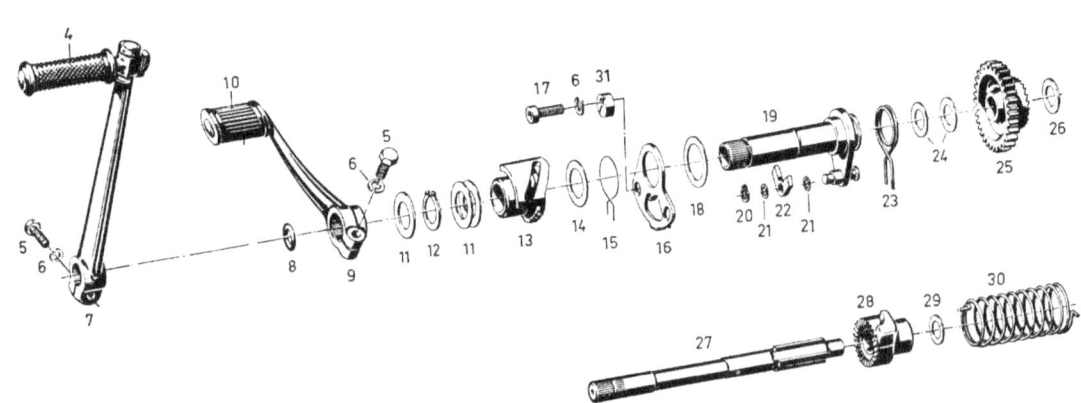

II

Ill. No.	Description	Order No.	Pcs.
I	**Gear-changing lever, Main shaft, Gearbox**		
1	Shifting fork	0248 135 100	1
2	Shifting lever, upper part	0648 106 000	1
3	Eccentric bolt M 6	0640 110 000	1
4	Shifting lever, lower part	0648 105 100	1
5	Locking washer for M 10 with inner lug	1445 017 000	1
6	Nut M 6	0642 108 000	1
7	Sealing ring 12.2 x 15.4 x 1.5	0250 118 000	1
8	Pivot screw M 12 x 1	0240 133 100	1
9	Selector rod	0619 004 001	1
10	Selector key	0619 001 100	1
11	Shim 25.2 x 39, page 39	0644 105 103	x
12	Main shaft	0637 102 101	1
	Main sh. ass'y., with ill. 9, 10 and 12...15	0685 102 101	1
13	Cup	0649 105 000	2
14	Pressure spring	0639 100 100	2
15	Plug	0663 002 000	2
16	Sliding pinion 1st gear (46 and 34 teeth)	0634 106 101	1
17	Ring 42 x 49 x 2.8	0647 101 001	
	Ring 42 x 49 x 2.7	0647 101 002	x
	Ring 42 x 49 x 2.6	0647 101 003	
18	Sliding pinion 2nd gear (41 teeth)	0634 107 001	1
19	Sliding pinion 3rd gear (39 teeth)	0634 108 001	1
20	Sliding pinion 4th gear (36 teeth)	0634 108 002	1
21	Sliding pinion 5th gear (33 teeth)	0634 109 001	1
22	Sliding pinion 6th gear (31 teeth)	0634 110 001	1
23	Shim 25.2 x 39, page 39	0644 105 000	x
24	Sprocket 14 teeth	0636 106 000	1
	Sprocket 13 teeth	0636 107 000	
25	Spring washer for ⌀ 20	0944 019 000	1
26	Nut M 20 x 1 (lefthand thread)	0642 103 001	1
II	**Starting device, Gear-changing**		
4	Rubber sleeve	0260 017 000	1
5	Screw, hexagon head, M 6 x 20	0240 005 002	1
6	Spring washer for M 6	0245 023 002	3
7	Kickstarter crank ass'y., straight, incl. ill. 4, 5 and 6	0289 028 001	1
8	Sealing ring, round, 11.3 x 2.4	0250 148 000	1
9	Gear-changing pedal	0248 144 100	1
10	Rubber sleeve	0660 000 000	1
11	Shim 20.5 x 28.5, page 39	0944 046 000	x
12	Circlip for ⌀ 20	0945 064 000	1
13	Selector boss	0286 317 001	
	Selector boss	0286 317 021	1
14	Shim 20.2 x 32, page 39	0244 118 000	x
15	Pawl spring	0239 119 000	1
16	Selector adjusting plate	0248 133 001	1
17	Screw, hex. sock. hd., M 6 x 25 f. gr. lock	1940 114 000	2
18	Washer 25.3 x 34 x 0.5	0246 008 001	1
19	Select. sh. ass'y. w. lock. lev. ill. 19...22	0290 106 211	1
20	Circlip for ⌀ 6	0945 105 000	1
21	Shim 6.2 x 10, page 39	0244 100 000	x
22	Selector pawl	0248 136 000	1
23	Torsion spring	0239 120 000	1
24	Shim 14.5 x 24, page 39	0244 055 000	x
25	Starter gear	0634 111 000	1
26	Washer 14.5 x 24 x 1.0	0244 055 002	1
27	Starter shaft	0237 122 200	1
28	Ratchet wheel	0634 005 001	1
29	Washer 12.1 x 18.5 x 1.0	0244 102 102	1
30	Torsion spring	0239 122 000	1
31	Stopping bush for gear lock	0647 103 000	2
	Gear-chang. ass'y., incl. ill. 11, 12, 13 (sel. boss 0286 317 021), 14...16 and 18...23	0690 002 001	1

Clutch side crankcase cover, Clutch, Layshaft

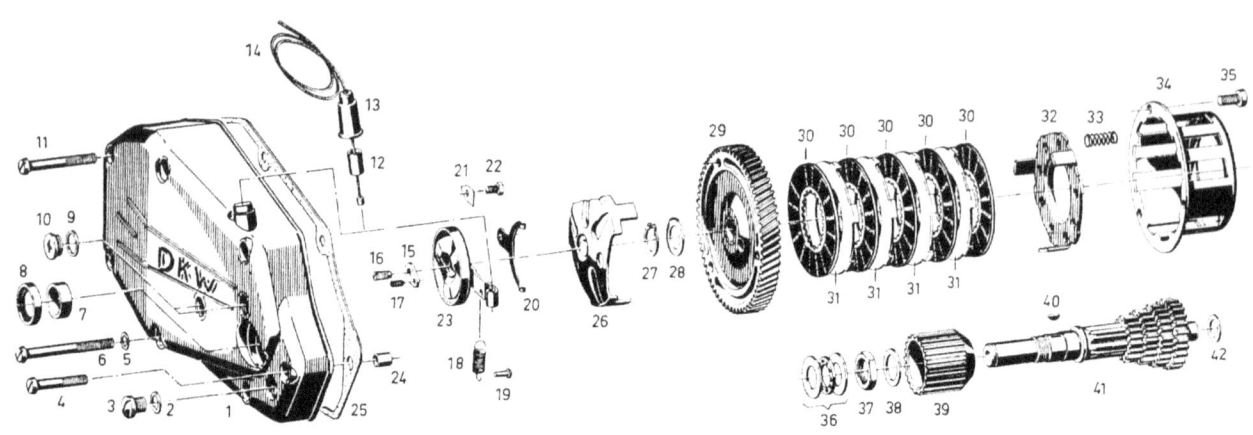

Magneto side crankcase cover, Speedometer drive

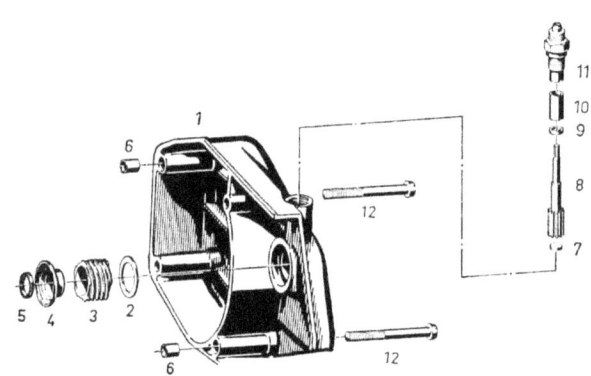

Ill. No.	Description	Order No.	Pcs.
	Clutch side crankcase cover, Clutch, Layshaft		
1	Crankcase cover	0611 114 104	1
	Crankcase ass'y., including illustr. 1, 5, 7...10, 12...23	0677 001 102	1
2	Sealing ring 10 x 14 x 1.5	0230 015 000	1
3	Screw M 10 x 10	0241 053 100	1
4	Screw M 6 x 38	0241 040 001	2
5	Sealing ring 6.5 x 11 x 1	0250 112 100	1
6	Screw M 6 x 65	0640 011 102	4
7	Bush 20 x 24 x 9	0232 131 000	1
8	Oil seal 19 x 28 x 4	0250 128 000	1
9	Sealing ring 14.1 x 17.2 x 0.5	0250 131 000	2
10	Plug M 14 x 1	0240 140 000	2
11	Screw M 6 x 52	0240 120 002	1
12	Nipple 10.4 x 15	0299 141 000	1
13	Cap, protective	0260 125 000	1
14	Wire with solder nipple 0291 006 000	0291 007 000	1
15	Locking plate with tap M 8 x 1 and M 4	0251 107 001	1
16	Adjusting screw M 8 x 1 x 13.5	0640 107 000	1
17	Grub screw M 4 x 6	0240 139 000	1
18	Tension spring	0239 123 000	1
19	Grooved pin 3 x 8	0949 003 002	1
20	Fork	0239 126 000	1
21	Locking plate	0245 112 000	1
22	Screw M 5 x 10	0941 087 000	1
23	Cam cup with tap M 8 x 1	0684 003 000	1
24	Dowel tube 8.5 x 10	0949 090 000	2
25	Gasket	0650 106 000	1
26	Thrust plate	0684 002 000	1
27	Circlip for ⌀ 16	0245 020 005	1
28	Shim 16.3 x 25.8, page 39	0246 015 000	x
29	Layshaft wheel with bush 0632 113 000	0685 100 000	1
30	Inner plate	0284 007 000	5
31	Outer plate	0259 109 000	4
32	Thrust plate	0658 003 000	1
33	Thrust spring ⌀ 9.5 (6 coils)	0639 106 000	9
34	Clutch case, 41.5 mm high	0658 002 100	1
35	Screw, hexagon socket head, M 6 x 15	2740 024 002	3
36	Ball cage ass'y. with 2 washers	0686 209 000	1
37	Nut M 18 x 1	0242 106 005	1
38	Washer 18.3 x 27 x 2	0644 106 000	1
39	Clutch hub	0658 001 000	1
40	Key 3 x 3.7	0246 005 000	1
41	Layshaft	0685 101 001	1
42	Shim 12.1 x 18.5, page 39	0244 102 000	x
	Magneto side crankcase cover, Speedometer drive		
1	Magneto side crankcase cover	0611 113 002	1
	Magneto side crankcase cover ass'y.	0677 002 001	1
2	Washer 15.7 x 24.8 x 0.5	0244 082 002	1
3	Spiral gear	0234 071 000	1
4	Bearing cup	0246 052 000	1
5	Sealing ring 13.8 x 19 x 2.5	0650 017 000	1
6	Dowel sleeve 8.5 x 10	0949 090 000	2
7	Washer 8.8 x 2	0644 017 000	1
8	Spiral pinion (11 teeth)	0234 070 110	1
9	Washer 6 x 9 x 1	0246 047 000	1
10	Bush	0232 151 000	1
11	Connecting screw M 12 x 1	0241 049 100	1
	Rubber cap	0260 041 000	1
12	Screw M 6 x 60	0940 119 102	4

Magneto-generator

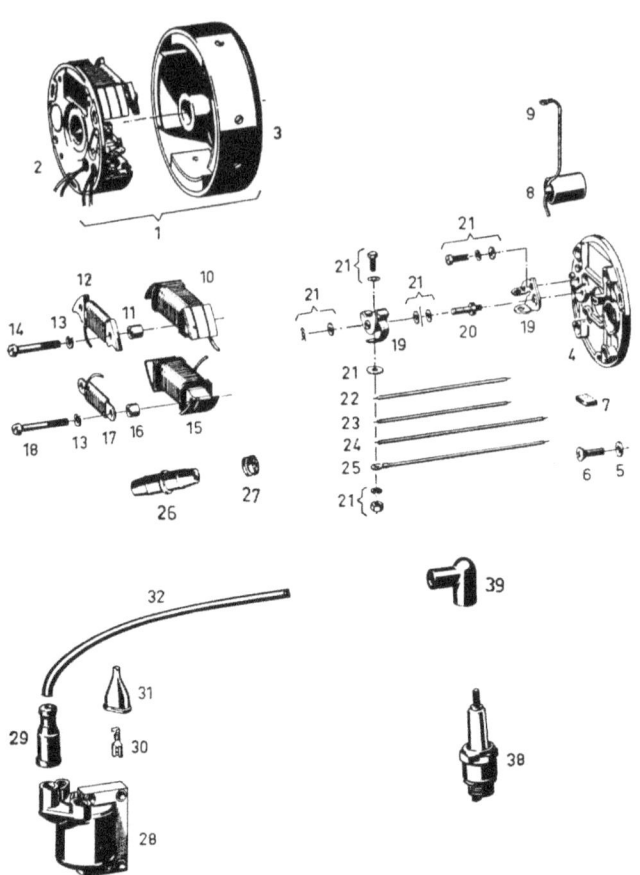
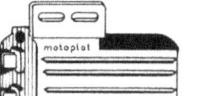
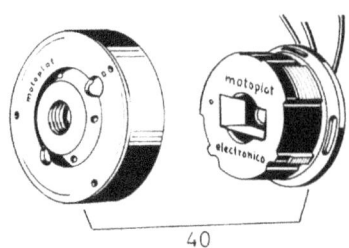

Ill. No.	Description	Order No.	Pcs.
	BOSCH-magneto-generator up to engine No. 9031 500		
1	Magneto-generator 6 Volt	0283 100 404 B	1
2	Armature base plate ass'y.	0283 105 017	1
3	Flywheel	0283 108 023 B	1
4	Armature plate	0265 140 009	1
5	Washer 4.1 x 9 x 1.2	0244 108 000	3
6	Screw M 4 x 14, Philips type	0240 106 100	3
7	Lubricating felt	2865 008 000	1
8	Condenser	0965 091 000	1
9	Connecting cable to condenser	0265 077 001	1
10	Ignition armature	0265 139 012	1
11	Bush	0247 106 005	2
12	Stop light armature	0265 139 014	1
13	Spring washer for M 4	0245 023 000	4
14	Screw M 4 x 30	0240 122 002	2
15	Generating armature	0265 141 004	1
16	Bush 4.2 x 8 x 7	0247 106 001	2
17	Tail light armature	0265 139 013	1
18	Screw M 4 x 32	0240 153 000	2
19	Contact breaker set	0283 101 100	1
20	Pivot pin	0240 066 009	1
21	Set of spares for contact breaker	0283 107 000	1
22	Lighting cable ⎫	0299 059 009	1
23	Tail light cable ⎬ quote required lenght	0299 059 016	1
24	Stop light cable ⎪	0299 059 026	1
25	Generating cable ⎭	0265 137 002	1
26	Cable terminal	0265 073 000	2
27	Rubber grommet	0665 119 000	1
28	Ignition armature	0283 109 000	1
29	Cap, protective	0265 150 000	1
30	Cable terminal	0265 152 000	2
31	Cap, protective	0265 151 000	2
32	Ignition cable ⌀ 7	0665 016 101	1
38	Spark plug W 260 T 1	0298 087 011	1
39	Spark plug connector ass'y., not screened, including. 1 x 1465 011 000 spark plug 1 x 1439 014 000 spring 1 x 1442 006 000 connecting nut	1465 011 001	1
	Ignition cable ass'y., including ill. 39	0283 110 003	1
	MOTOPLAT-magneto-generator from engine No. 9031 501		
40—41	Motoplat-magneto-generator cpl.	0683 006 001	1
41	Electronic-part with ignition coil	0283 124 000	1

37

Carburettor

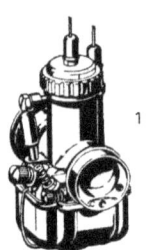
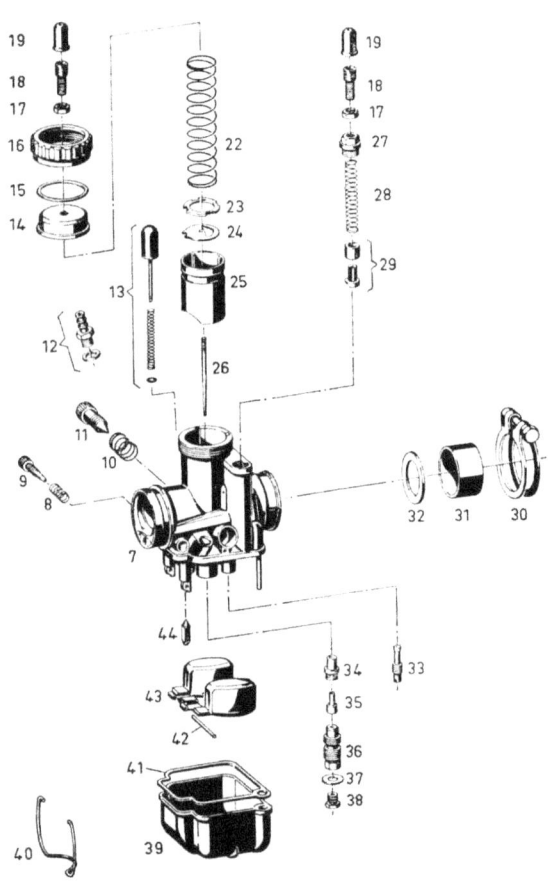

Ill. No.	Description	Order No.	Pcs.
1	Carburettor ass'y 1/27/19	0681 005 112	1
7	Carburettor body	0661 125 000	1
8	Spring	0961 067 000	1
9	Air adjusting screw	0640 105 000	1
10	Spring	0639 103 000	1
11	Adjusting screw	0640 106 000	1
12	Hose socket ass'y.	0986 432 000	1
13	Tickler ass'y.	0661 110 000	1
14	Cover plate	0661 119 000	1
15	Sealing ring	0650 111 000	1
16	Cover, to be screwed on	0642 106 000	1
17	Nut	0961 018 001	2
18	Adjusting screw	0961 081 000	2
19	Cap, rubber	0260 024 001	2
22	Spring	0639 105 000	1
23	Washer	0644 111 000	1
24	Retaining plate	0661 113 000	1
25	Throttle slide	0661 120 001	1
26	Jet needle, No. 5	0661 114 001	1
27	Plug	0661 007 000	1
28	Spring	0661 005 000	1
29	Starter slide ass'y, with sleeve	0686 100 000	1
30	Clamping ring	0651 102 000	1
31	Insulating bush for carburettor	0947 125 000	1
32	Insulating washer for carburettor	0644 110 001	1
33	Idle jet (quote required size) = 45	0661 118 000	1
34	Vaporizer	0661 115 000	1
35	Needle jet, size 2.76	0661 116 001	1
36	Mixing tube	0661 117 000	1
37	Washer for main jet	0962 083 000	1
38	Main jet (quote required size) = 140	0961 106 000	1
39	Float chamber	0661 122 001	1
40	Stirrup	0639 104 000	1
41	Gasket	0650 110 000	1
42	Pin for float	0649 103 000	1
43	Float	0661 121 000	1
44	Float needle	0661 112 000	1

Dimensions of shims

Order No.	Dimensions	Order No.	Dimensions	Order No.	Dimensions
0244 055 000	14.5 x 24 x 0.2	0246 008 000	25.3 x 34 x 1.0	0644 105 004	25.2 x 39 x 1.0
0244 055 001	14.5 x 24 x 0.5	0246 008 001	25.3 x 34 x 0.5	0644 105 103	25.2 x 39 x 0.8
0244 055 002	14.5 x 24 x 1.0	0246 008 002	25.3 x 34 x 0.3	0644 105 104	25.2 x 39 x 1.0
0244 055 003	14.5 x 24 x 0.3	0246 008 003	25.3 x 34 x 0.2		
				0944 003 000	8.4 x 14 x 0.3
0244 100 000	6.2 x 10 x 0.2	0246 015 000	16.3 x 25.8 x 0.3	0944 003 001	8.4 x 14 x 0.5
0244 100 001	6.2 x 10 x 0.3	0246 015 001	16.3 x 25.8 x 0.5	0944 003 002	8.4 x 14 x 0.6
0244 100 002	6.2 x 10 x 0.5	0246 015 002	16.3 x 25.8 x 1.0	0944 003 003	8.4 x 14 x 1.0
0244 100 003	6.2 x 10 x 1.0	0246 015 003	16.3 x 25.8 x 0.15	0944 003 004	8.4 x 14 x 0.4
0244 102 000	12.1 x 18.5 x 0.2	0644 104 000	35.2 x 44 x 0.3	0944 046 000	20.5 x 28.5 x 0.2
0244 102 001	12.1 x 18.5 x 0.5	0644 104 001	35.2 x 44 x 0.5	0944 046 001	20.5 x 28.5 x 0.3
0244 102 102	12.1 x 18.5 x 1.0	0644 104 002	35.2 x 44 x 0.6	0944 046 002	20.5 x 28.5 x 0.5
0244 102 003	12.1 x 18.5 x 1.5	0644 104 003	35.2 x 44 x 0.8	0944 046 003	20.5 x 28.5 x 0.4
		0644 104 004	35.2 x 44 x 1.0	0944 046 004	20.5 x 28.5 x 0.8
0244 118 000	20.2 x 32 x 1.0			0944 046 005	20.5 x 28.5 x 0.15
0244 118 001	20.2 x 32 x 0.8	0644 105 000	25.2 x 39 x 0.2	0944 046 006	20.5 x 28.5 x 1.0
0244 118 002	20.2 x 32 x 0.5	0644 105 001	25.2 x 39 x 0.3		
0244 118 003	20.2 x 32 x 0.3	0644 105 002	25.2 x 39 x 0.5		
0244 118 004	20.2 x 32 x 0.15	0644 105 003	25.2 x 39 x 0.8		

Wiring diagram of the DKW "Enduro"

with BOSCH-magneto-generator   up to frame-No. 428 000 581
up to engine-No. 9031 500

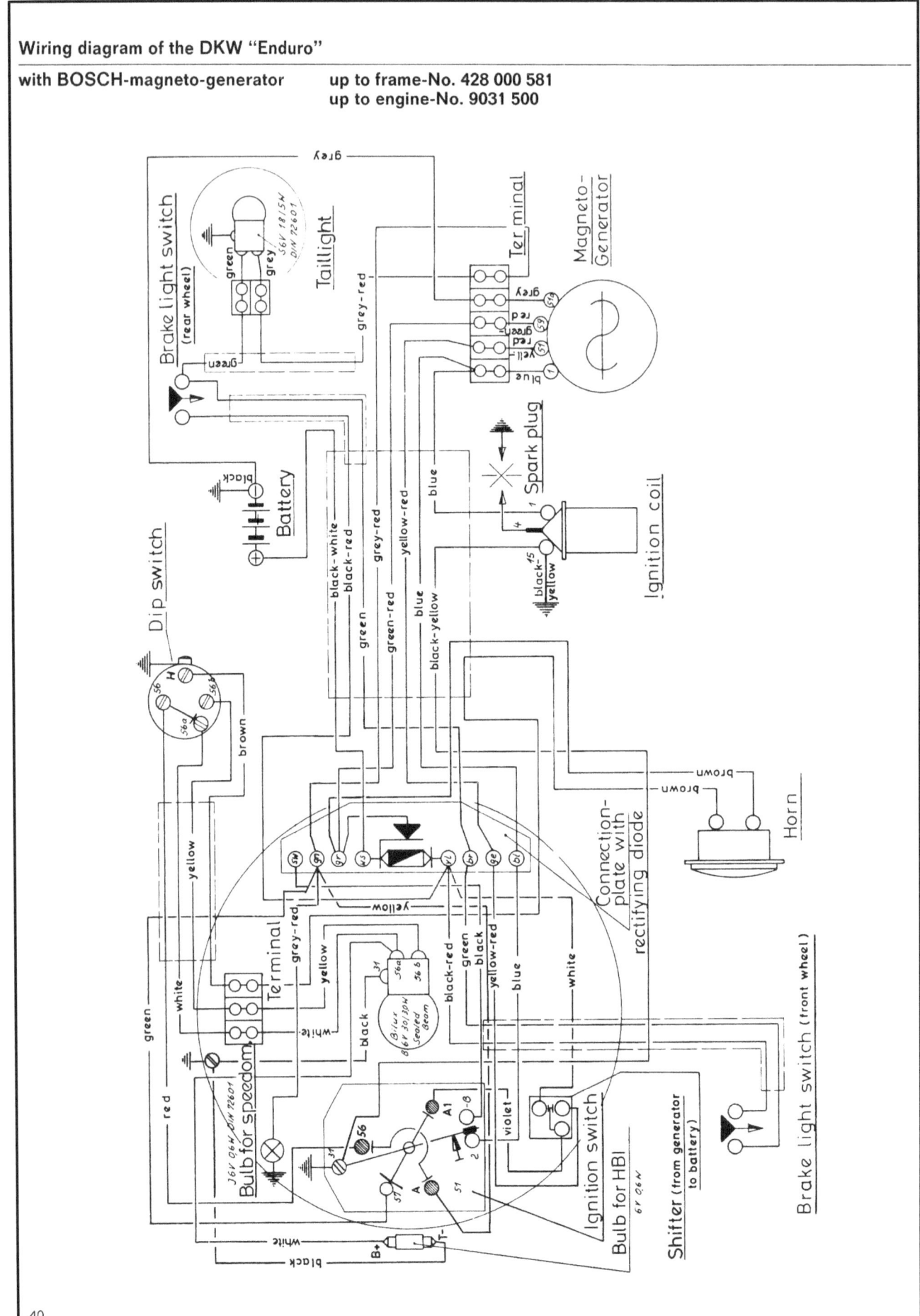

Wiring diagram of the DKW "Enduro" and "Boondocker"

with MOTOPLAT-magneto-generator   from frame-No. 428 000 582
                                    from engine-No. 9031 501

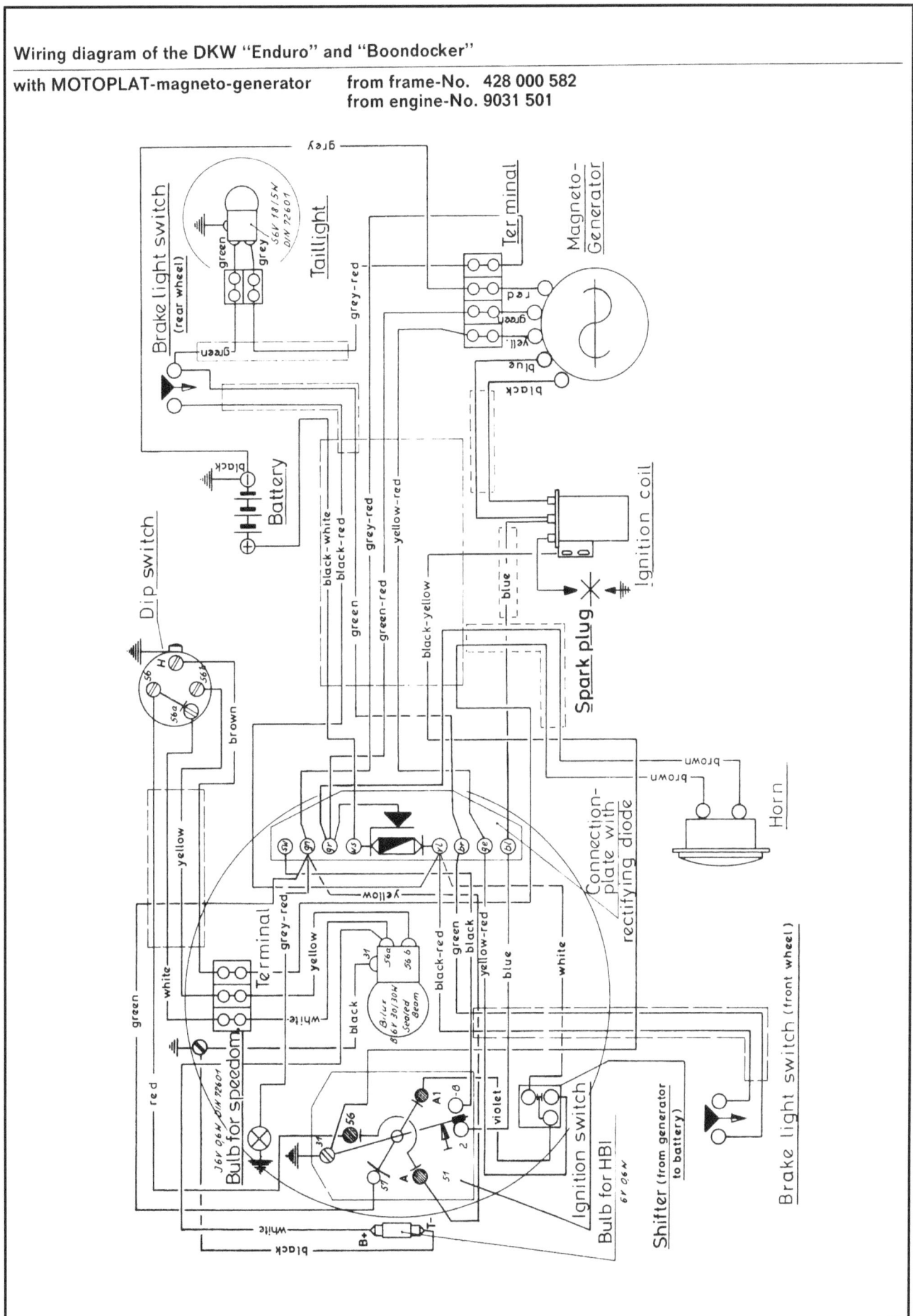

Wiring diagram of the DKW "Moto-Cross" and "Hornet"

with MOTOPLAT-magneto-generator   from frame-No. 428 000 582
from engine-No. 9031 501

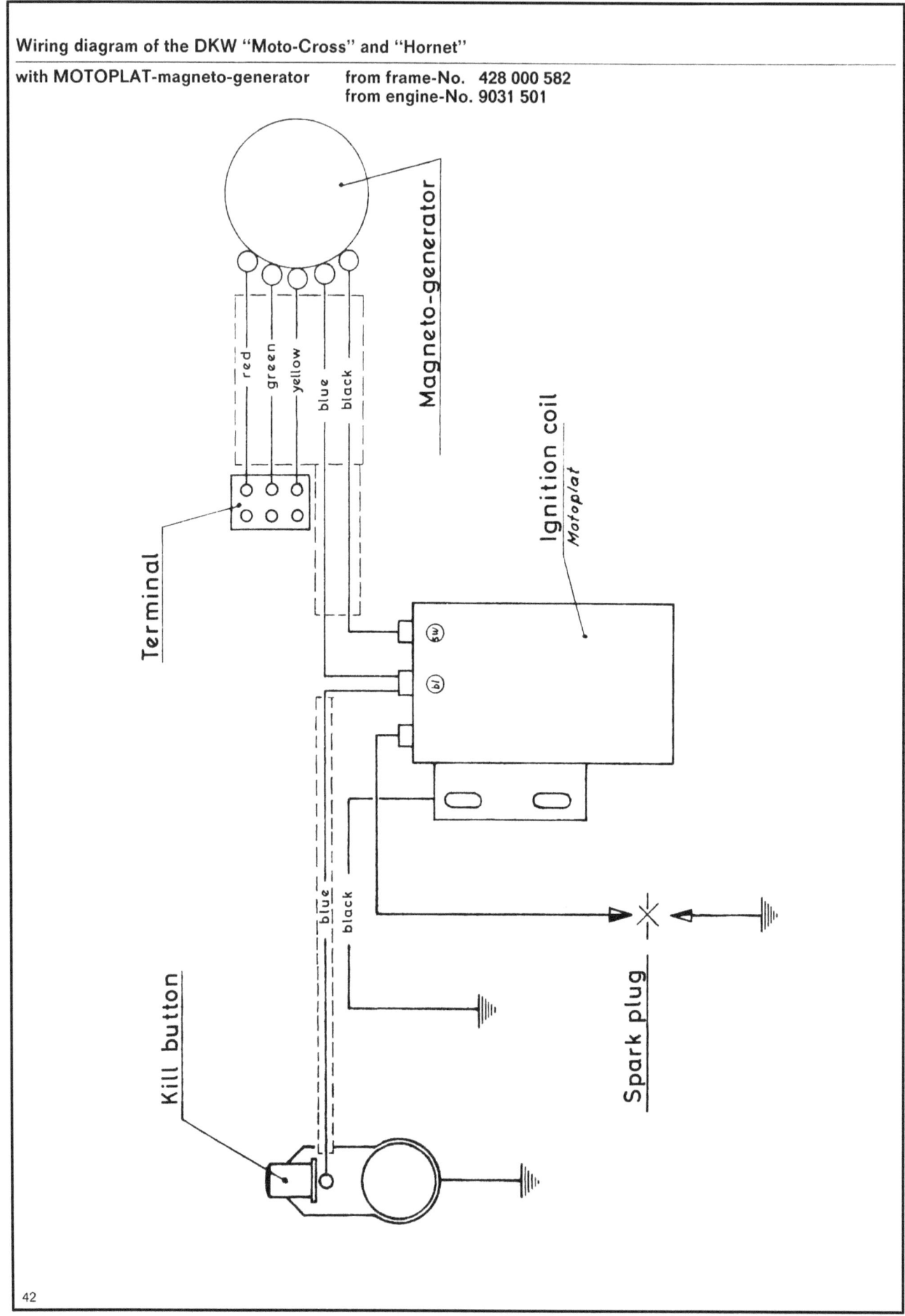

Wiring diagram of the DKW "Moto-Cross"

with BOSCH-magneto-generator   up to frame-No. 428 000 581
up to engine-No. 9031 500

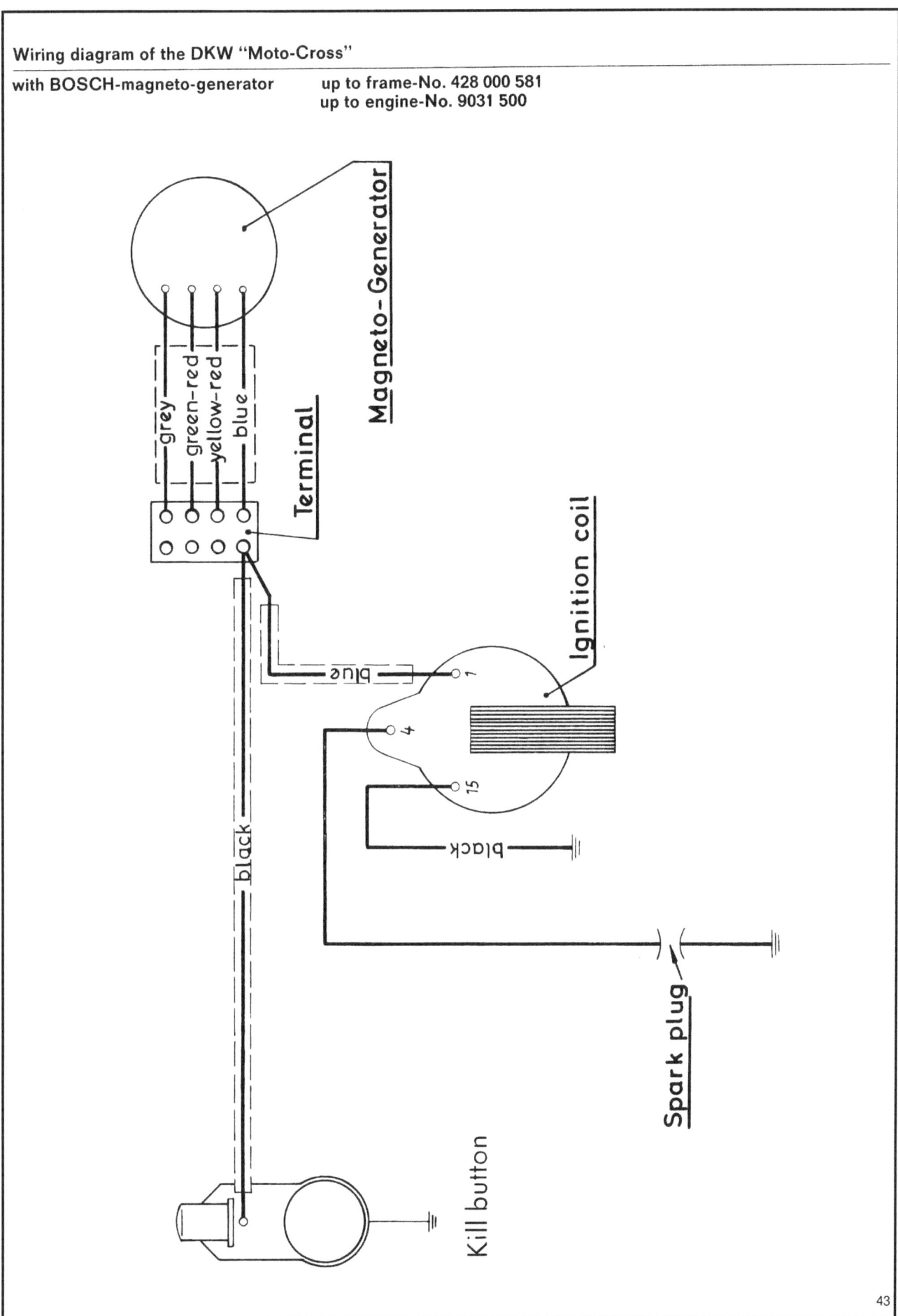

VELOCEPRESS MANUALS – MOTORCYCLE BY MAKE

AJS 1932-1948 SINGLES & TWINS 250cc THRU 1000cc (BOOK OF)
AJS 1945-1960 SINGLES 350cc & 500cc MODELS 16 & 18 (BOOK OF)
AJS 1955-1965 SINGLES 350cc & 500cc (BOOK OF)
AJS 1957-1966 FACTORY WSM - ALL SINGLES & TWINS
ARIEL UP TO 1932 (BOOK OF)
ARIEL 1932-1939 PREWAR MODELS (BOOK OF)
ARIEL 1933-1951 (WORKSHOP MANUAL)
ARIEL 1939-1960 4 STROKE SINGLES (BOOK OF)
ARIEL 1958-1964 LEADER & ARROW FACTORY WSM & PARTS LIST
ARIEL 1958-1964 LEADER & ARROW (BOOK OF)
BMW R26 R27 (1956-1967) FACTORY WORKSHOP MANUAL
BMW R50 R50S R60 R69S (1955-1969) FACTORY WORKSHOP MANUAL
BRIDGESTONE 90 SERIES FACTORY WSM & PARTS CATALOGUE
BRIDGESTONE 175 SERIES FACTORY WSM & PARTS CATALOGUE
BRIDGESTONE 350 SERIES FACTORY WSM & PARTS CATALOGUES
BSA SERVICE SHEETS MASTER CATALOGUE ALL MODELS 1945-1967
BSA BANTAM D1 TO D7 1948-1966 FACTORY SERVICE SHEETS MANUAL
BSA BANTAM ALL MODELS FROM 1948 ONWARDS (BOOK OF)
BSA DANDY FACTORY WORKSHOP MANUAL (COMPILATION)
BSA SINGLES & V-TWINS UP TO 1927 (BOOK OF)
BSA SINGLES & V-TWINS UP TO 1930 (BOOK OF)
BSA SINGLES & V-TWINS UP TO 1935 (BOOK OF)
BSA SINGLES & V-TWINS 1936-1939 (BOOK OF)
BSA C10, C11 & C12 1945-1958 FACTORY SERVICE SHEETS MANUAL
BSA OHV & SV SINGLES 250-600cc 1945-1959 (BOOK OF)
BSA C15 & B40 1958-1967 FACTORY SERVICE SHEETS MANUAL
BSA OHV & SV SINGLES 250cc (ONLY) 1954-1970 (BOOK OF)
BSA B31, B32, B33 & B34 1945-60 FACTORY SERVICE SHEETS MANUAL
BSA OHV SINGLES 350 & 500cc 1955-1967 (BOOK OF)
BSA M20, M21 & M33 1945-1963 FACTORY SERVICE SHEETS MANUAL
BSA TWINS A7 & A10 1948-1962 FACTORY SERVICE SHEETS MANUAL
BSA TWINS A7 & A10 1948-1962 (BOOK OF)
BSA TWINS A50 & A65 1962-1965 FACTORY WORKSHOP MANUAL
BSA TWINS A50 & A65 1962-1969 (SECOND BOOK OF)
DOUGLAS 1929-1939 PREWAR ALL MODELS (BOOK OF)
DOUGLAS 1948-1957 POSTWAR ALL MODELS FACTORY SHOP MANUAL
DUCATI 160cc, 250cc & 350cc OHC MODELS FACTORY SHOP MANUAL
HONDA 50cc ALL MODELS UP TO 1970 INC MONKEY & TRAIL (BOOK OF)
HONDA 90cc ALL MODELS UP TO 1966 (BOOK OF)
HONDA TWINS & SINGLES 50cc THRU 305cc 1960-1966 (BOOK OF)
HONDA TWINS ALL MODELS 125cc THRU 450cc UP TO 1968 (BOOK OF)
HONDA C100 50cc SUPER CUB O.H.C. 1959-1962 FACTORY WSM
HONDA C110 50cc SPORT CUB O.H.C. 1960-1962 FACTORY WSM
HONDA 50-65-70-90cc O.H.C. SINGLES 1959-1983 FACTORY WSM
HONDA 100-125cc SINGLES CB/CD/CL/SL/TL 1970-1984 FACTORY WSM
HONDA 125-150cc TWINS C/CS/CB/CA 1959-1966 FACTORY WSM
HONDA 125-160-175-200cc TWINS 1965-1978 WORKSHOP MANUAL
HONDA 250-305cc TWINS C/CS/CB 1961-1968 FACTORY WSM
HOHDA 250-350cc TWINS CB/CL/SL 1968-1973 FACTORY WSM
HONDA 250-360cc TWINS CB/CL/CJ 1974-1977 FACTORY WSM
HONDA 350F & 400F 4-CYLINDER 1972-1977 FACTORY WSM
HONDA 450cc TWINS CB/CL 1965-1974 K0 TO K7 WORKSHOP MANUAL
HONDA 500cc & 550cc 4-CYL 1971-1978 FACTORY WORKSHOP MANUAL
HONDA 750cc SHOC 4-CYL 1969-1978 K0~K8 WORKSHOP MANUAL
INDIAN PONYBIKE, BOY RACER & PAPOOSE ILL PARTS LIST & SALES LIT
J.A.P. ENGINES 1927-1952 & MOTORCYCLES 1934-1952 (BOOK OF)
MATCHLESS 1931-1939 ALL MODELS 250cc THRU 990cc (BOOK OF)
MATCHLESS 1945-1956 350 & 500cc SINGLES (BOOK OF)
MATCHLESS 1955-1966 350 & 500cc SINGLES (BOOK OF)
MATCHLESS 1957-1966 FACTORY WSM - ALL SINGLES & TWINS
NEW IMPERIAL ALL SV & OHV FROM 1935 ONWARDS (BOOK OF)
NORTON 1932-1939 PREWAR MODELS (BOOK OF)
NORTON 1932-1947 (BOOK OF)
NORTON 1938-1956 (BOOK OF)
NORTON 1945-1963 MODELS 16H, Big4, ES2, 19 & 50 WSM'S & PARTS
NORTON 1955-1963 MODELS 19, 50 & ES2 (BOOK OF)
NORTON 1948-1970 DOMINATOR TWINS FACTORY WSM'S & PARTS
NORTON 1955-1965 DOMINATOR TWINS (BOOK OF)
NORTON 1960-1970 TWIN CYLINDER FACTORY WORKSHOP MANUAL
NORTON 1970-1975 COMMANDO 850 & 750cc FACTORY WSM
NORTON 1975-1978 MK 3 COMMANDO 850 cc FACTORY WSM
PANTHER 1932-1958 LIGHTWEIGHT MODELS 250 & 350cc (BOOK OF)
PANTHER 1938-1966 HEAVYWEIGHT MODELS 600 & 650cc (BOOK OF)
RALEIGH MOTORCYCLES 1919-1933 (BOOK OF)
ROYAL ENFIELD 1934-1946 SINGLES & V TWINS (BOOK OF)
ROYAL ENFIELD 1937-1953 SINGLES & V TWINS (BOOK OF)
ROYAL ENFIELD 1946-1962 SINGLES (BOOK OF)
ROYAL ENFIELD 1952-1963 700cc TWINS FACTORY WORKSHOP MANUAL
ROYAL ENFIELD 1958-1966 250cc & 350cc SINGLES (SECOND BOOK OF)
ROYAL ENFIELD 1962-1970 INTERCEPTOR WSM'S & PARTS (Compilation)
RUDGE 1933-1939 (BOOK OF)
SACHS 1968-1975 100cc & 125cc ENGINES WSM & M/CYCLE PARTS LIST
SUNBEAM 1928-1939 (BOOK OF)
SUNBEAM 1946-1957 S7 & S8 (BOOK OF)
SUZUKI 50cc & 80cc UP TO 1966 (BOOK OF)
SUZUKI T10 1963-1967 FACTORY WORKSHOP MANUAL
SUZUKI T20 & T200 1965-1969 FACTORY WORKSHOP MANUAL
SUZUKI TWINS 1962 ONWARDS 125-500cc WORKSHOP MANUAL
TRIUMPH 1935-1949 SINGLES & TWINS (BOOK OF)
TRIUMPH 1937-1951 (WORKSHOP MANUAL)
TRIUMPH 1945-1955 FACTORY WORKSHOP MANUAL
TRIUMPH 1945-1959 TWINS (BOOK OF)
TRIUMPH 1956-1969 TWINS (BOOK OF)
TRIUMPH 1963-1970 UNIT CONSTRUCTION 650cc FACTORY WSM
TRIUMPH 1963-1974 UNIT CONSTRUCTION 350-500cc FACTORY WSM
TRIUMPH 1968-1974 TRIDENT T150 & T150V FACTORY WSM
VELOCETTE 1925-1970 ALL SINGLES & TWINS (BOOK OF)
VELOCETTE 1933-1952 MOV-MAC-MSS RIGID FRAME FACTORY WSM
VELOCETTE 1954-1971 MSS-VENOM-THRUXTON-VIPER FACTORY WSM
VILLIERS ENGINE UP TO 1959 INC. 3 WHEELERS (BOOK OF)
VILLIERS ENGINE UP TO 1969 (BOOK OF)
VINCENT 1935-1955 (WORKSHOP MANUAL)
YAMAHA 1961-1967 YA5 & YA6 (WORKSHOP MANUAL & ILL PARTS LIST)
YAMAHA 1971-1972 JT1& JT2 (WORKSHOP MANUAL & ILL PARTS LIST)

VELOCEPRESS TECHNICAL BOOKS – MOTORCYCLE

1930'S BRITISH MOTORCYCLE CARBS & ELEC COMPONENTS (BOOK OF)
1930'S BRITISH MOTORCYCLE ENGINES (OVERHAUL & MAINTENANCE)
1930'S BRITISH MOTORCYCLE GEARBOXES & CLUTCHES (BOOK OF)
CATALOG OF BRITISH MOTORCYCLES (1951 MODELS)
LUCAS ELECTRONICS BRITISH M/CYCLES REPAIR & PARTS (1950-1977)
MOTORCYCLE ENGINEERING (P.E. Irving)
MOTORCYCLE ROAD TESTS 1949-1953 (Motor Cycle Magazine UK)
SPEED AND HOW TO OBTAIN IT (Motor Cycle Magazine UK)
TUNING FOR SPEED (P.E. Irving)
WIPAC (COMBO) MANUAL NUMBER 3 + M/CYCLE & SCOOTER MANUAL

VELOCEPRESS MANUALS – SCOOTERS BY MAKE

BSA SUNBEAM SCOOTER WORKSHOP MANUAL 1959-1965
BSA SUNBEAM SCOOTER 1959-1965 (BOOK OF)
LAMBRETTA 1947-1957 ALL 125 & 150cc MODELS (BOOK OF)
LAMBRETTA 1957-1970 LI & TV MODELS (SECOND BOOK OF)
NSU PRIMA 1956-1964 ALL MODELS (BOOK OF)
TRIUMPH TIGRESS SCOOTER WORKSHOP MANUAL 1959-1965
TRIUMPH TIGRESS SCOOTER (BOOK OF)
VESPA 1951-1961 (BOOK OF)
VESPA 1955-1963 125 & 150cc & GS MODELS (SECOND BOOK OF)
VESPA 1955-1968 GS & SS (BOOK OF)
VESPA 1963-1972 90, 125 & 150cc (THIRD BOOK OF)

VELOCEPRESS MANUALS – MOPEDS & MOTORIZED BICYCLES

CYCLEMOTOR (BOOK OF)
NSU QUICKLY 1953-1963 ALL MODELS (BOOK OF)
PUCH MAXI N & S MAINTENANCE & REPAIR (3 MANUAL COMPILATION)
RALEIGH MOPEDS 1960-1969 (BOOK OF)

VELOCEPRESS MANUALS - THREE WHEELER'S

BOND MINICAR THREE WHEELER 1948-1967 (BOOK OF)
BMW ISETTA FACTORY WORKSHOP MANUAL
BSA THREE WHEELER (BOOK OF)
RELIANT REGAL THREE WHEELER 1952-1973 (BOOK OF)
VINTAGE MORGAN THREE WHEELER (BOOK OF)

VELOCEPRESS MANUALS – AUTOMOBILE BY MAKE

ALFA ROMEO GIULIA WORKSHOP MANUAL 1300 TO 2000cc 1962-1975
ALFA ROMEO GIULIA TECH MANUAL CARBURETED CARS FROM 1962
ALFA ROMEO GIULIA TECH MANUAL FUEL INJECTED CARS FROM 1969
ALFA ROMEO GIULIETTA & GIULIA 750 & 101 SERIES 1955-1965 WSM
AUSTIN-HEALEY SPRITE & MG MIDGET WORKSHOP MANUAL 1958-1971
BMW 600 LIMOUSINE FACTORY WORKSHOP MANUAL
BMW 600 LIMOUSINE OWNERS HAND BOOK & SERVICE MANUAL
BMW 2000 & 2002 1966-1976 WORKSHOP MANUAL
CORVAIR 1960-1969 WORKSHOP MANUAL
CORVETTE V8 1955-1962 WORKSHOP MANUAL
FERRARI HANDBOOK ROAD & RACE CARS (SERVICE/SPECS) 1948-1958
FERRARI 250/GT SERVICE & MAINTENANCE MANUAL 1956-1965
FIAT 500 FACTORY WORKSHOP MANUAL 1957-1973
FIAT 600, 600D & MULTIPLA FACTORY WORKSHOP MANUAL 1955-1969
JAGUAR E-TYPE 3.8 & 4.2 SERIES 1 & 2 WORKSHOP MANUAL
JAGUAR MK 7, 8, 9 & XK120, 140, 150 WORKSHOP MANUAL 1948-1961
METROPOLITAN FACTORY WORKSHOP MANUAL
MGA & MGB OWNERS HANDBOOK & WORKSHOP MANUAL
MG MIDGET TC, TD, TF & TF1500 WORKSHOP MANUAL
PORSCHE 356 1948-1965 WORKSHOP MANUAL
PORSCHE 911 2.0, 2.2, 2.4 LITRE 1964-1973 WORKSHOP MANUAL
PORSCHE 911 2.7, 3.0, 3.2 LITRE 1973-1989 WORKSHOP MANUAL
PORSCHE 912 WORKSHOP MANUAL
PORSCHE 914/4 & 914/6 1.7, 1.8, 2.0 LITRE 1970-1976 WSM
TRIUMPH TR2, TR3, TR4 1953-1965 WORKSHOP MANUAL
VOLKSWAGEN TRANSPORTER, TRUCKS & WAGONS 1950-1979 WSM
VOLVO 1944-1968 ALL MODELS WORKSHOP MANUAL

VELOCEPRESS TECHNICAL BOOKS - AUTOMOBILE

HOW TO BUILD A FIBERGLASS CAR
HOW TO BUILD A RACING CAR
HOW TO RESTORE THE MODEL 'A' FORD
MASERATI OWNER'S HANDBOOK
PERFORMANCE TUNING THE SUNBEAM TIGER
SOUPING THE VOLKSWAGEN
SOLEX CARBURETORS (EMPHASIS ON UK & EU AUTOMOBILES)
SU CARBURETORS (EMPHASIS ON UK AUTOMOBILES)
WEBER CARBURETORS (EMPHASIS ON ALFA & FIAT)

VELOCEPRESS BOOKS & GUIDES - AUTOMOBILE

COMPLETE CATALOG OF JAPANESE MOTOR VEHICLES
FERRARI 308 SERIES BUYER'S AND OWNER'S GUIDE
FERRARI BROCHURES AND SALES LITERATURE 1968-1989
FERRARI SERIAL NUMBERS PART I - ODD NUMBERS TO 21399
FERRARI SERIAL NUMBERS PART II - EVEN NUMBERS TO 1050
HENRY'S FABULOUS MODEL "A" FORD
MASERATI BROCHURES AND SALES LITERATURE

VELOCEPRESS BOOKS – RACING

CARRERA PANAMERICANA - MEXICAN ROAD RACE (BOOK OF)
DIALED IN - THE JAN OPPERMAN STORY
VEDA ORR'S NEW REVISED HOT ROD PICTORIAL

www.VelocePress.com